THE US, THE UN, AND THE MANAGEMENT OF GLOBAL CHANGE

UNA-USA POLICY STUDIES BOOK SERIES

The United Nations Association of the USA is a private, non-profit organization dedicated to broadening public understanding of the activities of the United Nations and other multilateral institutions. Through its nationwide membership and network of affiliated national organizations, UNA-USA conducts a broad range of programs to inform and involve the public in foreign affairs issues.

The UNA-USA Policy Studies Program conducts projects involving research and analysis on a wide spectrum of policy issues of concern to the international community. The Program brings together panels of interested and knowledgeable Americans to study and make recommendations on specific problems of U.S. foreign policy and multilateral activities. As part of this process, a number of papers are commissioned from leading specialists.

The UNA-USA Policy Studies Book Series contains books based on rewritten and edited collections of some of these papers. UNA-USA is responsible for the choice of the subject areas and the decision to publish the volumes, but the responsibility for the content of the papers and for opinions expressed in them rests with the individual authors and editors.

Already published:

Disaster Assistance: Appraisal, Reform and New Approaches, edited by Lynn H. Stephens and Stephen J. Green.

The New International Economic Order: A U.S. Response, edited by David B. H. Denoon.

The Politics of Human Rights, edited by Paula R. Newberg.

The Future of US-China Relations, edited by John Bryan Starr.

Arms Control: The Multilateral Alternative, edited by Edward C. Luck.

THE US, THE UN, AND THE MANAGEMENT OF GLOBAL CHANGE

Edited by
TOBY TRISTER GATI

New York University Press
New York *and* London
1983

Library of Congress Cataloging in Publication Data
Main entry under title:

The US, the UN, and the management of global change.

(UNA–USA policy studies book series)
Includes bibliographical references and index.
1. United Nations.   2. United Nations—United
States.   3. United States—Foreign relations—1945–
4. International relations.   I. Gati, Toby Trister.
II. Title: U.S., the U.N., and the management of
global change.   III. Series.
JX1977.U7 1983   341.23   83-2304
ISBN 0-8147-2986-X
ISBN 0-8147-2987-8 (pbk.)

Clothbound editions of New York University Press books are Smyth-
sewn and printed on durable and acid-free paper.

To Daniel with love

CONTENTS

LIST OF ABBREVIATIONS

ACABQ   Advisory Committee on Administrative and Budgeting Questions

ACC   Administrative Committee on Coordination

ADB   Asian Development Bank

AFDB   African Development Bank

ASEAN   Association of Southeast Asian Nations

Brandt Commission Report   Formally known as the Report of the Independent Commission on International Development Issues, Willy Brandt, Chairman

CERD   UN Committee on the Elimination of Racial Discrimination

CIEC   Conference on International Economic Cooperation

CIOMS   Council for International Organizations of Medical Sciences

CONGO   Conference of NGOs in Consultative Status

COW   Committee of the Whole of the UN General Assembly

CPC   Committee for Program and Coordination

DAC   Development Assistance Committee of the OECD

DD3   Third UN Development Decade

DPI   Department of Public Information

Committee of 24   UNGA's Special Committee on Decolonization

ECA   UN Economic Commission for Africa

ECE   UN Economic Commission for Europe

ECLA   UN Economic Commission for Latin America

ECOSOC   United Nations Economic and Social Council

ECWA   UN Economic Commission for Western Asia

EPTA   Expanded Program of Technical Assistance

EPU   European Postal Union

ESCAP   UN Economic and Social Commission for Asia and the Pacific (formally ECAFE)

EURODIF   European consortium for the production of enriched uranium

FAO   Food and Agricultural Organization

FFHC   FAO's Freedom from Hunger Campaign

GA   General Assembly

GDP   Gross Domestic Product

GNP   Gross National Product

Group B Countries   UN grouping of the Western industrialized countries that includes members of the OECD plus the smaller European states that are members of UN bodies

Group D Countries   UN grouping of countries comprised of the Soviet Union and its East European allies

G-10   Grouping of industrialized nations (plus Switzerland) for discussions of international monetary issues

G-24   Grouping of 24 developing countries (with equal numbers from Asia, Africa, and Latin America) for discussions of international monetary issues

G-77   Group of developing countries of the UN that started with 77 members in 1964 and now numbers over 120

IAEA   International Atomic Energy Agency

IAPL   International Association of Penal Law

IBRD   International Bank for Reconstruction and Development (part of the World Bank)

ICAO   International Civil Aviation Organization

ICDA   International Coalition for Development Action

IDA   International Development Association (part of the World Bank)

IDB   Inter-American Development Bank

IDS   International Development Strategy

IEA   International Energy Agency

IFAD   International Fund for Agricultural Development

IGO   Inter-Governmental Organization

ILO   International Labor Organization

IMCO   Inter-Governmental Maritime Consultative Organization

IMF   International Monetary Fund

IO Bureau   International Organization Bureau of the US Department of State

IPC   Integrated Program for Commodities

ITO   International Trade Organization

ITU   International Telecommunications Union

IWY   International Women's Year

JUNIC   Joint United Nations Information Committee

LDC   Less Developed Countries

MTN   Multilateral Trade Negotiations

NATO   North Atlantic Treaty Organization

NGO   Non-Governmental Organization

NICs   Newly Industrializing Countries

NIEO   New International Economic Order

NIIO   New International Information Order

NPT   Non-Proliferation Treaty

OAS   Organization of American States

OAU   Organization of African Unity

OECD   Organization for Economic Cooperation and Development

OEEC   Organization of European Economic Cooperation

ONUC   United Nations Operation in the Congo

OPEC   Organization of Petroleum Exporting Countries

PLO   Palestine Liberation Organization

SALT   Strategic Arms Limitation Talks

SC   Security Council

SDR   Special Drawing Rights

SELA   Latin American Economic System

START   Strategic Arms Reduction Talks

TCDC   Technical Cooperation among Developing Countries

UN   United Nations

UNCTAD   United Nations Conference on Trade and Development

UNDP   United Nations Development Program

UNEF I and II (1956 and 1973)   United Nations Emergency Force in the Middle East

UNESCO   United Nations Educational, Scientific and Cultural Organization

UNFPA   United Nations Fund for Population Activities

UNFICYP   United Nations Force in Cyprus

UNGA   United Nations General Assembly

UNHCR   United Nations High Commissioner for Refugees

UNICEF   United Nations International Children's Emergency Fund

UNIDO   United Nations Industrial Development Organization

UNIFIL   United Nations Interim Force in Lebanon

UNITAR   United Nations Institute for Training and Research

UNRWA   United Nations Relief and Works Agency for Palestine Refugees

UNTAA   United Nations Technical Assistance Administration

UNTSO   United Nations Truce Supervisory Organization

UNYOM   United Nations Observation Mission in Yemen

UPU   Universal Postal Union

URENCO   European consortium for the production of enriched uranium

WHO   World Health Organization

INTRODUCTION

TOBY TRISTER GATI

For almost four decades the United Nations has been part of the international landscape. Certainly that is long enough to draw some conclusions about what the UN system can and cannot do. It should also be long enough for the United States to have developed a set of priorities and a consistent pattern of utilizing multilateral institutions as a tool of foreign policy. In reality, however, there is no consensus in this country on what the UN is best equipped to do; if anything, there is growing concern and confusion about how the US should use the United Nations.

The American public's uncertain attitudes toward the United Nations are reflected in its general support for the organization tinged with a good deal of skepticism. While there are still groups that see the UN in extremes of either black or white—a place dangerously hostile to US interests or humanity's best hope for a just and peaceful world—the vast majority of Americans are realistic, if questioning, about the UN's specific, if limited, accomplishments and its proper role in US foreign policy.

The essays in this book all have in common a search for the broad, underlying principles that have guided the UN in the past and an attempt to explain the assumptions and expectations that have conditioned US action in the United Nations. They present diverse approaches to the historic record of UN successes and failures and different ways of assessing US participation in the United Nations. Each explores a wide range of issues central to determin-

1

ing the role the UN system will play in the international system in the years ahead and the role the US will play in the specialized agencies and other international organizations that constitute the UN system.

It is impossible to talk about the United Nations today without constant reference to the past—to the hopes of 1945 and the changes in the UN's membership, as well as to the unfulfilled expectations and the tasks still left undone. For that reason, many of the chapters in the first section of this volume offer a historical perspective on the United Nations, setting the stage for an examination of the UN's present role. Likewise, it is difficult to talk about the UN without frequent references to the future—for, in an increasingly interdependent world, the importance of international mechanisms for coping with global problems continues to grow. Thus, many of the contributors to the book have tried to combine discussion of the United Nations with an analysis of the way the organization might adapt to a changing international environment.

The rapid pace of change in today's world makes a reevaluation of the United Nations and of US policy in the UN especially appropriate at the present time. Although the goals enunciated in the Charter are not any less relevant today than they were 37 years ago, circumstances and the relative power of nations have changed to make a redefinition of roles and priorities essential. Given its size and complexity, what role can the United Nations play in the international system? Is American leadership in the UN necessary? By raising these and other questions, the chapters in this book assess the unique niche carved out by the UN during the postwar era against the reality of the still limited powers of international decisionmaking bodies to deal with changing global needs. They also assess the usefulness of the United Nations to US foreign policy by considering those past (and likely future) instances when the UN has adopted (and will adopt) policies not always in accord with our sense of the American national interest.

Such a reassessment will undoubtedly convey as much about our own willingness to engage other nations of the world in the great political and economic issues of the day as it will about the UN and its shortcomings. Indeed, several of the contributors stress the need for a closer connection between the evolution of the international system, particularly its capacity to adapt to global change, and the priorities of United States policy—if the two are not to work at cross purposes. This interconnection needs to be stressed particularly today because some political leaders and current critics of the United Nations have called upon the United States to disengage from multilateral forums at the same time that they are pressing for a reassertion of American leadership in other areas of foreign policy. It is certainly not self-evident that a selectively activist foreign policy can be a successful foreign policy.

Although the list of specific complaints against the United Nations is long and detailed, the criticisms of the United Nations heard most often in this country are that the UN provides a ready-made forum for articulating grievances against the West in general, and the United States in particular; that its effectiveness is seriously compromised by the organization's politicization, by an inefficient and swollen bureaucracy, and by a lack of proper program priorities; and that the international norms articulated in recent UN debates and resolutions are essentially hostile to US interests. While these are not new complaints, they do constitute real problems for the United States in its dealing with the UN system. The criticisms also carry considerable political weight because they reflect, to a large degree, the prevailing public position of the Reagan Administration towards the United Nations. As the United States Permanent Representative to the United Nations, Jeane J. Kirkpatrick, noted, ". . . the United Nations poses a problem for the United States. It's expensive, it's often ineffective, it seems particularly inclined to push policies that we do not desire to adopt, decisions from which we dissent, agreements with which we disagree." [1]

Are US policies at the UN very different now than they were under previous Administrations, Republican or Democratic? Certainly the Reagan Administration's rhetoric is different. The US more often rises to exercise its right of reply in order to put its adversaries on the defensive and it pursues a more aggressive policy of monitoring voting behavior in an effort to forestall easy potshots at the United States in General Assembly resolutions. In other words, the present Administration is less concerned with how "popular" the US appears to be at the UN; instead, it is interested in reversing what it has characterized as a "period of retreat" [2] in

US foreign policy at the UN and elsewhere. As Elliot Abrams, former Assistant Secretary of State for International Organization Affairs noted, "Our view is that we have our policies and our principles, and we carry them out at the UN, and if people like them, that's fine, and if they don't like them, that's fine."[3]

On some issues, the stridency of the rhetoric has not been matched by radical policy changes. For example, while the Administration has criticized the idea of the New International Economic Order in stronger terms than before, calling it "a product of a socialist ethos,"[4] it has grudgingly agreed to participate in UN-sponsored Global Negotiations whose aim is to restructure the international economy along the lines of the NIEO program adopted by the UN in the early seventies.[5]

On other important issues such as Namibia and the Middle East, what first seemed to be harbingers of shifts in US policies—statements indicating less pressure on South Africa to withdraw from its illegal occupation of Namibia and pledges to defend Israeli interests more strongly—have not been translated into a pattern of voting significantly different from what a previous Administration might have followed.

In several key areas, there has been a marked sharpening of the US response to long-standing issues, and in one important area there has been a substantial change in US policy. The United States has recently attached major importance to fending off attacks on freedom of the press in UNESCO by actively opposing efforts to restrict reporting or to license journalists. On procedural questions, the US used its muscle to ensure that the issue of self-determination for Puerto Rico was kept off the agenda of this year's General Assembly, and when Israeli credentials were suspended at an International Atomic Energy Agency conference in late 1982, the US made good on its threat to walk out of the proceedings. Denial of Israel's credentials by the General Assembly would have had the same consequences. A major policy reversal has been the Administration's refusal to sign the Law of the Sea Treaty, a document representing the culmination of almost a decade of intense negotiations on a wide range of issues from the right of free passage to the mining of manganese nodules on the ocean floor.

Yet, and despite its harsh criticism of the UN, the Reagan Administration has also supported many UN activities, particularly those clearly identified with humanitarian, health or development purposes, or those directed toward fulfilling functions that can only be performed by a multilateral agency. Thus it has supported the work of organizations such as the UN High Commissioner for Refugees, UNICEF, the World Health Organization and the UN Development Program, as well as the technical programs of specialized agencies such as the International Civil Aviation Organization and the World Meteorological Organization.

Underlying present US policy toward the UN, then, is a basic ideological distrust of multilateral negotiations and a shying away from any assumption of new international obligations. "Supra-national, international regulatory bodies," noted Elliot Abrams, "have all the disadvantages that national regulatory bodies do, multiplied . . . by the order of a hundred. . . ."[6] This general skepticism is reinforced by a sense that over the years the UN has turned away from its original mandate of ensuring peace and security and abused its authority to deal with international problems by allowing the specialized agencies to become increasingly politicized. The perception that the UN exacerbates conflict in its political organs and introduces "extraneous" political issues into its functional activities makes it highly unlikely that this Administration would consider bringing any important economic or political issue to the UN or would try to expand the organization's powers to manage international problems.

Somewhat ironically, perhaps, such criticism of UN activities is matched by an almost nostalgic attachment to the UN of yesteryear. This is reflected in a rather idealized image of the first decade of the UN's existence and a desire "to return the United Nations to the ideas and policies upon which it was founded."[7]

It is true, of course, that the organization was then controlled by the US-dominated bloc of Latin American states in the General Assembly (rather than the automatic majority of third world nations that now controls the Assembly). It is also true that more often than not it was the Soviet Union and not the United States that was on the defensive in the UN. But during this period, when the United States was so influential, were UN efforts to resolve the vital issues of the day, particularly those dealing with the maintenance of international peace and security, that much more successful? In point of fact, the UN's impotence in the face of international crises such as the Soviet invasion of Hungary in 1956 does not differ much from its response to Soviet intervention in Afghanistan almost 25 years later.

It seems that, irrespective of who "controls" the UN, it can be most effective in areas where the two superpowers' vital interests are not at stake. Given the nature of the problems before the world community, there is still much for the UN to do, especially in the area of North-South relations, human rights, and the management of political crises involving small- and medium-size states.

The UN serves other functions as well. After less than 6 months on the job, Jeane Kirkpatrick expressed her sense of the value of the UN to the United States in these terms:

> To an extent that I had not fully understood, the United Nations is a major center for international politics in which representatives of all the diverse nations in the world meet and discuss all the world's diverse problems. . . . Obviously, we need to be involved in these interactions. . . . It is a place, therefore, not only where we work, but it also has irreducible value for those of us charged with responsibility for making and implementing US foreign policy.[8]

As long as the UN performs this function, it is likely to continue to play an important role in the foreign policy of every country. This means that the United States—as well as other countries with a stake in world order—will have to address the difficult question of what the international community wants the UN to do and to be.

Stimulating serious thinking about these issues is the primary purpose of this book. The same goal served to motivate the work of UNA-USA's National Policy Panel on the UN system at 35, for which these papers were originally written. Guiding the work of this UNA program was a Steering Committee composed of scholars, government representatives, individuals with close professional ties to the United Nations, and members of local UNA Chapter groups. Many meetings were held in New York City to discuss each of the papers with a view to assessing the past record of international organizations and stimulating the public discussion necessary for reinterpreting and reaffirming the American role in multilateral institutions. During the same period, local study groups throughout the United States met to discuss the issues raised in the papers prepared for the project. Each local group committed itself to producing a narrative of its local meetings on particular study topics and, when consensus could be reached, preparing a report with recommendations for United States policy in the United Nations.

While taking into account the practical limitations of international institutions, as well as the limited capacity of the United States to influence other countries in the direction of our policy preferences, the Steering Committee proceeded from the assumption that the United States has an abiding interest in a stable international system and, furthermore, that the United States must continue to play a crucial role in international institutions if competitive economic pressures and regional political rivalries are not to overwhelm the search for peaceful solutions to global problems.

I would like to thank the members of UNA's Steering Committee, and in particular Donald Fraser, the Chairman of the Steering Committee, for participating in the panel's work. The diverse perspectives presented by the Committee members stimulated the serious reexamination of the United Nations' role in United States foreign policy that is essential for developing a realistic, forward-looking US strategy towards multilateral institutions. Mr. Fraser's leadership was a constant source of encouragement to paper writers and Steering Committee members alike. By keeping the group's attention on the need to develop reasonable and realistic US strategies and policy options in the United Nations, he added immeasurably not only to the quality of the essays in this volume but to the usefulness of the entire UNA project on the UN system at 35. I am also grateful to Nancy Sobieski and Cigdem Kurt for typing—and retyping—the various drafts of each paper. A special note of thanks is also due Paul D. Martin and Betty Starkey, whose help in the final editing of the book was invaluable.

Notes

1. Jeane J. Kirkpatrick, "The U.N. and the U.S.," cited in Midge Decter, Edwin J. Feulner, Jr., Ambassador Jeane J. Kirkpatrick, Burton Yale

Pines and Leonard J. Theberge, *The U.N. Under Scrutiny* (The Heritage Lectures 15, 1982), p. 22.

2. Dorothy Rabinowitz, "Reagan's 'Heroine' at the U.N.," *New York Magazine,* July 20, 1981, p. 36.

3. Transcript, "Ben Wattenberg at Large," Show number 205, 1981, p. 11.

4. Ibid., p. 4.

5. Despite Reagan Administration criticisms of Carter policies toward North-South issues, it should be recalled that the early phases of these negotiations were also stalemated during the Carter years by disagreements between the developed and developing countries over agendas and procedures.

6. Transcript, "Ben Wattenberg at Large," op. cit., p. 10.

7. Address by Elliot Abrams, Assistant Secretary for International Organization Affairs, before a conference of U.N. representatives of the United Nations Association-USA in New York, on June 5, 1981, United States Department of State, Bureau of Public Affairs, Current Policy Number 287, p. 3.

8. Statement by Jeane J. Kirkpatrick, Permanent United States Representative to the United Nations, before the Subcommittee on Foreign Operations, United States House of Representatives, May 12, 1981, quoted in *Third Planet,* published by the Illinois and Greater Chicago UNA-USA, Chicago, Illinois.

I

INTERNATIONAL ORGANIZATIONS AND US PARTICIPATION IN THE MULTILATERAL SYSTEM

1. THE UN SYSTEM IN PERSPECTIVE

DEVELOPMENT OF THE UN SYSTEM

LEON GORDENKER

INSTITUTIONAL ASSUMPTIONS: A RETROSPECTIVE ANALYSIS

The creation of the United Nations system rested on the assumption that maintaining international peace and security constitutes the basic issue of world politics. In every study prepared by the United States government, and in every international conference directed toward organizing the postwar world, peace and security was a fundamental aim. The United Nations Charter follows the pattern; its most specific sections and its widest grant of power to the organization concern keeping the peace.

As approached in the UN system of 1945, maintaining peace involved the prohibition of unauthorized use of force in international relations, rapid suppression of any such use of force, and a joint supervisory role for the great powers. If any member other than a great power did indeed use or threaten to use force, the UN was to have the capacity, directed by the Security Council, to suppress the outbreak. Thus, all members except the Big Five of the Security Council—China, France, the United Kingdom, the USSR and the United States—would face a deterrent to the use of force. It would become dangerous and expensive to resort to adventuring, let alone deliberate conquest, even on a small scale.

Yet disputes, as well as the disturbances that the Charter calls "situations," could arise. To deal with these, the UN system provides specific machinery for peaceful settlement of disputes and

11

some vaguer means designed to alter the basic international system. Because peaceful settlement would take place mainly in the context of the Security Council, the great powers could exercise their political persuasiveness and pressure. Frivolous or impractical schemes— that is those which the permanent members would not support— would be ruled out by the fact that the Security Council could act only on the basis of unanimity of the great powers.

The founders of the UN therefore assumed the continued existence of a twofold consensus as the basis of peace. To begin with, peaceful procedures would have a higher value than the use of force. A second implicit assumption was that grievances held by one government against another could in fact be settled and that they would not be allowed to fester into open conflict. Such a view had considerable merit in 1945, after the defeat of Germany, Italy, and Japan, whose behavior many understood as examples of what happens when violence becomes a primary instrument of policy. It was also assumed that generally the great powers would hold similar views about threats to the peace and would usually work together to maintain it. If they would not, no organization could force them to do so. The requirement of unanimity among the great powers for action by the Security Council ensured that lack of agreement on specific measures would be unmistakably proclaimed.

This twofold consensus was to have formed the background for a political process within the UN machinery. Practical recommendations could emerge with regard to specific disputes or situations that might threaten the peace. Such recommendations would conclude a process of negotiation and discussion or, when necessary, more elaborate methods of settlement, including specific plans for dealing with a disturbance. If violence broke out, the Security Council could act to mobilize worldwide pressure against the aggressor and even use economic or military sanctions against it. Such steps would be preceded by deliberation, discussion, and open decisionmaking by a Security Council in permanent readiness. Finally, the General Assembly and its associated organs could take steps to eliminate long-term, fundamental causes of disturbances to world peace. These steps also would emerge from a deliberative process, ending with clear-cut decisions to recommend courses of action to governments that were pledged to then give them serious attention. In all cases, either in the Security Council, the General Assembly, or elsewhere, decisions rested on the general principle of majority rule.

Over the last three and one-half decades, the process of negotiation and tradeoffs leading to General Assembly resolutions or Security Council action has developed in unanticipated directions, reflecting fundamental changes and challenges in the international environment in which the UN operates. It has mirrored realignments of attitudes on the part of governments, including the United States. It has displayed the effects of a more diverse membership in the UN organization and a more complex pattern of relationships among its members. And finally, it has provided a markedly altered setting for American policy toward the rest of the world.

The first extensive challenge to the UN system took the form of the Cold War. Antagonism between the Soviet and American governments undermined the assumption that the great powers held similar views about how to maintain peace. The challenge emerged almost at once after the San Francisco Conference, with the complaint by Iran that the Soviet Union was failing to withdraw its troops from Azerbaijan in accordance with an agreement between the governments. The discord between the US and the USSR was confirmed in the UN by their reactions to the civil war in Greece. The superpowers found themselves on opposite sides in other cases, such as that of unifying Korea; they also disagreed fundamentally on the treatment of nuclear weapons, on the provision of specific armed forces for the Security Council, on the handling of Berlin, and on the approach to the former enemy powers.

The outbreak of fighting in Korea in 1950 and the Security Council's response to American leadership ended any hope that the great power consensus could be restored, if indeed it ever really existed after the end of World War II. Nevertheless, the United States frequently was able to use UN machinery as a means of giving legitimacy and an operating framework to some of its policies. It successfully pressed for a greater role for the General Assembly in maintaining peace. It used the machinery to influence the outcome of the struggle over Palestine and to support the new Israeli state, treated the Korean and Greek disputes, and sought to embarrass and isolate the Soviet Union by forcing votes—and vetoes—in the Security Council.

The second challenge to the original assumptions of the system involved the smaller states and in part related to the failure of great power consensus. The Cold War obviated management of international peace by a club of great powers. Therefore, the lesser powers could logically perceive that, on the one hand, international institutions were leaving them to their own devices and that, on the other, they had reason to fear the individual embraces of the two superpowers. Consequently, the smaller countries increasingly developed a highly defensive attitude on issues touching on independence of policy or status. At the same time, the number of lesser powers among the membership began steadily to increase and, after 1955, when the United States and the Soviet Union stopped alternating their positions and agreed on universality of membership as a goal for the UN system, mounted rapidly to double and beyond their original numbers.

One consequence was a partial decentralization of the security system to regional bodies. In countries near to the Soviet Union and its allies, the United States attempted to organize alliances, claiming that these conformed to the UN Charter's objective of maintaining the peace. The most successful was the North Atlantic Treaty Organization (NATO). While the United States was the dominant partner, it could by no means absolutely control the behavior of the other NATO members and depended on negotiation and its attendant rewards and deprivation. NATO's success, together with the fears resulting from the war in Korea, called forth a competing decentralized security alliance in Eastern Europe. This was the Warsaw Treaty Organization, which answered invariably to the Soviet Union.

Elsewhere, decentralization of security machinery resulted in regional organizations that were less clearly dominated by great powers. The rudimentary inter-American system was explicitly turned into a full-fledged regional organization under the UN Charter. Although the United States gave an important and probably essential impetus to the creation of the new Organization of American States

(OAS), it had to give up any lingering pretense of completely dominating the hemisphere. OAS procedures attributed only formal equality to the United States and the organization made much of the sovereignty and integrity of all members. In Africa, not long afterward, pan-African idealism was transmuted into a continent-wide organization. Unlike the OAS, the Organization of African Unity (OAU) has no defense function and limits its activities to peaceful measures. Nor does it have any extra-African member or an official link to a great power. Elsewhere, too, regional groupings of various memberships and peace-maintaining pretentions developed, usually in the form of alliances.

A second consequence of the growing proportion of small states among the total membership of the UN system can be seen in the evolution of a well-organized, but informal, consultative mechanism which permits the majority in the General Assembly and elsewhere to criticize the great powers and the influential smaller countries at will. At the same time, this majority of third world states (known as the Group of 77 [G-77] although it now numbers more than 120) can shelter itself from recommendations by the General Assembly to which it objects. This consultative mechanism goes far beyond the corridors and tucked-away meeting rooms of the UN headquarters. It includes contact in meetings of the non-aligned powers and such bodies as the UN Conference on Trade and Development (UNCTAD) and the UN Industrial Development Organization (UNIDO), which the smaller and poorer countries treat as their advocates. It involves discussions in regional organizations and a great deal of ad hoc summitry and conferring at lesser levels. The majority of the General Assembly thus can identify issues to put high on the agenda, whatever the United States and other governments may say. Furthermore, governments with little individual capacity for developing programmatic demands in the General Assembly and elsewhere can concert their views and votes.

A third consequence of the failure of great power consensus has a superficially procedural character. It involves the confusion of roles between the Security Council and the General Assembly in relation to the original conception of the UN Charter. By collecting sufficient votes, any interested government can move the General

Assembly to give an opinion on matters actively before the Security Council. According to the UN Charter, such intermingling of roles should not take place.

It was the United States that led the General Assembly during the Cold War period to procedures which shifted discussion from the Security Council to the larger body, notably through the "Uniting for Peace" Resolution. In the General Assembly before the flood of new members, the United States could almost always obtain a recommendation to back its position. It did so during the Korean war when a General Assembly resolution asked members to treat the Communist government in Peking as if it had violated the Charter. Years later, the new members seized the procedural opportunities of the General Assembly, where they could control the agenda. Consequently the General Assembly has had a leading role in such matters of security as the Rhodesian case (before the United Kingdom brought it to the Security Council), the future of Namibia, and the situation in the Middle East. Led by the smaller states and the African group, whose views usually were harmonized in the OAU, the Assembly has branded South Africa as a breaker of the peace and has demanded the imposition of sanctions by the Security Council.

COLONIES AND HUMAN RIGHTS

The future of the colonial system and the maintenance of a standard of human rights are related to important secondary assumptions about the UN system. These assumptions in part were implicit but nevertheless quite real. During the San Francisco Conference, it was thought that the colonial system, which still extended over most of Africa and much of Asia, would change slowly, primarily in the direction of self-government rather than independence. The colonial powers would thus continue to have the main responsibility for managing the process of change and the United Nations would have only a slight role as overseer. The special case of the trusteeship system, which was to cover a growing but restricted number of territories, would allow the UN a stronger supervisory role that would be shared with the colonial powers. As for human rights, the United Nations was to promote respect for them as part of the effort to ensure the conditions for peaceful international relations. The wholesale violation of human rights had been part of the policies of the Italian, German, and Japanese governments—the enemies in the recent war—and thus was understood as an accompaniment to aggressive behavior.

Except by implication, however, the San Francisco Conference did not intimately connect human rights and colonialism. Human rights issues in the immediate postwar era had perhaps more to do with the immediate past than with the planned development of a future international order. The speed with which the General Assembly endorsed both the Charter of the Nuremberg Tribunal and the quickly drafted Convention against Genocide were indications of the sensitivity to the recent outrages. The adoption of the Universal Declaration of Human Rights in 1948, however, disclosed a broadening vision. Intended as a standard rather than a set of legal obligations, the document included familiar legal and political rights respected in the Western democracies. On the whole, these rights protect individuals against arbitrary treatment by governments. In addition, the Soviet Union and its friends, as well as gentler governments influenced by the social democratic tradition, added economic and social rights comprising positive benefits that individual citizens were to expect from their societies. For the United States, the economic and social rights seemed controversial because they included such items as the right to employment and to health care. In later attempts to turn the Declaration into binding covenants (these eventually were to come into force in 1976 with American accession), the political and civil rights were separated from the economic and social provisions.

As for colonialism, the San Francisco Conference dealt with the subject on the basis of two standards. The more far-reaching plans for the trusteeship system applied to the remaining colonies detached from Germany and Turkey after World War I for supervision under the League of Nations mandate system and any other that might be put into the category. (None ever were.) These Trust Territories fell under the supervision of the Trusteeship Council and were destined for self-government or independence. All other colonies were left politically undisturbed, although the General Assembly was to receive reports on their economic and social progress. The use to which these reports were to be put was deliberately left vague.

In treating both human rights and colonialism, the UN rested on the familiar assumption that a general, if not very certain, homogeneity of opinion held sway among governments. The United States foresaw a more rapid ending of the colonial system than did the British, French, Dutch, Belgian, and Portuguese governments, but the issue hardly seemed urgent. The stirrings among colonial peoples could be dealt with by the metropolitan governments, some of which already had plans for extending political and civil rights, including measures of self-government, to their colonial holdings. As for unrest in colonial territories, it was not considered a subject to be discussed in international forums as a threat to the peace but only as a technical issue for administrators. This was thought to be the case even in India and Burma, where independence was soon to come. In any case, the distance between the close supervision of some colonies within a Trusteeship System and the loose informational requirements for the remaining colonies clearly projected the intention of the colonial powers to reject outside meddling. Such was the attitude they almost always retained, even during the flood of decolonization after 1955.

Similarly, most governments at the San Francisco Conference either claimed to apply democratic standards or at least endorsed them. The victors in World War II were by some occult process made into the opposite of the tyrannies they defeated. The UN Charter strikes a liberal note with regard to democratic participation in government and even in international affairs. That the usual rhetoric masked wide differences of opinion about what such words as "the peoples of the world" really meant seemed less important than getting acceptance of Charter provisions that could be developed further sometime in the future. As the whole subject was deliberately combined with economic and social cooperation, human rights were not perceived by most governments as having possibly revolutionary effects. In any case, the UN could only make recommendations; furthermore, the organization was prohibited from dealing with matters that were largely within the domestic jurisdiction of governments.

Within a decade of the founding of the UN, an entirely new

perspective concerning the duration of colonial empires began to dominate the organization. The dissolution of the British Empire in India—as well as the independence of Indonesia, in which the Security Council and the United States had an important role—made it obvious that European governments could no longer employ simple violence to retain a hold on populous colonial empires. Neither the home population nor the other governments in international organizations would be content to treat large-scale liberation movements as matters for bureaucrats. Moreover, the membership of the UN increasingly included new states, whose governments found support for their anti-colonial sympathies among the traditional opponents of empire in the United States and Latin America. Within 15 years of the founding of the UN, the Algerian uprising and the growing pressure in sub-Saharan Africa demonstrated that time was running out on the remaining colonial empires.

Colonialism eventually became part of the general issue of human rights; in the process, the initial UN treatment of human rights underwent a series of metamorphoses. The original approach, which underlay the Genocide Treaty, the Universal Declaration and the long process of drafting the Covenants on Human Rights, emphasized the development of consensus among governments. This consensus could then be stated in legal forms and would become binding on governments that ratified the resultant treaties. It was a process typical of pre-World War II international institutions and generally fitted well with the procedures and tastes of the democratic governments of Western Europe. (The United States traditionally had more difficulty in following the treaty method, but did not oppose it for other nations.) Slow and painful and uncertain though it may be, the procedure had the virtue of ensuring that agreement from governments would also include a willingness to undertake the obligation to act.

The conventional process, however, soon became scrambled with other approaches. Self-determination was proclaimed as a human right by the General Assembly in 1960. The overwhelming support for this declaration, on which the United States abstained, made it obvious that the continuation of colonial government would be attacked more radically than ever before. Moreover, violations of human rights, which hitherto could be dealt with in the UN system only by the most gingerly and secluded persuasion, if at all, now became an increasingly political matter closely connected with the maintenance of the peace. The General Assembly and even the Security Council were brought into play, but selectively and on a case-by-case basis, rather than systematically as under the system envisaged in the conventional process. As a result, the denial of self-determination and general political and civil rights in Rhodesia and South Africa became the focus of system-wide political action intended to have immediate coercive effects, while other flagrant denials of human rights, such as those in Uganda, Burundi, Kampuchea, and Argentina, received little notice.

The broader political agenda that grew out of the new conception of human rights as a matter for immediate treatment in UN organs produced difficulties for the United States. Although by inclination an anti-colonial power, the United States had not contributed much to the process of drafting treaties about human rights. Indeed, from the Eisenhower through the Nixon-Ford administration the United States maintained that it would neither ratify such instruments nor recognize a need for them in this country. This was based on the assertion that its standards already were higher than the minimum proposed. Furthermore, coercive political action cut across other American commitments in the security field. It was thought in Washington that little support could be found in the electorate for such exotic and perhaps expensive undertakings as economic sanctions against South Africa. Indeed, much opposition, sometimes so effective as to carry the day, did arise to American approval of sanctions against the Ian Smith regime in Rhodesia. Elsewhere the United States faced claims, officially endorsed by UN organs, that its protegé in the Middle East, Israel, systematically violated the human rights of Arabs in occupied zones. Whatever the effect of such activities in domestic politics, however, the United States could not avoid taking difficult and sometimes unpopular positions in the Security Council and the General Assembly where, more often than not, alleged violations of human rights were identified with a breach of or threat to the peace.

Thus, the subject of human rights, conceived originally as part of the long-term program in the economic and social area, proved in fact to have a more short-term significance in the political arena.

Furthermore, the UN system extended its treatment of human rights beyond the concepts familiar in the liberal democracies which emphasized obligations of governments to provide welfare for their citizens. This gave the poorer countries grounds to argue that the economic and financial obduracy of the rich states prevented them from giving their poverty-stricken masses the help to which they were entitled.

The linking of human rights with threats to the peace, anything but unreasonable in the light of World War II, broadened the scope of UN concern with political affairs. It made possible the use of UN organs as sounding boards for opposition to the remnants of colonialism and gave an especially strong tone to complaints about racial discrimination. Inevitably, the management function of the great powers in the Security Council came into play and all Security Council members, including the United States, consequently faced difficult choices on a host of issues.

ECONOMIC COOPERATION AND THE SUPERVISION OF SOCIAL CHANGE

Promotion of economic cooperation and the supervision of social change at the international level entailed as much or more unanticipated revision of the original assumptions of the UN system than the colonial and human rights issues. Even more markedly than in the security field, the UN system initially foresaw the restoration of a prewar order that had been destroyed by the aggressive governments of the 1920s and 1930s. On the whole, a return to a liberal international economic system, or at least one managed along liberal lines, was envisaged. Even when far-reaching experiments were proposed, such as Keynes's vision of the International Monetary Fund (IMF), they tended to avoid any deliberate redistribution of income or concerted efforts to close the gap between rich and poor by means of development. The point received additional emphasis by the singling out of two financial institutions, the International Monetary Fund and the International Bank for Reconstruction and Development (the IBRD or World Bank), as different from the other specialized intergovernmental agencies. The result was that the coordinating mechanism for economic and social activity had little formal connection with the two principal operating agencies in the international financial realm.

The general principles intended for the postwar economic order can be read in the UN system's original emphasis on agreed intergovernmental cooperation. This emphasis represents a rejection of centralized management of the international economy. It favors a return to freer international trade, to a division of labor, and to careful direction by means of international treaties, as well as limited simultaneous governmental action based on recommendations and constant consultation in the UN Economic and Social Council (ECOSOC). The Council was intended to develop a technical competence that would command respect. It was also to serve as the coordinator of the work of the specialized agencies. Some of these, such as the International Labor Organization (ILO) and the International Telecommunications Union (ITU), had survived the war, and others, such as the World Health Organization (WHO) and the International Civil Aviation Organization (ICAO) were still being constructed. Operational programs, in which services were delivered directly to governments or their subjects on their own territory, would be rare and narrowly defined.

As for social issues, the UN's role would be mainly study and discussion. Only where the international ramifications of a social problem were inescapable (such as with the control of narcotic drugs) would international institutions take direct action. Most social problems that affected many countries, such as the creation of social security systems or regulation of dangerous occupations, either could be dealt with in specialized agencies by means of the treaty route or else, as with the status of women, were connected with human rights and could be handled under that rubric.

The notion that economic well-being necessarily underlay peaceful conditions in the world found a place in the UN Charter as a guiding principle for economic and social cooperation, but in fact this was largely lip-service. Few governments could permit themselves to join long-term efforts when their immediate interests or security became imperiled. Even if governments sought "peaceful change" (as scholars sometimes referred to it) as a way of eradicating the ultimate causes of conflict, they would enter uncertain ground, for it was doubtful whether the intervening steps between the generalizations on economic well-being and the attainment of peace could be put in terms of programs acceptable to all. Furthermore, a certain confusion entered the conception through the provision that the Security Council could call on the agencies in the UN system for help in case of a breach or threat to the peace. Such a provision suggests an immediacy that was usually discouraged elsewhere in economic and social activities.

The economic and social organs of the United Nations system evolved in unexpected ways. Most importantly, ECOSOC never fulfilled expectations. Even when it was a small body of 18 members, in contrast to its present membership of 54, governments failed to send their leading experts to it. In many respects, it was treated as just another diplomatic body with a special and, on the whole, dull and not very rewarding task. Nor did governments use the Economic and Social Council very often to display their best ideas in public. In part, the Council suffered from subordination to the General Assembly, since all really important recommendations and actions emerging from ECOSOC had to be endorsed by the General Assembly. As a consequence, a second debate was held on every issue in the General Assembly. Furthermore, participation in the Assembly was much wider, giving the smaller and poorer states a chance to present views that may not have been put before the Council and to vote accordingly. Canny politicians immediately understood that the General Assembly would provide the dramatic, public background that ECOSOC missed almost entirely.

The mechanisms for economic and social cooperation also were challenged almost immediately by governments and by events to stress short-term, operational programs at the international level. The aftermath of World War II was anything but cleaned up. The Council had to deal with problems of refugees and displaced persons, of disrupted regional trade and shortages of commodities. As early as 1948, it reacted to pleas for economic assistance from less developed countries by mounting a pioneering technical assistance mission to Haiti. Soon this was followed by general interest in technical assistance, a result of President Harry Truman's famous Point Four initiative.

Faith in technical assistance as a means of coping with the increasingly strident calls for aid from the less developed countries

(LDCs), which soon constituted the majority of UN members, led to the creation of broad programs to aid development. These were financed by the developed countries. Never enough to meet requests, the programs nevertheless did inject a visible UN presence in recipient countries and sometimes scored remarkable successes.

The centerpiece of the technical assistance system, constructed from two earlier agencies, is the UN Development Program (UNDP) which has had a budget as great as $500 million annually for operations in more than 120 countries. The agents employed for technical aid were from the beginning primarily the UN specialized agencies and the UN Secretariat. They responded quickly and often inventively to the opportunities to create new endeavors. Large parts of the expanding operations of the Food and Agricultural Organization (FAO), the UN Educational, Scientific and Cultural Organization (UNESCO), and the ILO operations were financed through UNDP; most other specialized agencies had at least a few UNDP projects to execute. Another related kind of international construction appeared in the World Food Program, attached to FAO. It furnishes short-term assistance in the form of surplus food for the people actually engaged in development projects. (This program owes its existence to American preoccupation with its surpluses and it has also increasingly taken part in emergency humanitarian programs.) Another short-term program executed by the UN International Children's Emergency Fund (UNICEF) at the end of World War II gradually evolved into an operation mainly intended to develop better conditions for children and mothers in place of immediate relief.

The consequence was an extension of the specialized agencies beyond the old functionalist pattern of research, agreement on common programs for execution by governments and responsiveness to a technical constituency. Increasingly, all of the specialized agencies offered services to their members and, during the last decade, such institutions as FAO and UNESCO have oriented their programs toward goals urged on them by the less developed countries, sometimes over the objections of the United States.

The remaining unanticipated change in the economic machinery had an even more remarkable character than the development of programs of service. In addition to the technical assistance and development programs, the UN system began to create institutions primarily to represent the views and demands of the less developed countries. These countries came to insist that fundamental changes in the world economic order were required so as to distribute a greater share of output and wealth to them. The same majority of less developed countries that had encouraged and fought for an expansion of services led the fight in the UN General Assembly to approve a reshaping of the UN's economic machinery with the stated goal of greater benefits for the LDCs, rather than the more limited objectives of the earlier, liberal approach.

This redirection of the UN system began with the creation of the UN Conference on Trade and Development (UNCTAD), approved by the General Assembly in 1964. The impetus for UNCTAD derived from a Soviet suggestion and was systematically opposed by the rich Western countries. Yet because of the third world majority, the new organization contrived generally to treat the socialist countries as little different from the capitalist lands. Both would be opposite numbers in bargaining with the LDCs in an effort to change the terms of trade, which were perceived, not altogether accurately, as continually reducing the poor countries' return. Creation of UNCTAD was soon followed by the establishment of the UN Industrial Development Organization (UNIDO), which was to be the LDCs' chosen instrument to push along industrialization in a way that, they believed, such older agencies as the ILO could not do.

Whatever the success of UNCTAD and UNIDO, the establishment underscored the readiness on the part of the LDCs to create machinery to confront the great economic powers of the world. LDC majorities in the UN structure permitted them to erect such institutions, and, in turn, the institutions encouraged the maintenance of solidarity among them. As a result, the LDC group was brought together with increasing frequency to consult on cooperative policies.

The high point of demands from the LDCs came with the Sixth Special Session of the General Assembly in 1974. It was there that the developing country majority designated the UN machinery as the vehicle for reaching a set of economic goals that had been explicitly fixed by means of an earlier political process. These goals were titled, rather provocatively, "A New International Economic

Order.'' The NIEO was the ultimate rejection of the notion that autonomous economic processes had to be nurtured through international cooperation in the UN system in order to raise the standard of welfare in the world. Nor could demands for repartition of the economic relationships be brushed aside by the wealthy countries as in the past: the Sixth Special Session of the General Assembly grew directly from the global crisis caused by the Arab oil boycott of 1973 and the sudden enormous increase in the price of petroleum, engineered through the Organization of Petroleum Exporting Countries (OPEC), not part of the UN system. Furthermore, it was obvious as never before that with the growth of world population, the rapid consumption of raw materials, and the power of cartelization of petroleum production, all governments had to admit a direct connection between international peace and economic issues. The changing conception of maintaining the peace was symbolized by the extensive North-South negotiations that have characterized the approach of the UN system to economic matters since the Sixth Special Session. In this set of negotiations, the United States has sometimes been an important participant but in no sense the dominant voice of two or three decades earlier.

Although some social change would accompany each economic initiative of the UN system, the Organization has never been able to treat social issues with the pointed determination with which it has sought economic reform. It has, nevertheless, taken up a long agenda of social problems. The UN soon recognized that its new technical assistance programs and financial assistance for development did directly affect society. As a result, the General Assembly endorsed the inclusion of social advice in technical assistance projects. The UNDP approved projects that related to difficulties with urbanization and town planning in developing countries and, in a quiet way, the specialized agencies took up social issues. The ILO, in particular, carried on and tried to extend its system of conventions to provide social protection of workers and spread its advisory services on such topics.

Contentious issues in the social field emerged as unexpectedly as they had in the economic area. Demographic statistics, gathered by the UN from national governments that often received technical assistance in the process, soon made plain that the world's population was increasing at a rapid, some said frightening, rate. Yet for the first 15 years or so, control of population could scarcely be mentioned in the UN system, so controversial was it. Gradually, means were found to provide some aid to governments interested in population control and by 1975 the whole subject opened up enough to become the focus of a political-level conference at Bucharest. The conference demonstrated that although controlling increases in population remained controversial, it was still possible for the UN to adopt a program of action for governments. Other social issues, such as the protection and shelter of refugees and the protection of the human environment, sparked the creation of new institutions and new international conferences. Even standards of nutrition and the significance and management of migration engaged parts of the UN system in differences of opinion. In the process, a political edge cut into the subjects that had long been the concern of technical experts, for it became increasingly clear that attempts to manage change along any one line of international cooperation involved interdependence with other programs, and eventually, political and financial choices.

THE EXPANSION OF THE INTERNATIONAL CIVIL SERVICE

Each time the United Nations system included new or broader subjects in its work programs, undertook new operations, or created new organs, the staff serving the organizations grew. This growth assumed startling qualitative and quantitative dimensions in comparison with the original assumptions of the UN system.

The San Francisco Conference, as well as almost all of the UN system, strongly endorsed the idea of an international civil service, owing allegiance to no one government and at the continuous disposal of the international institutions. Such officials were to have outstanding professional and personal qualifications and were generally to make a long career of international service. At the same time, the international civil service was to include personnel from a broad spectrum of countries to prevent it from becoming the exclusive preserve of any single country or culture. The organizational principle of the international civil service was simple enough.

A Secretary-General (in the case of the UN) or a Director-General (in the case of the specialized agencies) would be responsible for the staff and for providing the services required by international cooperation. Policies for execution by the international staff would be set by the various deliberative organs representing all governments.

The definition and adoption of the idea of an international career civil service accorded with both the practice and the inclinations of leading governments. The United States strongly favored an autonomous, energetic administrative arm, thus reflecting some of the fleeting thoughts of President Franklin D. Roosevelt. The British government favored the notion of an independent civil service that did its work in the background, following the model that Sir Eric Drummond, the first Secretary-General of the League of Nations, brought with him from his foreign office experience. The governments that had experience with the League, as well as many of its high officials, favored strengthening the powers of the Secretary-General so that on occasion he could assume a public, leading role. The Soviet Union did not object to such conceptions so long as the organs of which it was a member could issue directives and so long as some of its nationals had senior posts.

In many respects the assumptions about the international civil service that would serve the new UN system were those of traditional intergovernmental cooperation. A secretariat would set up meetings, provide basic documentation and research, and stay out of sight. In other respects, the innovative experience of the period between the world wars was to be carried on, for during that time an international secretariat had proved effective in putting forth ideas about international cooperation in the political field and especially in economic and social matters.

In one exceptional respect the new secretariat would have an overtly political role. This role was given to the UN Secretary-General, who was empowered to bring to the Security Council any matter that in his opinion involved a threat or breach of the peace (Article 99). Such a role had strong support from the United States and sympathy from many governments. Although it did not in fact go much beyond the discreet practice in the League of Nations, it surpassed any formal powers ever before given an international civil servant.

In important ways, each of the expectations about the international civil service was fulfilled, but as in other parts of the UN scheme, unanticipated developments led to challenges and partial redefinition of the original assumptions. On one level, the international civil service performed quite as expected. The usual services and preparations for international meetings and conferences were provided with high efficiency and diligence, and at times even innovatively. Such services, which have become routine to participants and observers, should not be undervalued, for they contribute to the efficiency of international cooperation as grease does to a wheel on an axle. Moreover, they consume a large segment of the budgets of international institutions.

The international civil service continued to influence organizational policies, as it had in Drummond's time at the League of Nations, if only as a result of its constant presence. In fact, it often actively sought innovation. Nowhere was this more apparent than in the elaboration of programs of technical assistance. The several secretariats of the UN system also provided the programmatic detail and bureaucratic memory for expansion in other areas, such as programs of population control and of distribution of surplus foodstuffs. Increasingly, they became involved in field operations: from furnishing highly technical consultations on a man-day basis to managing assistance for hundreds of thousands of refugees, from studying the developmental potential of a river valley to helping to redraft national legislation for the treatment of foreign corporations. In providing such services, the international secretariats, financed through the UNDP (itself the result of mergers designed and executed by international civil servants of earlier organizations) and frequently linked to loans through the World Bank, expanded enormously.

Building on the political role outlined in the UN Charter, the Office of Secretary-General also developed beyond the expectations of the original UN design. Although the Secretary-General might well have become a substantial innovator of programs affecting the general welfare, all of the holders of the office have emphasized those functions connected with maintaining the peace. Trygve Lie, the first Secretary-General insisted on his right to participate in and make suggestions to the Security Council despite the misgivings of some of its most powerful members. He also intervened in such disputes as the Berlin blockade of 1948. His support of the UN-sponsored enforcement action in Korea led to a boycott by the Soviet Union and eventual destruction of his effectiveness. Lie's successor, Dag Hammarskjöld, exploited the possibilities of his office to create the concept of peacekeeping—that military activity by the UN involving no overt violence or pressure beyond the implications of an international presence. His direction of the UN Emergency Force (UNEF) in the Sinai Peninsula after the 1956 Middle East crisis gave him enormous prestige and enhanced his ability to influence the whole of the UN's efforts to maintain peace and security. It also set the precedent that led to the UN operation in the Congo. The subsequent treatment of Hammarskjöld by the Soviet Union was reminiscent of that meted out to Lie.

The next two Secretaries-General could not have matched Hammarskjöld's creativeness, even had they tried, for the political atmosphere in the UN offered more complex crises and less scope for independent action. Nevertheless, U Thant found a useful function in the Cuban missile crisis, ended UN involvement in the Congo, tried to help stop the fighting in Indochina (openly criticizing the United States in the process), and superintended the placement of a peacekeeping force in Cyprus. He ended his term of office in 1971 as nobody's favorite but without having surrendered the right of his office to persuade, suggest, and criticize. His successor, Kurt Waldheim, also tried to remain part of the international political process. In a style different from his predecessors, he actively sought a negotiating and intermediary role and was sometimes successful in his efforts. He took part in negotiations in the Middle East, on arms control, on Rhodesia and Namibia, and on the American hostages in Iran, and developed new procedural approaches to refugee problems. His role became that of a roving ambassador, ever willing to lend assistance and to use his office in peacekeeping, relief, mediation, and provision of services. As a result he introduced a UN presence in a long series of negotiations, more frequently than not in the Third World where the UN's political role appeared to grow and perhaps to have an increasing utility. Waldheim managed, too, to avoid the direct, sharp criticism that damaged his predecessor's ability to continue in office. The efforts of the new Secretary-General, Javier Pérez de Cuéllar, in the Falklands crisis likewise indicate a willingness on the part of the Secretary-General to involve his office in sensitive political issues before the UN.

The political activities of the Secretary-General and especially the new programs of economic and social development have changed the visage of the international secretariats. Once thought of as a modestly sized collection of diplomats, the secretariats now include armed guards, warehousemen, radio operators, transportation specialists, technologists and consultants of a hundred stripes, managers of a catalog of activities and, of course, generalists who direct the new jungle of programs. Forming and administering policy for a civil service that has grown from hundreds to tens of thousands in three and a half decades has itself become an industry. This explosive growth raises questions of control and management that increasingly have become part of the discussion of the adequacy of the international civil services and of the United Nations itself.

At the same time, the international principles of the secretariats have been diluted. As early as Trygve Lie's term of office, it was apparent that the great powers did not entirely accept the notion of an international civil service whose officials did not represent governments. Accordingly, they parcelled out the second-rank posts in the Secretariat of the United Nations among themselves. Furthermore, the Soviet attacks on Lie, and under the impact of Senator Joseph R. McCarthy's noisome onslaughts, the concern of Washington about the loyalty of Americans working for the UN system tended to undermine the principle. Tunneling of this nature by the great powers never ceased. To it were added the demands by the new members that posts be given to their nationals. Thant and Waldheim bore the brunt of these demands and sympathetically used the flexibility of the civil service regulations to favor geographical—for which read national—representation above other standards.

There is no doubt that the international secretariats are more representative—in the sense of having nationals of more countries— than ever before. They are also bigger than ever before. The dilution of the principle of international service by the introduction of short-term appointments, the failure to develop career planning and development, the favoring of geographical appointments under the mantle of permissible levels for each member country, and the sensitivity to pressure by governments raises doubts about the impartiality and innovativeness of the secretariats of the UN system. It is ironic that such questions are most sharply posed by Americans, including members of Congress, many of whom were among the first to insist on responsiveness from the Secretaries-General.

INSTITUTIONAL ENDURANCE

Important assumptions of the UN system proved poorly grounded and had to be adjusted, sometimes radically, under the impact of developments in the wider political and social environment. While such developments deeply affect the UN system, the organization can neither control nor avoid them. What then is left of the institutions for the future? Do the present disappointment and disillusion, so marked in some American public groups, foreshadow both the uses and the fate of the UN system? To what extent can the battered assumptions still hold and to what extent do they represent adaptation to a world in which the fundamental power balances have shifted, in which the United States can only sometimes carry the day for its policy preferences, and in which a new and probably fundamental cleavage along North-South lines tends to dominate the agenda of the UN system?

In important respects, the assumptions of the UN system had more to do with the construction of institutions than with the policies followed by them. A fundamental assumption, which tends to get buried under the fallout of short-term controversy, has to do with the creation of permanent institutional structures in which political processes can carry on in reasonably predictable forms. The creation and nurturing of such structures represented a new degree of organization in a world robbed of almost all procedural certitude by a generation of warfare and social destruction.

The UN system consists of institutions that employ agreed procedures to seek agreed policies to cope especially with political developments. It makes a difference to all governments that they must deal regularly with the long agenda of the United Nations

General Assembly. Even the most cynical leadership has to find some responses to demands that it take a position on the resolutions introduced by other governments and by the comments emanating from the Secretary-General and his staff. On some questions, such as that of refugees recently, or the new awareness only yesterday of the importance of raw materials, including petroleum, the responses are broadcast. On such dramatic issues and a hundred lesser ones, interest groups around the world focus their professional and expert awareness. National political leaders have to reckon with the possibility, and on occasion the reality, that powerful voices in their own societies will echo the words of the General Assembly, as they have done on issues of colonialism, human rights, arms control, economic and financial reform, and humanitarian assistance.

To say that the regular, virtually inexorable, patterns of meetings, debates and pronouncements so typical of the UN system invariably or often explode into political pressures on a wide front would clearly be false. But such explosions have occurred and could again. Governments, especially those which like the United States permit active, visible political debate, must take into account the potential of such forum institutions as the General Assembly. Even if they sometimes do no more than create a nuisance, they nevertheless exist and quite likely will continue to do so, whatever the views of the United States. Such, incidentally, is the lesson of the rather petulant American withdrawal from the International Labor Organization (ILO) in 1975. The United States has now returned to membership, not necessarily with greater prestige.

The forums created in the UN system have become institutionalized in several important respects. Fixed on the political calendar, they entail deadlines that governments must meet and require decisions as to national policies, reports for the organizations involved and the selection of delegations, their instruction and their supervision. Ever more frequently, financial obligations arise from participation in the process.

The requisites of participation have led to the creation of bureaucratic structures at both the national and international levels. National governments need memories, experts, specialists, and policymakers to deal with international assemblies. Governments such as the United States, with wide interests, complex commitments, and an active and controversial domestic political life, soon must either try to develop the necessary structures for coordination or else inevitably appear to their fellow governments as amorphous in idea and confused in execution. Accordingly, the United States government has from the earliest days of the UN system maintained a rather elaborate bureaucratic network to deal with policy toward international organizations. The argument here is that such a network, whatever the quality of its work or its influence, can be understood as a component of institutionalization and an active factor implying long-term existence of the UN system.

The creation of bureaucratic structures at both the international and national levels results in the formation of a geometrical figure of relationships in which the various legs change in length and thickness, depending on the issues. Some issues, for example, involve peripheral Congressional attention in the United States but a great deal of time in the General Assembly—a general declaration on the value of using the UN Charter would have such an effect. On other issues, national legislatures that have a role in appropriating public funds for international purposes would be deeply engaged—the United States Congress typically pays close attention to a replenishment of the World Bank's soft-loan window or to a large grant to care for refugees in Southeast Asia. Other legs of the figure represent interest groups, such as an industrial association giving its views in regard to a UN-drafted convention to control the activities of transnational enterprises. The possibility of involving diverse and fairly broad publics in the UN system thus has become institutionalized, at least in a rudimentary sense. Such institutionalization does not necessarily promise positive support for anything that the UN system undertakes or even preference for that system above other possibilities for cooperative intergovernmental or unilateral action. It does provide the nucleus of an informed public that can be depended upon to raise questions and make arguments that prevent the omission, by default, of recourse to the UN system.

The UN system, moreover, offers positive opportunities for national policymakers to organize support from a wide spectrum of governments and to seek an aura of legitimacy for their programs. In this sense, the UN system provides a ready-made structure for generalizing a national initiative and avoids the necessity to find prior agreements on the rules of discussions, their locations, and their auspices. In addition, simultaneous access to many governments is easy. When agreements are reached, they have wide endorsement, thus engaging the foreign policy establishments of many governments. The Security Council, for example, can still decide to organize a peacekeeping force, support resistance to the illegal seizure of an embassy and its personnel, try to encourage cooling pressure in a civil war (as in Lebanon), and offer a framework for negotiation and positive pressure on such issues as the future of Rhodesia and Namibia. The General Assembly can set in motion a lengthy, frustrating, but still important negotiation on the law of the sea. It can initiate examination of the whole international economic system and the progress of the resulting discussions and negotiations. All the agencies of the UN system can offer technical advice for dealing with both routine problems or emergencies. They can provide knowing criticism and suggestions on ideas for international cooperation emanating from governments. Such was the role of the Food and Agricultural Organization when the United States proposed a world conference on food, which resulted in the International Fund for Agricultural Development (IFAD).

At the same time, the existence of international institutions with fixed rules and procedures allows a government to demonstrate for all to see the limits of its tolerance and the margins beyond which it will not cooperate. The United States has increasingly used its veto in the Security Council to make plain how far it will commit itself on programs urged by the UN majority. It has, for example, used the veto to prevent the adoption of far-reaching proposals of sanctions against South Africa and has also protected its relationship with Israel by the same means. Furthermore, in voluntary programs, such as the creation of a UN capital fund, it has long used its right not to join. In the General Assembly, American representatives oppose all or parts of programs that the government believes are excessive, ill-founded or irrelevant to the stated purpose. Sometimes this opposition has been voiced with great éclat, as during the tenure of Senator Daniel Patrick Moynihan as the United States Ambassador to the UN. More often, opposition is announced in speeches noted mainly inside the institutions and by negative votes that have sometimes left the United States in isolation.

In fact, opposition from the United States has the effect of dampening, if not fatally damaging, most recommendations and programs undertaken by the majority without US collaboration. In addition, the United States usually carries some, if not all, of the Western European and other affluent countries with it, either in opposition or pointed abstention. More than any other single member, the United States has the capacity to disturb and even wreck the deliberative process in the UN system and unquestionably to cripple any program requiring administrative and financial action.

Yet the persuasiveness of the United States has sharply declined in the UN system as compared with the years immediately after World War II. The new members not only have different emphases in their national policies from those of the more like-minded original membership but they also have the ability to dominate the political process. There is little the United States can do, for instance, to reverse the groundswell of governmental opinion that produced the call for a New International Economic Order, even if it can interfere with the programmatic implications of such a demand. Furthermore, the United States and its closest friends, acting together, cannot win over the Group of 77 in UNCTAD to their view of the way to manage international trade in primary commodities. Nor can it eliminate in the short term the suspicion on the part of many governments of poor countries that American espousal of freer international trade merely cloaks the domination of the third world's economies by uncontrollable multinational corporations.

Nevertheless the United States and other experienced and affluent governments have possibilities for persuading the majorities or substantial parts of them on many issues. The positive response to the American position in the Seventh Special Session of the General Assembly, which took up the New International Economic Order from the previous year's much more bitter session, clearly signified the attraction that well-integrated suggestions from the United States can have. Similarly, the United States has been able to lead the way on agricultural cooperation in the World Food Program and IFAD and has been able to widen the participation and adjust, probably beneficially, the assistance given refugees in Southeast Asia. The American role in the UNDP remains strong. On the broader stage of the General Assembly, American support remains valuable and worth bidding for. The United States, as well as other participants with wide interests, often can still use the fixed institutional practices to organize support for their positions and to gain adjustments of majority views in order to accommodate American needs. They can, moreover, posit the credible threat of turning programs of action that they find unsatisfactory into nullities. But such use of the political process in the UN requires well worked-out positions and the investment of a great deal of effort in negotiating agreements with others. Even then, it will not always be possible to find agreement, but it may be impossible less often than seems generally to be believed outside of specialist circles.

It appears then that important institutional aspects of the UN system have not been fatally damaged and may even have gained in flexibility as a result of adaptation to new conditions. Certainly dealings among the member governments involve more possible approaches than ever before. The fixed procedures of the UN system on balance remain an advantage to all the members as compared with an unorganized world. They often faithfully represent the opinions of governments, thus limiting commitment on the one hand and, on the other, making hard-won substantive agreements more secure. The danger is always present that unpleasantness will be papered over with formulas to permit an international assembly to agree on something, but such flimsy constructions usually have no meaning. What does have significance is the use of normal procedures to reach understood, cooperative positions based on negotiation and give-and-take. Governments with wide interests can probably take part in such a process with high effectiveness; certainly the United States is far from bereft of influence, even if it cannot count on emerging triumphant from each session of each institution in the UN system.

THE NEW BALANCE OF ISSUES

Established primarily in a desire to protect international peace, the UN system seems at first glance to have been transformed into a multi-part set of tools to deal with issues of development, economic distribution, and the aftermath and remnants of colonialism. The security functions have neither grown as much, measured in terms of expenditure, staff, or complexity of institutionalization, as those promoting the general welfare. Is the original central function of the UN system hopelessly overshadowed by new issues of development and distribution of wealth? Does an attempt to strike the balance between security and other issues merely disclose a new distortion? Has the heart of the UN system shrunk traumatically?

One approach to answering such questions involves estimating the strength of institutionalization of the system. If the security functions can be carried out by an active and vital Security Council that in fact is available for action, the relative balance struck in terms of time and institutional growth may have little significance. The Security Council has in fact remained alive and ready for action. It has been used repeatedly in dealing with the Middle East, with Cyprus, with Southern Africa, and with complaints from other quarters, including some from Southeast Asia, from North Africa, and from Latin America. The ambassadors, especially those representing the major governments, have usually had high prestige and respect both in their own governments and abroad. In this sense, the UN system still operates.

Furthermore, because the Security Council deals with actual or potential breaches of the peace, its agenda gets the serious treatment that governments and those publics interested in foreign affairs reserve for imminent danger. In addition, the Security Council offers a forum for displaying ideological wares in connection with strife over political power. This time-worn function of the Council has never ceased, even if some of the explanations have become tired and flabby. Yet even such speeches can sometimes signal an opportunity for agreement or adjustment.

Yet the Security Council and the UN generally remain far from the main supervisory centers for directing the maintenance of peace. Rather, they are used selectively and not always with much visible effect. This situation poses for policymakers the question of whether this old function could be revitalized and whether there would be any profit in doing so.

It is impossible to deal simply and convincingly with such a query. It could be argued that without an active, comprehensive security function, the UN system runs the danger of rejecting fundamental activities involving power relationships in favor of treatment of derivative and secondary matters. Obviously, a world war would indeed upset international cooperation to foster the general welfare. But it is not clear that the use of the UN system to deal with short-term threats to the peace in fact strengthens the entire system. Such threats often could be dealt with outside the system and, indeed, the UN Charter makes clear that the system is to be used after the more traditional diplomatic methods have been found wanting. Furthermore, it could conceivably be more important to have an institution that functions well on selected occasions rather than one that takes up all matters and does so with little success.

The existence of manifold means for dealing with security lends strength to the argument that American policy might best reserve for treatment by the United Nations those issues that can best be handled in its forums. As a leading world power, the United States has open to it bilateral and regional channels for approaching security questions. It has, in fact, long ago agreed with the Soviet Union that such long-term issues as strategic armaments should be negotiated for the most part in bilateral talks. The United States can also employ regional organizations, as in Latin America, and in some instances alliance structures such as NATO, as in the continuing friction between Greece and Turkey. It is also possible to shift from one forum to another.

The United Nations offers the advantage of procuring a wide consensus for those negotiations in which it is successful. It also has a way of focusing pressures on the parties under a mantle of legitimacy. Thus, for instance, the Security Council remains a highly useful instrument for dealing with problems of Southern Africa. These require both ample public display, because of the emotional and ideological implications, and sustained attention from several governments. Even slow progress toward managing such an issue underscores the usefulness of the UN system. Furthermore, agreements reached in other negotiations can be given general ventilation and support through the UN mechanism.

Other matters involving international security have such broad implications that it is advisable to bring a wide spectrum of governments into the discussion. This is surely the case with such an issue as the international control of nuclear materials or the suppression of international terrorism. Such items do not necessarily imply treatment of an immediate crisis, but they have a distinct bearing on long-term international security.

A critical situation such as the seizure by Iranians of the American Embassy and its personnel in Teheran illustrates the sort of issue that can usefully be treated by a broad discussion of international practice. Even if the United States at first hesitated to bring the matter to the Security Council for fear of creating yet another, possibly fatal, complication, the impartial approach of the Secretary-General, who summoned the Council on his own initiative, still was available.

Using a selective approach would not bring the United Nations to a central, directing place in international politics. Yet it would fit perfectly well with the explicit assumptions of the UN Charter, which direct member states to try to settle their difficulties by their own means and to come to the Council only when they cannot. In addition, the United States can try to induce the Council to intervene, in accordance with its stated powers, in matters that could develop into a threat to the peace. Usually such an attempt to produce a broad discussion will succeed at least in permitting the United States to exert its persuasiveness and influence on a given issue.

As for cases involving the outbreak of hostilities, it is likely that many of these will appear on the UN agenda, no matter how the United States believes they should be approached. Even so, some issues will not get full treatment, as was the case with the war in Vietnam. In that instance, the United States at least twice sought discussion in the UN forums but did so in what was perceived by other governments as an unpromising manner. Probably that perception grew out of a lack of clarity about what outcome the United States really sought from UN involvement.

On other matters of quite real importance, such as peacekeeping in the Middle East and the management of conflict and its inhuman aftermath at the time of the severing of Bangladesh from Pakistan, the UN machinery allowed American participation on an agreed and limited basis. American policymakers could well expect similar crises in the future and prepare for UN involvement in them. American participation can be effective to the degree that the United States really knows what it seeks and what it is prepared to give to the UN effort. If it is not ready to proceed on the basis sought by others, it has the ultimate right to refuse. But if it can join, it has the possibility of influence and even outright leadership to achieve its own goals, although these goals will always be examined in the light of commitments made in the UN system. If that is done, then selective backing of UN action by the United States can benefit both international institutions and the United States. The importance of the security function would not be denigrated and attempts to use it for blatantly chauvinistic purposes would tend to be discouraged.

TECHNICAL OPERATIONS AND PUBLIC PERCEPTIONS

Much of the work of the UN system, even in connection with sharp crises involving international security, must take place at an almost invisible technical level. Permanent civil servants at both the national and international level are charged with negotiations, decisions, and operations. Nowhere is this more true than in the areas of greatest expansion of the UN system, those involving international cooperation for development and redistribution. Furthermore, although most formal decisions in the UN system are taken openly in organs sitting in full view of outside observers, generally such gatherings involve narrowly defined agendas and a great deal of earlier consideration and investigation. Thus, much of the work of the UN system has neither drama nor simplicity. It lends itself badly to treatment in 45 seconds on television or in 250 words in a popular newspaper. On those rare occasions when the UN system poses dramatic issues—usually in matters of war and peace or of desperate human need, as among the refugees from Cambodia—it gets much display to large audiences, especially in the developed countries.

Technical treatment of specialized subject matter does, however, have its defined publics. Their representatives often appear at meetings in the UN system as observers and sometimes as participants. The United States delegation to the World Administrative Conference on Radio Communication of the International Telecommunications Union in 1979 included both civil servants and industrial personnel. The technical press carries reports on progress and results and disseminates criticism. Similar comments could be made about the attention ecologists, international lawyers, agronomists, development economists, pharmacists, statisticians, advocates of human rights, and trade unionists give various parts of the UN system.

The existence of specialized publics that have contact with the UN system does not guarantee either sympathy or willing involvement. It merely means that an opportunity for understanding technical aspects of international cooperation is offered to large numbers of trained people. While some theorists have dreamed of converting opportunities for understanding into firm loyalties, such an outcome can hardly be predicted with confidence.

If the existence of multiple publics reflects the growth of the UN system, it also highlights the mounting sophistication of both the institutions and their programs. What the UN system does, the way it proceeds, the manner in which it explains itself, all have grown in complexity. Like national governments everywhere, the UN system does not represent only agreed views among men of good will but rather a range of ideas and decisions, some of which contradict others. The clarity of aims in 1945—maintaining the peace first and then some cooperation to help that process in the long run—has given way to entangled and complex goals intended to satisfy new and changing interests.

Initial notions that the UN system could count on generalized, favorable mass support in the United States have become harder to sustain in the face of the consequences of institutional development and more varied behavior by governments. The mass public that gives fleeting attention to the UN system has probably not comprehended the more recent patterns. (Nor have some elites.) To an extent, disillusionment among American publics may be the result of excessive expectations. A more telling explanation may perhaps be found in naive ethnocentric views of international politics among broad segments of the American population. A yet more significant fact appears to be the close correlation between the attitude of governmental elites, especially the President and his immediate advisers, in the United States and the way in which the UN system is viewed. In periods of strong leadership away from multilateral diplomacy (as during the late days of the Johnson presidency, most of the Nixon presidency and now again in the Reagan tenure) the use of the UN system, which continues in most respects despite the attitude of the White House, gets little credit.

If a wider understanding of the purposes and uses of the UN system is sought, it probably can be reached more efficiently through patient explanation of the American approach to the UN system on particular issues than in a mass exhibition of superficial loyalty. At the same time, when American policy in international agencies needs mass support, as in the case of coping with the refugee flows of Southeast Asia or feeding the starving of Kampuchea or Bangladesh, policymakers can no doubt rely on the deep compassion that Americans have often demonstrated in the past.

The UN system could be encouraged by governmental decisions to build understanding and perhaps respect among defined American publics. The device of special conferences on defined issues, such as those on the environment, food problems, population, and others, has the effect of engaging specialists and interest groups. When they are well prepared, include the participation of leading American experts and interest groups, and point toward some practical outcomes, even if these are no more than a better definition of problems, they probably serve a useful purpose. Nevertheless, the proclamation of years of special attention for children, refugees, human rights, women, and other issues and the holding of special conferences can be overdone, destroying the effectiveness of the entire approach. American policy should therefore assess such conferences with a critical eye, weighing both the positive and negative effects. Where positive outcomes may result, an American contribution can often be crucial. Where there may be serious negative consequences, either in terms of solving problems or threatening existing cooperation, United States participation can excusably be restrained or even withheld.

Contact between specialized American publics and the UN system can also be maintained efficiently by high quality international secretariats that produce imaginative research and policy suggestions. Americans should participate in these secretariats, contributing both from the special reservoirs of national competence and by maintaining connections to various publics in the United States. As the international secretariats have expanded, it has not been the case that outstanding young Americans have chosen to make careers in them. In part, they have been discouraged by the lack of a consistent attitude of support for their participation on the part of American administrations. They have also been held back by the turgidness of the UN personnel system, by a lack of information, and by the very small number of leading Americans in the international civil service with whom they could have contact. Furthermore, the United States has not always been able to furnish its most able candidates for posts in the UN system. One consequence of this is the often tenuous liaison between Americans who are international officials and the natural domestic publics who would follow their work. To reverse this outcome will take much effort over the long term on the part of the American leadership at senior civil service and political levels. Yet much could be gained from the investment of more and better defined effort, especially that aimed at encouraging and protecting the careers of outstanding young Americans who could contribute to the international civil service. Their contribution might eventually help raise the standards of work in the service, add to understanding in crucial specialized publics, including the Congress, and encourage the kind of constructive criticism that is useful to policymakers.

However strengthened the connections between the UN system and specialized American publics may become, complaints of "politicization" may be expected to continue with regard to the functioning of parts of the UN system. Such complaints will in part represent the defeat of particular groups seeking policies congenial or rewarding to themselves. In part, they will concern the tactics used in international organizations. In fact, the term "politicization" itself creates difficulties of understanding. The growing scope of the UN system implies that more and different governments see in it a chance for influencing choices to their advantage. Such has been the American course in the UN system from the beginning and it would be naive to expect much else from other members.

There have been other complaints about inappropriate subject matter being taken up in parts of the UN system, with the result that actions are undertaken that are irrelevant to the main work of the various UN bodies. Such complaints multiply when, for example, a resolution condemning Israeli handling of occupied territories is pushed in the setting of an institution such as the UN Development Program or some specialized committee of the World Health Organization. In part, such distortions can be accepted philosophically as reflecting the zeal of representatives who want to preach to converted publics at home. At the same time, it must be remembered that it has been part of past American policy to involve specialized agencies in issues of peace and security, as in Korea and the Congo, and to view humanitarian problems as inseparable from political issues, as with the Palestinian refugees under the care of the UN Relief and Works Agency. It cannot have come as a surprise to the United States that other governments can also comprehend humanitarian and technical issues as offering opportunities to make statements about who should rule, who should benefit and how.

A more serious difficulty arises when the time and resources of technical agencies suffer from substantial diversion into propagandistic quarreling, arbitrary allocation, and incompetent decisions. In such instances, the United States does not lack the ability to create pressure and to withhold its often vital support. It can use its strength and persuasiveness to limit wasteful approaches to technical matters and to seek tactics that will produce better results. Nevertheless, the United States and other governments can scarcely expect to dominate the work of the UN system. As a result, tactics leading to short-term payoffs for some members in terms of publicity, doctrinal support, and shows of solidarity can be anticipated alongside possibly serious work. Whether the balance between useful results and inappropriate rhetoric is acceptable to the United States ought to be determined both in the light of current programs and future potentials.

SOME CONCLUSIONS

The creators of the UN system expected it to develop and adapt to changing international circumstances. In many respects, it has done precisely what was expected. It has become universal, its agenda has reflected the needs of its new membership, and the United States has released its earlier position of overweening influence on all matters before the world system. The United Nations itself no longer is busy with matters of peace and security before all else and the former enemy states of World War II have been integrated into the world organization. Yet 38 years after the founding of the UN, the world remains insecure and the UN machinery to provide security has never developed fully or as expected.

However, the UN system continues to expand and the demands placed on it evidently are without end. The new agenda emphasizes economic and social change at the international level; such change involves questions of justice and human rights at the national level. In a sense, then, the agenda has not changed at all. Although the mode of approach and the institutional arrangements have been adapted, the UN agenda still inevitably deals with human rights, justice, economic efficiency, and the adjustment of changing societies. The UN system, whatever its specific agenda, must still rely primarily on member states for the execution of programs agreed to at the international level. As a backdrop to all this activity, the dark shadows of national political insecurity and violence still threaten to undo accomplishments in these other realms.

The United States can find positive opportunities for beneficial international cooperation in this complex machinery. To use such opportunities, it must take part in the process of negotiation within the UN system, but, like other members, it is under no compulsion to support wasteful, misdirected, or repugnant efforts. In fact, its capacity to refuse has been used more often during the last 18 years than during the first 20. In retrospect, such a development appears reasonable and normal in a rapidly changing world of new demands, many of which the United States is not yet prepared to meet. Some of these demands, which imply admission of a feeling of guilt for past policies or involve acts of retribution for real or fancied grievances, will no doubt never evoke a favorable reaction from the United States government, whatever the attitude of some American political groups.

Participation in the contemporary United Nations system requires a great deal of sophistication among both policymakers and domestic publics. The United States participates across a broad front of UN activities and therefore what the UN system does has significance for a large number of publics, even if the consequences are not immediately evident. Problems of coordination in the vastness of the United States government and its political entourage become more difficult as policy choices involving international organizations are at once more delicate and more numerous, reflecting both institutional complexity and longer international agendas. In any case, the old visions of friendly and cooperative town meetings of the world on the shores of the East River have had to give way to a more selective and expert approach. The process of attitudinal change that follows from selective cooperation and a nuanced approach to the UN system probably is far from complete. As a consequence, support by American publics for participation in the UN system often seems confused and frequently inappropriate.

Such support can be greatly influenced by the tone adopted by political leadership. If the current complexities of the UN system demand an approach different from the earlier one of generalized support, then political leaders must try to demonstrate how particular aims in American policy can best be met and served through participation in the UN system. By doing so, they can also build understanding of how the system works in a world in which American deeds and words evoke responses very different from those of 1945.

MAJOR OBJECTIVES AND FUNCTIONS OF THE UN: THE VIEW FROM ABROAD

IVOR RICHARD

In order to try and analyze the different perceptions and expectations that the various groups of countries have in the United Nations, it is necessary to view them against the background of the changes that have taken place since 1945. That there have been profound changes is undeniable. It may, however, be useful to analyze the nature of those changes and to ask the question: what can we realistically expect from the UN as the number of problems that require global management continues to increase?

PERSPECTIVES AT THE UN: THEN AND NOW

For the United States and the Western nations (including my own) the UN was perceived initially as an organization that grew out of the disasters of the 1930s and out of the victorious alliance of World War II. It was envisaged by Roosevelt and Churchill as an institution that could provide a framework for world order founded on intervention by the great powers on the side of peace. The basic assumption was that the victorious alliance, as represented by the five permanent members of the Security Council, could and would continue after the war as "quasi-umpires" whose collective authority could be invoked if international peace and security were seriously threatened.

Contrary to popular belief, the enforcement machinery in the Charter was not drafted by naive, over-idealistic men. Whatever one thinks of the triumvirate of Roosevelt, Churchill, and Stalin, naiveté and an excess of idealism are not the two qualities which come to mind.

Given agreement between the five permanent members, there is little wrong with the enforcement provisions of the Charter. The Military Staff Committee of the Security Council has met monthly for the last 38 years. At each meeting they agree on the agenda, read the minutes of the last meeting, fix the date of the next, and then adjourn. It is worthwhile keeping the machinery oiled in case political agreement should prove possible in the future, but it must be said that the responsibility for its disuse lies with the membership and not with the institution. Were political agreement to prove possible, the machinery could be made to run perfectly well.

The price for Big Five agreement to the Charter in its present form was the inclusion of the veto powers of the permanent members. It was never envisaged that that power would be used in the way that it has been (by both sides). The assumption was that only in extremis would a country resort to the veto to protect its vital national interests. It was felt (on the Western side at least) that global considerations would usually override national interests.

Again the practice has proved entirely different. In terms of radically altering the perception of national interests by member states, we are still only at the beginning of a process whose end is not yet in sight.

The second assumption on which the enforcement provisions of the Charter were based was that in the event agreement were possible it would be feasible to enforce the peace by military intervention. That aggression would change its character over the course of the next several decades was not foreseen, nor could it have been. Aggression is no longer simply a matter of crossing borders with military expeditions, but can involve manipulation of the economy and of social conditions, political infiltration, propaganda, and the maintenance of ideologically based spheres of influence. These possibilities are nowhere mentioned in the UN Charter. For these reasons, notes UN Under Secretary General for Special Political Affairs Brian Urquhart, ''In the postwar situation, clear acts of

aggression were hard to identify and even harder to agree upon.''
When this was coupled with the revolutionary rethinking of the
meaning of war prompted by the development of atomic weapons,
concludes Urquhart, ''the Charter idea of collective security [be-
came] increasingly irrelevant to postwar realities.''[1]

So far as the Security Council is concerned, the Big Five fell out
early. As a result, the structure envisaged for peace enforcement
has remained relatively unused. In situations where agreement, or
at least acquiescence, has proved possible, then the Security Council has functioned in a reasonably successful way. Discussion in the
Security Council has at various times helped avert major hostilities
between Iran and Iraq, between Greece and Turkey over Cyprus,
between Morocco and Algeria over the Spanish Sahara, between
Portugal and Indonesia over Timor, between Greece and Cyprus
again over the Aegean islands. Peacekeeping forces in Cyprus and
the Middle East helped maintain a lower level of tension. What the
Security Council has not been able to do is resolve the major political problems facing the world. It cannot solve the problem of Cyprus; it cannot solve the issues in the Middle East or in southern
Africa. What it can do is attempt to prevent hostilities from either
breaking out or escalating, provide a forum within which discussions can take place, buy time in situations in which time is in itself
frequently a victory, and provide international forces to try and separate potential combatants.

Nor can the Security Council settle the major problems between
the superpowers or their respective alliances. Bloc-to-bloc disarmament is unlikely to be successful when pursued within the UN
context, and the ideological divisions in the world will hardly be
resolved by discussion in New York. Despite the Security Council's successes, however, if one were to compare the operation of
the Council in practice with the expectations placed in it in 1945,
one would have to conclude that it has failed to conform to those
expectations.

The growth of the Third World and, more significantly, that all
the major powers now find it necessary or desirable to pursue policies that do not upset too many Third World countries at once, has
provided an unforeseen brake on national freedom of action. Almost all countries now feel this inhibition. That is not to say that

the inhibition always successfully inhibits, but even the superpowers now find it desirable to pursue policies or at least to present their policies in ways that do not offend the Third World too deeply. It was notable that when Vietnam invaded Cambodia, and again when the Soviet Union invaded Afghanistan, the combined voting power of the nonaligned members of the Security Council forced the Russians in each instance to veto an action that they would clearly have preferred to avoid. The same is true of Western policy toward South Africa. That we are now collectively engaged in an attempt to ensure a peaceful transition in Namibia is directly due to the pressure exerted on the West in the Security Council in 1977 and 1978.

It is likely that the peacekeeping activities of the Security Council, though nowhere explicitly envisaged in the Charter, will in the future expand. There is something dramatic and attractive about the possibility of a global institution inserting its soldiers into an area of high tension in an attempt to keep the peace. That the peace has not always been kept is hardly surprising. What is surprising is that the UN and its members have developed mechanisms for neutral interventionism, and this at a time in history when ideological divisions have run deep. When Israel invaded Lebanon in March 1978, the Security Council met in emergency session, the necessary resolutions were all passed in two days, and 24 hours thereafter the first UN troops were moving into position. In that instance the machinery of the Security Council worked in precisely the way it was meant to. What was significant, however, was that it functioned in this way because the non-aligned and Arab countries were able to overcome Soviet reluctance to support such an intervention. Although the Security Council cannot always respond so successfully or so rapidly, as more countries gain UN peacekeeping experience this side of the Security Council's work is likely to grow.

If expectations that the Security Council would be able to operate effectively to enforce global peace have proved to be unrealistic, the early approach to the General Assembly has turned out to be equally misguided. Senator Vandenberg's much-criticized view of the General Assembly as a "global town meeting" has proved to be inaccurate. The citizenry of the town have failed to agree on much, save that we are all living on the same planet. The Western assumption in 1945 was that the General Assembly would proceed by rational argument to objective decisions of profound persuasive effect. While the decisions were not to be binding, it was nevertheless felt that men of good will calmly reasoning together at a high international level would be able to produce sensible solutions. At no time was it envisaged that the Assembly would turn out to be a meeting place for groups of countries with special interests and a forum within which those special interests would be advanced. Rather, it was believed that the Assembly would be an institution in which global interests would predominate and in which national interests would be subordinated. Also implicit in the early Western view of the assembly was the belief that votes held in a quasi-parliamentary manner could help to determine international issues. Nothing has proved to be further from the truth. If a vote has to be taken in the General Assembly (unless it is intended to be a purely declaratory exercise), then even the winners of the vote have, in reality, lost. Agreement on substance has proved to be much more important than the mathematics of majority decisions. Consensus voting, and indeed consensus diplomacy of the kind now practiced in New York, was foreign to the signatories of the Charter. That it would become the basis for multilateral negotiating was unforeseen.

There is no longer a Western majority in the General Assembly, but there is no Eastern majority either. The Assembly is now dominated by Third World countries and is therefore much less predictable than it ever was in the past. While this makes life difficult for Washington or London, it makes it equally difficult for Moscow or Peking. The Russian delegation in New York often seemed unpleasantly surprised when it was confronted by the mass of newly emerging nations. This group is collectively much less predictable, more difficult, more "uppity" than pleases either of the superpowers or their allies, used as they are to more regulated and formalized methods of diplomatic bargaining.

It is sobering to realize that the three main developments in world politics since 1945 were all unperceived at the time the Charter was drafted. The Cold War was not foreseen, decolonization was thought of as a much slower process than it turned out to be, and economic development in the Third World was little more than a pious hope.

Moreover, the economic assumptions that the West held in 1945 were that the status quo ante could be restored. The world economy was perceived essentially in terms of modified capitalism, and the arguments that then took place were about the extent of the modifications necessary to adapt that system to a postwar world. There was no suggestion that the world economy could be centrally directed or that there should be effective global management. The IMF and the IBRD were institutions designed to protect the flow of world trade in Western directions and to maintain currency stability between the major trading nations. The Third World, if considered at all, was perceived as a group of nations whose main economic function was as primary producers, and whose political systems would gradually and paternalistically move out of the colonial era to independence and Western styles of government. There was no serious talk of global economic development in the sense that we now understand it. Relief and aid were envisaged but no one in 1945 thought in terms of a major restructuring of the world economic system.

Many of the assumptions that the US and its allies held in 1945, and upon which the UN as an instrument of international cooperation was based, have thus proved to be either inaccurate or invalid. The world has just not behaved in the way that it was supposed to, and if the world is different, then so is the UN. It is, however, a tribute to the flexibility of the Charter and the adaptability of those working in the UN that it has proved able to adjust to these new conditions.

Hammarskjöld once wrote that the UN represented "the beginning of an organic process through which the diversity of peoples and their governments are struggling to find common ground upon which we can live together in the one world which has been thrust upon us before we are ready."[2] More recently, Harlan Cleveland has written extensively on the need for new structures to manage a new interdependence.[3]

Both these viewpoints are correct. The world has not yet proved able to create institutions at a global level that are capable of managing the problems of an increasingly interdependent planet. The real issue is whether we can create out of the present UN an organization for world order that is both relevant and effective. We are now in a period of intense and accelerating transition, and against this background it is worth considering what each group of countries can realistically expect from the UN.

Why do we find it necessary and useful to expend so much time, diplomatic effort, and money in maintaining delegations in New York and in participating so fully in UN activities? The answer must vary according to each group.

THIRD WORLD PRIORITIES AT THE UN

For the Third World the motivation is fairly clear. Newly emergent from the colonial era, they share a common heritage of poverty, underdevelopment, and vulnerability. Nowhere in the other international institutions do they have such voting strength or comparable influence. There is an inevitable tendency to "huddle together for warmth" when they confront global forces, both economic and political, infinitely more powerful than those they can themselves summon. It is the collectivity of the confrontation that makes the UN so attractive to Third World countries. Of course they differ in their ideologies (though almost all profess non-alignment), their stages of development (e.g., Singapore and Upper Volta), their geographical position in the world and hence their immediate interests, and their systems of government (e.g., Algeria and India). But what binds them together seems to be stronger than those forces that tend to drive them apart. Even the oil and non-oil producers profess and accept a degree of common purpose greater than their differing economic interests.

What seems to unite the Third World are three basic issues: the state of the world economy and their place in it; the Middle East; and southern Africa. Of the three, the most important and enduring will most likely prove to be the first.

Southern Africa is, in a sense, an easy issue for a Third World country at the UN. It has colonial overtones and therefore its virtue is apparent. The lead can be taken by black Africa; in addition, there is little likelihood of any non-African Third World state being called upon actually to do much about it, since the pressure on South Africa is perceived as being vicarious and capable of being applied only by the industrialized West. It is thus an issue that has morality on its side and unites at little cost. Who could wish for more? It is, moreover, an issue eminently suitable for UN discussion. Political pressure can be applied on the West in the Assembly or the Security Council in a public and declaratory way that is unlikely to produce adverse reactions from the Western nations themselves. Deep down, most of the industrialized democracies recognize at least the rough justice of much of what is said about apartheid. They are not prepared to impose economic sanctions against South Africa, but equally they are not prepared to penalize those countries or groups of countries who demand loudly that we should.

The Middle East is more complicated, particularly since Camp David, but even here there seems to be more uniting the Third World than dividing it. The rights of the Palestinians have become a Third World issue based not on a desire to curry favor with the oil producers but rather on the principle of the non-admissibility of territorial acquisition by force. Were it otherwise, many of their own borders would be seen to be quite vulnerable. It is this principle, too, that accounted for Third World reaction against Vietnam's invasion of Kampuchea and its condemnation of the Soviet invasion of Afghanistan. Again, the Palestinian issue has the attraction of being vicarious in the UN context and, again, it is an issue that, for all the public declarations, is unlikely to be resolved by public pressure inside the UN.

But what really provides the cement holding the Third World together is the whole complex of economic and politically related issues in the demand for a New International Economic Order. In brief, the developing countries are demanding radical changes in the functioning of the world economy with deliberate (even "affirmative") action in their direction. Their demands include greater access to Western markets for their goods, particularly their manufactures; higher and more stable prices for their raw materials; freer access to Western technology; curbs on the operation of the multinationals, particularly in the extractive industries; lower and inflation-proof prices for their imports from the developed world; and, finally, a far greater share in the management of the world economy. It is a formidable list that, on any view, will require much time to negotiate and a difficult period of adjustment for the West to accept.

If made individually, or even regionally, those demands could safely be ignored by the West. Some countries (including, I regret to say, my own) seem to believe that they can be ignored even when made collectively by the Third World as a whole. This is unlikely to be either possible in the long term or desirable in the short and medium terms. World economic stability in the twenty-first century depends on there being a reconciliation of the claims of the Third World and the desires of the industrialized nations. At the most basic and fundamental level the world cannot persist and prosper when one-third of it is rich and getting richer and two-thirds is poor and getting poorer. That is a recipe for revolution, not for progress.

Given the nature of these demands and the necessity for making them forcibly and collectively, it is hardly surprising that the UN is extremely attractive to the Third World as the principal forum within which they are to be negotiated. The proof of this particular pudding lies in its past eating, and the record is there to be read.

In explaining the reservations put forward by the United Kingdom on the Program for Action for the establishment of a new international economic order adopted at the Sixth Special Session of the General Assembly in April 1974, I said in a resounding cliché "things will never be the same again"—nor have they been. In 1974 there was a feeling prevalent in many Western capitals that this pressure for a NIEO was something that need not be taken seriously. Certainly the Sixth Special Session caught the West totally unprepared for what was to follow. The documents that emerged in the form of the Program of Action were comprehensive and detailed, far too much so as it turned out. But they were a political expression of the determination of the Third World to achieve major changes in the world economy and their part in it. The West was given warning of what was to come unless it took the NIEO seriously, as all now do.

US Ambassador John Scali, when at the UN, said in October 1974 in a speech that was both perceptive and prophetic, "We in the industrialized world have received fair notice that we must cooperate in creating a more equitable distribution of the world's bounty or risk finding ourselves isolated in a world of hostile nations and desperate men."[4]

By 1977 the Western attitude had changed somewhat, at least at a political level. We were by then all taking the North-South dialogue seriously, and discussion was joined.

The significance of this episode lay in the fact that the Third World had successfully used the UN as an instrument of pressure on the West and had thereby achieved a distinct change of political attitude. The UN is important to the Third World precisely because it enables them to exercise a collective clout which individually they could not conceivably possess. It also accounts for what appeared to many Western observers to be a quite extraordinary passivity of the Third World in the face of OPEC's price increases of 1973–74 and 1978–79. What was not realized was that to many developing countries OPEC was not only a catalyst but also an example. Their action was one in which a group of small, developing, and relatively poor countries took on the mighty West and won. As such it induced admiration rather than anger, and envy rather than hostility.

To many a developing country the institutions of the UN (with one major exception), if not perfect, are by no means unacceptable. Voting procedures in the General Assembly, Third World domination of ECOSOC, the opportunities the UN gives smaller countries to play more important diplomatic roles than they ever could bilaterally, the use of the UN as the principal forum for negotiating the NIEO, the operation of the specialized agencies as development and relief mechanisms, the sensitivity of the Secretary-General and his staff in dealing with Third World issues—all these tend to warm the developing world towards the UN as an institution (perhaps the only major one) in which they receive the weight and attention they believe themselves entitled to.

The major exception to this within the UN system is, of course, the Security Council. It is difficult to argue that the veto is a device of democracy. It is not. It is equally difficult to envisage any realistic circumstances in which it is likely to disappear. It represents too great an accretion of power to those countries fortunate enough to possess it for any of them to be prepared to relinquish it voluntarily. To replace it with a democratic system of voting in the Security Council would tend to downgrade the Council rather than increase the power of non-permanent members. A mini-General Assembly concerned with international peace and security is hardly likely to be more effective than the present system.

In short, a Third World country at the UN can expect support from its colleagues and peers, greater collective influence than it possesses bilaterally, an opportunity to make its views heard on a world scale, cheaper diplomatic representation since everyone else is also in New York, a greater understanding and airing of its own problems and, most important of all, a forum for discussing the great economic issues of the world in which the debate and the voting is not weighted, as they would see it, in the direction of the more advantaged.

In terms of the future politics of the world, this process has much to commend it. These new nations have to be brought into the world community in a way that enables them to participate relevantly and effectively. The diplomatic learning process is shortened considerably if a country can acquire experience and skill in the company of 156 others.

Nor should we be surprised if against this background there is a tendency to politicize the work of other UN institutions. Seen as a means of defining and exerting pressure, the specialized agencies are just as convenient a mechanism as is the General Assembly or ECOSOC. It may irritate the functionally minded Westerners, but in a way that is the object of the exercise.

SOVIET OBJECTIVES AT THE UN

The Soviet perspective on the UN is narrower and cruder. It is perceived primarily as a threat and secondly as a means of extending its influence in the Third World. I detected no sign whatsoever during my time at the UN that the Russians were prepared to participate in the establishment of a system of world order that might inhibit their national freedom of action. I saw little indication that they were even beginning to think kindly of supranationalism save on their own very restricted terms. The cold warriors of the 1950s were still very much alive in the sense that world politics were perceived largely in confrontational terms. The Soviet Union was often extremely difficult to deal with: narrow, introverted, suspicious, with a slow bureaucracy and a pervading security service. It was not that they were particularly Communist. It was that they were extremely Russian, and as such heirs to all the complex psychology of the Slavs' relationship with the West. To the Russians and their allies, the UN is an institution to be used to further their national interests, particularly as a forum for embarrassing the West. I can recall no Soviet initiative that struck me as an attempt to advance global cooperation, either in the Security Council, the Assembly or ECOSOC, where their contribution was invariably ideological and never financial. They are, however, often forced into acquiescence by the combined weight of the non-aligned states and the West. Nonetheless, their consent to peacekeeping activities, for example, is grudging and reluctant. For them, Security Council activity is at best peripheral to their real interests, unless over southern Africa and the Middle East, where the West and Israel are in the dock. Otherwise, the Russian attitude toward Security Council intervention is usually lukewarm verging on chilly. This may not be entirely surprising, given their view of world politics, but it is discouraging. One had the impression at times that the last thing they were interested in was world stability. Instability, provided it did not directly touch them, seemed to be preferable.

I imagine that Soviet strategic thinking still believes that their interests are best served by neutralizing the effectiveness of the UN rather than by building it up. Certainly their performance seemed to indicate this.

While seeing the UN as a threat to its freedom of action, the decolonization process did give the Soviet Union political opportunities for extending its influence in the Third World. Political support for a liberation movement was, moreover, cheap; votes in the UN, limited military assistance—mainly confined to small arms and equipment or training—and a certain amount of cash, which was rarely as much as the West chose to believe. Now that most liberation movements have succeeded in gaining independence, Soviet influence in the Third World seems to me to be on the wane. As more and more countries turn their thoughts and energies to economic development, more and more the Russians are finding themselves irrelevant to this dialogue, and for a nation that purports to be a world power irrelevance is perhaps the cruelest blow.

The fact is that the North-South dialogue is between the Third World and the West, not the East. If it succeeds, the political beneficiaries will be Western rather than Eastern. The Russian contribution to these great economic discussions is limited to some verbal encouragement for the developing countries' more extreme demands. They are, in short, in a wholesome dilemma. To participate more actively might prove expensive, since in global terms they are clearly a developed country and demands might be made of them. Yet not to participate is to leave the negotiating field clear to the West. So far they have squared this particular circle by giving verbal support for the NIEO while arguing that since global poverty is the result of colonialism and exploitation the bill should be presented to the West and not to the Soviet Union which, as is well known, has exploited no one. As an argument it is specious; as a defense it is wearing pretty thin.

For the Soviets, then, one of the dangers they perceive in the UN is that it might actually begin to resolve these economic issues. Their interests seem to lie more in the continuation of the grievances of the Third World, not in their resolution. On the other hand, they find it difficult to interfere too brutally in the course of the negotiations. Not being an aid donor of any consequence or size, they cannot bring the process to an end without antagonizing the developing world. As such, their best-case scenario would probably be one in which the dialogue dragged on with little in the way of concrete results while, as a consequence, Third World irritation with the West mounted.

WESTERN INTERESTS IN THE UN

Finally, there is the rich, benighted West, which for all its faults still possesses the system of government and the standard of living most admired by the rest of the world. That the United Nations has not lived up to our earlier expectations is clear, but the fault lay perhaps in the expectations, not in the institution. What can we hope for and, perhaps more important, what can we realistically expect in the future from the UN?

We cannot really answer this question unless and until we are clear about what it is that our participation in the UN is designed to achieve. What in short is the object of the exercise?

Great Britain participates in the UN to the considerable extent that it does partly out of self-interest and partly out of a sense of global altruism. We can be damaged by what goes on in New York. Our vital economic and political interests could be seriously affected, for example, by resolutions in the Security Council calling for sanctions against South Africa, or some form of action against Israel.

Our bases in Cyprus could be jeopardized. We could find ourselves committed to a program for world disarmament on a selective basis that is unpalatable and dangerous, unless we are there to present our views. In short, damage limitation is, and will continue to be, one of the principal motivations for British membership in the UN.

This UN is, however, also one of our main contact points with those countries that make up the majority of mankind. We can obtain there a unique overview of Third World trends and opinions. There is no other institution in which so many are represented where they are so accessible. It may not be the ideal "town meeting" of mankind, but at least all the potential citizenry is present under one roof. It is, moreover, the principal forum in which the Third World has chosen to present its demands for a New International Economic Order, and short of declining to play that particular game at all—a decision that none save the most insulated and foolhardy would be inclined to take—we have little option but to participate on the field of their choice. If the great economic and political problems of Third World development are to be resolved, it can only be done through an international institution in which the Third World has faith and trust, and not in some cosier and narrower grouping that would perhaps be more acceptable to us and to our allies.

At the end of the Eleventh Special Session of the General Assembly devoted to development, the Third World position was expressed clearly, even brutally, by Ambassador Mishra of India, the spokesman for the Group of 77. He said that "In their view the session had been a failure and had missed the historic opportunity of tackling the great issues of the day arising from the interdependence of problems and interdependence among nations in the field of development in an organized political manner.'' Responsibility for the failure, he said, lay with a very few delegations whose perceptions he charged ''are not global but parochial . . . they are more interested in maintaining their entrenched position than in an orderly change in the common interest of all . . . the perceptions of our partners in the developed countries continue to be influenced by considerations of short-term gains and they still consider international cooperation to be a zero-sum game.''[5]

As a British Ambassador at the UN, I regarded my primary purposes as threefold. First it was to try and participate as effectively as I could in helping to maintain international peace and security through the machinery of the Security Council itself, an effort that was at times intensely frustrating, sitting as I was for five and a half years next to the Soviet Union. At times it was, however, extremely rewarding, particularly when it involved the UN in a peacekeeping role. Secondly, I regarded myself as obligated to do what I could to try and extend British influence and preserve British interests, a policy based on the perhaps naive belief that British influence in the world was good—at least for Britain—and first among my work in this field was the UK's relations with the Third World. Finally, I regarded it as part of my function to try and make the UN itself work a little better, an attempt that led to certain differences of view with the then US Ambassador, now Senator Daniel Patrick Moynihan. Confrontation for its own sake never seemed to me to be a particularly effective way of reconciling differences.

The importance of the UN for the West lies precisely in its capacity to reconcile. We in Britain have a direct interest in world stability as we are indeed dependent on world trade for our existence and prosperity. We therefore have a major interest in the use of the UN as the forum for negotiating the NIEO. The same is, I think, true of the United States. The US too has global economic relationships that are growing in importance to the American economy, and I would therefore have hoped for a more perceptive approach on the part of both our countries toward the North-South dialogue. That we have an interest in a successful outcome to this dialogue is surely undeniable. It follows from this that we have an irreversible interest in the UN's handling of these discussions.

To return to the opening questions of this chapter: What is the nature of the changes in the UN since 1945? And what can we realistically expect from it in the future?

The most profound change in the UN since 1945 is the reflection of the profound changes that have taken place in the world since that date. The planet is now too small to admit of domination by any one nation or group of nations. We can expect the UN therefore to continue to mirror these changes. No doubt it will be imprecise and at times difficult. Political revolutions usually are, but we in the West must expect that the reconciliation of the differences that exist in the world will take time to resolve. There is nothing in the experience of the postwar era that leads me to believe that we should despair of the UN as the primary global institution within which they can be resolved.

Notes

1. Brian Urquhart, "International Peace and Security: Thoughts on the Twentieth Anniversary of Dag Hammarskjöld's Death," *Foreign Affairs*, Vol. 60, No. 1 (Fall 1981), and *Hammarskjöld* (New York: Alfred A. Knopf, 1972), p. 5.

2. SG/420, March 28, 1955. Cited in Urquhart, *Hammarskjöld,* op. cit, p. 47.

3. See, for example, Harlan Cleveland, *Governing A Pluralistic World* (New York: Aspen Institute, 1981).

4. Quoted in an address by Ambassador John Scali, United States Representative to the United Nations, to the 7th Annual John Hancock Awards Dinner for Excellence in Business and Financial Journalism, Atlanta, Georgia, October 30, 1974. See United States Mission to the UN, Press Release USUN–149 (74).

5. UN Document A/S–11/PV.21 (1980).

PROBLEMS OF GLOBAL MANAGEMENT

ROBERT W. COX

ON THE NOTION OF PROBLEMS

Everyone accepts that problems change with the times, and one would therefore expect that the inventory of issues confronting international organizations in the 1980s will be different from that present to the minds of those who framed the Charter of the United Nations in 1945. What may be less readily apparent is that the very meaning of the term "problem" can also change. There are, broadly speaking, two contradictory ways of understanding the notion of problems or needs. The first of these adopts the perspective of the world as a system of interacting political, economic, social, and material forces, an ecological-anthropological whole. Such a system can be understood to have a kind of natural equilibrium or condition of peaceful motion. Broadly accepted norms of political and economic behavior and collectively agreed policies with regard to the material environment of the system are required to sustain its equilibrium—or in other words, the condition we call peace. Seen from this perspective, "problems" are events and tendencies that threaten to disrupt the equilibrium and must be brought under control or regulation by the institutions of the system.

The other way of understanding the meaning of the term "problem" is in the perspective of the contending forces: the power struggle. The definition of problems is then part of the pursuit of goals by rival powers. Each of these rival powers has a different view of the desirable equilibrium of the system as a whole and thus a difference of opinion as to what norms and policies are required. Their priorities and preferences are different. In the first perspective, defining problems is a technical task, one of devising indicators of stress in the system and policies appropriate to restore equilibrium. In the second perspective it becomes essentially a political task. With regard to institutions, the first perspective thinks naturally of a series of task-specific agencies linked together by some central coordinating mechanism—a set of instruments corresponding to the different areas of policy required to manage the system, together with the possibility of achieving coherence in their use. The second perspective tends to regard any available institution as a potential vehicle for pursuing the conflicting goals of the contending powers and subordinates the purposes to be served by the institution to the prior question of who controls its use.

These two opposed perspectives may at first appear as an issue of moral or aesthetic choice. The idealist or utopian will be attracted to the first, the political realist to the second. But though personality may predispose individuals to one or the other, it is much more important to note the extent to which each perspective is historically conditioned. The first alternative, the system perspective, seems to correspond to reality when the world is organized under a stable dominance. Then the structure of world power among countries can be so far taken for granted as to be virtually forgotten, so that the notion of power becomes transferable from a structure of dominance among countries to the world system of which this structure is the guarantor. Insofar as the notion of power remains in political thought, it applies then less to the capabilities of countries for achieving national goals and more to the capability of the world system for maintaining itself. The extent to which this transference in the notion of power is an ideological fiction becomes apparent only when the underpinnings of the system, the structure of dominance among countries, is undermined. Then it is that the second alternative, the realist, or power struggle alternative perspective, seems to correspond more to the actual condition of the world. Thus the mental frameworks for the definition of the problems of global management are historically conditioned. Habits of mind, however, tend to persist beyond the circumstances in which they were shaped, and it behooves us to reflect upon how well adapted our structures of thought are to changes in these circumstances.

FACTORS AFFECTING INTERNATIONAL ORGANIZATION

Two relatively brief periods in modern history can be characterized as periods of stable dominance. In the first, Great Britain was the dominant power and guarantor of a world system for a number of years in the mid-nineteenth century. In the second, the United States played a similar role for the world system from World War II to the beginning of the 1970s. These periods have certain common traits: in negative terms, international relations were organized in such a way as to prevent any major war and to contain local wars (one can find parallels between the Crimean and Korean wars); in positive terms the world system was organized as a world economy with relatively free movement of goods and capital and broad acceptance and enforcement of certain norms of economic conduct. Free trade and the gold standard were the basic norms of economic conduct in the pax Brittanica. British sea power was both the ultimate sanction of economic behavior and the source of Britain's ability to play the role of balancer in Europe so as to prevent any combination of continental powers from disrupting the political equilibrium underpinning the world economy. After World War II, the Bretton Woods agreements setting the objectives of fixed and stable exchange rates, and the pursuit of progressive trade liberalization, were somewhat more flexible substitutes for the nineteenth-century economic principles. A combination of alliances under US leadership contained the Soviet sphere and created the political conditions for the unfolding of a global economy. The pax Americana was more prolific of formal institutions than was its nineteenth-century predecessor, but whether more or less formally institutionalized at the international level, these world systems can both be described in terms of economic ties with a political underpinning.

The demise of the pax Brittanica can be attributed to a combination of factors: the emergence and increasing power of new states (in particular Germany), the long depression of 1873–96, the rela-

PROBLEMS OF GLOBAL MANAGEMENT 67

tive decline of British economic power, the growth of rival powers (Germany, Japan, the United States) pursuing protectionist policies contrary to the erstwhile economic norm, and the new imperialisms of the late nineteenth century that greatly extended the area of politically administered spheres (as distinct from regions merely economically penetrated). The period running from the last quarter of the nineteenth century through to World War II can be seen in retrospect as the gradual fracturing of the world economy, punctuated by efforts after World War I to patch it together again. These efforts failed because Britain no longer had the capability to sustain the burden of world power and no other country was able or willing to take on the task until the United States did so after 1945.

The major question that hangs over the analysis of international relations today is whether or not something analogous to what happened to the nineteenth-century world economy is happening once again now, since about 1971.

The foregoing considerations suggest a framework of ideas in which to examine the possibilities and limitations of international organization. The term "international organization" is used here to refer to an historical process, and not to a set of institutions (the United Nations, etc.) taken as given. International organization in this sense is the process of institutionalizing and regulating conflict or potential conflict, both among countries and among economic and social interests that cross national boundaries. Reference to conflict does not mean that international organization is concerned exclusively with adversary situations. Institutions may also be able to transform into cooperation and concerted action situations which, in the absence of institutions and accepted rules, would see divergent interests working at cross-purposes. Institutionalization may not only contain or moderate conflict but may in some cases be able to transform potential conflict into cooperation. This institutionalization, it must be stressed, is not a cumulative, one-way process moving progressively from precedent to precedent toward greater harmony. Historically, the process has moved towards greater or less regulation, greater or less authority for the institutions. The important thing is to identify the conditions that determine the direction.

This process takes place within the context of world power relations. Often world power relations have been interpreted too narrowly as referring only to states and their interactions, whereas a broader range of forces emanating from societies as well as states have to be taken into account. Indeed, it has been suggested that under certain historical conditions—those of stable dominance in the structure of power among states—state power becomes a backdrop for the action of non-state forces, while under other less stable world conditions the non-state forces rush for cover behind more active state power.

World power relations have two aspects. Their objective aspect is the relationship of material forces, military and economic. Their subjective aspect is the acceptance of certain rules of international conduct and a recognition of legitimacy in the hierarchy of world power. These are the manifestations at the world level of the duality of all power: Machiavelli's centaur, coercion and consent. In a stable system, there is a fit between the objective and subjective aspects. Accepted norms are consistent with the hierarchy of power. A system becomes unstable when a hiatus develops between the two due to a shift in real power and the emergence of an ideological challenge to the erstwhile prevailing consensus. In a stable system, coercion is obscured by consent (which is to say that although the potentiality of coercion is present it rarely has to be used because of the force of consent). In an unstable system, coercion is more apparent, though less effective, and consent is eroded.

THE PATTERN OF INTERNATIONAL ORGANIZATION DURING THE EARLY YEARS OF THE UNITED NATIONS

The United Nations Charter began a period of relatively stable dominance, although paradoxically it did not take the form envisaged by many who helped draft the Charter. The terms of the Charter, and particularly the provisions for the Security Council and its Military Staff Committee, were predicated upon a continuance of the Grand Alliance that emerged victorious from World War II. The Cold War quickly demolished that assumption. The Marshall Plan, the North Atlantic Treaty Organization, and the other alliances built up an alternative security apparatus under US leadership. The United Nations during those years continued to dramatize the division of the world into Soviet- and American-led spheres with the vast majority of UN members being counted more frequently among the latter.

The institutional arrangements for matters other than security were very much of US inspiration. They took the functionalist form of a series of agencies charged with responsibility in specific areas of public policy. At the core were the institutions of the world economy, the fruit of the Bretton Woods negotiations—the International Monetary Fund (IMF) and the World Bank—with the General Agreement on Tariffs and Trade (GATT) filling in for an abortive International Trade Organization (ITO). On the fringes were a variety of specialized agencies, some old, most new, dealing with specific policy areas—the International Labor Organization (ILO), the Food and Agricultural Organization (FAO), the International Civil Aviation Organization (ICAO), the International Telecommunications Union (ITU), the World Health Organization (WHO), the United Nations Educational, Scientific and Cultural Organization (UNESCO), and so forth. In the early years, many of these agencies had US citizens as their chief executive officers, and where they did not, US citizens nearly always occupied the number two administrative positions. That the Soviet Union either did not join or withdrew from participation in the specialized agencies until after 1954 accentuated the formative influence of US leadership.

Of course, all did not move smoothly in this institutional complex. The Bretton Woods institutions could not get started quickly and were, in effect, put into cold storage for a time while other ad hoc and more limited membership bodies, the Organization of European Economic Cooperation (OEEC), the European Payments Union (EPU), etc., worked in more piecemeal fashion towards the same goals of stable, convertible currencies and liberalized trade relations. The coordinating role envisaged for the UN Economic and Social Council (ECOSOC) did not work very effectively—one reason being the presence of the dissident Soviet bloc in the UN. For the most part, coordination problems during those years reflected bureaucratic rivalries, not fundamental differences of goals or policy.

The whole complex of institutions outside of the security field reflected a single, consistent, and dominant view of the world in which economic liberalism was perceived to be the generator of material well-being, rising productivity the solvent of social ills, and pluralism both a social and political good in itself and a condition for the attainment of economic liberalism and higher productivity. The kind of qualifications or limited exceptions to these general principles considered to be necessary were only such as to accommodate welfare states of the Western European type and especially to avoid excessive unemployment. There was a high degree of coherence between the form of international institutions, the norms they embodied, and the US leadership that provided the key guarantee to the system. The general acceptance of the values upon which the non-security institutional system was premised meant that issues dealt with through these institutions could be considered as "technical." They posed problems of means rather than of ends. This contrasted with the polarization present in the United Nations, where issues typically involved some form of East-West confrontation, and where issues were resolved by what in Soviet eyes was then a Western automatic majority.

THE CHANGED SITUATION OF THE 1970s

From the standpoint of the 1970s, all that has changed. Somewhere during the 1960s, under the impact of a loosening of alliances, a more articulate Third World, and a more than doubling of UN membership, the automatic majority of the early 1950s disappeared. On the threshold of the 1970s one US Ambassador to the United Nations reversed the image and spoke of the "tyranny of the majority"—the new majority of Third World countries—and his successor as US Ambassador spoke of the United States as being "in opposition." These expressions reacted to the change but they overestimated the decline of US influence. That influence remains considerable even today.

The objective power relationships underpinning the institutional system have, of course, altered. The growing economic strength of Western Europe and Japan, both products of the period of stable US dominance, mean that on some issues these powers define their interests differently from the United States. They may look for US leadership but are not always prepared to follow it. The emergence of China enhanced US options while at the same time being a factor in the relative diminution of US world power. In some respects, the new power configuration resembles a conventional balance of power model, although in strategic matters it still seemed reducible to bipolarity. The greater fluidity of relationships among the major powers opened the way for greater initiative by Third World countries, and the control some of these countries have over oil supplies to Japan, Europe, and the United States gave them (since 1973) a new political leverage.

So, too, the norms basic to the postwar era no longer prevail. Bretton Woods laid the foundations of principle for a global economy with fixed exchange rates, currencies related to a fixed value in gold, and multilateralism or "most favored nation" treatment in trade. By the mid-1970s fixed exchange rates had to be abandoned, reverse discrimination in favor of newly industrialized countries was recognized as legitimate, protectionism was mounting in older industrialized countries, and gold had become an officially demonetized speculative hedge in a world in which many were losing confidence in paper currencies. The erosion of economic norms has historically been contagious with respect to other values, as for example, during the runaway inflations of the post-World War I period, which sapped loyalties to political values. Third World and Soviet-sphere countries criticize the norms of the post-World War II system as a Western imposition, challenging their universal validity.

Nowhere is the resulting confusion more marked than in human rights. For Western liberals, human rights are still essentially the rights of individuals and of interest groups. For some others, human rights are essentially collective—national, ethnic, racial, or class rights—and arise in the context of decolonization, claims for national territory, or social revolution. The former give individual rights priority over the claims of collectivities, while the latter would subordinate or set aside individual rights on the grounds of the need for unity in collective struggle. The ILO's tripartism, which reflects the acceptance in Western capitalist societies of collective bargaining by trade unions and employers within a legal and administrative framework provided by the state, has become an ideological victim of this kind of confusion. The ILO asserted as universal principle something that corresponded to social practice in only part of the world. So long as that part effectively controlled the organization, it hardly mattered. When countries in which the principle did not effectively apply became a sizable group, even a majority, the contradiction between principle and practice became blatantly obvious.

New problems have gained prominence during the 1970s—broadly defined problems that are interrelated, such as the environment, population, food, and industrialization—and in respect to which different groups of countries have quite different priorities. The interrelatedness of the problems seems to justify or even to necessitate management through global institutions, but the differences in priorities makes difficult the achievement of consensus on the norms that could be the basis for such management.

Ecology is thus a rich-country issue if it means taking the status quo as a point of departure (i.e., countries that have gained a position of dominance by virtue of having been the major resource depleters and polluters of the past are able to keep their relative positions, but everyone agrees on conservation of resources and limitation of pollution for the future). Development in the form of industrialization becomes a poor-country counter issue, presented in terms of a demand for transfer of capital and technology. The development issue is then redefined by the rich in the form of a new international division of labor to be brought about by the internationalizing of production through transnational enterprises that, in turn, will transfer mature technology and standardized production to the newly industrializing countries, while retaining control and innovation in the rich countries. The result is that international institutions have become forums for debate and negotiation, and sometimes for confrontation, over what is to be done, where once they appeared rather more as technical agencies designed to carry out agreed tasks on behalf of their members.

The functional specificity of the various specialized agencies has also become very blurred. In part this is a consequence of the ambitions of their own staffs, who have tended to interpret the breadth of the new interrelated issues as mandates for organizational expansion. There is a bureaucratic aggrandizement at work through which FAO seizes upon food or agrarian reform, or ILO upon employment and the satisfaction of basic needs as opportunities to define an enlarged span of activities in which these organizations can play a leading role among the others. In part, too, it is a consequence of member countries testing out any convenient forum as a vehicle to press their priority goals. Thus developing countries disappointed with the results of the fifth United Nations Conference on Trade and Development (UNCTAD) in May 1979 at Manila as regards prospects for their exports to the rich countries, were quick to raise this issue again the following July at the special conference on agrarian reform convened by FAO in Rome. Broad programs lend themselves to the attachment of particular claims. Not surprisingly, many of these claims appear to be "political" to the more established powers.

As suggested, some US reactions seem to overestimate the loss of US influence. The Atlantic Council's report *What Future for the UN?* [1] pointed out the contrast between US and European assessments of the changes that have taken place. European expectations for the UN were never as high as US expectations, and Europeans are inclined therefore to see a "crisis" not in the UN but rather in US attitudes toward the UN. Bearing in mind the changes that have taken place in the structure of world power and its normative content, it seems futile to reassert the virtues of functionalism, to castigate the "politicization" of international agencies, or to come forward with schemes for tinkering with organizational structures or procedures. These approaches all basically assume conditions that prevailed in the 1950s but, in fact, these have since changed. More useful is the effort to adjust expectations and policies to what can realistically be achieved in the changed conditions of the 1980s. This goes beyond the question of the feasibility of achieving US policy goals through international institutions. More fundamentally, it touches the question whether the United States does not share a minimum common interest with other countries in the maintenance of dialogue, even when the norms Americans accept as self-evident do not appear to be so accepted by all the others.

LEARNING TO LIVE WITH THE PRESENT

Thinking about international institutions and what they may be able to do has to begin with an assessment of the emerging config-

uration of world power. Policies with regard to international organization reflect preferences as to the future shape of world order
and are in turn calculated to bring about that preferred configuration. Schematically, three different future configurations can be
considered as directions of movement: (1) the Trilateral Commission's aim of reconstructing a collective form of stable dominance,
in which the Federal Republic of Germany and Japan together with
some other countries share with the United States in the management of world economy; (2) a fragmentation of the world economy
into a number of blocs—economic spheres each hinging upon a
major power—each following protectionist neo-mercantilist policies
and endeavoring to achieve a measure of autarky particularly with
regard to necessary raw materials; and (3) Third World aims to
achieve relative autonomy of national development free from dependency either upon a unified core management of the trilateralist
type or upon any leading power within a bloc. This is expressed in
forms ranging from increased bargaining power and more favorable
terms of trade with the industrialized countries to the extreme of
decoupling from the world economy with autocentric development.

The struggle of these divergent tendencies is not only, or perhaps
even primarily, a struggle among states. It is also a struggle within
states. The struggle between trilateralism and neo-mercantilism involves two different forms of capital: capital engaged in the internationalizing of production and in international banking requires
reliable rules and predictable management at the world economy
level; capital fixed within national boundaries and trade unions fear-
ful of the displacement of jobs look rather to the state for protection. The "state classes" of the Third World are in the delicate
position of having to steer their course between two outcomes favored by the different fractions of advanced country capital, neither
of which would fulfill their aims. The oil-rich may be tempted by
the trilateralist blandishment of cooptation into junior partnership in
the central management of the world economy (the "embourgeoise-
ment" of the Organization of Petroleum Exporting Countries
[OPEC], as one scholar put it)[2] or, alternatively, by preferential
deals trading oil for new industries within a bloc context. However,
counteracting Third World pressures stress political solidarity of the
less developed as the only way to maintain their momentum toward

an economic order more conducive to autonomous development. It is very difficult at this time to see any clear indications of a resolution, one way or another, of the struggle among these divergent tendencies. Most likely, uncertainty of outcome will remain together with a certain unstable ordering of objectives: the trilateralist goal as official policy of the United States and some other industrialized capitalist countries, limited by the recurrent and perhaps growing presence of neo-mercantilist reflexes by influential interests within these countries and by the recurrent political and economic necessity of meeting demands from the Third World—in other words, interdependency with incoherence. The practical problem is learning to live with such an unstable system so as to maximize safety and the chances of survival. This means not only building upon limited areas of agreement, but also anticipating and facilitating longer-term adjustments.

In this present political conjuncture, it would be unrealistic to search for a new "vision" for international institutions that could serve as the foundation for a new consensus. Such a vision was possible in the environment in which the UN Charter was written because it could be ideologically based on a power structure of stable dominance. Since there is no such power structure today, visions can only be particularistic, and those who imagine them to be universally acceptable court disillusionment and possibly danger. There are rival visions of a future world order today and the first lesson might be to learn more fully what they are, to try to understand them in their own terms, This need not and should not mean abandoning anything vital in one's own vision. A sensitivity to others' views of desirable world order will, however, facilitate the search for areas of limited consensus.

It follows that international institutions are to be thought of not primarily as the embodiment of norms—since there can be little agreement upon norms—but as bargaining forums. One precious survival from the liberal world order of the past is the habit of negotiation. Its survival probably owes less to liberal convictions in the virtues of rational discussion than to the perception that the consequences of breakdown in negotiation range in their unpleasantness from mutual nuclear destruction to disruption of economies, loss of life, or injury to self-esteem.

Negotiation is a continuing and, in present conditions of world power, a seemingly endless process. Negotiations do not lead to definitive decisions, after which someone or some agency is charged with getting on with the job. Negotiations rather plot out limited areas of agreement among some of the parties, defining perhaps a lowest common denominator among all the parties, or leading to confrontation between significant groups. Negotiations about particular questions, moreover, proceed in disjointed ways, taking place often at the same time in different forums with different combinations of participants or shifting from one forum to another with a different composition. All of this tends to separate the structure of issues from the structure of inter-institutional relationships. GATT and UNCTAD both deal with trade, but deal with it in different ways and with different combinations of participants. The New International Economic Order is debated at one time in the limited forum of the Conference on International Economic Cooperation (CIEC), at another time in the all-inclusive forum of the UN General Assembly. These parallel or sequential negotiations have a relationship to one another. They influence each other. When something may appear to be settled in one forum, it can be reopened and challenged in the next.

International institutions are being considered less and less in terms of the specificity of their formal mandates, and more and more in terms of who most influences their decisions. This was the most striking distinction between the first generation of specialized agencies revived or set up after World War II and the newer bodies like UNCTAD and the United Nations Industrial Development Organization (UNIDO), created under pressure from less developed countries during the 1960s. It was not so much that there was a gap in functional mandates that needed to be filled, but rather a sense on the part of the poor countries that their interests were being neglected or subordinated. The choice of forum is one part of the strategy of negotiation.

Faced with this fluidity and inconclusiveness of the negotiation process, some Americans have been attracted by the prospect of creating limited membership organizations for specific tasks, "coalitions of the willing" as Lincoln Bloomfield put it in the Atlantic Council report cited above.[3] The Organization for Economic Cooperation and Development (OECD) is a group of countries having generally more in common with each other in policy matters than each of them has with most others outside the group; the International Energy Agency (IEA) is an example of an organization set up within that framework to deal with a common and specific problem. Such initiatives seem likely to continue. They cannot, however, be abstracted from the broader, more complex pattern of negotiation. In this illustration, the IEA can never be more than one element in the total energy picture, no matter how fully the members agree among themselves. "Coalitions of the willing" may be considered as areas of temporary agreement in a situation in which cleavages extend outside the limited circle and in which outside groups of countries have means and influence with which to pursue their objectives. What is done within the limited forum thus has to take account of the larger complex and realistically should be considered as only part of the total negotiation process. Otherwise the coalition may just be brewing a storm.

Another consequence of the proliferation of international agencies and their bureaucracies, together with the weakening of the normative content of international institutions, has been to place the concept of an international civil service under considerable strain. Americans in particular have criticized the alleged politicization of the staffs of the United Nations and specialized agencies. In this regard, two points need to be distinguished. One is the attempt to make these staffs and particularly their upper levels more fully reflect the diversity of membership, a policy that usually bears the name of "equitable geographical representation." This must be regarded as both sound and necessary insofar as a diversity of norms and modes of reasoning sets the context in which international issues arise; therefore the institutions set up to channel negotiations about these issues should be capable of comprehending this diversity. The other point is the prevalence of patronage in making appointments, a practice that undermines both morale and effectiveness. It is often alleged that representation is thus gained at the expense of competency. One should be very careful about the meaning of competency. If it turns out to mean assimilation into a conventional dominant outlook, then one ought to be suspicious (my way of dealing with the issues is scientific, yours is ideological). If it refers to quality of mind, capacity for work, and talent for interpersonal relations, then it must be insisted upon. In an era of stable dominance, the international civil service aspires to be the predictable, professional servant of established norms, i.e., of a conventional wisdom. In an unstable system, it can most usefully aim to be the empathetic neutral, sensitive to the relativity of values and facilitating the negotiation process by its comprehension of the different perspectives on world order that confront one another. The criterion of competency changes with the change in the system.

The processes whereby demands and program proposals are initiated for international consideration has not heretofore been given sufficient emphasis. Frustration with the apparent inconclusiveness of negotiation often takes the form of institutional tinkering and procedural devices (the main practical results of which are often the creation of new official posts). Yet a clearer comprehension of the thought processes that lead up to negotiating positions might be more effectively conducive to a moderating of conflicting interests. Dialogue could be pushed back to the origins of differences. Working backward, three stages in the development of negotiating positions deserve attention: (1) formal international institutions are used as instruments for aggregating positions by different groups of countries (UNCTAD by Third World countries, OECD by rich developed capitalist countries, etc.) and the Secretariats of such institutions play an important role in distilling their group consensus; (2) formalized coordinating bodies constitute continuing mechanisms for arriving at common positions among different groups of countries (the non-aligned conferences, the Group of 77, the Geneva group of principal contributors to the UN and other international organization budgets, and so forth); and (3) less formal networks have been created to do some of the initial thinking, planning, and mobilizing of support (the Third World Forum, the Trilateral Commission, the Club of Rome, etc.). Levels 2 and 3 are probably the least studied and may be the most critical parts of the current political process of international organization.

SOCIAL FORCES AND THE SHAPE OF THE FUTURE

Up to this point the problems of global management have been discussed in terms of the configuration of world power among states, the extent of ideological diversity and consensus, and the limits and opportunities these set for international institutions. There is more. Behind the states, overflowing the states, are social forces. State policies attempt to channel them, but these forces in turn condition the nature of states and thus, indirectly, the nature of the world system. These effects are, however, worked out over long periods of time. Social forces remain very largely inarticulate in the international negotiating forums, yet politicians and negotiators would be imprudent to ignore their potential impact on the world system. The viability of present international organization can be gauged by the widening or narrowing of the hiatus between the demands of emerging social forces and the responses of international institutions.

Such a large subject cannot be dealt with systematically here. It is, however, possible to suggest certain lines of inquiry into the potential consequences of emerging social forces for change in the world system. As a connecting thread it is useful to consider the effects on societies of a growing interrelatedness of national economies and, in particular, of the internationalizing of production.

For the leading industrialized countries, the internationalizing of production implies industrial strategies that encourage a shift of low-productivity activities to less developed countries and a concentration on the production of sophisticated services and technology. The world economic conditions for continuing internationalization of production also require reasonable stability in exchange rates of the dollar and other major world currencies. Policies to ensure currency stabilization and industrial changes of this kind would adversely affect some groups, notably workers in low-productivity industries and those generally disadvantaged groups or people who live in depressed areas and depend on state transfer payments. At the very time when additional state aid would facilitate change by alleviating the plight of those most directly affected, the state is caught in a fiscal crisis that causes it to limit or cut back social services. In some countries, e.g., Britain, this has been extended to challenging the acquired power of unions.

It is important to underline the contrast between the situation today and the outlook of the 1960s. Then moderate inflation was accepted as a concomitant of growth, and continuing growth allowed for an allocation of increments to relieve areas of potential social conflict. Now, low or negative growth accompanied by higher inflation and budget cutbacks shifts attention to the more intractable issues of distributive social justice. Increasing social conflict within the advanced industrial countries might be contained by a coalition of powerful interests—a new social contract of labor and capital within the framework of a welfare state—but this would almost certainly involve a shift in a neo-mercantilist direction.

In the newly industrializing countries of the Third World, the internationalizing of production is mobilizing a new working class. Most frequently this process has gone on under authoritarian governments of a military-bureaucratic type that have either suppressed unions or, more usually, allowed the new workers to join unions controlled by the government or ruling party. Despite the effectiveness of the repressive apparatus of such regimes, there are indications that they are not indefinitely durable. At some point the social reality of this new working class will be translated into politics. We may assume it will take a form of radical nationalism.

Even if industry moves rapidly into the Third World and governments are able by and large to keep control over the new work force, most of the population of these countries may see no improvement, and quite possibly may see a deterioration in their condition. Industrial jobs lag far behind increases in the labor force and changes in agriculture dispossess or marginalize many in the rural population. International agencies like the World Bank have been most preoccupied lest such conditions undermine the prospects for the continuing internationalization of production. Programs for global poor relief and riot control packaged under ideologically attractive labels like "self-reliance" seem disproportionately small for the size of the problem, although they may buy some time.

The issue on the formal agenda of intergovernmental negotiations is a redistribution of the world's productive resources among countries, a new international division of labor. Excluded from the formal agenda, because it concerns domestic matters, is the hidden item of redistribution of opportunities within societies. This issue, and the social conflicts to which it gives rise, affect the advanced industrial societies, the newly industrializing countries, and the least developed countries in ways likely to be much more acute in the 1980s than in previous decades.

Notes

1. *What Future for the UN? An Atlantic Dialogue,* policy paper of the Atlantic Council (Washington, DC, 1977).

2. Roger Hansen, "The Political Economy of North-South Relations: How Much Change?" *International Organization* 29 (4), Autumn 1975.

3. *What Future for the UN?*, op. cit., p. 34.

2. THE UNITED STATES IN THE UN: PAST AND PRESENT

US PARTICIPATION IN THE UN SYSTEM

RICHARD E. BISSELL

The American view of the United Nations and its many agencies has been, even in its most euphoric moments, ambivalent. In times of conflict between the purposes of American foreign policy and the expressed posture of the majority of UN members, the American reaction has ranged from hostility to indifference. The implications of such a view of the United Nations from the people of the world's most powerful country cannot help but have a significant impact on international politics. For that reason, this chapter attempts to trace some of the roots of the American response to the UN (through specific forms of interaction during the postwar years) as well as some American views of where the UN should go from here.

An essential characteristic of American foreign policy frequently overlooked is that many policies develop without a strategy; in general, American foreign relations are *managed,* rather than going through an orderly policy-formation process. Such is not to distinguish American foreign policy from scores of other countries, but major implications thus arise for the role of the United States in the UN. Those who manage a set of foreign relations are primarily interested in reducing the conflict aspects of a problem as easily and expeditiously as possible. In nearly all cases, the concern of the relevant managers is to resolve the immediate problem, not to search for a comprehensive solution and not to use the problem as an opportunity to restructure the international system. The short timeframe takes precedence over the long-term. Thus one sees the desire to settle each issue in the ''council of the fewest.''

The preference of American foreign relations managers is to deal with issues bilaterally, since two is the smallest number of countries that could deal with an international issue. If the issue calls for wider consultation, some traditional allies may become involved (as in the case of the negotiations with South Africa over Namibia). To involve the Soviet Union and China, which would occur when an issue is taken to the Security Council, requires a commitment by foreign policy managers to a prolonged and uncertain negotiating process. Because of this pragmatic approach to American foreign policy problems, there has also been an increased resistance to taking issues to the General Assembly. In this way, the US has assumed a ''defensive'' posture at the UN and other multilateral agencies, as the initiative on UN agenda items generally is taken by other states. The extent to which the United States does initiate participation in UN activities represents a striking departure from tradition and from the instincts of managers in the US State Department charged with the execution of foreign policy.

BACKGROUND

Consider briefly the atmosphere at Dumbarton Oaks in the late summer of 1944. The future shape of the United Nations Organization was being negotiated against a background of the American capture of Guam, the liberation of Brussels and Paris, and the arrival of Russian forces on the border of East Prussia. Military power as a force in international politics and in the struggle for justice abroad had been vindicated as the fascist threat appeared on the verge of extinction. The role of the Security Council was clearly at the heart of the discussions among the delegates from the major powers. James Reston of the *New York Times* was a witness at the consultations, where he reported the Allied powers agreed ''that there should be a council with executive authority to apply military sanctions and an assembly of all the peaceful nations of the world, the assembly to have advisory powers.''[1] Such was the fundamental vision that motivated the drafters.

Importantly, there was little more vision than that. As Reston pointed out in his dispatch of August 20, Dumbarton Oaks "is a conference not of idealists but technicians. The delegates are concentrating not so much on how to abolish war as on what to do when it breaks out. This is the first obvious fact about the Dumbarton Oaks conference so far. The talk here is not of ideals but of machinery, not of principles but of plans." [2] Such an approach to world peace, at the formative stage of an international organization, conveyed no sense of an escape from failure, no radical search by statesmen in political misery. They were people tinkering with the international system, people who had the power to enforce a new system, and wanted to maintain it with minimal expenditures of power in the future. The concept of sanctions was carried over from the League of Nations, but most envisioned it to involve deterrent sanctions (through the threat of force) rather than the progressive decentralized sanctions preferred by the League, which all believed to have failed. But the League, according to participants, was hardly mentioned at Dumbarton Oaks; it had an odor of failure clinging to it that caused the Allied coalition to shun it, to engage not in rebuilding but in a new construction.

The American agenda for the new organization reflected the priorities at Dumbarton Oaks. There was no attempt to outlaw the use of force. Instead, there appeared a distinction between legitimate force (Chapter VII and Chapter VIII of the Charter) and illegitimate force (Article 2). It was conceded that conflicts would occur, but that the organization would have to devote its resources to restraining such conflicts from growing into general and all-out wars. Participants such as Dean Acheson had developed a strong distaste for the Wilsonian faith in the "perfectability of man." Cordell Hull spoke to this problem directly: "It is generally agreed that any peace and security organization would surely fail unless backed by forces to be used ultimately in case of failure of all other means for maintenance of peace." [3] The use of force in the cause of peace is the language of victors, of people who feel they have defended their moral order with the use of that ultimate arbiter, war.

In the American view, however, the use of force could not be legitimate without the underpinning of some quasi-legislative process. Here the Americans faced a quandary. John Foster Dulles spoke grandly about the need to "establish a world order based on the assumption that the collective life of nations ought to be governed by law,"[4] but the mechanisms for creating that law were beyond the willing reach of the victors of World War II. Dulles was careful to say that the Charter "does set forth certain general principles; but these are expressed as self-denying ordinances, not as law which the Organization enforces." He went on to say; "The Assembly is directed to encourage the development and codification of international law. But neither it nor the Security Council is given any authority to enact law."[5] Instead, the prevalent image in this country of the United Nations became not that of a lawmaking body, but with Senator Vandenberg's encouragement, it became a forum "where, so far as possible, we can talk things out instead of shooting them out."[6] As a victor in the war, the United States found it uncomfortable to contemplate the formal surrender of sovereignty to an international organization—most eloquently expressed by the anxieties of the US Senate, so prominent in the American abstention from the League. The legislative process that emerged from the American imagination was that of customary lawmaking: if all the nations talk long enough to arrive at a consensus, and they all act upon that consensus, Americans were willing to say that the United Nations could function, in that sense, as a lawmaking body. The authority of the UN, essential if a supranational system was to be created, was limited primarily to moral pressure and rhetoric; the extent of authority by enforcement was strictly circumscribed.

In a third area, the United States was able to make a major contribution, even though its commitment to that approach waned as the years passed: attacking the causes of war. The social sciences had reached the point of development in the United States and in Europe by 1945 that some relationships between socio-economic variables and the outbreak of war had been identified. Many perceived, for instance, that Lord Keynes's analysis of the Versailles settlement had been vindicated—that the punitive economic treatment of Germany by the victors after World War I had driven the German populace in the direction of authoritarian government. To punish a nation collectively appeared to encourage the development of nationalistic reactions (resulting, for instance, in the legal approach of the Nuremburg trials where individuals, not states, were tried for crimes against mankind). The social sciences, however, had not reached the point of examining to any degree the relationships between socio-economic variables and conflict outside the Eurocentric cultural frame of reference. Thus, the commitment to eliminating the domestic causes of war, which was so dramatically vindicated by the European economic recovery in the late 1940s and early 1950s, was a commitment made within limited cultural bounds. It was intuitively concluded by most social scientists, to be sure, that the logic of the Marshall Plan could be applied anywhere in the world, and that money plus deregulation would result in prosperity and democracy in any environment. That expectation must be kept in mind when considering the American disenchantment with the United Nations several decades later, as the Group of 77 (G–77), representing the development challenge of the 1970s, attempted to change the approach to development that emerged in Europe in the 1940s.

The United States thus entered the UN with a certain agenda, even if not explicitly formulated, that reflected the results of World War II as well as traditional American values. The priority goal of this grouping of governments was to be peace; the means to obtain that peace were twofold: an armed deterrent ("speak softly and carry a big stick") available to the UN acting as the frontier sheriff if necessary, and the creation of sufficient material prosperity that all states would have a stake in avoiding destructive conflict. The United States was initially willing and able to serve as the principal sponsor in both aspects.

THE VALUE OF MULTILATERAL DIPLOMACY

As the 38 years of UN experience have unfolded, the United Nations has functioned remarkably well in the pursuit of peace—due perhaps initially to the American commitment, but probably more as a result of the design of UN procedures. The UN has functioned as a standing peace conference and has demonstrated its willingness to provide peacekeeping forces where the consent of local governments has been obtained. Much derision has been focused on Vandenberg's formulation of the utility of the UN as a global town meeting, but surprisingly, it is from the periodicity of UN General

Assembly meetings that its function as a standing peace conference is derived. Adversaries that would otherwise not meet have the opportunity to encounter one another in an annual meeting. Examples are to be found in the Asian conflicts in the 1960s and 1970s, when certain major actors were not represented at the UN. Alternative forums, such as the Geneva conferences, have never been as effective because the convening of such meetings required a deliberate decision to meet with political adversaries. Such is not to say that the UN can or does function as an on-the-record forum for substantive negotiations. Talks on war and peace rarely take place in public forums; the utility of the UN has been as a catalyst or convenor of parties to armed conflicts, after which the substance was settled elsewhere. That many substantive negotiations were moved outside the locus of the UN after initiation does not comment unfavorably on that organization's value in multilateral diplomacy. Its proceedings were meant to be public; substantive negotiations generally cannot be public, and the UN fulfills the equally important function of generating the underlying value consensus vital to long-term peace.

It is also in the nature of foreign policy that an issue that can be settled by bilateral negotiations will be treated that way rather than submitted to the complications of multilateral negotiations. A particular issue may be some variant of the two; the negotiations over the Namibia issue, for instance, were launched in large part through the United Nations, but generally involved South Africa and the "Western five" powers. The United Nations will then, presumably, serve as an institution of ratification of an agreement when it is reached and needs to be labelled as legitimate by the international community. The United Nations, however, has rarely summoned military power as an enforcement tool; its largest efforts were in the Congo and in Korea, where the purpose was to restore order or to restore prewar boundaries. UN forces have served in the role of peace maintainers, frequently without drawing weapons, and they have obtained a degree of effectiveness through the widely respected international norm of not engaging UN peacekeeping forces in armed combat.

If one can say that the period since 1945 has been characterized by remarkably little interstate conflict, however, it is equally clear that domestic violence has become the major headache for an organization committed to the maintenance of the peace. Even where internal violence is quite manifestly fed by external supplies (such as by one of the great powers), the UN has not achieved any consensus among its members to control such sources of war. Such internal violence, too, frequently spreads across international boundaries, but the effectiveness of the UN in these instances has been severely limited due to the existence of Article 2 (7),[7] and the unwillingness of most governments to have the UN become involved in conflicts where any examination of the sources of war would involve judgments of internal political processes. Southeast Asia during the last 25 years is a prime example.

Any number of civil wars (Chad, Nicaragua, Rhodesia/Zimbabwe, Pakistan, and Lebanon) can also illustrate the quandary faced by the UN when regional violence is precipitated by the collapse of a national government, particularly where sectarian violence is involved. The norm was quite different in the League of Nations, where the rights of minorities within certain nation-states were considered issues for treatment by the League, with peaceful adjustments of boundaries and populations acceptable courses to follow. That norm does not exist in today's United Nations, for better or for worse, but it is clear that the UN has great difficulty grappling with situations of domestic anarchy before they become interstate wars. All nations have hidden behind the provisions of Article 2 (7) in order to exclude items of key domestic political concern from the UN agenda. Dealing with civil disorders will remain an important challenge of the 1980s.

In the area of legislation, the UN has performed essentially as the United States expected. It has been most effective in the area of consensus formation, but able to act decisively only where existing authority wishes to abdicate its responsibility. Consider, for example, one area where the UN is frequently identified as a prime mover in the postwar world: decolonization. Through perennial debates (where the United States originally stood with those arguing for rapid decolonization) in the General Assembly, and later in a variety of special committees, the UN established an international norm for the decolonization of the Western European empires. But the implementation of that norm came only when the colonial powers decided they were willing to do so.

The greatest test of the decolonization norm, however, is not in the original movement involving the colonies of European powers. The essential completion of the Euro-centered decolonization process has given birth to a recognition that group rights have no well-defined role in the UN and international law. Many states are empires in all but name, where ethnically alienated populations resist political relations with the capital city. Ethnic divisions start wars, yet there are no accepted norms in the UN on this issue, with decisions of the General Assembly appearing to be legally whimsical. Thus, the UN did nothing when Pakistan was split into two nations, yet it holds extensive hearings annually on the independence movement in Puerto Rico. Because much of the American impetus for support of the decolonization movement came from a belief in political stability deriving from the ''consent of the governed,'' the turn of ideology at the UN today has left many Americans confused. In turn, the United States has lost much interest in the UN as a norm-creating body, as can be seen in the increasing frequency of the American presence in the voting minority of the General Assembly.

In seeking the sources of international tensions in social and economic phenomena, the United States has also provided an agenda for the UN that ultimately serves to undermine many traditional American institutions. One example is the search for sources of misery and conflict in the Third World, where much blame is placed on the ''exploitative'' activities of foreign economic entities. Indeed, the entire American approach to problems of conflict, first formulated in the special European atmosphere and then widely applied in the Third World, has come under attack. The American view has consistently been that human rights of a political nature must precede or emerge parallel with economic rights. Many states today want the prosperity that they see in the United States, without the political democracy that Americans see as corollary. Others develop autarkic economic organizations along with Western-style political institutions. American multinationals are pressed to behave not in their own self-interests, but in the interests of other societies.

That American institutions believe they can "do good while doing well" is no longer accepted by much of the world, with the external assault on American multinationals additionally increasing the doubts of Americans about their own domestic institutions. Tensions between the United States and the Group of 77 on economic issues have thus been increasing, for the original effort by the United States on this score—intended to extend certain economic "rights and freedoms" to the Third World—has been turned back on the United States and interpreted as economic "duties" of the developed countries toward the Third World. Such a fundamental conflict in interpretations has become a test of wills, and is certain to remain a source of American alienation from the UN in coming years.

Finally, the record of the UN has been disappointing for original and continuing American expectations with regard to the relationships between the General Assembly/Security Council complex and the specialized agencies. The GA/SC grouping was created to deal with international political problems and the structure of the specialized agencies, largely held over from the League period, was preserved in order to enhance the autonomy and "functional" approach of those organizations. The specialization of those agencies to deal with particular transactional problems of inter-state life was an essential aspect of the functional theory of international integration. Such a complex of international organizations mirrored in many ways life in the United States at the mid-point of the twentieth century: a limited role for the political kingdom, and a multiplicity of practical, problem-solving institutions that maintained the normal routine of international life. Over time, the UN abandoned that model, and the specialized agencies have increasingly come under the watchful eye of the General Assembly, not so much regarding their performance on mandated issues, but concerning their conformity to political resolutions of the General Assembly. Thus, the rising hostility to Israel and to South Africa in the specialized agencies trailed the growth of hostility in the General Assembly. In addition, the transformation of economic issues (such as energy) into issues of "high politics" has led to their being considered by the General Assembly. The United States, of all major developed countries, is perhaps least willing to accept such a shift in the international policymaking environment.

HAS THE UN MISSED OPPORTUNITIES?

Where major issues of importance to world peace or to the United States have not been treated by the United Nations, a variety of explanations can be advanced to explain such omissions. In most cases, however, such missed opportunities were unintentional by-products of the drafting of the Charter.

The United Nations, a place where negotiation is the paramount tactic for solving an issue, finds it difficult to bring weak states to the negotiating table. The UN is no different from any other negotiating environment, in that a state will not negotiate a dispute from a position of weakness, and the UN has rarely shown itself able to compel a state to negotiate. Little would be accomplished by the United States enlisting the UN in a particular issue unless the other interested parties were willing to deal with the UN.

The United States has also hesitated in taking issues to the UN due to uncertainty about the rules by which the issues will be judged. There is no standard body of international law or dispute settlement that will predictably be invoked. Not only has traditional international law experienced repeated challenges from non-European cultural traditions being incorporated into the international system (with no new integrated body of international law yet emergent), but there is also repeated ad hoc reinterpretation of the Charter.

The major opportunity missed by the United States, particularly during the last decade of faltering Presidential leadership and in the American national mourning over Vietnam, has been the failure to take visionary new ideas for world order to the United Nations. The visions propounded at the United Nations for at least the last decade have not been American in origin. In effect, the United States has abandoned the concept of Senator Vandenberg's town meeting. Americans rise in the General Assembly primarily to answer the charges of others, not to take the initiative. When it consistently abstains from setting the agenda, or participating in choosing from the menu, the United States can hardly complain about what is served. Under the original concept of the UN, ideas can be introduced without any expectation of adoption—indeed, the most important ideas should be considered for many years before any action whatsoever. Surely it should fall to the United States, with some of the best planners in the world, to introduce to the agenda of the UN those items that will predictably be of crisis proportions in the 1990s.

STRUCTURAL CHANGE AT THE UNITED NATIONS

For the last decade, a broader concept of change has been under consideration at the UN: depending upon the speaker, an issue is framed as a revision of the Charter, or as using the UN to change the structure of international political and economic relations. Of importance to this issue is the attitude of the United States, holding a veto in the UN Security Council and a major determinant of the international political atmosphere.

It is first necessary to recall that the United Nations Organization was founded (as was the preceding League of Nations) to introduce a greater degree of order into the relations of sovereign nations. In effect, it was judged that an international order that would allow World War II (or earlier, World War I) to occur was a manifest failure, and that new rules or mechanisms would have to be established to direct the decentralized international system in a new direction. Such is to state the obvious. What has not been adequately analyzed, however, is the way in which the nature of the process and participants in such a change of the system would affect the new international order. There is quite a different result when a new system is developed by those who consider themselves the winners, as opposed to those who see themselves as losers. The issue is akin to the debate among scholars of revolutionary change, who argue constantly over the motive power of revolutions: does it come from desperation and starvation, or from rising expectations? In the founding of the United Nations, there exists an ambiguity about its origins, because the public support for such an organization came from people who felt that the previous system had failed, and that the failure of political organization must result in a new order. On the other hand, the negotiation of the UN Organization was undertaken by the "winner": the alliance of nations that organized militarily to defeat the dual threat from Germany and Japan in World War II. Those who lose are willing to transform radically the international order. Winners are generally more interested in affixing their temporary advantage into the rules of international politics, allowing change not through redistribution, but primarily where growth enriches all parties.

This behavioral problem of changing an international system is not restricted to the actual drafting of the UN Charter. Indeed, many of the tensions most irritating to Americans in the last 38 years of UN actions can be attributed to attempts by nations on the "losing" side (economically and politically) of international conflicts to undertake radical change precisely in areas where it is in the natural American interest to avoid such change. Therefore, any expectations of radical change in the rules of international politics or economics that would be negotiated by those who perceive themselves to be "winning" from the old rules will necessarily be disappointed. This is not to suggest that the North-South split is demarcated by this division over the process of change. Indeed, the divisions among the nations of the South are all too clear: Many (now called the Newly Industrializing Countries [NICs]) find themselves doing well by traditional international rules and will not press for the radical change that Americans have come to expect from the Third World. Insofar as the UN is an organization with universal membership, then, structural change is unlikely to occur in the international system until an overwhelming number of its members perceive the system, or a particular part of the system, to be a failure. The United States is certain to oppose structural change until a dramatic failure of the system occurs.

THE IMPACT OF THE UN ON THE UNITED STATES: WHAT SCARS?

The closer participation of the United States in the world, and in world organizations, since 1945 has left certain indelible marks. Most of all, it has made Americans realize how different they are from the rest of the world. The UN, as a reflection of the world, presents in stark contrast the differences between cultures. Despite the myths fostered by elementary-school geography books, where the globe was divided into blue and red areas but otherwise was all the same, the differences between countries are real. Even the widely noted common concerns of humankind (food, shelter, warmth) do not imply that men will organize at all similarly to deal with those needs. The dramas at the United Nations, and the communications revolution of the last decades, have convinced Americans that they are quite different from other people.

As a corollary of the differences between nations and cultures, Americans have become aware of the Third World challenge. The crisis of confidence that overcame American leadership in the late 1960s has had a lasting impact in the shaping of the agendas of international forums. The United States perceives the challenge not only at the United Nations, but most visibly there, because the treatment of specific issues (now generally raised by countries other than the United States) requires specific responses. In the multitude of proposed projects for funding by United Nations agencies, the United States has realized that the abdication of leadership does not imply that American resources are any less avidly requested by the Third World.

The challenge takes many different forms (depending upon peoples' perceptions), just as it assumes different shapes in the various UN organizations. No longer is the Third World perceived in simplistic formulations—e.g., poor people who just needed political independence in order to have opportunities to pull themselves up by their bootstraps—and the complexity of Third World demands on the first world has increased. The American government and elites are confused about the proper response to such a challenge. Institutionally, should the United States create special ambassadors for multilateral affairs? Should it instruct all US embassies to place multilateral issues at the top of their agendas with respective foreign ministries? Is the Third World challenge simply an outlet for frustration, or is it a diplomatic initiative that has to be dealt with on its merits? The challenge has been of great benefit to the United States in removing the blinders that history placed over American eyes, but finding a coherent response will be a long process.

Another impact of the United Nations on the United States has been to increase the international linkages of domestically based

American organizations. The role of non-governmental organizations (NGOs) in the specialized agencies has given the NGOs much
enhanced power in the domestic political struggles over issues. Not
only do the frequent meetings of international organizations ensure
consultations between the NGOs of various countries (e.g., the UN
Environment Program [UNEP] has provided a useful coordinating
role for conservation groups in the US), but the distribution of
physical resources provides support for domestically based NGOs
(e.g., research and program money available to the UN Fund for
Population Activities). Where issues in the United States were once
decided on their domestic merits (à la Fortress America), Americans have become increasingly sensitive to international opinion;
the role of former UN Ambassador Andrew Young was illustrative
in his mission to interpret the world to American domestic opinion.
Another recent illustration of this phenomenon is the American energy policy: the role of the International Energy Agency (IEA) in
placing pressure on American policymaking has been largely the
result of a deliberate decision by American policymakers who needed
outside pressure on American thinking to take strong action. While
the UN is formally an organization of governments, the tremendous
amount of consultation that occurs between NGOs suggests that the
balance of international power does not reside entirely in favor of
governments. Indeed, the continuing controversy over the role of
"transnational forces" suggests that strong pressures exist on both
sides of the debate.

It cannot be avoided, however, that the emphasis within the General Assembly and Security Council debates themselves is on the
actions and attitudes of governments. A long-term identity crisis
exists for the UN as to whether it represents its members (the governments) or the world (the people). Should the UN, in its regular
programs, focus on servicing national governments or serving as
advocates for individual interests?

The confusion on this score can be best witnessed in changing
policies on human rights issues, for few issues are as sensitive to
national governments as possible violations of human rights. The
struggle to introduce some scope for individual redress of human
rights violations in the UN system has been a long one. Within the
last few years, there has been some broadening of access, both in

cases brought before the Human Rights Commission (Sub-Commission on Minorities), and in connection with the Optional Protocol of the International Covenant on Civil and Political Rights (1966). Where the UN has less binding authority, as in the General Assembly, a growing tradition exists of enlisting individuals in particular causes. Individuals and other legal persons (such as corporations) have been urged to action in resolutions on ending apartheid, and they have testified in their personal capacity before General Assembly Special Committees. In addition, the servicing of individuals' needs has grown particularly as a result of UN interest in national liberation movements, as in the UN Trust Fund for Southern Africa providing scholarships for young displaced South Africans. The impact of such moves on the United States has been minimal to date, but the potential impact is significant. Fundamental forms of authority are being created at the global level, with international organizations relating to individuals and not to states; such a development needs to be monitored much more carefully in the United States—not to halt this move, but rather to protect its long-term utility. Such individual access, so basic to creating a larger supranational community, can generate a damaging backlash in the US and elsewhere if it is harnessed exclusively to short-term political goals.

INSTITUTIONAL CONFUSION IN US POLICYMAKING

After three decades, Americans are increasingly confused by the continuing turn of events in the UN. International tides of opinion beyond the experience of most Americans cause the UN to appear to shift and move without apparent explanation. The degree to which Americans understand the UN certainly diminishes as American newspaper coverage declines. American foreign policy bureaucracies are stretched to their limits dealing with present challenges and cannot spare the manpower to provide the UN with an imaginative agenda. For the American people, the UN has done little to rate a full minute on the evening news in recent years—so how could it be important?

The United Nations has not appreciably simplified the problem of dealing with over 150 sovereign nations. In that sense, the UN has failed. One can read that failure in the condition of the International Organization (IO) Bureau of the US State Department. Priorities in the State Department appear to ensure that the geographical bureaus are favored for policy implementation over the IO Bureau. The traditional bias of the State Department to work with the fewest nations possible (preferably bilaterally) has weakened the IO Bureau, but the UN has also done little to enhance the position of the IO Bureau. Instead, the US State Department faces a continuing problem of overlap and duplication of effort involving that bureau. A partial reading of organization theory at the time of creating the IO Bureau appears to have done the UN a disservice. Creating that bureau could have enhanced the status of the UN in American thinking, but only if accompanied by changed procedure and priorities. Instead, it is now evident that programs of lesser priority given separate organizational slots actually suffer in substance, being that much more isolated from the main run of policy. A separate IO Bureau can be justified primarily if there is a separate agenda for US foreign policy at the UN; in fact, however, that agenda has been very limited. Incorporating the current functions of the IO Bureau into other structures might provide for greater American realization of the domestic implications of what is called "complex interdependence." The process by which we unintentionally seal off the UN from the ordinary run of American diplomatic concerns simply serves to make Americans less interested in the functioning of the UN system.

THE CONFLUENCE OF INTERESTS, OR KEEPING THE US IN THE UN

It is essential to establish, first, that the UN has in many respects been a success during the first 38 years. World War III has not occurred. In fact, most of the countries of the world have not known war during the last three decades, and all of them have experienced rising standards of living. If some portion of that success can be attributed to the UN, and presumably it can, several major interests of the United States have been achieved. At the same time, the US has seen its leadership position in the UN eroded steadily, as has occurred throughout the international system. The American vision of the future that gave the impetus to leadership in the 1950s and 1960s has become an object of international derision. Until the US and the UN majority reestablish some common path to the future, American participation is likely to be lukewarm at best. Where can Americans look for the creation of that common vision?

It can find a useful communications forum at the UN, but not an antidote for wars. The UN provides a channel to talk with any other country, without any assurance that such talks will be productive. Negotiations, for the reasons laid out above, necessarily take place between the parties seriously interested in an agreement, not in a universal forum. In those cases where the issue must be treated universally, as in the creation of new international law, the UN is a useful place. This has been demonstrated by the International Law Commission's work. The process is time-consuming, but any negotiation involving over 150 countries necessarily takes a great deal of time. Instances when common interests that will lead to serious negotiation in a UN-wide forum can be identified will be rare, but these can be grasped as they appear.

Issues at the United Nations might usefully be divided into two categories: conflict and cooperation. Conflict situations, where two or more parties claim a single resource (territory, a piece of technology, political legitimacy), are unlikely to be resolved at the UN, but the Charter provides numerous encouragements for states to deal with conflicts peacefully, rather than through war. Cooperative situations, where several parties can each gain to some degree through international agreement (use of the sea bed, air space, radio waves, etc.), can be provided with lasting solutions. Too frequently, American expectations do not appear to differentiate between the two categories.

Much speculation in recent years has focused on the American response when disagreements appear at the UN. The US has withdrawn from and rejoined the International Labor Organization (ILO), as well as certain specialized committees of the General Assembly, to highlight US disapproval of certain UN actions. At other times, various groups have advocated selective participation in the UN, limitation of budgetary contributions, and other gestures.

It has already been maintained that disagreements with the majority will be frequent. However, in order to determine the proper

US response, it is necessary to distinguish between two types of disagreements: (1) constitutional (i.e., changes in the rules of operation of an organization as they existed when the United States joined) and (2) issue-oriented (where the action is constitutional within the terms of the Charter or founding document of the organization). The more serious case, clearly, is the constitutional question. Given the continuing interest of the United States in maintaining a clear relationship with organizations to which it has surrendered some of its sovereignty, it will weigh such changes carefully, including consideration of termination of membership. With regard to specific issues, however, the United States can recognize the inevitability of losing some votes on specific issues and then resolving to do its diplomatic homework better before subsequent meetings.

The American view of the UN has become mired in the conflicts between blocs, in the issues where Solomonic decisions are required in the absence of an accepted Solomon, and in the short-term issues where public diplomacy has the least chance of success. The shared sense of vision—necessary to rekindle an American commitment to the UN—will not come from overweaning attention to such issues. The changing of international rules and the resolution of zero-sum conflicts require decades or more for a "settlement" to emerge. The need to manage such conflicts will not be met, moreover, unless attention is equally paid to the areas of cooperation where the US and other members of the UN community are working on the basis of willing agreement. The US is not responsible alone for the apparent imbalance between conflict and cooperation; we live in an era of self-help redistribution (whether OPEC's setting of oil prices or Vietnam's occupation of neighbors), but the US, by virtue of its past leadership and its present size, can influence the shape of the UN debate. From the American side, the problem is partly structural (the role the UN plays in American foreign policy priorities), but is also partly the result of the weakness of the American vision about its own future.

The United States and its participation in the UN system has suffered from both inflated expectations and the trauma of the rejection that was sure to follow when those expectations were not met. The UN continues to perform small functions, as it has during its entire history. In small measure, it oversteps its powers from time to time, and has sometimes been pulled back into proper marching order. In other cases, it has undergone constitutional changes that were appropriate to the changing times. At its founding, the UN was envisioned by American delegates as being devoted, most of the time, to "encouraging" solutions to human problems: to encourage the development of international law, to serve as a forum for exchanging ideas, and to foster peace. But rarely was the UN expected to "decide" issues, for decisions were generally left in the hands of the sovereign nations adhering to the UN Charter—particularly the right to collective or individual self-defense. The US has an interest in fostering the original catalytic functions of the UN, for too many problems have accumulated on mankind's agenda without imaginative solutions being proposed. Attempts by the United States and others to abandon the UN have inevitably been only temporary retreats, for the UN remains the best repository of a global vision yet created, and the US will inevitably be part of that future.

Notes

1. *New York Times,* August 21, 1944.

2. Ibid.

3. Cordell Hull, *The Memoirs of Cordell Hull,* Volume II (New York: The Macmillan Company, 1948), p. 1676.

4. John Foster Dulles, *War or Peace* (New York: The Macmillan Company, 1950), p. 198.

5. Ibid., p. 199.

6. Arthur H. Vandenberg, Jr., *The Private Papers of Senator Vandenberg* (Boston: Hougton Mifflin Company, 1952), p. 198.

7. Article 2 (7) reads, "Nothing contained in the present Charter shall authorize the United Nations to intervene in matters which are essentially within the domestic jurisdiction of any state or shall require the Members to submit such matters to settlement under the present Charter. . . ."

UNITED STATES FINANCING OF
THE UNITED NATIONS

ROBERT F. MEAGHER

Writing in 1964, John Stoessinger stated: "The financial crisis of
the United Nations has aroused acute anxiety among many observers who see it as the unmistakable symptom of an early death of
the organization. . . ."[1]

In recent years, these anxieties have reappeared and have been
exacerbated by world inflation, the fluctuating value of the American dollar (the currency of the United Nations), and a division within
certain sectors of the United States government over the cost and
usefulness of the Organization. In 1964 Stoessinger could argue,
"The financial plight of the United Nations is *not* the expression of
a struggle over the Organization's existence."[2] Various Congressional actions such as the passing of the Helms Amendment in 1978
raise the question today of whether or not the combination of the
actions of some US officials coupled with those of some members
of the Group of 77 will result in the destruction of the Organization.[3]

THE US FINANCIAL CONTRIBUTION TO THE UN

Current US policies have evolved over a period of years reflecting
reactions to structural, political, and economic factors within both
the United Nations system and the United States. The peacekeeping

operations of the United Nations in the Middle East and the Congo precipitated a major financial crisis in the 1960s when both the Soviet Union and France refused to pay assessments to finance these operations. This led to a series of actions by the United States, including support for a UN bond issue, a decision to invoke Article 19 of the UN Charter to take away the voting rights in the General Assembly of those in arrears, and the request for an advisory opinion of the International Court of Justice on the issue of the legality of financial assessments for peacekeeping operations.[4]

Threats by Congress or by any official within the United States government are taken seriously by everyone connected with the United Nations because of the importance of the US contribution to the Organization. In 1946 the United States provided close to 40 percent of the assessed budget. Over the years, new members and the improvement in the economies of many states have led to a decrease in US contributions. Nevertheless, the United States remains the largest contributor by far, providing 25 percent of the assessed budget today.[5]

In general both the executive and legislative branches of the government have supported the central role of the United States in UN financing. On occasion particular events have raised doubts in the minds of some, particularly in Congress, of whether this role should be continued. The expulsion of the Republic of China (ROC), the passing of the resolution equating Zionism with racism and the resolutions on the New International Economic Order (NIEO) were three such events. In these cases criticisms emanated from both houses of Congress and demands were made to either cut US contributions or in some cases to withdraw from the UN. The executive branch, through the State Department, joined in the criticism of the actions but did not endorse either a cut in contributions or withdrawal.

In September 1978, Congress placed a restriction on funds appropriated for US assessed contributions to UN agencies, prohibiting their use for technical assistance activities (the Helms Amendment). Because UN agencies cannot accept conditional assessed contributions, this prohibition jeopardized many UN programs and the UN itself. Subsequently, in the next budget year, this provision was dropped in the authorization legislation but not without strong disagreement on the part of many in Congress.[6]

What has caused the US Congress to raise doubts about future contributions to the United Nations? Is this the whim of an individual or a small group of individuals adopted through the positive efforts of a few and the indifference of the majority? Are there reasons to believe that in the future US contributions may be substantially reduced or cut off? If so, can and should something be done to reverse this trend?

Several causes of Congressional disaffection with the UN can be discerned:

1. The loss of US and Western European controlling influence in the Organization.

2. Disagreement by Congress with various political actions of the General Assembly.

3. The use of the United Nations by the developing countries to bring about a redistribution of wealth and power through the creation of a New International Economic Order.

4. The nature of financing for technical assistance programs.

5. The dissatisfaction of Congress with recent decisions of the Committee on Contributions of the General Assembly.

6. The size and growth rate of the budgets of the UN and the specialized agencies.

7. Other issues.

The central issue that both the US government and the public must answer is whether it is or is not in the national interest to maintain its current level of the support for these institutions or to modify its current approach to them.

1. THE LOSS OF UNITED STATES AND WESTERN EUROPEAN CONTROLLING INFLUENCE IN THE ORGANIZATION

The United Nations and its many related institutions, such as the specialized agencies (FAO, UNESCO, ILO, to name a few), the financial institutions (IMF, World Bank group) and voluntarily supported agencies (UNDP, UNICEF, etc.) have each received strong US support both in their inception and in their development over the years. Both financially and from a management perspective the

United States has been their dominant supporter. The US has served them well and they in turn have served the US well.

However, the environment in which these organizations operate is far different from the clubby, more personal world of the League of Nations and the early days of the UN. It is not that personal factors have become irrelevant in international relations but rather that the heterogeneous nature of today's world, with its more than one hundred newly independent states, requires more and more specialized international institutions to deal with matters of great international import. Governments have reluctantly given up more and more sovereignty to international bodies; thus when particular events arise that question the wisdom of this delegation of authority, the institutions are rescrutinized and the decisions reconsidered.

During the postwar era the interaction between the new and the old states evolved through stages of tutelage, joint decisionmaking, self-reliance, and finally interdependence. This is well illustrated by the history of technical assistance programs within the United Nations. When the Expanded Program of Technical Assistance (EPTA) was created, the money was divided up and parceled out by the specialized agencies from their "agency shares."[7] The enabling legislation spoke of countries making their own decisions, but for the most part the attitudes of the developed countries was "we know what is best for you." As political concerns concomitant with independence became less all-encompassing, the LDCs began to set up planning boards and turned their attention to their economic and social priorities. At this stage they still needed help but they also had their own inputs; thus EPTA developed "planning shares" and decisionmaking became more of a joint enterprise. By the late 1960s, under the "consensus" and the recommendations of the Jackson Report, countries made their own decisions at their own pace and self-reliance became the dominant doctrine.[8] Finally, it became apparent to ministers of finance in the developed countries and ministers of development in the Third World that interdependence is a reality that cannot be wished away through rhetoric. The resolutions on the New International Economic Order and the Charter of Economic Rights and Duties of States emphasize various aspects of the interdependence theme.

The evolution in attitudes toward technical assistance programs and development aid has spilled over into all areas of discourse with developing countires. The poor of the world are asking for an international redistribution of wealth and power and, in order to make their demands, they are utilizing the very forums the United States nurtured over the years. When created in 1945 the United Nations had 51 members. Today it has 157. When created, voting was predictable and in the interest of the founding members. Today it is unpredictable and in the interest of the overwhelming majority of poor members. This poses a dilemma for the United States and other founding members. Do they or do they not want a world organization in which world problems can be discussed? Would they prefer to return to the club atmosphere of the past? Is it even realistic to think about going back?

These questions lead directly into a discussion of the financing of the United Nations. First, a few background facts: In 1946 the UN budget was $15.6 million. For the period 1982–83 (biennium) the General Assembly approved a $1.5 billion budget or $750 million per annum. The US share, currently fixed at 25 percent, is $187.5 million per annum. If all mandatory international organization contributions are combined, i.e. treaty obligations to specialized agencies, the US obligation rises to approximately $300 million. The 23 leading contributors to the United Nations provide over 90 percent of its funds.[9] Although the United States pays a higher percentage of the budgets and voluntary contributions to the United Nations system, it is much lower on the list if one judges contributions on a per capita basis and much further down the list if one ranks contributions as a percentage of GNP.

Is the United States getting its money's worth or should it pick up its chips and leave the game? To some the issue is, if we can't control the game, why play? The United States is virtually the only country in the world with that option. During the debates over the removal of Nationalist China from the United Nations a *New York Times* reporter interviewed an anonymous Soviet diplomat who said:

In the old days, the United States always had the votes so you could afford to be enthusiastic about the United Nations and play the role of world hero. Then the Soviet Union stood alone, or had only a few votes. We had to use the veto and thus we appeared the villain. Now the United States cannot get the votes for what it wants. So the United States is being realistic and changing its attitude.[10]

The clash within each national legislature is frequently "What is in our short-term national interest?" versus "What is in the long-term international interest?" It is not surprising that the short-term interests tend to win on the international level as well. When the UN or other international organizations make extreme political or economic demands during a period of economic contraction or when they unduly criticize the view Americans have of their own policies, Congress as well as the American public begins to question the value of the institutions and US membership in them.

2. DISAGREEMENT BY CONGRESS WITH VARIOUS POLITICAL ACTIONS OF THE GENERAL ASSEMBLY

Two issues serve as good examples of the effects of Congressional disapproval of General Assembly actions: the exclusion of Nationalist China from the United Nations and the Zionism is racism resolution.

From late 1949, when the Communist Party seized effective control over mainland China, until 1971, the United States was successful in rounding up sufficient votes to keep the PRC out of the UN. When the issue of admission came up in the 1950s the United States argued persuasively that countries should not be allowed to "shoot their way into the United Nations." In 1971, despite US objections, the People's Republic was seated. Although some Americans still favored a two-China approach, neither the Nationalists nor the People's Republic supported such a position. One Senator who supported a two-China policy, Senator James Buckley of New York, threatened that "a complete reassessment" would be made of US financial support to the UN if his preferences were not followed. (At that time the United States was providing 31.5 percent of the UN budget and had promised a $20 million contribution toward an $80 million expansion of the UN enclave in New York.) To give emphasis to his point he gathered the public support of 21 Senators and 35 members of the House.[11] Within Congress note was made of the fact that 43 countries supporting the Nationalists' expulsion were receiving $1.5 billion of US aid and 12 abstaining countries were receiving an additional $813 million.[12] Clearly it was assumed—as it has been on several more recent occasions— that certain obligations went along with the receipt of US bilateral aid. (No such comments were made about US NATO allies most of whom also voted for the expulsion.)

In the executive branch, however, there was some ambivalence over the vote. President Richard Nixon was about to visit Peking and, although he took exception to the UN decision, he was somewhat less strident than his record as a member of Congress would have suggested. Secretary of State William Rogers welcomed the People's Republic to the United Nations and opposed the ouster of the Nationalists. He was more guarded when discussing future US contributions to the UN, arguing that the US should not cut its financial contribution because of the unseating of the Nationalists. However, he then went on to say that he might not oppose cuts on other grounds, since the UN was spending too much.

During the Nixon Administration US annual payments to the United Nations were cut from 31.5 percent of the Organization's annual budget to 25 percent. Although Samuel De Palma, then Assistant Secretary of State for International Organization Affairs, said that the decision was based on "a matter of principle and not in retaliation for recent events," Representative John Rooney, Chairman of the House Appropriations Sub-Committee said soon after the vote to oust "our Nationalist Chinese friends" that the US payments to the United Nations "will be cut further after this cut [to 25 percent] is approved."[13] The Sub-Committee then failed to appropriate the promised $20 million contribution for UN expansion.

The *New York Times,* in an editorial opposing the Congressional cut in the US assessed budgetary contribution, advised:

> The proper and legal way is to seek General Assembly action next fall to set a 25 percent ceiling and then press the Committee on Contributions to lower the American share toward that same goal when it meets next year to revise assessments.[14]

The visceral reaction to the expulsion of a long-time friend from the UN highlighted the declining US support for the United Nations. One writer, arguing that the "United States can no longer be counted on as the cornerstone upon which most of the strength of the United Nations rested," outlined three reasons for this pessimistic conclusion: (1) cuts by the State Department in the staff of its Mission to the UN; (2) that Chief of Mission George Bush "does not have as important an advisory role in developing foreign policy as did most of his predecessors"; and (3) the continued importation of chrome from Rhodesia into the US in the face of a legally binding international embargo for which the US voted in the Security Council. Noting that President Nixon's foreign policy was based on five major centers of power—the United States, the Soviet Union, the People's Republic of China, Japan and an enlarged European Community—he added that "the great majority of the member nations of the United Nations in Africa, Asia and Latin America are outside these blocs."[15] It was, of course, the votes of these countries that ensured the ouster of Taiwan from the UN.

A second major decision that elicited a strong negative reaction from Congress was the General Assembly Resolution equating Zionism with racism. This vote was the culmination of efforts by the Arab states to rally third world support in and outside the UN for their position. This pressure manifested itself within various UN forums such as the ILO, UNESCO, and the General Assembly.

In October 1975 the General Assembly's Third Committee (Social, Humanitarian and Cultural) passed a resolution equating Zionism with racism and racial discrimination by a vote of 70 to 29, with 27 abstentions and 16 absent. Despite the public outcry throughout the world, and the passage of a formal resolution by the US Congress urging the GA to reject its Committee's resolution, on November 10 the General Assembly passed the resolution by 72 for, 35 against, with 32 abstentions. Congress unanimously adopted a resolution calling for the reassessment of the American relationship to the world body and condemning the vote. Legislators who had either warned that passage of such a resolution might lead them to oppose further funding for the UN now suggested that it was time for the United States to pull out of the United Nations. (Congress had already held up funds for UNESCO and the ILO because of the activities of the Arabs in these organizations.) Senator Richard Stone advised that he was preparing a bill that would cancel voluntary contributions to the United Nations (i.e. all non-assessed payments).[16]

As a result of the United Nations vote, the United States announced that it would not participate in or help finance the United Nations Decade for Action to Combat Racism and Racial Discrimination. Representative Matthew J. Rinaldo said that he planned to introduce legislation suspending further US participation in the General Assembly until Congress determined that the climate in the UN had improved. He also declared that he was introducing a bill to limit US financing of the UN to 5.6 percent of the Organization's budget. (This percentage would have been assessed on the basis of the share the United States population represented in the UN.)[17]

Although none of these legislative actions were subsequently enacted, it would be a mistake to believe that the UN resolution had no effect on Congressional attitudes and actions. The liberal coalition, the principal supporters of UN funding, were badly divided about the proper US response to this UN action and there was a great deal of resentment at being forced to trade off oil security with an anti-Zionist resolution.[18] The effect of the resolution on UN financing is difficult to evaluate. The growing importance of oil has muted but not eliminated criticism of anti-Israeli moves, but many traditional UN supporters also identify with Israel. Steps to withdraw from the UN were contained, but support for US financing of UN projects was weakened. Certainly this issue set the stage later on for a concerted drive by anti-UN forces in Congress to hamstring the organization.

3. THE USE OF THE UNITED NATIONS BY THE DEVELOPING COUNTRIES TO BRING ABOUT A REDISTRIBUTION OF WEALTH AND POWER THROUGH THE CREATION OF A NEW INTERNATIONAL ECONOMIC ORDER (NIEO).

The issues underlying the NIEO are substantive. The documents and resolutions speak in terms of goals and attempt to answer the question: What kind of a world do we want? Despite the similarity in goals of the poor and the rich nonetheless a number of differences remain on how they might be achieved.

The two movements for political independence and an end to economic dependency have absorbed the energies of the Asian, African, and Latin American states that entered the UN since World War II. These movements came together in 1964 when the United Nations Conference on Trade and Development (UNCTAD) became a permanent subsidiary organ of the General Assembly under the leadership of Raul Prebish, its first Secretary-General. Using UNCTAD as a meeting place and research center, the developing countries coalesced into the Group of 77, which then formed a coherent, albeit controversial, approach to third world development.

By the early 1960s, voting power within the United Nations had passed to the Group of 77. Few if any within this variegated group, containing the poorest of the poor and a limited number of relatively well-off developing states, believed that they could change the world by passing resolutions in the General Assembly. True, they had close to 80 percent of the votes, but they supplied only 10 percent of UN and specialized agencies' budgets. Then came the 1973 Arab-Israeli war and the Arab oil boycott. A new sense of power infused the nonaligned movement. Focusing its attention on economic issues for the first time, the nonaligned concluded that "a new type of international relations" was necessary. Algeria, a member of both the non-aligned and the Group of 77, called for the convening of a special session of the General Assembly on this topic.

The General Assembly's Sixth Special Session developed into a nasty confrontation between the poor and the rich. Clearly the poor overestimated their power, but at the same time the developed countries underestimated LDC power. This led to a more serious discussion of issues than one might have anticipated, and out of this meeting issued the resolution on a New International Economic Order and a Program of Action to implement it.

At the 29th General Assembly another key resolution was passed, the Charter of Economic Rights and Duties of States, a document embodying the past achievements, present activities, and future hopes of the Group of 77.[19] These meetings, with their acrimony and confrontation, led United States Ambassador to the UN John Scali to direct a strongly worded speech to the Group of 77 with an equally strong and only thinly veiled threat. It read in part:

Last year the United States Delegation sought to call attention to a trend . . . to adopt one-sided, unrealistic resolutions that

cannot be implemented. . . . This trend has not only continued but accelerated.

. . . The most meaningful test of whether the Assembly has
succeeded in this task of bridging the differences among member states is not whether a majority can be mobilized behind
any single draft resolution, but whether those states whose cooperation is vital to implement a decision will support it in
fact. . . . When the rule of the majority becomes the tyranny
of the majority, the minority will cease to respect or obey it,
and the parliament will cease to function. Every majority must
recognize that its authority does not extend beyond the point
where the minority becomes so outraged that it is no longer
willing to maintain the covenant which binds them.[20]

Despite the fact that fully 85 percent of the provisions of the
Charter of Economic Rights and Duties passed without dissent, three
articles dealing with private foreign investment (Article 2), producer associations (Article 5), and indexation (Article 28) were opposed by several states, and the United States in particular.[21] Discussions of these issues tended to become polarized between
complete central control of all economic decisionmaking and a
complete laissez-faire approach to the world. In fact, most industrialized states, including the US, the Federal Republic of Germany, and Japan tend to intervene more substantially in their economies than their arguments at the UN would suggest. Experiments
in decentralization and limited competition in various Eastern European economies portend a fairly widespread belief in a wide-
ranging variety of mixed economies; many of the LDCs combine
elements of both approaches as well.

Yet the issues raised at the UN are quite fundamental. Perhaps
they are not as conflictual as the political issues that divide East
and West—but then the Eastern bloc has not asked the Western
countries for the capital or technical assistance to transform the international system. The developing countries, to some extent, are
doing just that.

4. FINANCING BY THE UNITED NATIONS AND THE SPECIALIZED
AGENCIES OF TECHNICAL ASSISTANCE PROGRAMS

In recent years the extent to which technical assistance should be
financed as a normal part of the regular, assessed budgets of the

specialized agencies (as opposed to voluntary contributions through the central mechanism of the UNDP) has been a subject of international debate and concern. The genesis of the problem lay in the delays and cancellations of project delivery caused by a UNDP financial liquidity crisis in 1975–76. This crisis was the result of a United States cutback on its voluntary contributions, a reaction to the resolution equating Zionism with racism. It stimulated pressure from developing countries for more funding through assessed budgets "to avoid the vagaries and uncertainties of voluntary funding."[22]

The practice of financing technical assistance through regular budgets was not new. The United Nations had done this since 1948 and the constitutions of UNESCO, WHO, and FAO each provide for these activities to be funded from their regular budgets. In 1949 these regular budget sources of funds were supplemented by an Expanded Program of Technical Assistance (EPTA) financed through voluntary contributions.[23] These funds were utilized by the specialized agencies and in areas where there were no such agencies by the United Nations Technical Assistance Administration (UNTAA), a part of the United Nations itself. In 1958 another institution, the United Nations Special Fund, was added to assist developing countries in "pre-investment" projects, i.e., in surveys of natural resources, in the establishment of training institutions, and in the development of research facilities, funded also through voluntary contributions. These two programs were merged into a new organization, the United Nations Development Program (UNDP), which came into operation in 1966. However, the activities of both the Special Fund and UNTAA continued under the more centralized form of administration that had previously characterized the Special Fund, and funding continued to be through voluntary contributions.

When the practice of increasing technical assistance through assessed budgets came to the attention of various members of Congress they attempted to cut off this source of funding completely and force all technical assistance grants through the voluntarily financed UNDP. In 1977 and 1978 the Senate added up the amount of technical assistance earmarked from regular budgets of the UN and the specialized agencies and deducted this amount from US contributions to the regular budgets. In 1977 this provision was eliminated in conference; in 1978 the provision was not removed in conference. This legislation, called the Helms Amendment, was attached to the appropriation of the total international organization regular budget funds. It stated:

> For expenses, not otherwise provided for, necessary to meet annual obligations of membership in international multilateral organizations, pursuant to treaties, conventions, or specific Acts of Congress, $327,676,000, of which no part may be made available for the furnishing of technical assistance by the United Nations or any of its specialized agencies.[24]

None of the international organizations concerned could accept contributions to their regular budgets if conditions were attached; therefore the Helms Amendment in reality cut off the obligatory contributions of the United States to the United Nations and the specialized agencies. (Supporters of the Helms Amendment argued that the concerned organizations could and would accept the conditional funds. Such was not the case.) The Secretary-General of the United Nations, warning that the United Nations could be destroyed unless the United States Congress removed this restriction, said:

> If the restrictions were allowed to stand, it would destroy the principle of collective financial responsibility and with it the economic and political viability of the entire United Nations system.[25]

When the fiscal 1980 appropriation bill came up for consideration in 1979 the debate continued. Congressman Dante Fascell, in opposing the Helms approach, argued:

> It is a hard way to get at the problem but it is totally effective if you are trying to get the United States out of the United Nations. If you are trying to destroy the United Nations, that is what this amendment would do.

On the other hand, Congressman Robert Bauman, a supporter of the Helms tactic, argued otherwise. He noted that:

> . . . from the beginning [of the UN], the understanding of the United States was that these agencies would be financed by voluntary contributions of the members for the most part.

Pointing out that the amount of technical assistance being spent from regular budgets was rising rapidly moving from $19 million in 1978 to $27 million in 1979 and finally to $41 million in 1980, he concluded:

> . . . the issue is whether an agency of the UN is going to appropriate tax money that belongs to the American Treasury and its taxpayers or whether Congress is going to appropriate.[26]

In the fiscal 1979 supplemental appropriation bill the funds deleted by the Helms supporters were restored and the conditions were removed. The 1980 appropriations bill was also approved without restrictions, but not without much debate and many close votes.

What the Helms Amendment did was to bring attention to an attempt by the developing countries to assure a continuous and probably increasing flow of technical assistance from the assessed budgets of the United Nations and the specialized agencies. The Helms Amendment was an effective, albeit heavy-handed, way to dramatize concern over this fact. Undoubtedly the proper way to change the practice is by changing or limiting in some manner the financial powers of the concerned organizations. However, this is easier said than done: voting structures are heavily weighted in favor of the Third World countries, which stand to gain if no changes are made. In the long run, some compromise must be worked out if the United States participation is to continue in these organizations. At issue is really not whether Helms or others are for or against particular programs of technical assistance (for the sums involved are really relatively small), but rather who will decide on the amount of funds to be appropriated for such activities. This larger question is still far from being resolved.

5. THE DETERMINATION OF ASSESSMENTS

Who will pay how much and what the criteria will be for determining assessments within the United Nations are among the most important questions within the United Nations system.

The General Assembly both considers and approves the UN budget. As Article 17.2 of the UN Charter says, ''The expenses of the Organization shall be borne by the Members as apportioned by the General Assembly.'' This rather general clause raises both procedural and substantive issues.

Procedurally it would have been quite difficult for the delegates of 51 countries (never mind the current 157 members) to sit around and attempt to decide the assessment issue. Thus, the task of preparing a detailed scheme is entrusted to a 10-person expert Committee on Contributions whose members are to serve for ''relatively long terms,'' be selected on the basis of ''broad geographical representation and experience, and be nationals of different states.''[27] Its recommendations are sent to the Fifth Committee (a standing committee of the General Assembly), which discusses the decisions made and sends its recommendations to the General Assembly for a final determination.

Substantively the assessment scale is based upon member states' capacity to pay, which in turn depends upon four criteria: national income, per capita income, war-caused economic dislocation, and ability to acquire foreign currency.[28] A moment's reflection brings forth the realization that none of these criteria are or were self-evident. National income accounting, the basis for the first criterion, suggests that countries had comparable statistics and that they were up to date. The second, that population figures were accurate and up to date. The third, that war-caused dislocation could be determined in a reasonable time by an expert committee and, fourth, that the ability to acquire foreign currency could be evaluated with some ease.

The original assessment for the United States was set at 49.89 percent of the UN budget. The US delegation argued against this figure on two grounds: first, it was not an accurate reflection of the US capacity to pay; and secondly, it would be unwise to make an international organization so dependent upon the contribution of any one member. The US believed that no state should pay more than one-third of the total budget but agreed to a temporary assessment of 38.89 percent for 1946. This amount continued to decline annually until 1954, when the US contribution was reduced to one-third.[29]

As statistical data improved and postwar reconstruction continued at a rapid pace, the Committee on Contributions began in 1956 to set assessments to cover three-year periods, with minor adjustments to take account of new members, most of whom were very poor. For the most part these countries were assessed the minimum contributions, then set at 0.04 percent. By 1961, the scale of assessments had created a situation in which:

. . . Fifty countries constituting 50 percent of the membership are assessed only a little over 3 percent of the budget. Twenty countries constituting 20 percent of the membership contribute almost 90 percent of the total. The Big Five are responsible for almost two-thirds, the United States for almost one-third.[30]

As difficult as assessment questions were, they became even more so when the United Nations decided to send peacekeeping troops first to the Middle East (1956) and later to the Congo (1960). In the case of the Middle East a special account outside of the regular budget was established. This raised questions as to whether or not members were bound to pay assessments under UN Charter Article 17 and, if they did not, whether they would find themselves without a vote under Article 19. At this time the United States accepted the lion's share of these expenses. Thus, financing was partly allocated on the basis of assessments through the regular budget and partly on voluntary contributions. The US agreed to pay 25 percent (as its assessed share) on the first $10 million annually and half the amount in excess of $10 million (through a voluntary contribution), provided other governments contributed the remaining half. This resulted in a total US contribution of 43 percent. Assessed payments for the UN Emergency Force resulted in numerous arrears in default but, as Stoessinger notes, "UNEF never threatened the financial structure of the UN itself."[31]

When the Congo operation arose in 1960 the Security Council, in order to ensure the withdrawal of Belgian troops and the maintenance of order until the new government could establish itself, authorized the Secretary General "to provide the Government with such military assistance as may be necessary until, through the efforts of the Congolese Government with the technical assistance of the United Nations, the national security forces may . . . meet fully their tasks."[32]

The figure the UN came up with was $48.5 million. In the Fifth Committee the question was how to apportion this expense. There were almost as many formulas suggested as there were UN members. Some said it should be a part of the regular budget and paid for under the 1960 assessment formula. Others wanted an ad hoc account clearly stipulating that the costs were expenses of the Organization under Article 17 and that the assessments created binding legal obligations. (This group also suggested voluntary contributions to reduce the assessments of the countries with the least capacity to pay.) The Eastern bloc nations stated their intention not to contribute to any part of the expenses, which they believed should be paid by Belgium, the former colonial authority. Although the Soviets supported the actions of the UN in both the Congo and the Middle East, they refused to pay for either out of the assessed budget. The Latin Americans, on the other hand, wanted the expenses to be paid largely by members of the Security Council.

The problem was solved for 1960 using the ad hoc account approach, assessed on the basis of the 1960 scale. The expenses were thus considered to be a binding legal obligation under Article 17. In 1961 costs were estimated at $135 million, although it was hoped that reimbursement waivers and economies would reduce the sum to $120 million. The amount of money involved led to a reopening of the question of how it should be paid. The US favored the principle of collective responsibility on the basis of the 1960 assessment and once again offered a waiver of over $10 million of reimbursement rights and a contribution of up to $4 million to reduce the assessments of governments with a limited capacity to pay. The Soviet Union argued that since the action came under Article 48 (a Security Council action), the Security Council, and not the General Assembly, should decide the matter. This would have given them a veto on the expense question. Other formulas were also suggested. Mexico came up with a unique formula: 70 percent should be borne by the five permanent members of the Security Council, 25 percent by those states whose investments in the Congo exceeded $1 million, and only 5 percent should be apportioned under the regular assessment scale.

It was finally agreed that $100 million would be apportioned under the 1960 assessment scale to cover the period from January 1, 1961 through October 31, 1961, with an amendment included that reduced the contributions of poorer states. No specific reference was made to Article 17, and the resolution did not state specifically that it was a binding legal obligation; instead the special responsibility of the permanent powers of the Security Council for the financing of peace and security operations was emphasized.

In the case of military operations a major problem has been to determine what expenses are to be covered under the assessed budgets. This has been a problem in financing technical assistance as well. Throughout the 1950s the developed countries were protected from what they feared would be extravagant technical assistance expenditures voted by developing countries by the rule requiring a two-thirds majority vote on budgetary questions. By 1961, however, the developing countries had more than two-thirds of the votes in the General Assembly.

At the 34th General Assembly in 1979 the Committee on Contributions summarized current criteria for assessments. Not surprisingly they still found comparative estimates of national income to be prima facie the fairest guide.[33] However, over the years, new minimum and maximum rates have been decided upon. The minimum has gone down from 0.04 (1946) to 0.02 (1972) and is now 0.01 (since 1976). The maximum, originally at close to 40 percent for the United States, dropped first to one-third and is now 25 percent. Other criteria for determining the level of contributions include: the disparity between the economies of developed and developing countries; special problems of countries with the lowest per capita income; the mitigation of extreme variations between two successive scales of assessments; and excessive variations of individual rates of assessments between two successive scales. The differences between the initial and current criteria reflect the evolution from an essentially East-West confrontation within the UN to a North-South one.

Up until 1968 debates over the scale of assessments centered largely around two issues already touched upon in this chapter: the principle of a ceiling on contributions and the principle that no member's per capita contribution should exceed the per capita contribution of the member with the largest assessment (the US). In the early period the socialist states complained that, due to their different economic system, their assessments were calculated at too high a rate. Later on, there was a clash between the US and the Soviet Union over the US insistence that its assessments gradually be lowered.

Special provisions for low per capita income countries began in 1946 and have been under continuous review, the most recent amendments being made in 1979. In essence these provisions permitted low per capita income countries to pay smaller assessments than would have been the case if only national income criteria had been taken into consideration.

In 1972 the United States proposed in the Fifth Committee that its assessment should be reduced to 25 percent. Pointing out that it had been the US position from 1946 on that no one country should contribute more than 25 percent of the budget, spokesmen went on to say that the proposal represented no shift in United States policy nor a diminution of interest in or support for the United Nations. It was also stressed that the proposal related exclusively to the administrative budget of the Organization and not to its programs financed by voluntary contributions.[34] This did not create any serious concern to members because both East and West Germany were about to be admitted and would immediately take up the slack created by the reduced US contribution.[35] The reduction in the US assessment meant that several other countries were making higher per capita payments to the United Nations than was the US. According to a compromise agreed to in 1956, those countries affected were entitled to a reduction in assessments. Canada, Denmark, and Sweden all agreed to forego lowered assessments, leaving only Kuwait and the United Arab Emirates with a reduction. Since application of this principle shifted the main financial burden from high to medium or low per capita income countries, a number of developing countries asked the Committee on Contributions to look into it and to report to the 1974 General Assembly. The provision was repealed in 1974.[36] It is interesting to note that the great increase in oil prices in 1973 would have permitted five additional countries from OPEC to gain from the continuation of this principle. The vote for repeal was 101 for, 7 (all OPEC) against, and 13 abstaining. Kuwait said that an economy based on one depletable resource was ephemeral and subject to risk.

In 1975 the Committee on Contributions was aware that due to great changes in the world economy steep increases in the next scale of assessments would be unavoidable. It explored a wide range of indicators including per capita energy and food consumption; the percentage of gross domestic product originating in manufacturing; the percentage of economically active population in other than agricultural fields; infant mortality rates; number of physicians per 1,000 inhabitants; and literacy rates.[37] Lack of reliable data, particularly from developing countries, made it impossible for the Committee to explore systematically all those indicators. The Committee requested additional information from the Secretariat on external public indebtedness, a factor they felt to be significant.

The new scale of assessments presented to the 31st General Assembly (1976) for the Triennum 1977–79 became the subject of much conflict and debate. Based on national income statistics for 1972–74, it included for the first time sharp increases of income for many of the OPEC countries as well as others.[38] The OPEC countries tried to defer a new scale until 1978 and also wanted to limit the increases in individual rates of assessments between triennial scales to 30 percent. However, many developing countries complained that a continuation of the existing scale for two more years would increase the burden on the developing countries whose economies had suffered reverses, while those whose economies had improved would unfairly gain. Finally, in a compromise approved by the Group of 77 and other regional groups, it was decided that the General Assembly would adopt its new scale for 1977 only and would have the entire scale of assessments reviewed at the 32nd General Assembly in 1977.

Both the US and the Soviet Union opposed the OPEC position. During the debate in the Fifth Committee the Soviet delegate voiced his regret that:

. . . a group of countries, whose contribution was to be significantly increased as a result of the very considerable increases in their national income, had objected to the new scale and had put forth proposals which were inconsistent with the existing criteria and, in many cases, completely unjustified.[39]

When the General Assembly took up this issue the following year it had in hand the Committee on Contributions report, which concluded that it was:

. . . unable to develop a workable, universally and directly applicable system of limitations, either in percentage or absolute terms, to be imposed on changes, both upward and downward. Moreover, most members of the Committee felt that the imposition of such limitations would depart essentially from the basic principle of capacity to pay laid down by the General Assembly at its first session. . . .[40]

As a result, the Committee had decided that the great variations from the previous to the current assessments should be mitigated by extending the base period calculation from the three years 1972–74 to a seven-year base period 1969–75. After debate, the new assessments for 1978–79 were approved in both the Fifth Committee and the General Assembly.

The US abstained on the new schedule of assessments both in the Fifth Committee and in the General Assembly, noting that:

. . . in the 1977 scale, 117 developing countries were assessed at 11.73 percent of the Organization's budget, while the remaining 27 Member states financed 88.27 percent of the budget. Under the 1978–79 scale these 27 countries would pay 89.04 percent. [It is] anomalous that developing countries with huge national incomes and sizable amounts of available foreign currency had been afforded reductions at the expense of other countries with severely depressed economies.[41]

After two years of heated debate the 33rd General Assembly adopted the Contributions Committee report by consensus. At the

34th General Assembly (1979) a new scale of assessments was approved, but not before many of the old questions were reopened.

It was evident that many developing countries are still unhappy that national income, with its maximum and minimum levels plus a series of per capita adjustments for developing countries, is still being used as the basis for determining assessments. However, the development of a consensus on other methods of assessment has proven to be extremely difficult. Thus, the search for a fair and equitable approach—a search begun in 1946—continues.

6. THE SIZE AND RATE OF GROWTH OF THE UN BUDGET

The UN budget has grown from $19.3 million in 1946, when it had 51 members, to $149.7 million in 1970, when it had 111 members, to $750 million in 1982, when it had 157 members. During the last decade alone, the assessed budget of the specialized agencies (including the International Atomic Energy Agency [IAEA]) has jumped from a combined $209.4 million to $692.8 million annually.

What is one to make of these figures? One can argue that the absolute sum has gone up substantially. However, given that most of UN's new members were former colonies from the poorest parts of the world, it is also evident that the per capita budget has gone up much more slowly. To give some additional perspective on the budget figures, they must also be recalculated in real terms, for few economists or laymen put much faith in absolute figures in this era of rampant inflation. In 1980, prices rose close to 14 percent in the United States and they have increased over 150 percent since 1967. On the other hand, the US dollar, the currency of the UN, used to be worth 4.25 Swiss francs; in 1979 it was worth 1.50 Swiss francs. Due to the decreased value of the US dollar, the real increases in the UN budget are not that great.

Nonetheless, the perception that the UN spends enormous sums of money remains. At the 33rd General Assembly, concern over the rapid increase in the UN budget led the United States to cast its first negative vote on the question of the UN budget.[42] Without a doubt, the words of John Stoessinger still ring true: "Seldom have so many important people argued so tenaciously about so little money."[43]

7. OTHER ISSUES

There are many other issues to be explored if one is to gain an international perspective of the many institutions linked closely to the United Nations. Space allows for only a brief mention of the more important of these. There are questions of how the international financial institutions and the specialized agencies are spending their money. There is the deteriorating international economic scene and the fluctuations in raw material supply and prices. There is the alarming increase, almost day by day, of economic nationalism, with cries for high protectionist tariffs and restrictions on imports. There is also the US Presidential election process which, in its own self-centered way, asks the rest of the world to pause for one or two years while rhetoric rather than policy dominates. And finally, there is a generalized feeling of annoyance over the lack of appreciation of past US contributions to the international development through the UN. Each of these, and many other issues, must be understood if US financing of the United Nations is to be put in proper perspective.

CONCLUSIONS

The United States, a designer and principal supporter of the United Nations in the past, has in recent years begun to hinder United Nations operations by imposing conditions on the use of US assessed financial contributions, a clear violation of treaty obligations. These conditions not only limit US funding of UN programs, they cut funding off entirely, because the United Nations may not accept conditional payments of assessed contributions.

The various rationales for changing US attitudes have been set forth in this chapter. They are the result of a greatly enlarged UN, many of whose members have goals and approaches different from our own; short-term political factors such as the Zionism is racism resolution and the expulsion of the Republic of China; and decreased support for an international perspective in Congress at a time when the world is growing increasingly interdependent.

Some members of Congress, never strong supporters of the United Nations in the past, have spent many hours decrying attempts by the United Nations to increase technical assistance to the poor nations of the world through the assessed budgets of the UN. This ignores two crucial facts: first, that this move was necessitated by a cutback in US voluntary contributions to the United Nations Development Program, and second that the arguments as framed by supporters of the Helms Amendment are not a genuine issue. UN technical assistance through the assessed budget is nothing new; it began in 1946. In addition, the constitutions of a number of specialized agencies (including UNESCO, WHO and FAO) provide for technical assistance activities to be funded through the assessed budgets; the US Senate ratified US membership in each of these organizations in the 1940s. Ironically, it was the American Director-General of the ILO, Mr. Bradford Morse, with Congressional and US labor support, who first turned that specialized agency from a standard-setting institution into a technical assistance organization, an approach pursued by the ILO for approximately the past 30 years. It is important to be aware that the amount of money being contested is minuscule for the wealthier countries of the world.

The United States has served the United Nations very well over the years and has in return been well served by the United Nations. In the post-World War II era the United States has been faced with two continuing problems: the first, a struggle with the Soviet bloc and the second, a search for techniques to bring development and stability to the developing countries. In the East-West struggle, time and again the developing countries have rallied to the support of the United States, beginning with the Uniting for Peace Resolution (which enabled the United Nations to enter the Korean War on the side of South Korea) up through the 1980 GA resolutions opposing Soviet intervention in Afghanistan and the taking of US hostages in Iran.

In the second arena of North-South issues the world has seen repeated on the international level issues identical to those confronted by the developed countries within their national borders over the past 200 years—a demand by the poor for a more equitable distribution of wealth and power. The developing countries have used the only international forum available to them to voice these demands, the General Assembly of the United Nations, although they are only too aware that the passing of resolutions is, at best, a very slow, incremental way to bring about change. They have also spearheaded the huge expansion in UN development and technical assistance programs that has aroused such negative response in this country.

The desire of developing countries to improve their economies is understandable; the efforts to increase their role in international decisionmaking is perhaps inevitable. That the developing countries as a group are now the largest market for American exports makes it self-evident why the development of these countries is in the US national interest. The efforts of those in Congress who oppose US involvement in the United Nations and who seek to put conditions on our assessed payments to the UN budget are not only violating treaty obligations but are, in addition, acting against the US national interest in the areas of both security and trade. A careful consideration of the US national interest in both these areas should incline the Reagan Administration to give strong support to meeting US financial obligations to the United Nations.

Notes

1. Stoessinger and Associates, *Financing the United Nations System* (Brookings Institution, 1964).

2. Ibid, p. 293. Emphasis added.

3. For a definition of the term and other terms related to these issues see Robert F. Meagher, *An International Redistribution of Wealth and Power* (Pergamon Press, 1979), Appendix B, p. 200.

4. These events are described in John G. Stoessinger, "Financing of the United Nations," *International Conciliation,* No. 535 (Carnegie Endowment for International Peace, November 1961), pp. 30 ff., and William W. Bishop, *International Law* (Little, Brown and Company, Third Edition), pp. 262 ff. See also *New York Times,* April 25, 1972 for a summary of the problems.

5. The State Department provides Congress with annual reports entitled *US Contributions to International Organizations.*

6. *Thirty-Fifth Annual Congressional Quarterly Almanac,* pp. 131, 133, 134, 136, 194, 196, 197, and 204.

7. For an elaboration on these matters see G. Mangone, ed., *UN Administration of Economic and Social Programs* (New York: Columbia University Press, 1966).

8. See UNDP, "Consensus Approved by the Governing Council," *Report of the Governing Council Tenth Session* (June 1970), Annex, pp. 35–48. For a history of these events see Volume II, Chapter 2 of the United Nations publication, *A Study of the United Nations Development System*. For the recommendations of the Jackson Report, see Vol. I, Chapter 1.

9. United Nations, Department of Public Information, *United Nations: Image and Reality*, DPI/641, September 1979, p. 28. The United States is far and away the largest contributor followed by the Soviet Union (11.6 percent), Japan (8.64), the Federal Republic of Germany (7.7), France (5.82), China (5.5), United Kingdom (4.52), Italy (3.38), and Canada (3.04). Nine countries pay between 1.04 and 1.54 percent. The rest pay less than 1.0 percent; 67 countries pay the lowest assessment of .01 percent.

10. *New York Times*, May 25, 1972.

11. *New York Times*, September 29, 1971.

12. *New York Times*, October 27, 1971.

13. *New York Times*, December 3, 1971 and May 16, 1972.

14. *New York Times*, May 19, 1972.

15. *New York Times*, May 25, 1972.

16. *New York Times*, October 22 and November 12, 1975.

17. *New York Times*, November 16, 1975.

18. During this period, but not related to the anti-Zionist resolution, the US advised the ILO that it was giving the necessary two-year constitutional notice to withdraw from the ILO. This was only partially linked to the seating of the Palestine Liberation Organization (PLO) observers at ILO meetings. The more fundamental reason was the belief of George Meany, then President of the AFL-CIO, that Director-General Wilfred Jenks of the ILO had failed to honor a pledge not to appoint a Soviet Undersecretary of the ILO in return for US support of his selection as Director-General. The US did not return to the ILO until 1979.

19. Included within these various resolutions was support for state-run producer associations; indexation of raw material prices and capital goods; the use of local tribunals employing local law to settle investment disputes between foreign investors and host governments; codes of conduct for transnational corporations and the transfer of technology; and the stabilization of commodity prices at an equitable level.

20. Reprinted in "Review of the 1974 General Assembly and the United States Position in the United Nations," *Hearings* before the Subcommittee on International Organizations of the Committee on Foreign Affairs, 94th Congress, First Session, February 4–5, 1975, p. 10.

21. *UNGA Resolutions* 3201 (S-VI), May 1, 1974 and 3202 (S-VI),

May 1, 1974. Article 2 expanded the definition of permanent sovereignty over natural resources, spoke of regulation and supervision of transnational corporations, permitted unqualified nationalization of foreign property, provided for "appropriate compensation . . . taking into account [the States'] relevant laws and regulations and all circumstances that the state considers pertinent," and, in case of dispute over compensation, for settlement under "the domestic law of the nationalizing State and by its tribunals" unless concerned states agree otherwise. The United States, with fully 50 percent of all foreign investment controlled by its nationals was categorically opposed to this article, preferring a formula that provided for "prompt, adequate and effective" compensation under international law.

Article 5 gave states the right to associate in producer associations. Coming at a time when one such association, OPEC, had just radically raised the price of oil, this was a difficult pill for any of the major oil-importing countries to accept.

Article 28 called for indexation of the prices of exported primary products against the prices of imported capital goods. The interference with the market mechanism was unacceptable to the United States and subsequently many of the Group of 77 realized that this might not be the best approach to an extremely complex process.

22. *Congressional Record,* April 5, 1979, H2014.

23. For a discussion of these programs see Mangone, cited in note 7 above. See also Uner Kirdar, *The Structure of United Nations Economic Aid to Underdeveloped Countries* (The Hague: Martinus Nijhoff, 1966); H. L. Keenleyside, *International Aid: A Summary* (New York: H. James Heineman, 1966); M. Nashat, *National Interests and Bureaucracy versus Development Aid* (Geneva: Tribune Editions, 1978).

24. State Department Appropriations Bill for FY 1979 (P.L. 95–431).

25. *New York Times,* April 19, 1979.

26. *Congressional Record,* April 5, 1979, H2021 and H2022.

27. *Report* of the Committee on Contributions, GAOR: 1st Session (1946).

28. Ibid.

29. Stoessinger, "Financing the United Nations," op. cit., p. 8. and US Congress, *US Contributions to International Organizations,* House Document No. 111, 86th Congress, 1st Session (Washington, DC: US Government Printing Office, 1959), Table 31, p. 114.

30. Stoessinger, "Financing the United Nations," op. cit., p. 12.

31. Ibid., p. 23. The preceding paragraphs on these issues are a summary of Stoessinger's comments on pp. 14–30.

32. Ibid., p. 23.

33. *Report* of the Committee on Contributions, GAOR: 34th Session, Supplement No. 11 (A/34/11), 1979. It is possible that the recently developed and constantly refined purchasing power index will some day replace national income and gross national product statistics; at the moment this is not the case. Professor Irving Kravis of the University of Pennsylvania has been carrying out studies of this nature for the World Bank for more than five years. A number of reports have already been produced by the Bank.

34. *1972 Yearbook of the United Nations,* p. 712. Resolutions 2961B (XXVII) adopted by the General Assembly on 13 December 1972. In 1946, the US had argued that no state pay more than one-third of the budget.

35. Resolution 2961D (XXVII) adopted by the General Assembly on 13 December 1972.

36. *Report* of the Committee on Contributions, GAOR: 29th Session, Supplement No. 11 (A/9611), 1974, pp. 3, 4.

37. *UN Yearbook 1975.*

38. *UN Yearbook 1976,* pp. 891 ff.

39. Ibid.

40. *Report* of the Committee on Contributions, GAOR: 32nd Session, Supplement No. 11 (A/32/11), 13 September 1977, p. 14.

41. A/C.5/32/SR22, p. 7, paragraphs 24 and 25.

42. United Nations Association of the USA, *Issues before the Thirty-Fourth General Assembly of the United Nations* (UNA-USA: September 1979), p. 121.

43. Stoessinger, ''Financing the United Nations,'' op. cit., p. 3.

II

UN FUNCTIONS AND US OPTIONS IN AN INTERDEPENDENT WORLD

1. THE UN SYSTEM AND THE MAINTENANCE OF INTERNATIONAL PEACE AND SECURITY

CONTRIBUTIONS OF THE UN TO INTERNATIONAL SECURITY REGIMES

DEBRA L. MILLER

One of the main purposes of international organizations throughout history has been the preservation of peace and security.[1] The League of Nations and the United Nations, both constructed in the wake of world wars, were each designed with the prevention of the previous war in mind.[2] Thus, one sees in the Covenant of the League of Nations the requirement of a three-month "cooling-off" period before antagonists were legally allowed to escalate a conflict into armed warfare—perceived as a scheme through which states could possibly have averted the chain reaction that led to World War I in July 1914.[3] In a similar vein, the UN Charter provides for the establishment of a permanent UN military force at the disposal of the Security Council for use by a concert of great powers against aggressor nations, again an attempt to avoid the collapse of collective security that foreshadowed World War II.[4] However, the League's emphasis on rational discussions, legal formulas, and democracy could not prevent World War II, and the Great Power concert that the UN's founders envisaged never materialized, leaving only the bitter taste of the Cold War as a reminder of dashed hopes.

The poor track record of statesmen and diplomats in predicting how crises may develop in future systems makes it rather difficult to offer suggestions about the multilateral management of new threats to peace which may appear in the next decade. Given the stake of the United States in a peaceful international system, however, the suitability of the UN for handling new types of threats to peace in a way that is consonant with American interests should be of concern not only to academics but to policymakers as well.

This chapter examines constraints on the UN in the security field as well as its traditional functions, and why a country might or might not turn to a universal international organization rather than smaller multilateral or bilateral forums to deal with security affairs. It also attempts to provide insights regarding the possible handling of ''new'' threats to the peace—specifically, problems involving nuclear proliferation, human rights, and energy security.

FUNCTIONS OF THE UN IN THE SECURITY FIELD

Too often the United Nations is thought of as only a debating society or bargaining forum that is inhospitable to US interests. Often the UN is seen largely as an impotent organization, incapable of bringing disputing parties to settlement or enforcing the collective will of the General Assembly against aggressors. The UN, however, has had some notable successes in maintaining peace. These successes are of several different types, but the end result has been a positive UN contribution to the construction of various regimes designed to enhance security. This chapter will use Robert Jervis' definition of a security regime:

> . . . Those principles, rules, and norms which permit nations to be restrained in their behavior in the belief that others will reciprocate . . . The concept implies not only norms, and expectations which facilitate cooperation, but a form of cooperation which is more than the following of short-run interest.[5]

It is not easy to think of arrangements that fit this definition, let alone ones to which the UN has contributed.[6] Before discussing the UN's functions in the security field, it may be useful to examine why cooperation in the security field, particularly regarding arms control issues, is so hard to obtain. First, security, more than any other issue, is most closely related to a nation's sovereignty. Compromising the ability for independent action in this area may diminish a state's ability to respond as it wishes to protect its integrity or its existence.[7] Second, cooperation in this area is difficult to achieve because conditions approximate those of the "Prisoner's Dilemma" game.[8] That is, whereas it might be optimal if (in a world of two states) both State A and State B agree to limit their arms, if one state reduces or controls its level of armaments and the other does not, then the state applying the controls loses more than if no agreement had been made. Conversely, the state that does not restrict its arms according to the agreement gains an advantage. Thus, although the state which implements arms controls is only living up to its agreement, it may be unwittingly making itself more vulnerable. In general, the policy preferences of each state can be ranked as follows:

1. Agree to arms control arrangements and then cheat;
2. Do not agree to arms control limitations; or
3. Agree to arms control limitations and adhere to them.

The only way to make adherence to agreements (option 3) the preferable outcome—as it should be—is to make it too costly or too difficult for states to cheat. Thus, cooperation in this area, more than any other, demands assurances of reciprocal behavior, usually through some sort of monitoring by other states.

If monitoring requires a state to submit documentation about its armaments levels or to agree to on-site inspections by other states or the personnel of international organizations, there may be times when these conditions can in themselves pose an obstacle to cooperation. Many states do not like the idea of non-nationals surveying and judging the extent to which they have adhered to international agreements and they do their best to resist such intrusions. This is particularly true of the USSR in the arms control area in the past, but it is also true of the US on some issues of concern to the international community, notably the monitoring of human rights violations and labor regulations.

In some cases then, agreement on limited surveillance, instead of being a compromise between total surveillance and no agreement at all, can become a way to circumvent international scrutiny. In actuality, partial surveillance may decrease security more than no agreement at all. For example, states may invite inspectors into their territory and authorize inspections of only those sites and items that conform with international agreements, thus diverting attention from clandestine activities elsewhere. Inspectors may then report that a state is adhering to an agreement, even though it is not. Instead of enhancing the security of all states, such agreements can lull some states into a false sense of security.

These three obstacles to cooperation in the arms control and security area derive from the very existence of the current anarchical, decentralized international system of nation states. In order for a state to guarantee its own survival, self-help and independence (as opposed to cooperation and interdependence qua division of labor) are often required.

Obstacles to cooperation may arise on another level as well. Different states, with different forms of government, political interests, and security needs, may have different interests in this area. Consequently they also may have conflicting ideas about what constitutes an optimum security regime. Both the East-West division and the North-South cleavage have had a significant impact on the UN's ability to handle security problems. In post-World War II international relations, the East-West split has circumscribed, in geographical terms, the UN's involvement in particular disputes, limiting it to those areas outside of either superpower's sphere of influence, or as Dag Hammarskjöld described it, "beyond the no-man's land of the Cold War."[9]

The North-South split has limited the UN's role in the area of arms control too, although for different reasons. The superpowers have resisted discussing arms control issues in the UN partly because the great powers are mainly interested in the need for reducing horizontal proliferation (i.e., limiting the number of nuclear-weapons states) and in focusing on conventional arms, while the Southern (weaker) states prefer to focus on controlling vertical proliferation (i.e., limiting the size of the superpowers' nuclear arsenals). As a result, states have most often chosen to work outside of the UN in organizations limited to states with similar or complementary interests.

Despite the difficulty of constructing security regimes in this international system and the unwillingness of states to involve the UN, the United Nations has played an important role in the construction of regimes to enhance security. Basically, the Organization has three primary functions in regime construction and maintenance: consciousness-raising, standard-setting, and the implementation of standards.

First, debates at the UN can serve to raise the level of consciousness about particular global problems. Discussion, debate, and the ensuing publicity sensitize states to the issues involved as well as to other states' perceptions of problems. In this sense, the UN often serves to set the agenda for later international debates. At least in this area, the UN is peculiarly an egalitarian body. Non-governmental organizations, small states, and other actors traditionally thought of as having little influence in international politics have regular channels at the UN through which they can put items on the agenda without too much difficulty and then have some influence in framing the following debate and discussion. The effects of this process can be to the good if they heighten policymakers' sensitivity to the public's concerns about potential threats to peace. Arms control issues have received special attention at the UN lately. The Disarmament Centre at the UN in New York has been revived and expanded since 1978 and two Special Sessions on Disarmament have taken place with full participation of both governments and non-governmental organizations.

The situations in Namibia and South Africa have also come to the fore in part because of the emphasis placed on them at the United Nations. Although solutions to these issues have not been found at the UN, the publicity and pressure for solutions have had an effect on US policy. It is doubtful that the Reagan Administration would have attempted to help solve the Namibia problem, even outside of the UN within a smaller group as it is doing now, without being sensitized to the problem at the United Nations. Likewise, the Administration's proposal for START talks with the Soviet Union, which also are to take place outside of the UN, can be partially attributed to pressure generated at the UN and elsewhere to begin serious negotiations on arms control. One can find other such examples during the past 38 years, where the UN's sensitization role has catalyzed states to agree outside the UN to schemes that have inhibited conventional and nuclear proliferation. The 1959 Antarctic Treaty, although negotiated outside the UN, was first proposed by India in the General Assembly in 1956. The idea for the 1967 Treaty of Tlatelolco which established a nuclear free zone in Latin America was also proposed at the GA, but negotiated outside of the UN. Thus, UN consciousness-raising often has extra-UN consequences that can be critical catalysts to security maintenance.

The second function the UN performs in security-regime construction is standard-setting. The UN is a legitimizing institution, a place where states try to arrive at consensus about moral behavior in a system that does not necessarily reward moral acts. In fact, as discussed earlier, cheating is sometimes rewarded. In the area of peace and security, UN member states have supported countless documents that have enshrined norms promoting sovereignty[10] and peaceful settlement of disputes,[11] and have spoken out against aggression.[12] These have had a cumulative effect on the way nations justify their behavior, if not always on the behavior itself.

Critics of the UN suggest that aggression is hard to define (it is) and that the UN's 1974 clarification of the term did not make it any clearer (it didn't). Even more importantly, they suggest that the UN's promotion of the norm of decolonization[13] has sometimes conflicted with the norm against aggression, and that the Third World-dominated UN favors the first at the expense of the second. This is sometimes true, but at other times the results are surprising—in the 1982 dispute over the Falkland Islands, the Security Council condemned Argentina, not Great Britain. Despite the colonial overtones of the dispute, the norm against the use of force was reaffirmed by the General Assembly (compare the case with the 1961 dispute between Portugal and India over Goa, where the opposite occurred).

The UN has also contributed to the articulation of norms against the use of nuclear weapons. While the restraint of the superpowers in this area is due more to their perceptions of self-interest than to UN norms, the reluctance of weaker states to use nuclear weapons in local disputes may derive in part from the UN's norm against such an action and from the perception that sanctions (e.g., the cutting off of military assistance by one's allies) will be applied within the UN context against countries that violate that norm.

Although the role of the United Nations in the establishment of broad norms to enhance security is important, the Organization is more limited when it comes to significant treaty negotiation activities. Had the Great Power unity the founders hoped for continued after World War II, most of the work in this area would have taken place in the Security Council with the advice of a permanent Military Staff Committee (which never came into existence). Since this did not materialize, responsibility for the creation of legally binding instruments to enhance security fell to the General Assembly, even though the Charter forbids the GA from entering into anything but non-binding recommendations in this area. As a result, the First Committee of the General Assembly is limited to suggesting areas where fruitful treaty-making might occur. Any actual UN treaty-making occurs in Geneva at the now 40-member Committee on Disarmament which reports to but is independent of the GA. That Committee has been responsible for producing, in part at the behest of UNGA resolutions and First Committee suggestions (and always with the concurrent agreement of the two superpowers), the 1963 Partial Test Ban Agreement, the 1963 Hot Line Agreement between the US and the USSR, the 1967 Outer Space Treaty, the 1968 Non-Proliferation Treaty, and the 1972 Biological Weapons Treaty.

The existence of standards and norms can contribute to evolutionary change and to orderly and predictable behavior by states even when states are in conflict with each other. On the other hand, fault for non-adherence to such norms and standards rarely lies with the UN. Rather, it is a consequence of the existing anarchical international system where survival of the state is the top priority and each state pursues what it perceives as its own national interest, often regardless of international strictures.

The third function of the UN in the construction and maintenance of security regimes is the implementation of standards. Here, the UN's performance and the performance of its member states have been the most mixed. Implementation really requires two things: surveillance of activity and sanctions for inappropriate behavior. The reluctance of states to allow surveillance or to allow it only under certain circumstances compounds the problem of implementing agreed-upon standards. Thus the enforcement of agreements such as the Non-Proliferation Treaty (NPT) by the International Atomic

Energy Agency (IAEA) is limited because some states are not parties to the treaty, some do not allow on-site inspections, and some try to be selective about what the inspectors actually see.

Likewise, the UN and the specialized agencies are selective about what they enforce. UN bodies have discretion over what they will rule on, and they often use it. As a result, in certain areas, such as human rights, despite the vast number of complaints received from around the world, the UN has primarily focused on Israel, Chile, and South Africa. Other states, such as Argentina, have received disproportionately little attention in the UN. In other words, questions of implementation are very political: who you are and what group you represent can be just as important as what you have done.

Concrete sanctions for unacceptable behavior are even more difficult to obtain than simple verbal condemnations. If sanctions are actually to change the behavior of an offending party, they must be universally applied, promptly implemented, and have real teeth. In addition, the political benefits realized from acts of condemning or imposing sanctions on another country, or the benefits deriving from the changed behavior of the offender, must outweigh the economic costs for those states imposing the sanctions. The confluence of these factors has rarely, if ever, existed. The League of Nations agreed on sanctions to undermine Mussolini, but some states such as Switzerland and Austria did not comply for economic reasons, and others such as France and Great Britain were wary of inflaming Italy and thereby pushing Italy into a closer alliance with Germany. The UN has had the same problems as the League had with sanctions. The efforts to change Rhodesia's, and later South Africa's, behavior through sanctions failed not so much because of a lack of political commitment, but because of economic factors that led to a lack of universality.

Perhaps the most important and effective role the UN performs in implementation is peacekeeping. Peacekeeping can be classified as an implementation function because it assists in keeping conflagrations from growing and in maintaining cease-fires with the aim of achieving a norm promoted by the UN—the peaceful settlement of disputes. Peacekeeping is not specifically provided for in the UN Charter. Rather, it was created by Dag Hammarskjöld in response to the rivalries in the Third World, the site of almost all armed conflict since World War II. In the initial stages, most of these conflicts have had local causes, but in their secondary stages, they have become proxy wars for the superpowers, either because of a continuing stream of military assistance or because of direct intervention by either the US or the USSR. Hammarskjöld hoped to limit the size—and severity—of these conflicts by preventing them from entering the second stage. As Hammarskjöld envisaged it, the peacekeeping force was to be a neutral, interpositionary defensive force composed of soldiers from middle-level powers who would serve at the behest of the Security Council—or the General Assembly under the auspices of a Uniting for Peace resolution—with the consent of the belligerents. There have been over a dozen UN peacekeeping forces since the 1950s. Some have not conformed to the model outlined above. In the Congo, the force played a partisan role and initiated activities, rather than simply being a defensive force. In other conflicts, soldiers have come from allies of the superpowers (although never from the superpowers themselves).

Peacekeeping has not been an unmitigated success. When peacekeeping operations were undertaken as a result of General Assembly resolutions that overrode Security Council preferences, France and the USSR withheld a portion of their UN dues in protest. This caused a major crisis in the early 1960s when the US threatened to invoke Article 19 of the Charter against the USSR, which was then in arrears for three years. Such a step would have deprived the Soviets of their voting rights in the General Assembly. The Soviets countered with a threat to withdraw from the UN altogether, and the outcome was that the General Assembly did not vote at all in 1963 (everything was done by consensus). The UN subsequently found other ways of paying for its peacekeeping activities. Since then, the General Assembly has never overruled the Security Council on this issue, reinforcing the belief that effective peacekeeping requires the approval of the Security Council's permanent members as well as the approval of the belligerents. When Nasser dismissed the UN Emergency Force (UNEF I) in 1967, a force that had been in the Middle East since 1956, his action was not "illegal," although it certainly indicated that war was around the corner.

What can we conclude about the UN's role in the construction and maintenance of security regimes? Consistent with the findings of Zacher and Findlayson (see the next chapter), the UN's success in the construction and maintenance of security regimes is very much a function of the structure of the international system and of relations among sovereign states. Thus, the role of the UN in this most important area is severely constrained by both systemic and political forces. Despite this, the UN, because of the nature of the institution, the ingenuity of some of its staff, and the ideals of the member states, has been able to shape partial security regimes and to have some influence on the behavior of states, particularly in the area of consciousness-raising and in shaping the terms of the debate, in standard-setting, and in implementation. Even during the past troubled decade, the UN has served as much more than a debating society.

CHOICE OF FORUM

That nations often "forum shop" is not new, nor is it necessarily reflective of anti-UN sentiment that they often prefer to deal with problems outside of the UN. Most states look for the forum that is most hospitable to their interests on a given issue and for many reasons the UN's forums are hardly those they would choose. Thus, the US and many other countries consistently refrain from using the UN General Assembly on many security issues. Likewise, developing countries engage in similar shopping activities, especially on economic questions, where there are a large number of organizations with overlapping mandates but with very different missions. On security issues, however, the developing countries are often ambivalent about using the United Nations.

There are those who suggest that, especially in the area of politico-military affairs, states are more and more often using regional forums to deal with security problems and increasingly turning to bilateral or small multilateral working groups for the negotiation of difficult issues. The implication is that power and authority are being taken away from the General Assembly and the various UN specialized agencies. In general, this hypothesis has little validity. Issues are usually dealt with at a variety of different levels and in different-sized organizations. An organization may deal with an issue for a while, then drop it, only to pick it up again at a later stage of development. In addition, organizations tend to specialize in making a particular type of decision. For example, the Conference of the Heads of the Non-Aligned, the UN General Assembly, and the Pugwash Conference are all usually agenda-setters rather than rule-makers or rule-implementers.[14] Even at near universal organizations such as the UN Conference on Trade and Development (UNCTAD), in the end it is often only a small elite (i.e., the spokesmen for the various blocs, the President and Chairman of the Conference, along with a few Secretariat staff) who create rules, after consultation with their respective constituencies.

In short, a pluralistic and decentralized environment for international negotiation has developed in which the UN, its specialized agencies, regional groups, and bilateral diplomacy operate in tandem, feeding back one to the other. The process of international negotiation is not tending more toward centralization at the UN or decentralization at smaller bodies: it encompasses both.

What are the factors that states consider when choosing among different types of international institutions in which to pursue their interests? In general, they take into account the following four points:

Organizational mission. Many organizations have a "mission" or a decided ideological tilt. In other words, most Secretariats are sectarian.[15] As a result, countries may favor bringing an issue to a particular body because a particular preferred outcome can be predicted with greater certainty. Thus, on trade issues, the US favors the General Agreement on Tariffs and Trade (GATT) over UNCTAD, because GATT has a free trade, pro-competition bent in contrast to UNCTAD's emphasis on economic development doctrines. The developing countries have different preferences.

The structure of influence. The way decisions are made and voting is carried out is another factor that influences the choice of forum. The US prefers to have weighted voting or formal decision-making procedures that serve to protect US interests: the IAEA, the IMF, and the Security Council all have formal structures more conducive to US interests.

However, the informal structure of influence within an organization can be just as important as the formal one. Thus the US shies away from the UN General Assembly not only because of its one-nation, one-vote voting system, but also because of the anti-hegemonic, pro–Third World bias among the majority of delegates, the competition that takes place among industrialized states for diplomatic "brownie points" with the Third World, and the unlikelihood of forging effective coalitions with other delegations (North or South) that are mainly interested in toeing the rhetorical line. Even at UNCTAD, the US enjoys more informal influence, as a rule, than it does at the General Assembly.

Linkage politics and politicization effects. The term "politicization" is used by different authors in different ways. Some people use the word interchangeably with issue-linkage, noting than an issue is politicized if it is linked at the bargaining table to another issue not logically related to it. Others say that an issue is politicized when there is a high emotional charge attached to it for ideological or other reasons not particularly related to the merits of the issue, in a way that precludes so-called "rational, analytic" negotiation. No matter how authors use the term, however, they seem to agree that politicization of an issue or an environment affects diplomats' choice of forum and influences outcomes.[16]

For example, by the end of the 1970s, developing countries were dissatisfied with the progress they had made in the specialized agencies regarding the achievement of the Programme for a New International Economic Order. Thus, they suggested holding a universal, multi-issue conference known as the Global Negotiations, at which they could exploit the West's energy dependence on OPEC and make progress in achieving the NIEO by linking the granting of concessions on energy security to reciprocal Western concessions on monetary reform and technology transfer.

David Kay has suggested,[17] and Sidney Weintraub seems to concur,[18] that the specialized agencies were established in order to prevent such politicization and issue-linkage. These authors rue that both have occurred in the specialized agencies, and Kay goes so far as to suggest that the US downgrade its participation in those agencies where these phenomena are especially predominant.

Unfortunately, such a strategy is largely unworkable because there are very few issues that are not politicized. Even those issues considered in the so-called "functional agencies" cannot be decided in a purely apolitical, technical way. Ideology, the distributional consequences of decisions, and other such factors make negotiations controversial. This seems to be inherent in all political processes involving trade-offs. The important thing for statesmen is not so much to avoid all politicized issues and arenas (although this may sometimes be appropriate), but to understand *why* they are politicized and then to learn how to operate within the constraints of a particular situation, and even to exploit it.

Organizational size. Other things being equal, it has been argued that smaller organizations and bilateral relationships can afford greater potential for fruitful negotiation than larger organizations. This is not because of politicization, mandate, or influence factors (discussed above), but because of size alone. "Smaller is better than small," argues Kenneth Waltz, noting that it is often easier to strike a bargain among fewer parties. "The costs of bargaining increase at an accelerating rate as the number of parties becomes larger. . . . As numbers increase, each has to bargain with more others. Complications accelerate rapidly."[19] In addition, as a group grows in size, each party has less incentive to bear the costs of bargaining. In Waltz's words: "Each member of a pair expects to get about half the benefits of a bargain made; each member of a trio a third, and so on."[20]

Although it might indeed be easier to strike a bargain with fewer parties, much depends on who the parties are and what influence they bring to bear on a situation. In addition, the significance of the agreements reached cannot be measured solely on the basis of the number of parties involved. Thus, the statement that as a group grows in size each party has less incentive to bear the costs of bargaining because the benefits from negotiation decrease proportionately may be more false than true in international negotiations. Waltz's comparison between the costs of bargaining (time, money spent, and acrimony among states) and the benefits of negotiation (especially those that are collective goods such as monetary stability, international security, or clean air) is often an "apples and oranges" comparison when applied to the world of multilateral diplomacy.

Is it better or worse to have more signatories to an agreement? Fewer signatories may require fewer surveillance activities, as Waltz suggests; all other things being equal, there will probably be a smaller number of cheaters. These points may be true, but on the global level at least, they may also be irrelevant. No one would suggest that because France and India have not signed the NPT the world community is better off or more secure—despite the fact the community does not have to bear the costs of policing France and India's nuclear facilities. Universal adherence is often clearly preferable to partial adherence, especially in the security area.

There are situations in which the number of adherents can be more limited without adverse consequences. Agreements made between the US and the USSR on nuclear and other arms do not have to include any other parties to be considered significant achievements (the level and type of weapons are already limited to only a few countries because of their size and the level of technology involved). Similarly, agreements establishing regional nuclear-free zones may require only the participation of the states within the zone. However, even in these two cases, there might be additional benefits of more widespread interest or participation in the negotiations. Regarding the first case, many agreements between the superpowers have been spurred by pressure put on the two by other states at the UN and elsewhere. Regarding nuclear-free zones, most regional groups that wish to establish such zones are eager to gain security assurances from outside parties that they will not supply nuclear weapons to any nation in the region and that they will not be the victim of nuclear blackmail or aggression.

There is yet another reason that smaller may *not* be better than small. As noted in the first section of this chapter, one of the main functions of universal organizations is to legitimize certain norms, rules, and activities. This is particularly important to weaker states, or to states that are trying to gain international legitimization of their actions. Unilateral statements and bilateral or limited multilateral arrangements may make it more difficult for statesmen to adopt certain policies if they believe that others do not perceive these activities as legitimate. In the present system, universal international organizations seem to be able to offer such legitimacy better than other smaller forums whose decisions do not embody such widespread consensus.

There are other benefits of negotiating in large, universal organizations. One is educational. The US and other states have persuaded (or, on occasion, have been persuaded) that a proposed new standard or arrangement has more bad consequences than good ones; as a result, states have sometimes modified or changed their foreign policies. More than a few NIEO projects have been abandoned because Northern states have either convinced Southern states that, ultimately, the projects would not better them economically, or else because the industrialized nations have indicated their unwillingness to support the projects. Had the US refused to participate in such negotiations, this discussion might not have occurred.

At present, the US is not interested in particularly radical change in the present system, but other states *are* interested in such change. By participating in universal organizations where these states make radical demands or proposals, the US has the possibility of tempering some of these demands and other states have the opportunity to try to influence the US position. If a consensus does develop on some issues, this may have the effect of co-opting radical states into existing, or slightly changed regimes, thus giving them a stake in the maintenance of various arrangements for world order.

Conventional wisdom suggests that the US would do well to steer clear of large, universal organizations because of their size, current politicized character, type of mission, and structure of influence. Krasner, in his chapter in this volume, in essence concurs with this.[21] But the discussion above should put some perspective on the "small is beautiful" argument. Sometimes it is easier to negotiate and to bring US influence to bear with a smaller number of parties (especially if those not sympathetic to the US point of view are excluded), but there are also decided disadvantages to agreements among the few, especially if the behavior or actions of others are affected by or will affect the agreement. Only existing universal organizations can confer certain benefits, such as legitimization of agreements. Listening and responding in larger organizations to states interested in radical change allows the US to influence the negotiations, to educate, and perhaps even to co-opt new states into the system of existing agreements.

All of this does not negate the charge that the UN can be "a dangerous place" for the US if the pressure to agree to things contrary to US national interests becomes overwhelming, if the US is isolated from even its closest allies on issue after issue, or if the UNGA endorses notions such as Zionism is racism. Nor does it suggest that forum-shopping, according to the criteria discussed above, is not a wise activity. But the UN may be a far less dangerous place for us than some believe. Even though there are some risks in participating in the UN, non-participation cannot limit damage, nor can it have an effect on changing the rules of the game.

THE UN AND NEW THREATS TO THE PEACE

Energy security, the management of nuclear capabilities, and human rights issues have been increasingly accepted as peace and security problems. It is likely that these areas will become even more critical in the 1980s, and that multilateral management will be called for to keep the peace. The UN has already played a role in managing these issues, but it is possible that its role could be expanded because of the potential severity of the issues.

Human rights. Human rights is not really a new issue for the UN. The Charter suggests that the protection of human rights is one of the organization's main goals; indeed, the 1948 Universal Declaration of Human Rights was one of the first products of the UN. Most states have signed the Declaration, and many have ratified either one or both of its companion Covenants, one on economic and social rights[22] and the other on political and civil rights,[23] written later. In addition, declarations or conventions against genocide, colonialism, racism, and sex discrimination were approved by the General Assembly during its first 25 years.[24]

Human rights is also not a new peace and security issue. Statesmen perceived it as an international issue in the wake of Hitler and World War II, as had nineteenth-and early twentieth-century Anglo-American liberal political philosophers before them. Nevertheless, human rights violations are rampant today, despite the attempts to develop a relatively broad consensus on human rights standards. Human rights may present threats to intrastate and interstate peace as well. Thus the international community has focused on South Africa's apartheid policies and Israel's treatment of the Palestinian refugees. (Obviously, the United Nation's preoccupation with these two problems has much to do with the organization's deep sensitivity to ''colonialism.'') Even in cases where human rights violations are seemingly purely intrastate, however, such as those atrocities committed by the Chilean, Argentinian, or Uruguayan governments, it is often impossible to isolate the immediate and purely domestic from the potentially long-run interstate consequences (consider the ultimate consequences of the Shah's abuses in Iran and Somoza's in Nicaragua).

Although the work of the UN in human rights standard-setting has been lauded, much remains to be done in fully and consistently implementing those standards. Implementation is difficult, in part, because the existence of universal standards belies universal consensus on human rights issues. There is little consensus among states about which rights enunciated in the Covenants states must grant to their citizens and which are merely aspirations, or about which rights take precedence over others in conflict-of-rights situations.[25] In regional organizations such as the European Community, where lack of consensus is not as much of a problem, implementation of regional standards through quasi-judicial intergovernmental or supranational machinery is more complete and less politicized.

Implementation is also difficult because of the nature of human rights. Human rights are claims by the citizen against the state and, at least in the short run, the balance of power usually rests with the state. Furthermore, governments usually limit human rights for a purpose—that is, such restrictions are one of many instruments for achieving particular goals or for maintaining political stability. If a government believes that the full granting of human rights may jeopardize its existence, endanger the security of the country, or change the character of the nation, accusations by the UN against the state and admonitions to change will fall on deaf ears. What makes the Palestinian refugee problem and the system of South African apartheid so intractable is their close connection with the political configuration of each region.

Not all human rights problems are immediate threats to the peace. But for those that are, the problems states face in managing traditional peace and security issues arise in the human rights area as well. First, as suggested above, the "solution" to many human rights problems may jeopardize national or regional security or the basis upon which national sovereignty rests. Thus, most states guard jealously as their sovereign prerogative the extent to which they will grant human rights. Second, many states have little interest in international surveillance of their implementation of human rights standards. (This is true not only of authoritarian or third world states. The US also refuses to agree to legally binding treaties that would make the US accountable to the UN for its behavior in this area.) Third, the conduct of the UN as an enforcer of human rights standards is suspect because of the extreme degree of politicization about some issues, the politicized environment at the General Assembly when these issues are raised,[26] and the UN's inconsistent enforcement record. Even when the UN calls attention to human rights abuses in particular countries, it is very difficult for the organization to do much to remedy the situation. The UN's enforcement mechanisms in this area are limited to public assertions that a particular country is acting badly and to recommending that states impose sanctions against the country. But sanctions organized by the UN against human rights abuses have rarely been effective. Indeed compliance is almost always voluntary, or the result of extra-UN political tradeoffs, such as the Helsinki Accords.

Despite these factors, UN implementation machinery has been strengthened every year.[27] The UN Human Rights Commission hears more complaints and issues more condemnations than ever before. Indeed, in the years to come the UN may be able to improve significantly its performance in this area.[28] Several suggestions could be adopted to facilitate this process. First, states could reconsider the definition and notion of human rights abuses. Not all abuses are similar in character. Genocide and apartheid must be judged by the international community as more serious than the deprivation of the right to vote or to work. The UN ought to have options open to it other than either ignoring human rights violations or treating all types of abuses in approximately the same fashion—as if the governments that perpetuated them were "criminal." Resolutions and sanctions against states that emphasize the criminality of an offending state's actions may make that state deny the charges against it and reinforce a posture of intransigence. Rather than heavy-handed condemnation and suggestions for punitive sanctions, this lesser set of abuses could be treated as "civil" wrongs, publicized as such, and handled with a mixture of quiet diplomacy on the part of the Secretary-General's office and bilateral "carrots" aimed at remedying the situation. Some of these carrots might include guarantees of a state's security, if appropriate. This type of treatment might defuse some of the emotional charge that surrounds human rights issues and consequently depoliticize the UN's enforcer role. At the present time human rights violations are treated as civil wrongs in Europe, with some success.[29]

Current UN enforcement of human rights standards is incomplete and inconsistent. The UN selectively targets certain states and particular abuses for condemnation, with targeting based heavily on political considerations. If the UN changes its enforcement procedures as suggested above, there will be less of a need or an incentive to base implementation on political considerations. Consequently, enforcement attempts might be more uniform and consistent.

The mixture of UN and extra-UN diplomacy might also be constructive. If both the UN and a country's allies quietly press for corrective action, and reward a state for steps in that direction, the country may, over time, find it in its advantage to change. Extra-UN diplomacy would be useful in dealing with both the most serious and the lesser human rights problems.

Nuclear proliferation. While the potential for improving the UN's performance in the area of human rights may be great, the UN and the International Atomic Energy Agency's (IAEA) role in preventing the proliferation of nuclear weapons most likely will not be significantly enhanced in the near future. The difficulties of controlling vertical proliferation by the nuclear powers have already been discussed. The focus of this section will be on the prevention of horizontal nuclear weapons proliferation and ensuring that nuclear power is used only for peaceful purposes in non-weapons states. Despite the past UN role in this area, future initiatives in this area will most likely be taken outside the UN. There are many reasons for reaching this conclusion and, interestingly enough, it is also the view of the new Director-General of the IAEA and many national policymakers alike.

While it is generally believed that the fewer states that have nuclear weapons (outside the superpowers) the more global security is enhanced, three additional states currently maintain their own independent nuclear capabilities for reasons of national security or political prestige. (India also has a nuclear capability, as evidenced by its explosion of a "peaceful" nuclear device in 1974.) Many non-weapons countries have acquired or are acquiring the technology and materials needed to satisfy their energy needs through nuclear power. This situation is commercially advantageous for the US, USSR, and Western Europe, but fraught with potential danger, for nuclear power produces the spent fuel that is required for the production of atomic weapons. Most states have conflicting goals on these issues: the conditions for ensuring security at the global and national level are often different, and a weapons state's security interest may conflict with its commercial interest.

The Baruch Plan of 1946 envisaged that the UN would own and control nuclear power and activities rather than leaving them to national development and management. This plan was never realized, in large part because the Soviet Union did not want to legitimize the existing American nuclear weapons monopoly and rejected the plan. Since 1957, when the IAEA was founded, however, the UN has had a role in supervising the use of nuclear materials, albeit never the final say on who could or could not acquire nuclear technology. The international consensus that produced the IAEA was the product of the Atoms for Peace Program developed by the Eisenhower Administration.[30] The goal was to aid non-nuclear countries develop nuclear power capacities with the important proviso that recipient countries would not divert materials from civilian to military uses. The IAEA does this by requiring non-weapons member states to file reports with the IAEA on their nuclear activities and allow international inspectors to visit their nuclear facilities to verify these reports. This is the so-called "safeguards system."

The final step in the construction of the current international regime was the negotiation and ratification of the Nuclear Non-Proliferation Treaty (NPT) at the UN in 1968. Although Ireland first proposed the idea at the United Nations, it was the US and the USSR that convinced other states that the treaty should be negotiated and ratified.[31] The NPT offers the opportunity for non-weapons states to pledge that they will use nuclear power only for peaceful purposes and for weapons states to pledge that they will not aid in the development of nuclear weapons in other countries. In addition, the treaty requires that non-weapons state signatories open all their nuclear facilities to IAEA inspection and that weapons state signatories take steps to control their own nuclear arms race. In return for the promise to remain non-nuclear, non-weapons states were to be offered aid in the development of their civilian nuclear capabilities.

The NPT regime has never been completed, and compliance was by no means perfect even in its heyday in the late 1960s and the early 1970s. France and China never signed the Treaty, nor did India, Pakistan, South Africa, Israel, Brazil, Argentina, and several other near-nuclear states. In addition, the safeguards system is limited because the IAEA cannot be absolutely sure that no diversion has taken place, nor can the organization itself impose sanctions for misconduct. There are those who suggest, ironically, that the NPT may have encouraged nuclear weapons proliferation because its imperfect safeguards system lulls technology suppliers interested in commercial gain into complacency about security problems associated with the transfer of nuclear technology.

The NPT regime began to seriously erode in the 1970s. The oil crises spurred significant international interest in the development of nuclear power facilities. After the Vietnam War there was increased uncertainty about whether the United States, which had been the major impetus behind the regime, was still willing or capable of providing a security umbrella for its allies. In addition, the United States lost its position as the principal supplier of nuclear technology to the Third World and, as the Europeans began to exploit the growing demand for nuclear technology and materials, safeguards on the transfer of technology became weaker and weaker.

The reasons for the erosion during the past decade have largely been outside the IAEA or the UN's control. Hans Blix, the new Director-General of the IAEA, notes: "You can't stop proliferation with safeguards. Security considerations are decisive. If a country is secure it is more likely to invite us in. Insecure countries are more likely to seek atomic weapons."[32] The responsibility for controlling the spread of technology that makes proliferation possible lies with the states currently possessing nuclear weapons. Blix is critical of both the Carter and Reagan Administration's proliferation policies. Suggesting that President Carter relied too heavily on punitive sanctions to prevent countries from developing weapons capabilities, Blix is concerned that the Reagan Administration is promoting the export of nuclear technology for commercial reasons and passing the buck concerning responsibility for controlling proliferation to the IAEA—a task Blix maintains the Agency cannot handle by itself. At the same time, the Director-General praised the decision to provide substantial military aid to Pakistan in an effort to prevent that country from developing nuclear weapons. Blix thus closely connects a nation's desire for nuclear weapons with its legitimate security concerns in the belief that measures like these may be able to get to the heart of the nuclear proliferation dilemma and ultimately pave the way for more adherence to the existing regime. (It should be noted, however, that despite Reagan aid and Blix's suggestions and pressure, Pakistan has given no indication that it intends to sign the NPT, nor has it opened its nuclear facilities to outside inspection.)

Another expert in this field, former Carter Administration policymaker Joseph Nye, also suggests strengthening the non-proliferation regime through steps outside the UN. Nye urges US-Soviet bilateral leadership to control proliferation. Among other things, he proposes more regular, low political visibility talks between the US and the Soviets on proliferation problems; concerted, quiet efforts to urge more states to sign the NPT; and the imposition of joint sanctions or expressions of disapproval toward countries developing nuclear weapons rather than continued US-Soviet competition for the friendship and political alliance of new weapons states. Nye also suggests that the US and the Soviet Union require that spent fuel be returned from third countries to the country of origin. Although relations between the Soviet Union and the US are currently strained, Nye believes that cooperation on these points is possible, given the mutual interest involved here.[33]

Nye stresses the US-Soviet dimension, but it is also important that US-European consultation be strengthened. Discussions among the London Suppliers Group in the 1970s were sometimes acrimonious and perhaps limited in their ability to develop a real policy consensus, but continued cooperation is ultimately necessary to maintain the non-proliferation regime.

There may also be the possibility of greater multilateral management of the fuel cycle on a regional basis outside of the UN. For example, Lawrence Scheinman points to existing regional institutional arrangements such as EURODIF and URENCO as the harbinger of a politically acceptable alternative to national ownership and control of nuclear facilities.[34] This type of arrangement is more effective than an international safeguards system alone and more politically saleable than more ambitious universal schemes such as the Baruch Plan. Regional arrangements do require an enormous amount of technical and political cooperation within the region for them to work, as well as guarantees of fuel, if need be, from an outside party such as the US. Therefore it is likely that such institutional arrangements would not develop in areas of potential conflict such as Southern Africa, Southeast Asia, or the Middle East. This will sharply limit their utility. Moreover, the institutional arrangements will be smaller, extra-UN ventures. This is not to say that these arrangements would not have value in preventing nuclear weapons proliferation, but only that such arrangements will develop in areas where they are less needed for security reasons because countries involved have peaceful intentions toward one another. The UN's role will probably be limited to legitimizing these arrangements.

Although UN efforts to foster non-proliferation and manage nuclear power may not be very different in the future than they have been in the past, the United Nations will nonetheless continue to have a role in both areas. More than ever before, however, success will depend less on the IAEA and international arrangements and more on the responsible future management by nation states of nuclear technology transfer and control over the fuel cycle.

Energy security. When considering the potential for more extensive UN involvement in human rights and nuclear proliferation issues, one could argue that the Organization was building on a past record of considerable achievement. One cannot say the same for energy security. Even though the issue itself was at the top of most foreign policy agendas during the 1970s, the UN's involvement has been brief and relatively inconsequential. This does not necessarily mean that the issue is a non-starter for the United Nations, but it does indicate that the UN and other international organizations will have to attack this problem in a very different way.

Most efforts to promote multilateral energy security at the UN and elsewhere have focused on the political problems between energy exporting and importing states. For example, at the 1975–77 meetings of the Conference on International Economic Cooperation (CIEC) industrialized states tried to extract concessions on energy security from the oil-producing states in return for concessions on the New International Economic Order.[35] This failed. In the mid-1970s efforts were made to coordinate the energy and foreign policies of the OECD countries. These also failed.

Despite the poor record of global management, energy security has been less of an issue since 1980. Why? In simple terms, the market has changed.[36] Demand for oil is not growing at the same rapid rate as a decade ago, the West has conserved oil to some extent, and the recession has dampened energy appetites. Iran has recently begun to export oil again, changing the structure of the market, and global oil production is again on the rise despite changes in demand. In addition, OPEC has not been able to agree on production or price levels, both because of political squabbles among the members and various economic considerations.[37] The consequence of all this has been recurring oil gluts.

That there is no energy crisis now does not preclude another one in the future if supply and demand conditions change. Not only could OPEC once again regain its cohesion and raise prices or cut back production for economic or political reasons, but demand for oil could grow in the West if there is a sustained economic recovery. Thus, it makes sense for the international community to explore different methods for achieving energy security. A variety of different approaches taken by various groups of states, both importers and exporters, both on a regional and global level, are outlined below.

One problem states worry about is the abrupt supply cutback or cutoff. To guarantee energy security in this event, the 20 members of the International Energy Agency (IEA) (affiliated with the OECD) agreed in 1976 to an emergency allocation plan to be implemented by the IEA Secretariat in time of crisis.[38] However, shortfalls must be extremely severe before the plan is put into effect; it was not used in the 1979 crisis. Moreover, should the US oppose the plan at the time, it would probably not go into effect.[39] The difficulties of creating even a limited allocation scheme illustrate why it is extremely doubtful that states at the UN could formulate a universal energy-sharing plan in the next decade. Certainly neither the OPEC states nor the IEA states would have much incentive to participate, and agreement among parties would most likely be too difficult to obtain.

Several oil-importing states, such as France, have eschewed the multilateral route to energy security entirely; [40] others, such as Japan, have supplemented it with bilateral long- or medium-term supply arrangements with an oil-exporting state in which the importer usually offers economic or military aid, or political concessions, to entice the supplier into entering and maintaining the relationship. Japan has established such arrangements with Mexico, Saudi Arabia, and Iran; France with Iraq; and Italy with Venezuela.[41] The obvious potential disadvantage of these relationships is to the oil consumer, who must purchase oil from the partner even if cheaper oil (or other energy sources) becomes available elsewhere, a cost that is evidently acceptable if energy security is the paramount goal.

Multilateral emergency allocation schemes or bilateral long-term access arrangements between buyers and sellers do not seem to be a feasible option for oil-importing developing countries. These countries lack the hard currency or the technological expertise that could encourage oil suppliers or rich states to enter into agreements with them.

Another method for ensuring energy security is to attempt to change the structure of the market itself. Consumers can enjoy the benefits of more competition in the short run simply by making the market more transparent (i.e., providing information on price and supply). The IEA currently does this for its members,[42] and this type of project might be feasible for the UN as well. Obviously, not all UN member states would welcome UN efforts in this field. In the long run, however, energy security would be enhanced if the market becomes less concentrated and there were more economical alternatives to oil. To this end the IEA has encouraged joint energy research projects between its members, despite the difficulties of doing so. While sharing the common goal of reducing oil dependencies, states are still reluctant to share information on potential projects or on science and technology matters, and they have shown little interest in participating in joint projects. This has led the IEA to shift gears somewhat and focus instead on national research and development activities. It has had states elucidate common general goals in this area and has evaluated and loosely coordinated national efforts.[43] Other international institutions have also tried to change the structure of the energy market, thus reducing long-term dependence on OPEC. For example, plans for the World Bank's new energy affiliate call for funding energy projects in the developing world.

It appears that those multilateral efforts that have met with the most success in ensuring even limited energy security are not those aimed at changing the political conditions surrounding the 1970s' oil crises, but those directed at ameliorating some of the economic causes. In the long run, market restructuring schemes organized by the IEA and the World Bank offer the best hope for reducing dependence on OPEC oil, and thus for enhancing energy security. In the short run, bilateral buyer-seller relationships may be effective, but they are fragile, costly, and available only to a few industrialized states. Multilateral market allocation schemes in case of crisis have never been functional and there is at least some doubt that they ever will be, as long as disparities in political power and economic need persist. Given the realities of energy supply and demand, the UN would do well to avoid fruitless negotiation between OPEC and the oil importers and instead concentrate its limited resources on enhancing energy security by fostering reduced dependence on OPEC oil.

CONCLUSIONS

This chapter began by suggesting that international organizations have usually disappointed their founders when it came to handling traditional security problems. It then asked if perhaps the United Nations could deal with non-traditional threats to the peace better than it had with classical security problems such as arms control. Several conclusions suggest themselves.

Although the UN is severely constrained by both systemic and political factors in constructing and maintaining security regimes, it has contributed to, among other things, the legitimization of norms protecting sovereignty and condemning aggression, the promotion of arms control measures, and the development of peacekeeping. Considering the events in the Falkland Islands and Lebanon during 1982 and the many other incipient crises throughout the world, the UN and the good offices of the Secretary-General will probably be called upon to aid in the peaceful settlement of traditional types of disputes among nation states in the years ahead. Whatever new issues appear on the UN security agenda in the future, the traditional issues will not disappear and the UN's role in helping manage the latter should continue.

The new cluster of issues, such as the ones analyzed in this chapter, may not be easier for the UN to handle than the old ones. There are two main reasons for this. First, when aspects of human rights issues, nuclear power management, and energy security become potential threats to the peace, they also acquire most of the same problematic characteristics of traditional security issues, characteristics that hinder or preclude international organization management. Thus, human rights problems are most difficult to solve when the abuses are the instruments by which a government maintains its identity or achieves its security goals; energy security cannot be guaranteed to oil-importing states as long as oil is perceived by OPEC states as their most useful political weapon; and keeping nuclear weapons out of the hands of additional countries or developing systems of multilateral management of the fuel cycle is least likely in regions where some states have legitimate security concerns.

Secondly, if one looks at the past record, the UN (and the League of Nations before it) is only very seldom capable of transforming into cooperative relations the confrontational political relations that cause security problems to develop. Sometimes, indeed, the opposite is true and the inflammatory rhetoric of the General Assembly may even fan the fires. This is why (in contrast to the Brandt Commission report's conclusions) energy security should probably not be the subject of more international political negotiations, but rather, that intensified efforts should be taken to reduce dependence on OPEC oil; it is also why lesser human rights abuses should be in effect decriminalized (although not legitimized) and dealt with in a more consistent, quieter way.

New threats to the peace may pose challenges to the international community, but it does not necessarily follow that they can therefore be managed only at the global level, for at least two reasons. First, if there is no consensus on states' underlying goals, or if the consensus is weak, then implementing norms and standards is hindered or precluded—witness the difficulty in applying the Universal Declaration of Human Rights. Second, the extent to which universal organizations can manage problems is often directly dependent on outside multilateral and bilateral activity. Thus, the IAEA's task of reducing proliferation is made more difficult if the US or Europe continue to export nuclear technology without much regard for safeguards.

It is likely that threats to the peace in the 1980s will come from both old and new security issues. The UN will be challenged to deal with all of these problems. It will inevitably disappoint those who forget how limited are the powers of international organizations, and how constrained they are by political realities and the structure of the present international system. Despite these limitations, if the past is any indicator of the future, the UN can be expected on balance to further the peaceful settlement of disputes in limited, but still significant, ways.

Notes

1. See F. H. Hinsley, *Power and the Pursuit of Peace* (Cambridge: Cambridge University Press, 1963), for a history of multilateral schemes proposed by philosophers and statesmen to this end.

2. Inis Claude, *Swords into Plowshares,* 4th ed. (New York: Random House, 1971), pp. 41–80.

3. Covenant of the League of Nations, Article 12.

4. Charter of the United Nations, Chapter 7.

5. Robert Jervis, "Security Regimes," in *International Organization* 36, 2 (Spring 82) p. 357.

6. In fact, Jervis argues that no international security regime exists at present. He points out that the main forces responsible for the absence of major wars during the past forty years, those which have contributed to self-restraint on the part of states, are the bipolarity of the international system and the nuclear stalemate between the US and the USSR. These

systemic factors cannot properly be called a "regime," Jervis argues, and, in any case, the UN has had little to do with creating either of them.

7. Of course, not compromising has its attendant risks, too. Arms racing creates balances of power and deterrence that might facilitate stability and peace, but in some situations may contribute to the outbreak or continuance of war. See Kenneth Waltz, *Theory of International Politics* (Reading, Mass.: Addison-Wesley, 1979), pp. 102–129; and Robert Jervis, "Why Nuclear Superiority Doesn't Matter," in *Political Science Quarterly* 94, 4 (Winter 1979–80).

8. See Robert Jervis, "Cooperation under the Security Dilemma," *World Politics* 30 (January 1978).

9. Inis Claude, op. cit., p. 313.

10. For example, Article 2 of the UN Charter.

11. For example, Article 1 and 33 of the UN Charter. Over 130 disputes were considered by the Security Council and the General Assembly between 1946 and 1977. A. LeRoy Bennet, *International Organization: Principles and Issues,* 2nd ed. (Englewood Cliffs, NJ: Prentice-Hall, 1980), p. 120.

12. For example, the Preamble of the UN Charter.

13. See the Declaration on the Granting of Independence to Colonial Countries and Peoples adopted by the UN General Assembly, Resolution 1514 (XV), December 14, 1960.

14. For a discussion of the types of decisions made by various international organizations, see Robert Cox and Harold Jacobson, *Anatomy of Influence* (New Haven: Yale University Press, 1973).

15. Joseph S. Nye, Jr. coins this term in his article on UNCTAD in Cox and Jacobson, op. cit.

16. For a functionalist's view, see David Mitrany, *A Working Peace System* (Chicago: Quadrangle Books, 1966); for a fascinating treatment of the problem at present, see Ernst B. Haas, "Why Collaborate? Issue-Linkage and International Regimes," *World Politics,* 32, 3 (April 1980).

17. See David A. Kay, "On the Reform of International Institutions: A Comment," *International Organization* 30, 3 (Summer 1976), p. 536.

18. Sidney Weintraub in this volume.

19. Waltz, op. cit., p. 135.

20. Ibid.

21. Stephen Krasner in this volume.

22. The International Covenant on Economic, Social and Cultural Rights was adopted by the General Assembly on December 16, 1966.

23. The International Covenant on Civil and Political Rights was also adopted on December 16, 1966 by the General Assembly.

24. The Convention on the Prevention and Punishment of the Crime of Genocide was adopted in 1948; the Declaration on the Granting of Independence to Colonial Countries and Peoples in 1960; the International Convention on the Elimination of All Forms of Racial Discrimination in 1966; and the Declaration on the Elimination of Discrimination against Women in 1967. See Nigel Rodley's chapter in this volume for detailed information on the covenants and conventions.

25. See Jack Donnelly, "Recent Trends in UN Human Rights Activity: Description and Polemic," *International Organization* 35, 4 (Autumn 1981).

26. Ibid.

27. See Sidney Liskofsky, "The United Nations and Human Rights: 'Alternative Approaches,' " in David Sidorsky, ed., *Essays on Human Rights,* (Philadelphia; Jewish Publication Society of America, 1979).

28. The following discussion owes much to conversations with and ideas and suggestions from Professor Louis Henkin of Columbia University and Professor Nicholas Onuf of American University.

29. See Arthur H. Robertson, *Human Rights in National and International Law,* 2nd ed. (New York: Oceana, 1977).

30. The history of UN involvement in this area is detailed in Joseph S. Nye, "Maintaining a Non-Proliferation Regime," *International Organization* 35, 1 (Winter 1981).

31. Ibid., p. 19.

32. Judith Miller, "U.N. Aide Sees Little to Curb Spread of Atom Arms," *New York Times,* February 19, 1982.

33. Joseph S. Nye, Jr., "Nuclear Talks Must Go On," *New York Times,* January 23, 1982. Nuclear proliferation is one of several topics discussed at informal non-governmental bilateral meetings sponsored by the UNA-USA's Parallel Studies Program with the Soviet UN Association.

34. See Lawrence Scheinman, "Multinational Alternatives and Nuclear Non-Proliferation," *International Organization* 35, 1 (Winter 1981).

35. For the results of the CIEC, see Jahangir Amuzegar, "A Requiem for the North-South Conference," *Foreign Affairs,* 56, 1 (October 1977).

36. For a thorough discussion of recent changes in the structure of the oil market, see Brian Levy, "World Oil Marketing in Transition," *International Organization* 36, 1 (Winter 1982).

37. On the latter point, see Jahangir Amuzegar, "Oil Wealth," *Foreign Affairs,* 60, 4 (Spring 1982).

38. See Robert Keohane, "The International Energy Agency: State Influence and Transgovernmental Politics," *International Organization* 32, 4 (Autumn 1978), p. 934.

39. Ibid., pp. 935–6.

40. France does not belong to the IEA.
41. Brian Levy, ''World Oil Marketing in Transition,'' op. cit., p. 132.
42. See Keohane, op. cit.
43. Ibid.

THE UNITED NATIONS AND COLLECTIVE SECURITY: RETROSPECT AND PROSPECT

JOCK A. FINLAYSON AND MARK W. ZACHER

Twice in the twentieth century the hopes that nations and statesmen have placed in the idea of collective security have been revealed as exaggerated. After World War I Woodrow Wilson and others believed that the creation of the League of Nations would "go down in history as the date of the birth of the new world."[1] Similarly, the establishment of the United Nations signalled an attempt to prevent incidents of international violence by erecting a functioning collective security system. However, a sharper sense of political realism was exhibited by the framers of the UN Charter than had been shown by earlier proponents of collective security. Whatever illusions there may have been in 1945 regarding the role of the United Nations, they did certainly *not* include the view that the Organization could act to reverse military initiatives undertaken or supported by the major powers. Rather, there prevailed an eminently realistic appreciation that most states would not engage in military action against international aggressions explicitly or tacitly sanctioned by the most powerful actors in the UN system. The Organization was expected to enforce the peace as an agent of the Great Powers, or else it would not act at all.

The Cold War ensured that there would not be Great Power— and especially Soviet-American—collaboration against most military aggressors. The interest of both military alliances in expanding their spheres of influence meant that each side assumed very biased perspectives on the legitimacy of the use of force in interstate relations. Instead of reacting to military conflicts in terms of their compliance with universal norms, the main concern was how the victory or defeat of the conflicting parties would affect the relative strength of the major politico-military groupings. Not surprisingly, military outcomes that favored the relative position of their own grouping usually were defined as "just." This system of competitive alliances was inconsistent with the collective security system envisioned by the framers of the Charter, which was based on avoiding the "advance identification of friend and sometimes of foe" and presupposed "impartiality and flexibility on the part of members."[2]

This chapter presents an analysis of how past coalition configurations in international security politics have affected the collective security role of the United Nations in postwar conflicts. It then explores the likely outlines of international security politics and the potential for collective security in the next ten to fifteen years.

PAST PATTERNS OF UN INVOLVEMENT AND SUCCESS

The dominance of Cold War considerations in international security politics has often been overstated. However, with respect to the diplomatic response of most states to wars and crises in the global UN setting, judgments of the likely effects of alternative policies on the relative positions of the dominant politico-security groupings often have been crucial. Members of the Western, Soviet and nonaligned groupings have each been preoccupied—whether because of their own concern or because of "persuasion" by their alliance leaders—with how different diplomatic strategies and UN activities would impinge on the solidarity and growth of their (sometimes very informal) alliance systems. While the East-West axis of conflict has been the most important backdrop to the management of interstate conflicts in the UN, many of those occurring in Asia since the early 1960s have been strongly influenced by the emergence of China as a major actor and the competition among the US, the USSR and China and their "friends." To say that these bipolar and tripolar configurations have had the most important influence on the politics of conflict management in the UN is not to deny that many conflicts originated from grievances quite removed from these general rivalries, or that some states at times adopted policies for reasons quite independent of these rivalries. However, it does mean that the reactions of most countries in the global setting usually have been grounded in judgments of the effects of alternative outcomes on the fortunes of or balance of power among these central politico-security groupings.

Given this concern of the members of the major military groupings, as well as the nonaligned states, to prevent the reduction of their own influence and resources and, if possible, to increase them, their policies toward particular conflicts have been determined largely by the alignment affiliations of the aggressing and victim states. In order to facilitate analysis of post-war conflict situations, these have been categorized into five types: interbloc, intrabloc, nonaligned-nonaligned, aligned-nonaligned where the nonaligned is the aggressor, and aligned-nonaligned where the aligned is the aggressor. In most types of conflicts, the major groupings have *not* perceived it to be in their interests to oppose an aggressing state and/or to view the UN as the best forum in which to bring about cessation of a crisis or a war. In fact, of the little over 100 international crises and wars in the years since 1946, the UN has "intervened" (i.e., called for a ceasefire and withdrawal) in less than 20 percent of the conflicts, and in only about a half of these has the Organization met with "success"—namely, compliance by the parties *soon* after the UN directive.[3]

CATEGORIES OF CONFLICT

1. INTER-BLOC CONFLICTS INVOLVING ALLIES OF THE SUPERPOWERS
In such conflicts, the aggressor as well as the victim have had the backing of a major military grouping and the nonaligned states have usually been predisposed not to take sides. Thus, except for a few conflict situations in the late 1940s and early 1950s (i.e., the Greek Civil War and the Korean War), when the Western group commanded the support of over two-thirds of the membership, UN intervention (i.e., a call for a ceasefire and withdrawal) has not oc-

curred. In the first decade of the UN's life there existed what Stanley Hoffmann has called a "majoritarian illusion" that UN resolutions would sway the behaviour of combatants, but it soon subsided in the face of an "obvious discrepancy between votes and compliance."[4]

2. INTRA-BLOC CONFLICTS WHERE BOTH PARTIES ARE MEMBERS OF ONE GROUPING

During these types of conflicts the allies of the conflicting parties have usually sought to manage the crises or wars within organizations composed of their own members and to exclude the United Nations. Their concern was that UN involvement would provide their enemies with opportunities for influencing one of the conflicting parties to terminate or weaken its existing alliance ties by the offer of diplomatic support. For example, the US has been particularly successful in keeping Western Hemisphere conflicts out of the UN and dealing with them within the Organization of American States (OAS). In similar situations in other parts of the world, Western states have generally worked to bring about the termination of crises or wars by informal diplomatic mediation. Likewise, the Soviet bloc has sought to deal with its crises (the invasions of Hungary in 1956 and Czechoslovakia in 1968) within the Warsaw Pact system. Western countries could use UN debates and, in 1956, resolutions to embarrass the Communist invaders, but they did not expect to reverse the aggressions by these tactics. While the Soviet bloc states lacked the voting strength to prevent UN consideration of their internal problems, they most definitely had sufficient military strength to ignore the sentiments emanating from the banks of the East River.

3. CONFLICTS INVOLVING NONALIGNED STATES

It has often been posited that the UN can play a constructive role in moderating disputes between nonaligned states. However, in the relatively few conflicts that fall into this category (e.g., the wars between Algeria and Morocco in 1963, Somalia and Ethiopia in 1964, and Tanzania and Uganda in 1979), most nonaligned countries have not been anxious for the Great Powers to become involved in conflict management through the UN. Their primary concern has been that Great Power backing of certain parties could draw nonaligned states into the competitive alliance systems. Concurrently, the Great Powers themselves have usually opted not to take partisan positions for fear that this might encourage one of the parties to align with the rival Cold War bloc, and have preferred to see such conflicts managed on the regional level. In the recent Iran-Iraq war the UN has called for a ceasefire (but not a withdrawal) and has launched a mediatory mission. However, the bloc leaders have neither adopted partisan position nor pressured the parties to stop their fighting and accept a settlement.

4. CONFLICTS INVOLVING NONALIGNED AND ALIGNED STATES IN WHICH THE NONALIGNED STATE IS THE AGGRESSOR

In such cases (e.g., Afghanistan–Pakistan in 1960–61, Iraq–Kuwait in 1961, Indonesia–Malaysia in 1964–65, Somalia–Ethiopia in 1977, and Algeria's sponsorship of the Polisario's intervention in Morocco and Mauritania beginning in 1976), UN involvement has seldom gone beyond the debate stage. The allies of the attacked or threatened country have generally been reluctant to condemn the aggressive nonaligned state because they fear driving it into collaboration with the rival coalition. Hence they have sought, not always successfully, to avoid UN debates in favor of extra-organizational mediatory strategies. The members of the other bloc, on the other hand, have tended to back the nonaligned state (US policy in the most recent Somalian-Ethiopian war being an exception) and have vetoed any resolutions aimed against the nonaligned aggressor. The nonaligned countries have generally tended to avoid taking positions in such conflicts. In such circumstances, the necessary constellation of support for UN action against an aggressor has not existed.

5. CONFLICTS INVOLVING NONALIGNED AND ALIGNED STATES IN WHICH THE ALIGNED STATE IS THE AGGRESSOR

This is the one group of conflicts in which all major coalitions have often opposed the aggressing party and backed UN action against it. Examples are the Suez crisis of 1956, the Congo crisis of 1960, the Cyprus crisis of 1963–64, and the Israeli intervention in Lebanon in 1978. It is perhaps obvious why nonaligned nations have opposed threats or acts of aggression against one of their own number, and why the members of the bloc to which the aggressing party did *not* belong have supported UN resolutions calling on the aggressor to cease its action. The motivations of the allies of the state initiating the crisis or war are less palpable. Essentially, allies of an aggressor have feared that its action could drive the attacked nonaligned state (and perhaps other nations in the same grouping) into greater collaboration with the rival coalition, and also that military assistance from the rival coalition to the victim state could lead to an inter-bloc war. While allies have also been concerned that their policy could alienate their own coalition member, more often they have judged that the continuation of its aggression would have deleterious effects on the global balance of power.

UN INVOLVEMENT IN SPECIFIC INTERNATIONAL CRISES

Brief descriptions are provided in the following paragraphs of the most important crises and wars in which UN diplomacy and actions were central to the termination of hostilities. Then the conflicts in which the UN intervened by passing a resolution calling for an end to hostilities but in which there was *not* short-term compliance are surveyed. Space limitations prevent consideration of conflicts that were either not debated at the UN or those that were debated but did not result in passage of resolutions calling for an end to a threat or act of aggression. The vast majority of conflicts in the postwar era have elicited either no UN debate, or UN debate but no resolution, and this in itself illustrates the limited effect of the UN in postwar security disputes.

The specific conflicts that fell clearly or partially into the category of aligned-nonaligned conflicts where the former was the aggressor (category 5) are the Suez war of 1956, the Congo crisis of 1960, the French-Tunisian war of 1961 (the Bizerte crisis), the Cyprus crisis of 1963–64, the Middle East wars of 1967 and 1973, the Portuguese intervention in Guinea in 1970, and the Israeli intervention in southern Lebanon in 1978. It is these crises and wars that have proven most susceptible to constructive UN involvement and where UN peacekeeping forces have been most active in supervising withdrawals of forces and preventing renewed fighting.

The Suez crisis was perhaps the classic case where the US, with the backing of many Western states, opposed the military initiatives of three important allies because it regarded these actions as certain to alienate the nonaligned countries, threaten a larger war, and undermine Western interests throughout the region. Canada's proposal to introduce a UN Emergency Force (UNEF) into the area sought to save face for its errant allies while getting them to reverse a policy damaging to global Western interests.

The majority of Western countries assumed a comparable stance regarding the Belgian intervention in the Congo in 1960. The UN peacekeeping force was viewed as useful not only in facilitating the withdrawal of a NATO member's forces from a nonaligned country, but also in stabilizing a domestic situation where continued instability could have led to external interventions on behalf of pro-Western and nonaligned factions. Most Western states were concerned that the imposition of a political solution in the Congo by certain of their allies might alienate the nonaligned and provoke certain Congolese parties to seek Soviet assistance, with the attendant possibility of a direct East-West clash.

In the cases of the French-Tunisian and Cypriot conflicts, the besieged and threatened parties (Tunisia and the Cypriot government of President Makarios respectively) wavered between affiliations with the nonaligned grouping and with the West, but their attempts to mobilize international support for their plights signalled at least a temporary nonaligned stance. In the case of the French invasion of Tunisia to secure the source of water for the Bizerte naval base, its own Western allies backed UN resolutions calling for withdrawal. And while de Gaulle did not immediately give in to such external pressure, he did so within several months. In the case of the Turkish threat to intervene in the civil war in Cyprus, the NATO states sought to restrict diplomatic crisis management to the alliance, but the Cypriot government of Makarios was successful (at least in part) in portraying Western (NATO and Turkish) designs as neocolonial in character. Rather than alienate the nonaligned forces rallying to the Makarios appeals, the Western states backed UN resolutions opposing the use of violence and setting up a UN peacekeeping force to prevent recurrence of the fighting, which had seriously destabilized NATO's southeastern flank.

The Middle East wars of 1967 and 1973 do not clearly fall into the category of aggressions by aligned against nonaligned parties, but the extent to which they do helps to explain a great deal about the nature and scope of UN involvement. In 1967, when Israel (with significant provocation) attacked Egypt, Syria, and Jordan, the first two Arab states were pursuing decidedly pro-Soviet and anti-Western foreign policies, while Jordan could have been considered as either pro-Western or, possibly, nonaligned. The main reason that the Western countries, and the US in particular, put pressure on Israel to curtail its advance and then backed a ceasefire resolution in the Security Council was a fear that a prolonged war might tempt the nonaligned forces in the Arab world to collaborate more closely with the Soviets or might result in escalation of the conflict. The Western states did not demand an immediate Israeli withdrawal, as they had done in 1956, since it was felt that the Arabs had provoked the attack and that Egypt and Syria were not truly "nonaligned" countries, but the management of this conflict makes it clear that it was in some respects perceived as an aligned-nonaligned dispute.

The initiators of the 1973 Yom Kippur War were Egypt and Syria. The former state (then under President Sadat) can be classified as nonaligned, while Syria had somewhat moderated its earlier pro-Soviet foreign policy. During the first week of the war, when Egypt and Syria were making military gains, the USSR vetoed a Western-backed resolution calling for a ceasefire. However, once the tide of battle changed and the Egyptians were on the retreat in the Sinai, the USSR came around to supporting a ceasefire and the Western countries increased their support for an end to the fighting. The conflict had suddenly taken on the appearance of an aligned state making gains at the expense of two nonaligned. The Western countries brought great pressure to bear on Israel to cease its advance lest the Egyptians, and the Arabs more generally, become further alienated from the West and turn to the Soviets for assistance.

In the cases of the Portuguese-backed incursion into Guinea in 1970 and the Israeli invasion of southern Lebanon in 1978, the Western states again opposed the actions of the allies. In the former case the UN sent out an investigatory body to corroborate the Portuguese involvement, and in the latter all major blocs supported the creation of a UN peacekeeping force (UNIFIL) to supervise the withdrawal of Israeli troops and prevent a recurrence of the fighting.

There have been a number of other conflicts in which the UN called for a termination of a threat or act of violence that cannot be classified into the category of aligned-nonaligned conflicts with the latter as the victim. However, in these cases there was seldom compliance with UN directives. The reasons for this provide some insight into the role of the UN in international conflict management.

UN resolutions against aggressors in the Greek Civil War, the Korean War, and the Soviet-Hungarian war of 1956 were all products of Western numerical predominance in the early years of the Organization. Given Soviet-bloc backing for the aggressions, the lack of compliance with organizational directives is understandable. However, in two early conflicts in which the UN "intervened"— the Indo-Pakistani war of 1947–48 and the Arab-Israeli war of 1948—the reasons for the UN's failure to elicit short-term compliance are less obvious. In the case of the war in the Indian subcontinent, the Soviet Union's adherence to the "two-camp doctrine" in the late 1940s meant that the USSR did not befriend either party— despite the fact that the Soviets could have achieved diplomatic gains (as they later did) by supporting India against the British-backed Pakistanis. With little concern that the Soviets would use their influence in the region, the Western states felt no strong motivation for pressuring the parties to cease their fighting. Instead, mediation efforts were undertaken, and efforts were made to promote a military stabilization after the two countries had fought to a standstill. In the 1948 Arab-Israeli War, both the Americans and the Soviets supported the Israelis who were initially attacked by the Arabs. Because the Israelis achieved victories in each round of fighting, the superpowers felt no incentive to exert strong pressure on the parties to end the war. (Soviet sympathy for Israel and Israel's tilt toward nonalignment in the nascent East-West conflict did not last very long and can best be viewed as a short-lived transitional period in Middle East politics.)

There were several conflicts in the Middle East and Africa in the

1960s and 1970s in which UN intervention was not able to secure an end to the violence. In 1963 the UN created an observer group (UNYOM) to verify the withdrawal of a large Egyptian force and a small Saudi contingent from Yemen. At that time, the US government was concerned that nonaligned Egypt's support of the republican Yemeni government against the insurgent royalist forces and their pro-Western Saudi allies would drive the republicans into greater reliance on the Soviets. When the Egyptians refused to withdraw, the UN force was dissolved (1964) and the issue was never discussed again at the UN. The Western states did not want to criticize Egypt's policy and alienate both Egypt and the republican Yemeni government by castigating their actions in a public forum. In yet another situation, the Turks invaded Cyprus (1974) after pro-"enosis" (pro-union) Greek Cypriots overthrew the Makarios government. The accession to power of a group which intended to establish dominance over the Turkish Cypriot community and to unite Cyprus with Greece led to a rapid decline in sympathy for the Greek Cypriot government among the nonaligned and Western nations. Hence, there was no strong effective pressure on the Turks to remove their troops, even though several UN resolutions calling for them to do so were passed.

There were three unique conflicts in Africa during the years 1975–77 that elicited UN resolutions but little compliance. In early November 1975 the Security Council opposed the invasion ("the Green March") of Moroccans into the Spanish Sahara. The Moroccan civilians soon withdrew, but regular Moroccan forces then entered the disputed territory along a different section of the border. During the crisis, diplomatic negotiations were undertaken within the Western grouping, and in mid-November it was formally announced that Spain would divide the area between Morocco and Mauritania. These decisions were made by the Western nations, Spain, Morocco, and Mauritania, with the UN playing a peripheral role. So, too, there was little early UN discussion of the Angolan civil war between pro-Soviet and pro-Western factions and their external backers (Cuba and then South Africa sent troops; Zaire provided base camps). It was only when a large group of African countries brought up the issue of South African involvement that the Security Council requested the withdrawal of South African forces. (These troops were removed after assurances were received from Luanda regarding the future supply of electricity from a hydroelectric project near the border.) The key point here is that within the UN, states could only agree to deal with what might be called the "racial" dimension of the problem; not surprisingly, they could not agree on the larger political (East-West) issues. The last African conflict that evoked a UN "cease-and-desist" order was the case of Rhodesian attacks against guerilla camps inside Mozambique in 1976. UN consensus was based on broad international opposition to the white-minority Rhodesian regime. However, UN condemnation did not result in a termination of the intervention, since Rhodesia continued to receive support from South Africa and strong pressure was not applied by other states.

A final group of three conflicts in which the UN passed resolutions calling for a termination of fighting occurred in Asia. In at least the first (the Indo-Pakistani war of 1965), the UN did achieve a certain measure of success. Both the US and the USSR were concerned that the fighting, initiated by Pakistan, would deepen Pakistan's reliance on China and might even lead to actual Chinese military involvement in the conflict. As a result of the degree of Pakistani reliance on the Western nations and the inability of China to counter that influence in the UN (China was not even in the UN at the time), the combination of Western and Soviet pressure and Indian military superiority was able to bring an end to the conflict. Of particular interest in this conflict is the concern of two Great Powers that a nonaligned state (Pakistan) might be driven into closer collaboration with the third Great Power (China). This led the US and the USSR to press the conflicting parties to terminate hostilities. In the Indo-Pakistani war of 1971 over the political future of East Bengal (now Bangladesh), the Soviets and Chinese supported the Indians and Pakistanis respectively, thus making Security Council action impossible, while the Americans "tilted" toward Pakistan. The General Assembly did pass a ceasefire resolution, but since its intervention was supported by a major power, India did not comply with the UN directive.

The last Asian conflict to evoke a UN response was the Indonesian absorption of East Timor in 1975. Neither the Indonesians nor the East Timorese advocates of independence had very clear international alignments, although the East Timorese had a more "left-ist" orientation. Probably Western sympathies for the Indonesians had to be muted because of the pique the Portuguese felt toward the pro-union East Timorese and the Indonesians, who were largely responsible for the hasty and unplanned termination of Portuguese rule. The Soviets (but probably not the Chinese) may have had a slight preference for East Timorese independence, but they were probably more concerned about alienating Indonesia, an important Southeast Asian country. The mixed sentiments of the major power groupings meant that no significant pressure was exerted on Indonesia to withdraw from East Timor.

The analysis above suggests that unless all major politico-security groupings perceive the consequences of a successful aggression undermining their global power position, UN actions will not succeed in bringing about the termination of threatened or actual aggressions. Verbal opposition may be expressed for domestic political reasons or in order not to offend certain countries, but unless this is accompanied by a clear sense that a successful aggression will have harmful effects on the power balance, insufficient pressure will be applied against an aggressor to cause it to cease its action. With few exceptions, a united and strong global opposition to aggression has only been possible when a member of one alliance system has threatened or attacked a nonaligned state, and then largely because the allies of the aggressor state have been worried about the possible effect of the conflict's continuation on the political orientation of the victim state and other nonaligned nations. Most of the conflicts the UN has dealt with successfully have involved threats or acts of military intervention by pro-Western states (especially NATO countries and Israel). They have not constituted a large percentage of postwar conflicts, and hence the successes of the UN in international conflict management have been quite modest in number. Indeed, as noted earlier, the United Nations has successfully intervened and brought to an end only about ten percent of the wars and crises that have erupted in the international system since the creation of the Organization. Without deprecating the role the UN has performed in resolving or stabilizing certain conflicts, it is a fact that the incidence of international conflict remains depressingly high despite the existence for almost four decades of an institution that was intended to be a second, more successful version of a global collective security organization.

THE FUTURE OF COLLECTIVE SECURITY

The nature of the UN's conflict management role in the decade ahead depends on the main characteristics of the international security environment, since it is this political milieu that largely shapes and circumscribes the potential for a United Nations role in international disputes. The tight bipolar model utilized by scholars to portray and describe the early postwar system is no longer suited to the more complex politics of the present era. There are still important elements of bipolarity in the security relations of the industrialized nations, but these are countered by marked polycentric tendencies in the Soviet and American alliance systems as a result of members' divergent goals and priorities. In addition, China has emerged as an independent "pole" in the international security system, in the Third World the politico-security ties of many countries with members of the two blocs have become more attenuated, and regional and North-South issues are increasing in salience.

In thinking about the future, it seems reasonable to hypothesize that these trends will continue. Thus, the environment in which the United Nations will seek to manage future conflicts will be characterized, on the one hand, by the existence of more major actors or coalitions and, on the other, by less cohesion and permanence in these blocs. The Western alliance system, although unlikely to become completely fractured in the next decade, will be significantly more polycentric, with Western Europe and perhaps Japan promoting their own interests in the Third World—particularly the Middle East—and exhibiting less of a willingness to subscribe to an American-centered view of security issues. Concern over the resources these countries should devote to defense could exacerbate the relationship still further. One result may be an American withdrawal into the Western Hemisphere, with certain remnants of a nuclear umbrella for the other North Atlantic countries remaining.[5] It is also conceivable that Eastern Europe may come to enjoy greater freedom from Moscow in the formulation of foreign policy, although such a loosening in alliance ties seems much less likely to occur in the East than the West. China, which since 1975 has been exhorting the noncommunist nations of Southeast Asia to "engage in security collaboration with one another and the United States," may in the years ahead begin to cooperate informally with a number of Asian countries (including Japan, with whom a Friendship Treaty was signed in August 1978).[6] Certain powerful Third World actors—such as India, Egypt, Nigeria, and Brazil—may well exert greater influence in their respective regions in the next decade. It is also quite possible that security relations with the major power blocs will decrease in importance for many developing nations.

Given these trends, to what extent will the future environment prove hospitable for UN management of international disputes? In what types of conflicts will the major politico-security coalitions agree to allow UN organizational involvement? Will a more multipolar and polycentric environment, in which more states have some influence over the levers of power and coalitions are more transient, lead to an increase in the number and types of conflicts that the global body can manage successfully?

Expectations that a more multipolar system will be more stable and free of major conflict—and thus conducive to broad agreement to resist military aggressions and hence to the practice of collective security—are in general unconvincing. As Richard Rosecrance has commented, "In a multipolar system, it may be difficult to persuade nations to engage in regulative action because in such an order it is not clear whose interests are primarily affected by a disruptive act."[7] In a system with more than two major coalitions, some significant differences among their members and a large number of nonaligned countries, nations may be less concerned about shifts in global alignments or modest changes in the relative power of various groups. In addition, they may be subject to cross-pressures in assessing their security and economic interests during periods of conflict. It is also possible that in a world of more and less cohesive politico-security coalitions the nonaligned countries will tend to adopt more diverse positions toward international conflicts. Their ties with and policies toward different coalitions could vary considerably, and hence they could adopt quite varied positions toward conflicts depending on the identity of the parties. They could, in fact, have little sense of common identity with nonaligned countries in other geographical regions, and this could mean that fewer states would come to their defense when attacked.

Given the above trends, what will be the future role of the United Nations in specific types of international crises and wars? In inter-coalition conflicts the UN will probably be no more effective than in the past, since the aggressing state will usually have a Great Power backer. (The recent diplomacy surrounding four disputes— the Angolan civil war, the Angolan intervention into Zaire, and the Vietnam-Cambodian and Vietnam-China wars—supports this point.) If the allies of an aggressor constitute a very small coalition, it may not be possible to prevent passage of a General Assembly resolution directed against the aggressor, but developments on the battle-field—and not diplomatic pressures—are likely to determine the outcome of the conflict. (If the 1971 Indo-Pakistani war is seen as a conflict between Soviet and Chinese allies [with the Western co-alition "tilting" toward the side favored by the Chinese], one can see that the support of a major power bloc for the aggressor stymied UN effectiveness—despite an overwhelming vote in favor of a ces-sation of hostilities by the General Assembly.) While the dynamics of interbloc conflicts in a multipolar setting will probably mirror those in a bipolar setting, this may not always be so. In a multi-polar world where alliance ties are more tenuous, it is easier to conceive of a small state allied with a Great Power initiating mili-tary violence against a member of another grouping without the approval and backing of its larger "protector." It is even possible, although not likely, that the protector would then oppose such an aggression and try to terminate its action through the UN.

In intra-coalition crises and wars, the allies of the conflicting parties will still be predisposed to try to resolve their conflicts within the confines of their own grouping. Western Hemisphere states will turn to the OAS as they have in the past, and it is possible that a new Euro-African organization with a comparable security role will evolve. However, the desire of coalition members to isolate conflict management within their alliance system is not likely to be as strong as it is in a rigid bipolar security system, since the prospect of a member shifting its foreign policy orientation may not be viewed as such a serious matter. Conflicting parties which belong to a ma-jor security grouping may also be more willing to resist allies' preferences and seek to involve other groupings through the UN. This would be particularly likely to occur if a victim state felt it was not being defended as vigorously as it should be (recall the Cyprus conflict), or if the aggressor was promoting a change in government along lines approved by other states. In general, intra-coalition conflicts will probably not be as resistant to UN involvement as they have been in the past, but effective consensuses to resist an aggressor may still be difficult to obtain.

With respect to conflicts between nonaligned states, there is probably no greater chance of great power opposition to an aggression, and UN involvement in crisis management, in a world of more, but less cohesive, security coalitions than there is in a rigid bipolar system. The likelihood that all or some of the members of a bloc will see some gains to be derived from supporting one party is greater if states are not very concerned about a growth in power of the other major bloc coalition in the event that the other conflicting party goes to it for assistance. However, in such a situation it is difficult to envisage a broad consensus against the aggressor in the UN. Hence, regardless of whether virtually all major countries and groupings are noncommittal or some adopt partial positions, the probability of a strong UN response to stop a war is very unlikely.

When nonaligned states threaten or initiate military action against a country aligned with a major security grouping, the pattern of UN involvement will very likely not vary from the past. One or more rival groupings will probably back the nonaligned state, and the allies of the victim will be predisposed to avoid public censure of the aggressor. The only development likely to alter this situation is the evolution of a consensus on a particular issue which the nonaligned aggressor violates. However, the chances of this occurring are not great. A recent conflict in this category has been the Algerian backing for Polisario rebel incursions into those parts of Morocco and Mauritania which once constituted the Spanish Sahara. The Western states (particularly France) have extensively assisted both Morocco and Mauritania, but there has been no effort to censure the Algerians, who have been backed by the Soviets.

The one type of conflict that still seems most susceptible to constructive UN involvement is a military initiative by an aligned state against a nonaligned. The only conflict that in recent years evoked a UN resolution calling for a ceasefire and withdrawal and the creation of a UN peacekeeping force falls into this category, namely, the 1978 Israeli intervention into southern Lebanon. In this case the Western powers were concerned that the Israeli action could alienate nonaligned countries as well as some pro-Western Arab states and that heightened tension might lead to a major war. However, given a more multipolar system the allies of an aggressive state could be less predisposed to oppose their ally since concern about alienating a particular nonaligned state or the entire nonaligned grouping might be reduced. With multiple centers of power, shifts in the foreign policy orientation of nonaligned states could be viewed less and less in "zero-sum" terms. Indeed, there might even develop greater recognition of the legitimacy of spheres of influence; in a multipolar world, military action might be seen as an acceptable act of preserving a particular sphere of influence (although this would probably not be admitted publicly).

There are two particular areas of global security politics in which some broad consensuses might develop which could then promote an expanded conflict management role for the UN. One is nuclear proliferation, an area where the two superpowers (and other developed nations to a lesser extent) do at times perceive themselves to have common interests, whatever the intensity of their rivalry. The US and the USSR have together supported several treaties and proposals, some negotiated under UN auspices, aimed at controlling both their own arms competition and the spread of nuclear technology to other, chiefly Third World, countries. The 1963 Partial Test Ban Treaty, the 1966 agreement to outlaw nuclear weapons in space, similar agreements relating to Antarctica (1959) and the seabed (1971), the 1968 Nuclear Non-Proliferation Treaty, the creation of a Nuclear Suppliers Group in 1975, and of course the various stages of the bilateral negotiations on strategic arms limitation all testify to a common interest in controlling nuclear weapons.

It is not at all implausible that in the future the nuclear powers (including even China) will increasingly find themselves at loggerheads with some non-nuclear countries over this issue. At some point, it might appear prudent to the nuclear countries to use the

United Nations—most probably via the Security Council—to assist in the control of conflicts whose continuation could create incentives for the acquisition or localized use of nuclear capabilities. Such a development depends of course on the attainment of a degree of consensus among the nuclear powers, including China and France, not exhibited so far. In the Third World there are also states—especially neighbors of potential nuclear states who do not themselves have the resources to go nuclear—that share an interest in discouraging nuclear proliferation. In addition, possession of nuclear weapons may increase Third World interest in preventing the development of situations where they would be tempted to use their newly acquired weapons. Even a limited consensus on this issue could provide the basis for effective collaboration through the UN.

Another important political and security issue on which a consensus among the main groups of countries may develop concerns South Africa's domestic apartheid policy and its occupation of Namibia. To many UN members, Pretoria's domestic and regional external policies are examples of what might be called "standing aggression" because of their colonial and racial overtones. Consequently, a large number of Third World and Soviet-bloc countries have sought for a number of years to impose various sanctions against South Africa through the UN. At the 32nd UN General Assembly, numerous resolutions were passed condemning the apartheid regime, one of which stated that any collaboration with the regime constituted "a hostile act against the purposes and principles of the United Nations."[8] The General Assembly has repeatedly called for sanctions against South Africa in connection with the latter's illegal occupation of Namibia.

Although Western members of the Security Council have vetoed the imposition of mandatory sanctions against South Africa, it is possible that the combination of internal conflict in South Africa and increased Third World pressure on Western nations might prompt the latter to reassess their policies. The Western nations seeking a peaceful transition to an independent Namibia had planned for a UN role during the transition period, as evidenced by the creation of a United Nations Transition Assistance Group. While the key Western states are not likely to alter their diplomatic positions in the next few years, this issue is one of the few security problems that might generate a significant convergence of views among all the major UN groupings.

As a response to the changing international security environment, it is sometimes argued that regional bodies are likely to be better able to resolve and control disputes among their members than the more fractious global organizations. This is based on the assumption that "by 'making peace divisible' (a sin in the Wilsonian world of global collective security), regional organizations isolate conflicts and prevent solvable local issues from becoming tangled with irrelevant problems and thus changing into insolvable global issues. In addition, geographical neighbors are more likely both to understand the factual background of a conflict."[9]

The Organization of American States (OAS) has exhibited considerable efficacy in most conflicts which have not concerned the communist issue. The interest of the US and most Latin American states in excluding the communist states from the management of Western Hemisphere conflicts, broad backing for the nonintervention norm in the region, and the resources of the US behind OAS actions have provided the foundations for organizational effectiveness in the past. There is no reason to believe that circumstances have changed so significantly as to inhibit constructive OAS action in most future inter-American conflicts. Both the Organization of African Unity (OAU) and the Arab League have been effective in the past only in conflicts confined to boundary conflicts. Divisions over relations with outside powers and over ideology have so fractured these two regional groupings that consensuses on other conflicts have been (and will continue to be) virtually impossible to achieve.

Regional organizations, much like the UN itself, have their particular roles in international conflict management, but there are few indications that these roles will expand significantly. With the possible exception of the Western Hemisphere, most conflicts are likely to be between members of hostile ideological and foreign policy groupings. Thus their "resolution" is likely to result either from military developments on the battlefield or diplomatic interactions outside formal organizational contexts.

In addition to the general conflict management role of the United Nations, there are two instrumentalities of UN involvement in conflict situations that deserve some comment. These are the use of peacekeeping forces and of mediatory action by the Secretary-General.

Peacekeeping forces have been utilized in virtually all conflicts in which the UN has intervened to bring about the termination of a war or crisis. Their functions have been to facilitate the separation and withdrawal of adversaries and to deter and prevent a recrudescence of fighting. Significant success has been achieved in performing these tasks although political agreement among the major world powers *and* the conflicting parties has always been a prerequisite for their creation and effective operation. Some differences regarding procedures for the creation and termination of peacekeeping missions, financial arrangements, and operational activities in the field do still exist, but many, if not most, have been resolved. The limited-time mandate (generally six months) by the Security Council has been broadly accepted as a solution to the creation and termination issues. Appropriations through the General Assembly have provided a sounder financial base, and the voluntary nature of some contributions—while undesirable from a certain perspective—has discouraged outright political opposition to undertaking certain peacekeeping tasks. As a result, peacekeeping operations are likely to be a continuing feature of UN efforts to terminate or discourage the renewal of conflicts, and there is little reason to think that the character of future UN peacekeeping operations will be greatly different from the recent past.

Since he often has direct access to the parties involved in conflicts, the Secretary-General can be a valuable mediator in some disputes. However, it is important to realize that any Secretary-General threatens his political life if he takes a public stand without the clear backing of virtually the entire UN membership. Governments—especially those of the major powers—do not take kindly to being publicly pressured and perhaps embarrassed by international officials. The Secretary-General, if he is skillful and tactful, can act as a conduit between hostile parties and can put forward valuable compromise proposals. But it would be foolish to place too much importance on his role in international security conflicts where states' vital interests are involved and where they are concerned about maintaining control over the diplomatic process.

CONCLUSIONS

Nations concerned with promoting the UN's contribution to international security should not seek to push the Organization into crises and wars where a consensus for effective action does not exist, or is highly unlikely to occur. Repeated failure to deter or stop hostilities only breeds cynicism regarding the utility of the Organization, even if such failures are not attributable to the UN per se. It is better that the United Nations should generally be effective—and be seen as effective—when it does formally consider international conflicts. The Organization always will be used to a certain extent as a public relations or propaganda forum (the Western countries were very adept in this area during the early years of the UN), but one can only hope that states will try to minimize their use of the Organization in this way so as to preserve its unique political role in conflict management.

Another important point to stress is that public commentators on the UN—whether they be officials, politicians, journalists, or academics—should avoid attaching blame to "the United Nations" when certain decisions are (or are not) made by its deliberative organs. Such an anthropomorphizing of a multilateral body not only fails descriptively to place responsibility where it belongs (on the policies of the member states), but it also tends to generate hostility to and alienation from an organizational structure that might provide a very valuable framework for collaboration in certain circumstances. The UN and most other international organizations are best conceived as standing diplomatic structures that can be used for collaborative action by member states. Their political products rest fundamentally in the hands of the members, and their successes and failures should be analyzed from this perspective.

Despite the limited realization of the norm of collective security since the creation of the United Nations, the concept will continue to engage the hopes and minds of scholars, statesmen, and nations. There will no doubt be occasions in the future when the United

Nations can play a vital and welcome conflict management role. Opportunities for peacekeeping, mediation, and other forms of pacific settlement will present themselves, and it is to be hoped that the Organization will seize such opportunities. It will not be the traditional form of collective security as defined by Woodrow Wilson, but whatever contribution the Organization can make toward conflict management, regardless of how undramatic it might be and the form it may take, it can only be welcomed.

Notes

1. M. Leon Bourgeois, first Chairman of the League Council, in Joel Larus, ed., *From Collective Security to Preventive Diplomacy* (New York: John Wiley and Sons, 1965), p. 13.

2. Wolfram F. Hanrieder, "International Organizations and International Systems," in Hanrieder and Richard Falk, eds., *International Law and Organization* (New York: Lippincott, 1968), p. 279.

3. Mark W. Zacher, *International Conflicts and Collective Security, 1946–1977: The United Nations, Organization of American States, Organization of African Unity, and Arab League* (New York: Praeger, 1979), Chapter 2. A theory of collective security and definitions of terms such as war, crisis, and alignment are contained in Chapter 1. Chapter 2 focuses on patterns of involvement and success of the UN. Chapter 6 compares the patterns of involvement and success of the UN and the three regional organizations. An appendix provides brief descriptions of all the conflicts analyzed in the study.

4. Stanley Hoffmann, "International Organization and the International System," *International Organization* 24, 3 (Summer 1970), p. 292.

5. Some observers see clear evidence that such a "regionalization" of interests and priorities has been under way for some time, at least in the economic field (Benjamin Rowland and David Calleo, *America and the World Political Economy* [Bloomfield: Indiana University Press, 1973]).

6. Sheldon Simon, "China, Vietnam and ASEAN: The Politics of Polarization," *Asian Survey* 19 (December 1979), pp. 1181–84.

7. Richard Rosecrance, *International Relations: Peace or War?* (New York: McGraw-Hill, 1973), p. 116.

8. General Assembly Res. 32/105k.

9. Joseph S. Nye, *Peace in Parts* (Boston: Little, Brown, 1971), p. 17.

2. *THE UN SYSTEM AND THE NORTH-SOUTH DIALOGUE*

US PARTICIPATION IN INTERNATIONAL ORGANIZATIONS: LOOKING AHEAD

SIDNEY WEINTRAUB

We never have known how to use the United Nations. The uncertainty stems not just from changing fashions—although that has something to do with it—but from real uncertainty.

For the most part, our ambassadors to the United Nations have been distinguished persons, but we do not know whether we want them to be spokesmen or initiators, the good cop or the bad cop, to behave like Moynihan, who was chosen because he would go into opposition or like Young, who would present a sympathetic side to the Third World, or somewhere in between.[1] We substantively sat out most of the Sixth Special Session of the General Assembly in 1974 but then exploded in anger at the very end against the procedure when the new international economic order resolutions were adopted by consensus; then, having learned some lesson from this experience, we took the initiative with a comprehensive statement on foreign economic policy at the very outset of the Seventh Special Session in 1975. We variously send senior delegates to UN economic meetings, or relatively junior persons, as at the UN Conference on Trade and Development (UNCTAD) in Manila in 1979.[2] We don't know whether we want to conciliate differences in the UNGA to get acceptable resolutions, since this would imply negotiation there and compliance, or just vote ''no'' and do our negotiating elsewhere.

184

Our message to the world has penetrated. For us, the United Nations is a place for debate and rarely for negotiation. We can accept with equanimity and even enthusiasm technical decisions in specialized UN agencies, but not important decisions affecting disarmament, the world's trading or monetary systems, the distribution of international investment, or significant transfers of resources to developing countries.

Our treatment of the United Nations and its various agencies may be exactly right, in that they should be used sparingly, but it may be totally wrong, since uncertainty tends to be equated with weakness.

Looking ahead, we should seek to define probable future US objectives as some guide for the use of international institutions—those of the UN system and others—in ways best suited to achievement of these objectives. The focus here is on the political-economic nexus of economic and social issues because these occupy a large and growing proportion of US and international efforts in international institutions. However, it must be kept in mind that US substantive and institutional choices will not necessarily be determining, since other countries have their own objectives and will have different institutional emphases.

US OBJECTIVES IN THE UN

With the explosion in membership, the United Nations, particularly the General Assembly, ceased to be a US-dominated organization. For economic and social issues that could affect the US economy, the United Nations never really was our chosen instrument, but US antipathy against it (epitomized best during Moynihan's tenure) never became active until we lost control of the organization. Even for peacekeeping issues, our use of the Security Council has diminished from what it was at the outset. It requires a rare event, like the Iranian seizure of the US Embassy and hostages in Teheran, to make us think of the Security Council as a useful instrument. The US preference has been and is still for the functional approach and the evolution of the UN only reinforced this.

It was always evident that some issues would cross functional lines and that it would be desirable to have some machinery available for the international community to look at the whole rather than just the parts. The Second Committee of the General Assembly and the Economic and Social Council could, in theory, accomplish this, but even these bodies were viewed by us as sideshows, not to be used for resolution of economic policy issues of consequence. Organizations could report in a pro forma way to ECOSOC, but decisions would be taken elsewhere. For decisionmaking, the US and the other industrial countries in a position to do so set up the International Monetary Fund (IMF) to deal with balance-of-payments issues and to regulate the exchange-rate system, the International Bank for Reconstruction and Development (IBRD) for mobilizing funds from world capital markets for providing reconstruction and development assistance, and the General Agreement on Tariffs and Trade (GATT) (when the International Trade Organization [ITO] failed to come into existence) for trade negotiations and as the forum for setting trade rules and settling trade disputes. Each of these functional bodies had its area of competence, and while their charters had provision for mutual consultation (such as obtaining an IMF seal of approval when a country sought permission from the GATT to impose trade restrictions on balance-of-payments grounds), the interconnections were not profound.

When new bodies were created in the crucial economic areas of trade, money, and development finance, the US preference was again for non-UN bodies or organizations affiliated only loosely with the United Nations. The International Development Association (IDA) was created as an affiliate of the World Bank precisely to keep it out of the United Nations proper. Regional development banks were established in Latin America and Asia separate from the UN regional economic commissions in those areas. To deal with issues that crossed functional lines, the United States took the lead in 1974 to establish the joint IBRD-IMF Development Committee outside the United Nations in order to have finance ministers debating economic issues, since they were considered more responsible (that is, less likely to politicize the debate) than officials from foreign ministries. The Conference on International Economic Cooperation (CIEC), the so-called North-South dialogue, which also was multifunctional, was established in 1975 outside the United Nations, consciously and deliberately, at US urging. The motivation in each case was the same: "responsible," functional officials would attend the meetings, rather than officials who would debate the philosophy of the new economic order or who was exploiting whom. Another motivation for creating these institutions was that the number of persons in attendance would be less than the full membership of the United Nations through constituency representation. When a similar attempt was made to limit attendance in the United Nations, it failed, and the result was the creation in 1978 of the Committee of the Whole (COW).[3] The US has no more desire to deal with the COW on economic and social issues than it does with the General Assembly itself or with UNCTAD.[4]

The UN functional bodies, mainly the specialized agencies, conform generally with the US preferred mode of action as long as they do not stray too far from their appointed economic and technical functions. Indeed, it has become routine for senior US officials to talk primarily about the specialized agencies and not the multifunctional bodies when they recount the major accomplishments of the United Nations in the economic and social fields.

Why functionalism? Is functionalism of the type preferred by the United States still viable in the face of the demonstrated preference of most developing countries for negotiating in multifunctional bodies and for "politicizing" the functional ones?

The stated reason for favoring functionalism is straightforward: this approach permits progress in one area, say trade, even while there is conflict in other areas, particularly in political relations. The more sweeping the issue linkages in a single negotiation, the more difficult it is to reach agreement.[5] It is no accident that foreign ministry officials predominate at multifunctional meetings, such as the General Assembly, UNCTAD, or the North-South dialogue, since they generally are not the technical experts but the synthesizers, whereas persons responsible for specific areas generally guide functional meetings. Central bankers come to Basel for meetings of the Bank for International Settlements, treasury officials attend meetings of the Group of 10 on monetary policy, agriculture officials meet at the Food and Agricultural Organization, health officials at the World Health Organization. The main business at hand in these organizations is economic or technical, and the issues are limited in scope. Disparate tradeoffs—more oil for the United States if it puts pressure on Israel to be more accommodating to Arab demands—are less likely at functional meetings.[6]

Even when the vision is a grand one, like the political and economic integration of Europe, or restructuring the world's economic system after World War II, it is normally approached in incremental steps, gradually extending the accomplishments to other economic areas and potentially to the political arena.[7]

The current US vision for the 1980s and beyond is not grand; it is incremental. We do not seek a restructured trading system but instead the avoidance of protectionism and some progress in reducing nontariff barriers. We do not seek a new monetary system. Managed floating, perhaps a return to a fixed but adjustable par value system if circumstances some years hence permit, and perhaps some reduced reliance on the dollar as the world's major reserve asset, are our more modest objectives. We are prepared to codify foreign investment procedures as long as the codification permits what is occurring in any event. We are satisfied with the rules of the current economic system, not in every detail but in the main. We would like to break the oil cartel, but we know this can occur only from our actions, not from negotiation. We are prepared to make concessions on the fringes of the system but not at the core.

It is possible to be even more precise. We are prepared, sometimes reluctantly, to enter into specific commodity agreements or even support a modest Common Fund, but we would not support indexation of commodity prices to the prices of manufactured goods in an effort to manipulate deliberately the terms of trade. We are prepared to alter reciprocity rules for developing countries in trade negotiations, but only if these countries make a contribution (concession) appropriate to their economic status and eventually graduate out of these special privileges. We are prepared to extend the scope of nonconditional lending by the IMF, for example by enlarging the compensatory finance facility, but we are not prepared to give up conditionality altogether. We sometimes are prepared (or were before the Reagan Administration), Congress willing, to provide more concessional funds for IDA and in our bilateral aid programs and to increase the capital of the IBRD and the regional development banks, but we cavil at aid automaticity, whether it be through an SDR-aid link or an international assessment based on GNP.[8]

For the most part, other industrial countries share these objectives.[9] The French might want to organize trade more than we would but not at any sacrifice to French industrial or agricultural interests. The Europeans and Japan generally are less enamored with flexible exchange rates than the United States, but the differences are only a matter of degree. There are developed countries, particularly the Nordics, which may be willing to provide concessional aid to poor countries on a more or less automatic basis, but this willingness does not extend to the major aid donors, such as Japan and Germany.

By contrast, however, there are important disagreements with this world vision on the part of developing countries. Most of them would prefer thoroughgoing nonreciprocity in trade negotiations and automaticity in aid giving. Much more significantly, the collectivity of developing countries, the so-called Group of 77, would prefer to play down functionalism and play up issue linkage. This may not apply to every member of the Group of 77, but thus far any differences have been mostly obscured. In straightforward functionalism, say in trade negotiations or the operations of the international monetary system, the collective power of the developing countries is less than that of the industrial countries. This power imbalance in functionalism is aggravated by the weighted voting in the principal functional institutions, namely, the IMF and the World Bank. The kind of confrontational negotiation which has been occurring with increasing intensity over the past 10 to 15 years requires unity of the developing countries as a source of strength, and this strength is given greatest meaning when there is issue linkage. Politicization of international institutions, as has been occurring, is done not out of contrariness, but as a tactic to gain power by transcending functionalism.

Developing country dissatisfaction with the GATT not only resulted in the creation of UNCTAD's mandate, allowing it to deal with trade issues, but also in the enlargement of UNCTAD's scope to deal with development assistance, other forms of financing, technology issues, and the operation of the monetary system. UNCTAD tried to seize authority in fields in which the industrial countries had created many separate institutions, such as the GATT, IMF, and the World Bank. The COW extends this coverage even more broadly than UNCTAD. In the third general session of the United Nations Industrial Development Organization (UNIDO) held in New Delhi in early 1980, the major agenda item that disrupted the conference was the proposal to establish a large fund to promote industrialization (or, put differently, to enter into the field of responsibility of the World Bank).

Politicization means different things to different countries. To the Group of 77, the control of the major functional institutions by the industrial countries is politicization, whereas to the US politicization refers to the effort by the Group of 77 to shift more activities to UN bodies where weighted voting does not exist. Which is politicization, the insistence by the North on maintaining enough of a weighted vote to be able to veto significant changes in functional institutions such as the IMF, or the effort by the developing countries to increase their weighted vote? The answer is obviously both.

The word "politicization" is clearly an oversimplified description of what normally occurs in international institutions, because political considerations enter into most economic and technical decisions. We have come to expect linkages (or "politicization") in multipurpose bodies like the General Assembly, the COW, or in the "global negotiations" of the United Nations, but we still recoil in anger when they occur in what we believe to be extraneous ways in functional institutions. We may not like the confrontational negotiation in the multifunctional UN bodies either, but we have accepted this as inevitable and indeed even logical. We did not withdraw from the General Assembly after the Zionism-is-racism resolution, and, indeed, never even officially considered doing so, but we did withdraw from the International Labor Organization (ILO) and we withheld funds from the United Nations Educational, Scientific, and Cultural Organization (UNESCO) because of the introduction of Israeli-Arab politics. We did not like it, but we accepted the majority decision to permit an observer from the Palestine Liberation Organization (PLO) in the General Assembly. This same issue was introduced by the Group of 77 at the IMF meeting in Belgrade in October 1979. The outcome here is uncertain, but the issue is more serious in this organization, which is probably the functional organization par excellence. The dam has not yet broken and functionalism has not yet lost its viability, but it is becoming more and more difficult for the United States to hold the functional line. This is particularly true for issues in which there is linkage to Middle Eastern oil, since most industrial countries tend to put oil first and functional purity second.

What can one conclude? US economic objectives favor a modified status quo, a willingness to accept changes at the margin but not at the heart of the institutions where international economic interactions are carried out. US institutional objectives reflect these underlying substantive goals. It is not an unreasonable outlook given our world position. There is no evidence, either, that the alternative approach of dealing with substance by issue linkage within institutions is more likely to advance the objectives of the world's poor. It is certainly hard to see how recognition of the PLO in the IMF can do this. The Group of 77 seeks to enhance its power—its political power and its economic leverage—by issue linkage in multifunctional institutions, and the US seeks to retain its power and enhance its economic interests by doing all significant economic business in functional institutions.

IMPLICATIONS OF CONFLICTING OBJECTIVES

A typology of institutional arrangements, and the business each type normally carries out, might be useful. There is no one channel for any given type of activity, since negotiation is multi-institutional. It is common for countries to make bilateral diplomatic approaches before upcoming meetings or votes in multilateral institutions; this usually involves some issue linkage. It is rarely as blatant as in 1964, when Haiti sold its vote to expel Cuba from the OAS by linking this vote to US aid.[10] However, any diplomatic approach connects bilateral relations with behavior in multilateral institutions. Ambassador Moynihan was proud of his ability to affect the voting behavior of many countries as when he convinced many not to support a vote on a resolution in favor of Puerto Rican "liberation" in the United Nations by making it known in capitals that the United States would consider their support of this vote to be an "unfriendly" act.[11] There are periodic attempts in the US foreign policy establishment to link the behavior of countries in multilateral institutions with US bilateral relations, especially aid. UN Ambassador Jeane Kirkpatrick recently made one such effort to make unfriendly votes costly. However, there is understandable reluctance to push this type of linkage too far because it would elevate the importance of votes in international institutions, and hence increase the opportunities for blackmail. In practice, the United States tends to link votes in international institutions with US behavior toward the country in question only when the issue is important to us. For example, the vote in the Security Council on December 31, 1979 to consider sanctions against Iran if the US hostages were not released within one week was undoubtedly one such issue.

The table below is a typology that tries to capture the flavor of current institutional arrangements. Several comments are needed to clarify the typology. There is a distinction in the listing between *universal* functional *technical* institutions and *near* universal functional *policy* bodies. There are no fully universal bodies, not even the United Nations, but the membership in the technical bodies normally includes the communist countries while most communist countries are not members of the policy bodies, that is, the IMF, the World Bank, or GATT.

The functional policy bodies have been labeled in the typology as major negotiating forums whereas the universal multifunctional ones are listed as less acceptable to many countries for negotiating purposes. This needs little further explanation beyond that already contained earlier in this essay. When UNCTAD puts on its commodity hat and calls for producer-consumer meetings on specific primary products, its competence to sponsor such negotiations is not questioned. Nor is this competence questioned in negotiating the details of a Common Fund. It is questioned when UNCTAD gets into areas that fall within the competence of what have been labeled the near universal functional policy institutions. The authority of the General Assembly to debate almost any conceivable international issue, or of the COW to debate issues of international economic or social significance, are not questioned, but there is major disagreement as to whether these bodies have negotiating responsibility.

This point will be returned to, since it is at the heart of the international disagreement that exists about the future role of the United

A Typology of International Institutions

Nature of Institution	Examples of Types of Issues Handled
1. Bilateral diplomacy	SALT/START Arms sales Much foreign aid Many trade problems Investment relations

2. Limited groups of like-minded nations
Examples:
  OECD
  DAC
  IEA
  Commodity groupings
  G-10
  G-24
  Summits of industrial nations
	Policy coordination
	Caucuses for upcoming meetings
	Specialized issues affecting those nations
	Effort to provide world leadership

3. Regional organizations
Examples:
  OAS
  The 5 UN regional economic commissions
  Colombo Plan
  Multilateral development banks
  SELA
  OAU
  ASEAN
  NATO
	Regional peacekeeping
	Regional economic analysis and development
	Regional caucusing

4. Universal functional technical
Examples:
  Most UN specialized agencies, such as:
    WHO
    UNESCO
    FAO
    ILO
    ICAO
    ITU
    UPU
    IAEA
	Study, technical assistance, agreement on policy in specialized field
	Focus world attention on critical issues

A Typology of International Institutions

Nature of Institution	Examples of Types of Issues Handled
UNDP	
IFAD	
Special meetings, such as on environment, food, women, science and technology, habitation and water	
5. Near universal functional policy Examples:	Establish international rules in functional field
IMF	Dispute-settlement forum
GATT	Major negotiating forums in areas of competence
World Bank	
6. Universal multifunctional Examples:	Debate issues in areas of competence
UN, including the GA, COW, and UNCTAD	Negotiation of concessions and policies, but less generally accepted than in functional policy forums
Special sessions, such as 6th and 7th special sessions of UNGA, and meeting on DD3	Seek to set North-South policies over long term
7. Security Council	Unique in its peacekeeping authority

Note: The meanings of abbreviations for the various UN bodies are found in the list at the front of this volume.

Nations. It is precisely this conflict of views that must be dealt with in future US policy on the use of the United Nations and other institutions.

One other point about the typology worth noting is that it is a partial listing of institutions, a typology by example rather than comprehensiveness. Many specialized agencies have not been listed and many sub-bodies of large institutions have been omitted. The decline in relative US economic and political power over the past two decades has resulted in a greater sharing of world leadership than when the US was the undisputed hegemonic power. The lack of a single leader has led to a proliferation of new organizations, some to suit our needs (such as the IEA within the OECD), but most others to suit the needs of other countries, particularly the developing ones. There seems almost to have been a deliberate practice: when in doubt about how to deal with a new issue (environment is an example), or how to give impetus to an old issue (agricultural development is an example) create a new institution. In this sense, the international system behaves much like national authorities dealing with special interest groups, with the possible difference that there are no international sunset laws. The interplay between bilateralism and multilateralism and among different international institutions is now extremely complex and growing more so annually. (This theme will be raised again in discussing management of this chaos.)

Several trends have thus been evident in the multilateral system: a politicization of the universal multifunctional institutions; a political contagion running from these to functional institutions, both of the technical and the policy variety; and a growing problem of institutional management as a result of the growth in the number of institutions. Three major operational consequences that have flowed from these developments are the following:

1. For North-South issues, the universal multifunctional institutions (and to some extent the large world conferences that are universal and functional) now set the agenda both for international debate and even for the negotiating content in the functional policy institutions. A few examples will suffice to show this. UNCTAD stimulated the debate on tariff preferences for developing countries, but the negotiations themselves were completed in the GATT. UNCTAD set the parameters of the international commodity debate and carried out itself the negotiations on the Common Fund and in special commodity groupings for particular primary products, such as cocoa. The General Assembly has set the issues for much debate in its NIEO resolutions, but the actions that followed are being played out mainly in other institutions. Since the NIEO resolutions, the IMF has several times expanded the scope of its compensatory financing facility and extended the terms of its lending in the extended Fund facility, and the GATT has negotiated a new frame-

work agreement. The Special Session of the General Assembly in 1980 not only worked out the elements of the third UN development decade, but was a major agenda-setting meeting on North-South issues.[12]

The universal multifunctional institutions are not unique in setting the international agenda for North-South issues, but they clearly are predominant. It already has been noted that special universal functional meetings, such as those that dealt with the issues of food, the role of women, population, environment, habitation, water, science and technology, and renewable sources of energy, play an agenda-setting role. The World Bank plays an important agenda-setting role in the annual speeches by its President to the Bank's Board of Governors and in the *World Development Reports*, which have been prepared yearly since 1978. Each institution sets its own agenda on the basis of problems in its particular area of competence and many of these agendas are internally generated.

However, and this point merits special emphasis, the tone and often the content of North-South issues are now mainly the result of debate and resolutions in the General Assembly, UNCTAD, and the COW. As much as these institutions are disliked by the functional policymakers in the United States and other developed countries, actions taken in them dictate how much time and effort these same policymakers will have to devote to issues selected by the multifunctional organizations. The practical results that emerge are rarely identical to the formulation of the issues as presented in the General Assembly or UNCTAD, but years are spent altering resolutions on such matters as a Common Fund or tariff preferences for developing countries in order to make them acceptable to the industrial countries.

2. Not only do the universal multifunctional institutions take the lead in setting the agenda for North-South negotiations, but they do so in a conflictual atmosphere in which ideology (politicization) is part and parcel of the substantive argument and—this is the main point—this politicization carries over into the functional institutions as well. A G-24 document issued before an IMF annual meeting is not terribly different in its content on monetary and balance-of-payments issues than a G-77 document issued before an UNCTAD

or a General Assembly session. There is no longer such a thing, if ever there was, as a nonpolitical international functional institution.

Having said this, however, there are differences between multifunctional bodies and functional institutions in the UN system, and between the three major functional policy institutions that are essentially outside the UN system. For one thing, the developed countries control the decisionmaking in the IMF and the World Bank. Resolutions cannot be passed by the sheer number of sovereign countries. When a decision is taken in the IMF or the World Bank, it will be carried out. When a resolution is passed in the General Assembly or other UN institutions, it need not be carried out by those countries which disagree. The developed countries cannot veto resolutions in the GA, but they can veto actions.

In the GATT, no country can be forced to give a trade concession against its will. For example, while the United States has accepted the principle of nonreciprocity, it has insisted in its negotiations in the GATT that nonreciprocity does not mean that developing countries need not make any contribution, but rather that the contribution need not be equivalent to the concession received. The GATT, in other words, operates on the basis of quid pro quo negotiations, whereas the General Assembly operates primarily on the basis of unrequited concessions by developed to developing countries. This does not remove the potential for politicization in the GATT, but it certainly reduces its effectiveness for developing countries in obtaining concessions as compared with multifunctional UN institutions.

3. The growing politicization of universal or near universal institutions has led to an increase in actions taken by limited groups of like-minded nations. The Group of 10 was a way in which some developed countries could escape from the generality of the IMF membership, just as the annual economic summits of Western leaders are a way to escape from the generality of even the OECD. The most significant discussions during the multilateral trade negotiations were among the United States, the European Community, Canada, and Japan. The developing countries were not ignored, but they were not central to the negotiations, in part because their individual trade is less than that of the major industrial countries, but

also because they wished to negotiate on a nonreciprocal basis. If the quid pro quo is negligible, why spend too much time giving concessions?

This point can be made in another way. If politicization, which is extraneous to the interests of the industrial countries, is felt to have become too extreme, these countries retain the option of conducting their main business in ad hoc groupings or in other institutions. Where decisions will actually be carried out once adopted, as in the IMF, behavior takes on a character different from that observable when conclusions can be ignored, as in a General Assembly resolution. The functional policy institutions are the ones to which economic policy makers in the developed countries devote most attention, because decisions taken in them can affect their own countries. These policy makers pay less attention to the multifunctional and technical functional UN bodies because countries can avoid any action they themselves do not wish to take. They are perhaps mistaken in this behavior, because even though they have negative power over decisions, in their aloofness, even disdain, they are losing sight of the agenda-making power of the universal multifunctional bodies.

To recapitulate briefly, the key elements of the analysis thus far are the following:

- The developed countries have business to do among themselves, and they rely on the IMF and the GATT to carry on this business in trade and monetary matters. Politicization they consider extraneous to this business will be avoided by almost any means, including taking their business elsewhere.
- The policy implications of extraneous politicization in the more technical UN bodies are usually less crucial in their effects on the internal economies of the developed countries; hence the tolerance of many policymakers for politicization is greater here, although still quite limited.
- Politicization is expected in the universal multifunctional UN bodies. Any resentment against this by policymakers in developed countries must certainly be tempered by the knowledge that economic progress often occurs only after political pressure is exerted.
- The US tends to look at its actions in the multifunctional

UN bodies as damage limiting, whereas it looks to the functional policy institutions for real accomplishments.

• What US policymakers often lose sight of is that, while damage can be limited for the moment, the North-South agenda for many other institutions is set in these multifunctional UN bodies. In order to limit damage, one has to look not only at an immediate resolution, but at how the elements of this resolution will become accepted wisdom as they are repeated in preambles of later resolutions, in speeches, and in proposals that later show up in the functional policy institutions.

If this analysis is essentially correct, it explains why the United States is uncertain in its attitude toward, and behavior in, the United Nations. Damage limiting is never as stimulating as creativity. If the quid pro quo for agreeing to a concession in a UN resolution is abstract—it will make for a better world—rather than concrete, this appeals more to idealists than to bureaucrats and technocrats. Participation in the multifunctional UN bodies is thus often left to officials responsible for political relations. This has long been an arena of internal conflict in the US government. Officials engaged in UN affairs often urge that the United States grant concessions for reasons of improving political relations with the South. Those involved in carrying out economic policy resist giving concessions either because there is no explicit quid pro quo, or because they believe the proposed concession will be damaging to US interests (US opposition to the SDR-aid link was of this nature), or because they fear that agreement to a concession can not be followed up by actual delivery of what was promised (US unwillingness to endorse the target of 0.7 percent of GNP for official development assistance is based to some extent on this concern).

LOOKING AHEAD

The following three questions are important ones to answer in trying to discover the shape of future US participation in the UN system and in other international institutions:

1. While admitting that functionalism is under attack from the collectivity of developing countries, is it dead? Should the United States forsake it in favor of multifunctionalism? To put the question

in less extreme form, should the United States diminish its emphasis on functionalism and increase that of multifunctionalism?

2. If the United States wishes to take more of a leadership role in the multifunctional institutions, what is the possible substantive content of this leadership? Can proposals advocating incremental change be the stuff of which leadership is made?

3. Both the foregoing questions presuppose a continued unity of developing countries, and hence an emphasis by them on issue linkage. Is this a legitimate assumption?

The third question might best be addressed first, since future pressures from developing countries may be substantially different from those of the recent past. For the most part, the Group of 77 has stuck together; the main impetus for multifunctionalism, issue linkage, and the current degree of politicization has stemmed from this unity. The high point of this unity came in 1974 when the NIEO resolutions were adopted by the General Assembly. Unity as a negotiating tactic had been developing for more than a decade, growing out of the nonaligned movement and the creation of the Group of 77 at the first session of UNCTAD in 1964, but the immediate stimulus for the NIEO resolutions was the effective use of price- and revenue-raising power by OPEC.

OPEC has been so effective in the years since 1974 that its very success now has become the main stimulus for the loss of unity among the developing countries. The rift between the oil-importing and the oil-exporting countries, long simmering beneath the surface, erupted into public view at UNCTAD-5.[13] Oil was the spark to fire aggressive unity of the Group of 77, just as it is the spark that is firing disunity. UNCTAD provided the locus for unity, just as it later provided the locus for open dissension among the Group of 77. The assumption that there is an aggregated group of 120 or so developing countries following a common economic and political interest is a risky foundation on which to base policy. The differences among the Group of 77 are too great to permit this simple assumption.

In 1980, the oil exporters had a current account surplus in their balance of payments of more than $100 billion, while the developing country oil importers had a collective deficit of about $70 billion.[14] The annual rate of growth of GDP of the non-oil middle-income countries during the decade of the seventies was 6.2 percent (3.6 percent per capita), while that of the low-income countries was only 4 percent (1.7 percent per capita).[15] This experience led Robert McNamara, then President of the World Bank, to suggest a disaggregation of goals for the third development decade, rather than an aggregate goal for all developing countries as in the second development decade, to give greater attention to this diversity.[16] The theme of concurrent heterogeneity and homogeneity of the Third World is one of the points stressed in the 1979 *Interfutures* report of the OECD.[17]

There are profound differences in substantive policy positions among developing countries because of their underlying heterogeneity. The poorest countries want debt forgiveness, while the more advanced middle-income countries want better access to private capital markets in order to continue to contract new debt. The latter group of countries should benefit substantially from the trade concessions made in the Multilateral Trade Negotiations (MTN), whereas these negotiations mean little to the poorest countries. In their economic policies, the more successful middle-income countries are more attuned to the status quo and to incremental change than to radicalism. They are slowly acquiring an outlook comparable to that of first world developed countries. They may not be at the point of graduation from the Third World, but for many of them, commencement cannot be too far away.

Certainly this changing constellation of players in the different "worlds" of countries must be factored into US decisions on institutions. Many of the potential graduates are apt themselves to prefer functionalism. There will be much ambiguity, perhaps for a decade or more, as they waver between functionalism and issue linkage as their primary thrust in international institutions, but even ambiguity implies that the future attack on functionalism from the developing countries will not be a replica of what we have witnessed over the past decade. This does not signify that there will be an end to politicization either in the multifunctional or functional institutions; as has been indicated, politics is part and parcel of international negotiation. It may, however, presage a diminution of

confrontation by unity. If many of the middle-income countries forsake or diminish the confrontational approach to achieving concessions and rely more on give and take in specific functional areas,
this will dramatically alter the tone of the North-South debate.

The first question posed above, as to whether the United States
should accept and make a virtue of the decline of functionalism,
can now be addressed more fully. The US preference for functionalism is based primarily on our perception of our self-interest. It
permits concentrated attention on specific issues without excessive
contamination from extraneous matters or disagreements outside the
functional area. Functionalism permits changes in the processes of
international economic interaction to take place incrementally and
in negotiations in which the quids are in the same field as the quos.
Despite politicization of both the technical and the policy functional
organizations, they function essentially as described above. A
meeting of the IMF's executive board, where day-to-day decisions
are made, bears little rhetorical resemblance to the General Assembly, and no US policymaker would suggest that we negotiate the
nature of the exchange rate system or the composition of international reserves in the multifunctional bodies. WHO still concen-
trates on health issues, the FAO on agriculture, the ILO despite its
politicization mainly on labor matters, and so on. Even though one
form of the question was stated in the extreme—is functionalism
dead?—this is clearly overquestioning.

It is hard to believe, either, that most developing countries would
wish to end functionalism. They certainly would not want to do so
in the technical bodies, nor probably in the policy institutions. We
must listen to national policymakers in developing countries to determine their priorities in such fields as money and finance, as well
as to the orators who attend the multifunctional meetings. The developing country policymakers undoubtedly would like more authority over decisionmaking in the IMF or the World Bank, but this
is not the same as wishing to terminate these institutions. The middle-income developing countries generally have benefited from this
institutional structure, since it undoubtedly contributed to their high
growth rates over the last 30 years.

For these reasons, it is hard to take seriously suggestions that the
United States should downgrade functionalism, despite the travails

in pursuing this course, because there is no evident substitute for getting specific business done. The potentially shifting composition of country groupings discussed above only reinforces this conclusion.

However, there is a caveat to this conclusion inherent in the way the second question was asked. Not only will functionalism continue to be in the US interest, but the agenda-setting role of multifunctionalism also is likely to persist. There are many reasons for this. A functional institution tends over time to become ingrown. The policy officials who attend the meetings and the Secretariat that prepares the papers develop a pattern of thinking that seems resistant to change. It already has been noted that the impetus for the compensatory finance facility in the IMF, and particularly its periodic liberalizations, and for trade preferences, came from multifunctional institutions.

In most cases—those cited and others—the United States has been dragged along kicking and screaming until the moment of capitulation. The US rarely takes initiatives in multifunctional institutions as it does in the functional ones (indeed, it is looked to for leadership in the IMF and GATT). Instead, the US almost invariably reacts. The one time this country did act first, at the Seventh Special Session of the General Assembly, the rest of the world was stunned by the novelty of the situation. Because the Seventh Special Session turned out to be a relatively nonconfrontational meeting, it has been suggested that we should regularly take leadership initiatives in the multifunctional institutions. Perhaps that way, the argument goes, we can set the agenda.

This suggestion is not easy to carry out. The initiatives at the Seventh Special Session were mostly advocacy of policies already being pursued, as in the trade field; that is, they were an extension of our initiatives in functional policy institutions. The one exception at the Seventh Special Session was US advocacy of a liberalized compensatory finance facility in the IMF as a counter to the proposals in the NIEO. This proposal was accepted, but beyond that the Seventh Special Session has been mostly forgotten. The rallying cry of the Group of 77 remains the NIEO, the resolutions of the Sixth Special Session.

It is hard to envision what initiatives can be taken at agenda-setting multifunctional meetings by a nation that seeks only incremental changes and that wishes to carry these out functionally. The initiatives that the US does take turn out to be the same initiatives taken at the functional institutions. This will hardly be seen as a pioneering effort by those intent on more drastic changes in the international economic system. The US cannot stun the assemblage regularly by repackaging its policy preferences, as was done at the Seventh Special Session. Nor, given its general posture of shunning dramatic change, is it likely to be able to take major initiatives changing US policy, unless this is done to prevent something that is considered worse—like consenting to general trade preferences in order to slow down the proliferation of special preferences, or setting up the IDA to prevent the establishment of a similar facility in the United Nations, or proposing an expansion of the compensatory finance facility in order to distract attention from many of the proposals in the NIEO.

No one can object to suggestions that the United States should be more bold and imaginative in its participation in the universal multifunctional institutions. It is generally a better tactic to take the initiative than to respond in ways that seek to limit damage. Recognition of America's interdependence with developing countries would also argue for a more cooperative US posture in these institutions. The rub, however, is to be able to delineate those imaginative proposals acceptable both to those who control the apparatus of the multifunctional institutions and to the US public as represented in the executive branch and the Congress.

This is not to argue that the United States is never able to take initiatives in the UN system. Indeed, as in the functional policy institutions, the US is looked to for some leadership at the universal functional meetings that have been sponsored by the United Nations. These special conferences tend to be reasonably congenial to us. Since they are functional, they permit us to mobilize the technical expertise that exists in the United States. However, there may be diminishing returns from these meetings; the 1979 Conference on Science and Technology for Development was more confrontational and had fewer concrete results than some of the earlier meetings, such as that on food.

In summary, the responses to the questions asked at the outset of this section are the following:

1. Functionalism is not dead. It is not in the US interest to forsake its preference for functional as opposed to multifunctional bodies for dealing with specific functional issues. Put more straightforwardly, from the US viewpoint, functional negotiation is best conducted in functional institutions.

2. It would be desirable if the United States could take leadership in the universal multifunctional institutions, since in this way it could be more influential in setting the agenda for the total structure of international institutions, but this is counsel that, at the moment, has little content. If the assessment is correct that the US objective for the 1980s is for incremental change, then the scope is limited for bold initiatives that would be generally acceptable in the United States.[18] There also is little merit in taking functional initiatives in the universal multifunctional organizations if the US desire is to strengthen the functional policy institutions as the main arena for substantive negotiation.

3. The changes taking place in what is called the South are profound. These are reflected in disparate rates of economic growth, in vastly different economic structures, and in distinct and often conflicting substantive priorities. It would be an error to plan future US participation in international institutions from the perspective of the confrontational unity of the Group of 77 of the past decade. Slogans like unity in heterogeneity, which spokesmen from the South tend to use, are just that, slogans. US policy must differentiate among the substantive needs of the different groups of developing countries, and this in turn must be reflected in our institutional behavior.

CONCLUSIONS

It is intellectually unsatisfying to come to institutional conclusions when the real issues are substantive, since there never is a unique institutional solution to important issues of foreign policy. Getting the substantive task done, based on what is possible in the US political context, must dictate the US institutional approach.[19] We are a nation in which conservatism is a powerful force, a nation that abhors shocks, and that looks mostly inward. These attributes condition our participation in international affairs.

The conclusions to be drawn from this assessment of the domestic context, from the changing international context in which unity of the developing countries is becoming increasingly unviable, and from the complex international institutional structure in which the US must operate, are the following:

1. The most important conclusion is that pursuing the US interest requires that our major attention in the critical policy fields of trade, money, and the transfer of resources to poor countries must continue to be given to the functional policy institutions. They are politicized, and may even become more so, but there is a quantum difference between the degree of their politicization and that of the universal multifunctional institutions.

2. However, since the multifunctional institutions do help set the agenda for much of the international substantive debate, including that in the functional policy institutions, the United States must devote more substantive expertise to multifunctional institutions than it has in the past, particularly to the General Assembly and its offshoots. It is unlikely that the United States will be able often to take major initiatives that will form the basis for North-South debate, but even this may be possible from time to time. Equally important to US participation in multifunctional institutions is the high probability that many of the emerging middle-income countries are apt increasingly to be talking our language. We need our own spokesmen who know our substantive language.

3. A final reason for this dual functional-multifunctional emphasis is that the interplay among institutions is substantial. Compromises are often worked out in a succession of floating meetings—some bilateral, some regional, some among like-minded nations, some purely functional, others in multifunctional settings—and we must play professionally in all the games. The complexity of issues, and that there now are many relatively powerful players, further complicates the negotiating task of reaching consensus on significant matters.

It is popular to talk of the impasse in North-South relations. It was this sense of stalemate, of talking past each other, that prompted the creation of the Brandt Commission as an agenda-setting group that could have more influence than the UNGA. Impasse there may be, but going beyond that, what we have been witnessing is an intricate negotiating process that takes place at many levels, in many forums, some with linked issues, other unlinked, and all of this complicated by the changing substantive situations of the negotiating countries. The essential institutional task for the United States is to manage this complexity, this apparent chaos.

Notes

1. Seymour Maxwell Finger discusses US representatives to the United Nations in *Your Man at the U.N.: People, Politics and Bureaucracy in the Making of Foreign Policy* (New York: New York University Press, 1980).

2. George Ball, an Undersecretary of State, came to the sessions at the close of UNCTAD-1. The most senior representative at the close of UNCTAD-5 was a Deputy Assistant Secretary of State.

3. The constituency representation really failed in the CIEC as well, since the developing country representatives were constantly looking over their shoulders and caucusing with their constituencies. It may be that constituency systems will not work well when significant issues that cross functional lines are under discussion.

4. The purpose of the COW is to assess progress in the institutions of the UN system in achieving the goals of the NIEO, or put more neutrally, in promoting development in the developing countries. There had been almost continual conflict as to whether the COW should be a body for direct negotiations, as the developing countries wished, or a forum for exchanging views, which the developed countries preferred. This dispute is certain to continue.

5. A clear expression of this viewpoint is contained in C. Fred Bergsten, Georges Berthoin, and Kinhide Mushakoji, rapporteurs, *The Reform of International Institutions,* a report of the Trilateral Commission, 1976. In listing the advantages of functional specificity over multifunctionalism, the report asserts that issue linkage which can deter functional progress is more easily avoided (p. 5).

6. The Jackson-Vanik amendments tying emigration from Communist countries to official export credits and most-favored-nation trade treatment from the United States are complicated precisely because the linkages are so disparate.

7. Ernst B. Haas, *The Uniting of Europe: Political, Social and Economic Forces, 1950–1957* (Stanford University Press, 1958) is an early exposition of the functionalist approach and the potential spillover effects from this approach into political unity in Europe.

8. The SDR-aid link would use the international monetary system to transfer resources to developing countries. The idea is to distribute SDRs, or reserve assets created deliberately by the international community, not on the basis of country quotas in the IMF (as is now the case), but rather to prefer developing countries in this distribution. At present, developed countries receive about 70 percent of the SDRs that are created and the less-developed countries 30 percent. The ostensible basis for US opposition to the SDR-aid link is that it could lead to manipulation of the international monetary system for aid purposes rather than to facilitate international trade and other economic transactions.

9. However, we are more insistent on obtaining a "contribution" from developing countries in trade negotiations than is any other industrial country. Graduation is an explicit issue for the United States but not for most other industrial countries.

10. The selling of the Haiti vote is discussed in a State Department memorandum (obtained in the LBJ Library after declassification) entitled "Haiti: Proposed Plan of Action for Period Beginning May 1, 1964," which unequivocally labels the Haitian proposal as "blackmail."

11. Daniel Patrick Moynihan and Suzanne Weaver, *A Dangerous Place* (Boston: Atlantic-Little Brown, 1978), pp.111–112.

12. I have in mind the launching of "global negotiations." The main area of conflict was almost predictable: the developing countries wish this mechanism within the UN framework to conduct substantive negotiations, while the developed countries, and particularly the United States, are willing to negotiate in the UN only in the sense of providing guidelines to the relevant functional institutions.

13. This divisiveness on oil prices is alluded to in an article on UNCTAD-5 in the IMF *Survey* of June 18, 1979, p. 186.

14. The estimates are from the IMF, *Annual Report* 1980, p. 17.

15. The World Bank defines a middle-income (developing) country as one with per capita GNP in 1980 of more than $410. The more populous middle-income countries are Argentina, Brazil, Mexico, Spain, Yugoslavia, Turkey, the Philippines, Thailand, South Korea, and Nigeria. The low-income developing countries are defined as those with per capita GNP in 1980 of $410 or less. Most countries in Africa fall into this grouping. The most populous low-income countries are India, Bangladesh, Pakistan, and Indonesia. China, for which GNP data are inadequate, probably would

fall into the low-income grouping. The middle-income countries with the highest annual average growth rates in GNP between 1960 and 1979 were Singapore (7.4 percent), South Korea (7.1 percent), Hong Kong (7.0 percent), Greece (5.9 percent), Portugal (5.5 percent), Yugoslavia (5.4 percent) Spain (4.7 percent), and Brazil (4.8 percent).

16. The data on GDP growth and the suggestion for differentiated goals come from McNamara's address to the Board of Governors of the World Bank, Belgrade, October 2, 1979. Cited in the McNamara Years at the World Bank: Major Policy Addresses of Robert S. McNamara 1968–1981 (Baltimore: Johns Hopkins University Press, 1981), pp. 565–609.

17. *Interfutures,* research report on "The Future Development of Advanced Industrial Societies in Harmony with that of Developing Countries" (Paris: OECD, June 1979), pp. 197 ff.

18. Several readers of this chapter argued that this vision of the United States as favoring a gradually changing relationship with the Third World may not prove valid because of growing US vulnerabilities in the 1980s. In addition to energy, these are likely to include our need for markets in the developing countries and access to raw materials from them, and the growing trade competition we will face from the more advanced middle-income developing countries. These vulnerabilities, it can be argued, will impel the United States to seek new forms of interaction with the Third World and may lead to bold initiatives on our part. This is possible. It is also possible, however, that the more advanced middle-income countries will become more like the current industrial countries and favor incremental change as being in their own best interest. Our relationship with Third World countries in the 1980s is likely to be both cooperative and competitive, as indeed it is now, and while this obviously will lead to changing US positions, I doubt we will wish to take initiatives to make these changes drastic or precipitate.

19. Much the same thought is expressed in *What Future for the UN?: An Atlantic Dialogue,* a policy paper of the Atlantic Council, Washington, DC, October 20, 1977: *"The main emphasis must be on getting the job done,* rather than dogmatically working within any particular institutional framework" (p. 11, italics in original).

THE UNITED NATIONS AND POLITICAL CONFLICT BETWEEN THE NORTH AND THE SOUTH

STEPHEN D. KRASNER

The contemporary international system has many unique character-istics, of which the power disparity between the countries of the North and the South is one of the most startling. Never since the beginning of the modern state system in the sixteenth and seven-teenth centuries have sovereign entities with such drastically differ-ent power capabilities operated in the same environment. There have always been small states, if size is measured by population or geo-graphic area, but size differentials have never been compounded by vastly different levels of development. At the beginning of the nineteenth century the widest difference in per capita income be-tween states was about two to one. The present ratio is above 30 to one.[1]

The international weakness of most Third World countries does not relieve their leaders of any of the imperatives of sovereignty. Like all political leaders they must resist external invasion and in-ternal disintegration; in addition, coups and revolts are a constant threat. Leaders try to secure national wealth not just to improve the conditions of their citizenry, but also to ensure the stability of the regime or their own tenure in office. The pursuit of wealth by Third World states, indeed by any state, is a political, not just an eco-nomic, act.

In pursuing wealth, Third World states confront a dilemma. The generation of wealth has almost always meant greater involvement with the world economy, but greater involvement has increased vulnerability—and involvement with the world market is inherently a threat to the state's control because it opens the society and economy to external shocks. Few states in the South have the resources to insulate themselves from such shocks. Falling raw material prices can threaten the stability of a regime. Protectionist actions by the United States or Europe can undermine, even destroy, a burgeoning new industry—Korean color TVs may be a graphic example.[2] Higher oil prices can wreck development plans. The IMF can impose stringent conditions on standby agreements. (Such conditions led to riots in Egypt and Peru.)

Industrialized countries, even small industrialized countries, have a much larger store of domestic capabilities that can be used to cushion external shocks. Their economic factors are more mobile. Workers can move from a steel mill in Ohio to an automobile plant in Pennsylvania more easily than peasants can move from countryside to city or switch from growing cotton to tobacco. Social insurance schemes can ease adjustment for workers. Consultative, even corporatist, political structures are more highly developed, particularly for small industrialized countries.[3] Thus, developed states are much better able to cope with the instabilities that are inherently part of an open economy.

North-South relations must be seen within the context of the profound structural weakness, both international and domestic, of most Third World countries. The behavior of the developing world is not simply a function of poverty. The South wants to enhance its control, not just to multiply its wealth.

VARIETIES OF THIRD WORLD POLICY

The interactions between rich and poor areas of the world involve a dizzying array of concerns: the regulation of multinational corporations, the establishment of freight rates at international liner conferences, the treatment of guest workers in Europe and migrants in the United States, the conditions for International Monetary Fund standby agreements, the renegotiation of official debt in Paris clubs, and the setting of quotas for international commodity agreements. The New International Economic Order (NIEO) is, then, but one of many programs pursued by less developed countries; it is but one of many pillars staked across the field of North-South relations. One pillar can be moved, or even removed, without altering the position of the rest.

The policies pursued by developing countries can be divided into three broad categories:

   1. Policies designed solely to enhance wealth without any concern for enhancing control.

   2. Policies designed to enhance wealth and to share control with actors from wealthier areas.

   3. Policies designed to establish effective control over institutional arrangements governing the international economic system with the enhancement of wealth over the long-term as a secondary consideration.

An example of a purely wealth-seeking policy would be the negotiations that take place when a multinational corporation interested in exploiting raw materials first approaches a developing country. The country does not have the expertise to develop the mineral deposits on its own. The company is not sure that the deposits are there. Corporate activity offers the promise of great wealth for the host country if the endeavor is successful. The corporation bears the risk. Under these circumstances countries have typically sought up-front payments with little concern for control of corporate activities.[4] Many *bilateral* trading arrangements are also dominated by purely wealth-seeking concerns.

The second type of policy, intended to enhance wealth and also to share control, has most often been directed toward regional or functional international organizations. International commodity agreements offer a particularly clear example. Their function is to stabilize, and possibly to raise, prices for primary commodities. Markets may be regulated through buffer stocks and export quotas. Management of these operations is overseen by legislative bodies, or international commodity councils, with one chamber composed of producing countries, the other of consuming countries. Agreement requires at least a majority of votes from each council. Thus, both exporting countries (usually exclusively LDCs) and importing countries (usually exclusively industrialized countries) have an effective veto. Power is shared.

Bilateral and regional regulation of multinational corporations offer another example of Third World efforts to enhance immediate wealth and share long-term control. Many developing countries have insisted that multinationals divide ownership with local nationals, hire indigenous personnel, limit profit repatriation, and provide technology. Such policies involve a challenge to the autonomous power of the corporation to allocate capital, labor, and goods; they are not merely an effort to secure higher payments for the host countries. There is, for instance, a great difference between the demand of oil-exporting countries for higher tax payments in the late 1940s and early 1950s and their assertion of the right to set prices and output levels in the 1970s.

Finally, Third World countries have pursued policies that are basically designed to assert effective control over the international environment; the accumulation of greater wealth has been a secondary consideration. The clearest example of this third kind of behavior is the package of proposals contained in the New International Economic Order (NIEO).

The NIEO has been primarily pursued in the universal órgans of the United Nations family, especially the General Assembly and the United Nations Conference on Trade and Development (UNCTAD). Acting through international organizations is an attractive strategy for the Third World. The institutions of the United Nations offer a way for the weak to compensate for their inability to act unilaterally, for the exiguity of their national power resources. Rules and norms generated within the UN can impose some restraint on the unilateral exercise of power by the strong and rich. Approval by international organizations accords legitimacy to particular forms of behavior, legitimacy that could not be obtained through purely national actions.

The Third World has been able to effectively use the United Nations system because of a peculiar historical situation: the gap between underlying power capabilities and institutional structures that can arise during periods of regime maturation. When the identity between actions taken by international organizations and the preferences of strong states weakens, the gap between power and institutions that develops during periods of regime maturation opens possibilities for weak states. At the present time, the Third World has captured much of the United Nations structure, a structure that it would never have been able to create for itself. The United Nations system has provided a forum as well as bureaucratic and technical resources for the South. American leaders, who originally endorsed giving each nation a single vote in many UN bodies, did not anticipate that American domination of these organizations would end. Yet the "one nation, one vote" system remains.

THE NIEO PROGRAM

What kind of program has the Group of 77 presented in the United Nations, particularly UNCTAD and the General Assembly? The New International Economic Order has generally been interpreted in the West as an effort to increase the level of resource transfers to the poor. In the estimation of many this view is profoundly mistaken. The NIEO is more a political program than an economic one. Its fundamental goal is to resolve the dilemma created by involvement in the world economy—the dilemma of securing greater wealth only at the cost of greater vulnerability. This resolution would be accomplished by creating new institutional structures, growing out of the existing UN system, to govern the world economy. These new structures would be controlled by developing states.

This is not to imply that less developed countries are interested solely in political control, or that they do not pursue purely wealth-oriented policies. But it is to assert that the NIEO, which is only one of many Third World programs, is basically a political rather than an economic challenge because it aims at control, not just at wealth. At the same time, there is nothing inconsistent in a country pursuing a moderate, "prudent" policy that does not challenge existing international norms and values in some areas, while at the same time endorsing immoderate, "imprudent" policies in others. For instance, under the presidency of Luis Echevarria, Mexico became a leader of the Third World movement at UNCTAD and the UN. At the same time, the Ministries of Development and Finance were welcoming foreign investment in several sectors of the Mexican economy.[5]

The specific *economic* proposals associated with the New International Economic Order are now quite familiar.[6] They all have in common the aim of increasing the wealth for at least some developing countries. Most of them have been on the international agenda for more than a decade. But it is not simply the binding of these proposals into one package that has led them to be recognized as a call for a "new" international economic order. Rather, it is that they have been accompanied by attacks on the basic assumptions of the existing order and by demands for effective control over international decisionmaking machinery. It is the *political* component of the Third World's position that distinguishes the present situation from earlier ones. This is revealed both in specific issue areas and in the general statements that have been associated with the NIEO.

In the area of the transfer of resources, the NIEO emphasizes automaticity. There is little interest in conventional aid programs that leave the allocation of resources to Northern states or the international institutions that they dominate. The distribution of funds would be based on universal principles rather than on the preferences of donors. A general debt rescheduling would eliminate the case-by-case negotiations that have taken place in "creditor clubs," where industrial countries have often imposed stringent conditions on debtor states. A link between the creation of new international liquidity and international financial aid would also limit the leverage of the wealthier countries. While the North would still influence the aggregate amount of liquidity created, it would not control its dispensation.

Mahbub ul Haq, former Vice President of the World Bank, who emerged in the late seventies as an important articulator of Third World positions, carried the South's position on resource transfers to its logical conclusion. Haq proposed the creation of a world development authority that would act under the aegis of the United Nations and would have authority over all international economic institutions.[7] It would be run by a board elected by the UN General Assembly representing all national blocs. Short-term credit would be provided by a world central bank, and would be based on growth potential, not on past levels of affluence. Long-term credit would be automatic and would come from such mechanisms as international taxation on activities that create social diseconomies, such as armaments spending. A tax based on arms budgets was proposed by the developing countries at the Spring 1978 UN Special Session on Disarmament. The adoption of such programs would mean a radical shift in the control of the flow of resources from rich countries to poor countries.

In the area of technology the LDCs have not only promulgated more stringent national regulations, but have also moved to fundamentally change the international regime. Most technology transfers in the present system are controlled by multinational corporations. The Third World wants a new international code that would be binding on states and private firms. This code would unbundle technology, lower prices, and regulate intracorporate transfers. The Group of 77 has also called for preferential treatment for developing countries, and a distinction between the treatment accorded national and international firms. They have called for the elimination of restrictions on the use of technology, such as contractual arrangements prohibiting the export of products that utilize a particular firm's technology if these exports compete with the firm's sales in other areas. The position of the developing countries is based on the principle that technology is part of the common heritage of mankind. Access to technology is viewed as a right, rather than as private property that must be purchased. Under the proposals made by the Third World, the fundamental purpose of the existing regime, which is to protect the position of those that generate and sell technology, would be supplanted by a regime that would favor the buyers and users of technology.[8]

In the area of sovereignty over raw materials, both the 1974 Declaration on the Establishment of a New International Economic Order and the Charter of Economic Rights and Duties of States assert that host-country governments have the right to nationalize multinational concerns. While the documents recognize that "appropriate compensation should be paid," any disputes are to be settled in terms of the national laws of the host country. International practices (that is, international law), international organizations, or home-country governments, are denied presumptive relevancy or the right to intervene. These proposals deny multinational corporations any effective power vis-à-vis host-country governments. If these proposals are adopted, a firm could not appeal to its own government or to international law, or engage in economic retaliation. "No State may be subjected to economic, political, or any other type of coercion to prevent the free and full exercise of this inalienable right" to nationalize or transfer ownership.[9]

In the area of raw materials trade, the Charter on Economic Rights and Duties of States supports basic restructuring of existing institutional arrangements. Article 5 reads: "All States have the right to associate in organizations of primary commodity producers" and "all States have the duty to respect that right by refraining from applying economic and political measures that would limit it." In essence, this article asserts that developing countries have the right to form cartels and that industrial states do not have the right to do anything about it. If such practices were accepted it would mean a dramatic shift in power in international raw materials markets.

An Integrated Program for Commodities (IPC) was adopted at the 1976 UNCTAD meeting in Nairobi. This program originally called for the formation or extension of international commodity agreements for some 18 primary commodities and for the creation of a Common Fund. The first window of this Common Fund will make loans to individual commodity organizations. Since decisions in international commodity councils require the approval of both exporting and importing countries voting separately, the first window would not mean any sharp departure from existing norms, rules, and practices, although it could make individual agreements more effective by coordinating policies among commodities with high cross-elasticities of demand, such as coffee and tea.

The second window of the Common Fund is more wide-ranging and novel in its conception. Under existing proposals it could make loans for activities such as diversification, productivity improvement, market promotion, and enhancement of the role of developing countries in marketing and distribution. The Group of 77 would also like the Common Fund to provide resources to regulate the market in commodities that are not covered by international commodity agreements. The Fund could, for instance, make loans to finance stockpiles in individual countries. The operations of the second window would be under the control of the Common Fund and might not, therefore, be subject to veto by commodity-consuming countries. Although not much progress has been made in recent years toward these objectives, if the provisions of the Common Fund were to be put fully into force and supported with significant resources, they would fundamentally alter the institutional arrangements under which trade in primary commodities takes place. There would be a basic shift in power from multinational corporations and consuming countries to producing states and the Third World as a whole.

A review of these NIEO proposals shows that all of its provisions imply a profound alteration in control over the world economy, not just a transfer of wealth. It may be, of course, that the stated position of the Third World is a bargaining device rather than a set of consummatory goals. Perhaps the less developed states are simply interested in resource transfer, and are not that much concerned with issues of power and control.

The evidence against this interpretation is scanty, but several developments over the last decade suggest the saliency of political goals for developing states. The most weighty evidence comes from the United Nations Law of the Sea Conference (UNCLOS), a negotiation in which the Third World relinquished economic benefits in an effort to achieve effective control through the structure of a new seabed authority to regulate the exploitation of deep seabed nodules. That the issue was fundamentally one of control is evident since the industrialized countries had already agreed to a mutual veto voting arrangement, indicated a willingness to restrict nodule output for twenty years, and agreed to share production between an Enterprise controlled by the Authority and multinational corporations. All to no avail. The Third World continued to insist on effective control of the Authority and a primary place for the Enterprise.

Early on in the seabed negotiations the Third World rejected proposals that would have provided far more aid resources by limiting the economic zone of littoral states to less than the 200-mile exclusive economic zone already agreed to at the conference and implemented by many states.[10] Virtually all of the oil and gas (by far the largest ocean resource) and fish are within this 200-mile zone. Now, however, the common heritage of mankind is restricted to the deep oceans where only seabed nodules offer any promise of significant economic aid. Had the Third World endorsed a narrow economic zone the resources available for global aid would have been far greater. But this path was eschewed largely because a number of Latin American states with long coastlines took the lead in pressing for an extensive economic zone. A split between land-locked and coastal states, the cleavage that would have been predicted by an analysis that explained state behavior in economic terms, did emerge in the early and mid-1970s but ultimately collapsed. The Group of 77 came to endorse greater national power for littoral states, many of which are developing countries,[11] while at the same time pressing for effective control for the Third World as a whole in the non-national areas of the ocean.

There were other possibilities for greater wealth as well. In 1970 the United States proposed the establishment of a trusteeship zone between the 200 meter isobath and the edge of the continental slope. Development of this zone would have been controlled by the littoral state, but some share of earnings from the zone would have been used to increase assistance to less developed countries. The trusteeship zone would probably have contained significant amounts of oil and gas. However, the proposal was dismissed by the Third World.[12] The trusteeship zone would have provided more revenue for LDCs but it would have precluded greater control.

Other international negotiating efforts have also stalemated over the control of new international institutions. However, in these cases the tradeoffs between economic benefits and political control are not so evident. The Common Fund for commodities was locked in a dispute over voting arrangements, with the South calling for a distribution of votes that would give developing and socialist countries a majority and the North calling for votes to be partially weighted by contributions to the Fund.[13]

Another example involves the non-tariff barrier codes negotiated during the Tokyo Round. Few of the developing countries have signed any of the new codes, even though all of them give the LDCs special and differential treatment without any obligation to offer reciprocal concessions. In addition, fewer than 20 developing nations have signed the tariff part of the codes. Greater access to the markets of industrialized countries would have positive economic benefits for a substantial number of developing countries and the GATT could be an important line of defense against growing protectionism, which is a greater threat to the newly industrializing countries of the Third World than to any other group of states. However, the GATT has not been an important institutional forum for them.[14]

The following pattern is suggested by the behavior of developing countries. Within existing institutions the Third World has pressed for revisions of decisionmaking arrangements that will give them at least an effective veto; for new institutions the Third World has sought effective control. This cannot be understood simply as an effort to secure greater financial resources, for such resources would be more easily secured by assuring the industrialized states of at least a veto power. It cannot be explained as a reaction against intransigence on the part of industrialized nations in existing organizations—even in most institutions with weighted voting developing countries can exercise an effective veto.

In the one nation-one vote universal multifunctional organs of the United Nations system, developing nations do exercise a preponderant influence. Even in some of the specialized agencies with weighted voting, the position of developing countries is stronger than is generally realized.[15]

In the World Bank and IDA, approval has been given to a number of loans that were opposed by the United States. In the African Development Fund, voting power is shared between African and non-African members, but the African states retain effective control over administration. In the Inter-American Development Bank borrowing countries have 53 percent of the votes; in the Asian Development Bank borrowing members have 45 percent.

Third World policy is, however, consistent with an argument that explains behavior on the basis of the relative position of developing countries in the international structure. Small and poor states are vulnerable to external developments over which they have little control. These developments are a threat to regime stability and even national integrity. The control of international institutions charged with establishing rules and norms for the international economic system is a way to influence a threatening and dangerous, yet unavoidable, global environment. (Of course, the application of national power resources would be usually a far more effective way to mediate external pressures, but few developing countries have the resources to implement such a policy effectively.) International organizations offer one of the few forms of leverage that are available to the weak and the poor.

CONCLUSIONS

The implications of the analysis presented here are not auspicious for either the United Nations or the future of world order. The United Nations has become the forum for the most political kinds of Third World demands, those that involve a shift in control over the world economy. More pragmatic economic objectives are pursued through national action, bilateral negotiations, and sometimes large but still nonuniversal arrangements such as the Lome Convention.

Agreement on political issues is exceptionally difficult. Politics is a zero-sum game; control by one set of actors denies control to others. It is unlikely that significant agreements will be concluded. The experience of the Law of the Sea Conference does not augur well for other attempts to create new international orders. Where agreements have been concluded establishing new institutional structures, such as the International Fund for Agricultural Development, the amounts involved have been modest. The Common Fund for commodities appears to be headed for the same kind of outcome. A modest fund will satisfy some symbolic purposes for both sides—the Third World will have a new institution and the industrialized countries will have demonstrated their willingness to compromise—but it will not satisfy any basic political or economic goals. Rather than being the conclusion of a negotiating process, it will be merely one step. Other demands will follow. The less developed countries have already broached the idea of a new compensatory finance facility that would be outside the Common Fund and the International Monetary Fund.

The UN will be the setting for discussion of the more intractable issues of power and control. Many more strictly economic issues, which are more susceptible to mutual agreement, will not be brought before international organizations. They will be settled in a pragmatic fashion in institutional settings with limited membership. Here interests are often complementary and compromise is possible. Multinational corporations want to invest in developing countries and developing countries need markets in industrialized countries; their sales dampen inflation and generate demand for capital goods and other exports from wealthier areas. Industrialized countries need more raw materials from the Third World and producing countries need higher foreign exchange earnings. Where mutual interests exist, the specific division of receipts will be settled by the bargaining power of the parties involved, not through universal negotiations. There may be many specific agreements between the North and the South, but there is little evidence that the wealthier and poorer areas of the world can move toward the creation of new institutional arrangements that would contribute to world order in the 1980s.

The causes of the disagreement between the North and the South are rooted in the fundamental structural characteristics of the present international system. It is the profound weakness of virtually all Third World countries, not their poverty, that has led them to try to secure greater power and control through international organizations. They lack the national resources to achieve such control by acting on their own. Although the commitment of Third World states to the NIEO program varies among countries and within the same country over time, the driving force for the NIEO—the disparity of national power capabilities among states—will not disappear.

POLICY IMPLICATIONS

The fundamental challenge for the United States is to manage the decline of hegemony. The extraordinarily ambitious goals that were pursued, often with great success, into the 1960s are no longer appropriate because they are no longer feasible. The United States cannot pursue ideological objectives such as the promotion of human rights and the fulfillment of basic economic needs because other more immediate interests will inevitably intrude and external events will increasingly threaten immediate and tangible American interests.[16] Oil in the Persian Gulf, instability in the Caribbean and Central America, automobiles from Japan, all pose threats that cannot be ignored.

With regard to the Third World, the American policy most likely to prove successful would be selective disengagement. Selective disengagement means concentrating in those areas where the United States has a clear stake in relations with particular Third World countries. Efforts to construct new universal norms, rules, and institutions should be downplayed if not completely abandoned.

The decline in American power and the persistent weakness of the Third World implies that there is no actor in the system capable of establishing new, mutually satisfactory universal arrangements, although regional and functional organizations may emerge that offer rules and norms acceptable to all actors in a particular issue area. Ceding power to the Third World, however, is not likely to lead to durable and effective organizational arrangements, because the Third World countries will only accept new institutions if they can exercise a preponderant influence.

In specific terms, a policy of selective disengagement for the United States suggests the following tactics:

1. The United States should downplay the role of universal organizations such as the General Assembly and UNCTAD. American involvement in such organizations should be more limited both symbolically and financially. The United States should not, for instance, treat the United Nations Ambassador as a cabinet official, nor should the appointment of the Ambassador be regarded as a major event.

2. The most promising arenas for successful agreements are those where all parties have a clear tangible, usually economic, interest in the issue at stake.[17] Such arenas will usually have limited membership. In general, they will not be associated with the UN because of its presumption of universal membership. International commodity councils that include only major producers are an example. The United States should pay relatively more attention to such arenas.

3. Proposals to negotiate global agreements should be approached with caution. The Law of the Sea conference was a mistake that should not be repeated in other functional issue areas. The major exceptions are issues involving problems of the global commons, such as the allocation of radio frequencies, where the failure to reach agreement can have high costs for everyone involved.

However, even in such issue areas there should be no illusion that an easy solution based upon purely technical criteria will be discovered. The Third World will demand greater control in return for acquiescence to new global regimes.

4. The United States should be prepared to accept frequent changes in negotiated relationships. In the absence of clear international norms, agreements will frequently be altered as the relative bargaining power of the actors changes. Because of fundamental differences about power and control, the United Nations system cannot effectively establish the international norms and rules that are a prerequisite for enduring, as opposed to fleeting, agreements among states and other international and transnational actors.

5. The industrialized countries will be compelled to create new international institutions that are limited in membership to settle issues that are vital to them. The International Energy Agency is an example. The non-tariff barrier codes concluded during the Tokyo Round are formally open to all the participants in the negotiations, but since few developing countries have signed, they are relevant mainly to the industrialized West. Indeed, some of these codes, such as the agreement covering government procurement, deal basically with issues affecting the industrialized countries alone.

The relatively stable institutional arrangements of the postwar period cannot be reconstructed in the present era, nor can substitutes be found. No actor in the system has the power to create such structures. The United States and developing countries share many tangible interests. In the areas where their interests coincide, bargains will be struck and some transitory rules may emerge. But there will be no agreement on new norms or on the creation of effective universal institutional structures. In an era of hegemonic decline the United Nations cannot contribute to the reconciliation of differences between the North and the South.

Notes

1. P.N. Rosenstein-Rodan, "The Have's and Have Not's Around the Year 2000," in Jagdish Bhagwati, ed., *Economics and World Order: From the 1970s to the 1990s* (New York: Macmillan, 1972), p. 29.

2. As a result of orderly marketing agreements signed with Korea, Taiwan, and Japan, the import of color TVs in 1979 was down 50 percent from 1978 levels. *New York Times,* March 8, 1980, p. 30. *World Business Weekly,* November 12, 1979, p. 5.

3. For a discussion of the importance of factor mobility see Albert Hirschman, *National Power and the Structure of Foreign Trade* (Berkeley: University of California Press, 1945).

4. Raymond Vernon, *Sovereignty at Bay* (New York: Basic Books, 1971) and Theodore H. Moran, *Multinational Corporations and the Politics of Dependence: Cooper in Chile* (Princeton: Princeton University Press, 1974) develop the concept of the obsolescing bargain. Once a discovery is actually made the host country may seek greater control as well as more wealth because its leverage has increased: the company has sunk costs; the state knows the resource is there.

5. John and Susan Purcell, "State and Society in Mexico: Must a Stable Polity be Institutionalized?" *World Politics* 32 (January 1980), especially pp. 214–217 for a discussion of Mexican policy under Echevarria.

6. Good discussions of the NIEO can be found in Karl P. Sauvant, "Introduction," in Karl P. Sauvant and Hajo Hasenpflug, *The New International Economic Order: Confrontation or Cooperation Between North and South?* (Boulder: Westview Press, 1977); Catherine B. Gwin, "The Seventh Special Session: Toward a New Phase of Relations Between the Developed and Developing States?" in the same volume; and Branislav Gosovic and John Gerard Ruggie, "On the Creation of a New International Economic Order: Issue Linkage and the Seventh Special Session of the UN General Assembly," *International Organization* 30, 2 (Spring 1976).

7. Mahbub ul Haq, *The Poverty Curtain: Choices for the Third World* (New York: Columbia University Press, 1976), pp. 187–197. Ronald Meltzer refers to Mahbub ul Haq's proposal in a somewhat different context in this volume.

8. Sauvant and Hasenpflug, op. cit., Part V.

9. United Nations, General Assembly, Resolution 3201 (S-VI), *Declaration on the Establishment of a New International Economic Order,* 4 (e).

10. Richard N. Cooper, "The Oceans as a Source of Revenue," in Jagdish Bhagwati, ed., *The New International Economic Order* (Cambridge: MIT Press, 1977), p. 112.

11. The largest beneficiaries of the extensive economic zone are the United States and the Soviet Union. The United States was split on this issue in the early 1970s, with military interests pressing for a narrow zone and mining interests for a broad one. American policymakers might have endorsed a narrow zone had the conference participants moved in that di-

rection. See Ann Hollick, "Bureaucrats at Sea," in Ann Hollick and Robert Osgood, *New Era of Ocean Politics* (Baltimore: Johns Hopkins University Press, 1974) for a discussion of policymaking in the American government.

12. For discussions of the trusteeship zone proposal see Cooper, op. cit., p. 112; Hollick, op. cit., pp. 28–40; and John R. Stevenson, "Legal Regulation of Mineral Exploitation of the Deep Seabed," *Department of State Bulletin* 65 (no. 1672), pp. 52–53.

13. See James P. Paragamian, "The Common Fund: Development, Mechanics and Forecasts," *Law and Policy in International Business 11,* 3 (1979) for an overview.

14. For a description of the Tokyo Round see Stephen D. Krasner, "The Tokyo Round: Particularistic Interests and Prospects for Stability in the Global Trading System," *International Studies Quarterly* 23 (December 1979). For a discussion of LDC policies to circumvent protectionist measures see David Yoffie, *The Advantages of Adversity: Weak States and the Politics of Trade,* Ph.D. dissertation, Stanford, 1980. For LDC particpation in Tokyo Round agreements as of February 1980 see Chamber of the United States, *International Report,* March 15, 1980.

15. In the International Monetary Fund, often regarded as a bastion of the rich, less developed countries now have 36 percent of the votes. Since major decisions require a 70 to 85 percent majority, the Third World has an effective veto. A detailed examination of voting in the International Monetary Fund is offered by Joseph Gold, "Voting Majorities in the Fund," *International Monetary Fund Pamphlet Series,* No. 20 (Washington: International Monetary Fund, 1977).

16. The relationship between a state's position in the international structure and the kind of foreign policy goals it pursues is examined in Stephen D. Krasner, *Defending the National Interest: Raw Materials Investments and U.S. Foreign Policy* (Princeton: Princeton University Press, 1978), Chapter 7.

17. For a rationalistic analysis concluding that membership in decision-making institutions should be limited to actors with a direct stake in that issue see Robert A. Tollison and Thomas D. Willett, "An Economic Theory of Mutually Advantageous Issue Linkages in International Negotiations," *International Organization* 33 (Autumn 1979), pp. 447–48.

THE UNITED NATIONS AND THE GLOBAL ECONOMIC SYSTEM

HOWARD M. WACHTEL

The political structure of the future world community was the meat for the United Nations' deliberations in its early days. Economic problems were relegated a secondary role and left primarily to other international institutions such as the World Bank and the IMF, created at the Bretton Woods Conference. (An exception to this was relief work which became part of the United Nations' mission immediately after World War II and has remained within the scope of its operations ever since.) Thus the important economic questions of how the international monetary system was to be organized in a postwar world, how trade was to be conducted among nations, and how capital was to move around the globe was explicitly precluded from the United Nations agenda. Separate international institutions were created in each of these areas to monitor global economic affairs.

This historical backdrop conditions the tensions between the North and the South today in the drama that is unfolding surrounding the debate over a New International Economic Order (NIEO). The majority of the developing countries, not having been present at the creation of the "old" international economic order, are persistent in their representations to be present at whatever new international economic order unfolds over the next years. But the United Nations, which has never been comfortable in dealing with economic problems, outside of direct relief, has found it difficult, if not impossible, to make progress on the needs of the nations of the South for economic development and a global redistribution of wealth through the creation of a New International Economic Order.

Moreover, there is a sharp resistance on the part of many nations in the North, including the United States, to introduce such issues into the United Nations framework. They claim that many of the agenda items for a New International Economic Order belong in existing institutions and they have not been receptive to the introduction of structural economic issues into the United Nations framework.

The beginning of the Third Development Decade may be an appropriate time to take stock of where the United Nations has been on these issues before more time is squandered on sharp debate that yields tepid results. Can the United Nations achieve its lofty ambitions of peace and social justice *without* possessing the instruments to affect *economic* justice in the world? Can the United Nations pursue its political ambitions with its economic hands tied behind its back? These are the central questions that confront the nations of the world today as they attempt to create a more peaceful and equitable world order.

POSTWAR WORLD SYSTEMS

The end of World War II offered the nations of the world an opportunity unique to human history. First, since virtually every major country in the world and every area of the globe was involved in the war, a reconstructed world order required that the global community collaborate in such an endeavor. Second, both the political and economic systems that governed relations among nation states had been disrupted irretrievably by the war. In the economic sphere this was perhaps even more a truism than was the case with world politics.

Starting around the middle of the war, the Allies began to turn their attention to the problem of what a reconstructed world economic order would look like. A conference at Bretton Woods, New Hampshire in 1944 produced a codification of the rules that were to govern the international economic system after the war. That system was to reign for some 25 years until it began to unravel in the early 1970s. Designed by economic visionaries, the Bretton Woods system heralded a period of economic growth and cooperation among the industrial nations of the world that heretofore had been unthinkable. The overarching purpose of the three institutions created at Bretton Woods was to promote free trade: a flow of goods, services, and capital among nations with a minimum of tariff restrictions and a maximum of monetary stability. The International Monetary Fund (IMF) was to stabilize the international monetary order through a system of fixed exchange rates; the International Bank for Reconstruction and Development (World Bank) was to facilitate capital mobility in the world; and the General Agreement on Tariffs and Trade (GATT) was to promote a rational system by which tariffs would be established among signatories to the treaty.

The Bretton Woods system affects relations between the North and the South today and has important ramifications for the United Nations. Virtually no nation from the less developed world was in on the creation of the Bretton Woods system. Outside of Latin America, what today are called the nations of the South were then merely colonial appendages of the major signatories to the Bretton Woods treaty: Great Britain, France, and the Netherlands. The deliberations concerning a new international economic order after World War II were split off from the negotiations that led eventually to the formation of the United Nations. The two principal meetings where the economic and political future of the world was being considered were separated by 3,000 miles—the one held in California, the other on the East Coast. Administratively, the major responsibilities were also divided between the two meetings. Economic affairs at Bretton Woods were handled primarily by the US Treasury and the equivalent finance ministries from other countries, while the major responsibility for staff work and negotiations in San Francisco was conducted by the US State Department and the foreign affairs ministries of the allied nations. While the Soviet Union was, of course, an important participant in the San Francisco meetings that produced the United Nations, it never ratified the Bretton Woods agreements that produced the postwar economic system for the world. The Soviet Union has been able to use its "outsider" status to its advantage by singing an anti-imperialist refrain while escaping any responsibility for the world economic system it unceasingly reviles.

The structure of voting power that was established for the United Nations was very different from that in the international economic institutions. In the former, the voting principle was one nation, one vote, with membership based on the idea of universality so long as a nation state was prepared to abide by the Charter of the United Nations. However, the economic institutions were established more on the market principle of one dollar, one vote. Voting is weighted, based on the capital subscriptions of member nations. As a consequence, the wealthier nations of the world exercise a degree of voting power based only on their wealth, not in proportion either to their population or to their membership in a particular cluster of countries, such as the OECD, the Northern industrialized nations, or the developing Southern bloc of states. The Hamiltonian principle of voting in accordance with property governs the world's economic institutions, while the Jacksonian principle of voting prevails in the world's political forum, the United Nations.

Looked at in this way, the United Nations represents the political structure of the postwar world, while the Bretton Woods system represents the economic structure. The two are really separate and distinct entities with little or no interface between them. They were established with very different geographic, administrative, and voting identities, and this has created a chasm that has remained ever since. Efforts to bridge the gap between the two world systems have never been successful. Their historical origins provide an insight as to why this is the case.

THE UNITED NATIONS AND PROBLEMS OF
ECONOMIC DEVELOPMENT

As more nations of the world became politically independent and gained entry into the United Nations, their inability to receive what they considered an adequate hearing at the Bretton Woods economic institutions led them to bring their concerns about economic development to the General Assembly of the United Nations.

The First Development Decade was followed by a second in the 1970s, and a third soon was adopted by the General Assembly in 1980. The adoption of General Assembly resolutions on the program for a New International Economic Order in 1974 and 1975 propelled the economic development agenda forward by authorizing UNCTAD, a body charged with fostering economic development in the South, to engage in negotiations on commodity issues, debt and finance, and foreign assistance. The preexisting Law of the Sea Conference became subsumed under an NIEO agenda in the eyes of many nations in the South, since natural resources and access to them was at the center of controversy in that forum. The role of transnational enterprises in the world and the transfer of technology became the grist for additional UN commissions, conferences, and generalized debate. Years of attention to the complex economic agenda of the South has produced limited results, except for a few commodity price stabilization agreements whose implementation remains problematical.

At the same time these developments were taking place in the United Nations, the world economy was buffeted by extraordinary economic events that have had dramatic effects on every nation's economy. The explosion in oil prices and economic stagnation in the industrial economies exacerbated the position of the poor nations in the South by closing off outlets of demand for their export products. International monetary disorder accompanied these economic developments in the price and production spheres, formally signalling an end to the Bretton Woods international monetary system as it had functioned for 25 years.

Cynics claim that the reason the less developed countries have turned to the United Nations is because that is where the South exercises political dominance. This, of course, is true. It is also no doubt true that many criticisms have been levelled at the Bretton Woods system by the South because in these institutions the poor nation majority exercises only a small minority voting power.

However, for progress to be made in the North-South economic dialogue now being conducted through the UN, such innuendoes of motives on both sides must be put in the background. Of greater consequence for the future of the economic development problems of poor nations is the artificial bifurcation of the political from the economic that took place after World War II, when the principal organs of the United Nations were created.

THE FUNCTION OF THE UN SYSTEM IN NORTH-SOUTH ECONOMIC PROBLEMS

Aside from relief efforts, the UN system has played a limited role in the operations of the international economic system, while at the same time it has become a focal point for debate over a reconstructed world economic order. This political debate has been vitriolic and rather unconstructive precisely because it has been divorced from any real effect on the actual functioning of international economic affairs that are lodged in other institutions. So long as the separation of the economic from the political remains, the debate will continue to be conducted on a plane of irresponsibility; the very conversion of the debate to something more meaningful will, over time, move it toward responsibility and a heightened seriousness.

Where will this emerge, if at all? In the 1980s, the critical problem for the poor nations of the South will be debt and the financing of balance of payments deficits. It has become evident in recent years that the accumulation of debt by poor nations of the South is unsustainable.[1] Moreover, one particularly critical period for the repayment of those obligations is upon us, because in the early 1980s the debts accumulated after the first OPEC price explosion are coming due.

Creative thinking on this problem has long been absent from the official forums in which this matter is normally discussed: the IMF, World Bank, and finance ministries. The South's proposal for a complete write-off is both impractical and bad economics. The United Nations could have played a significant role in this area by making this problem the focus of its work in its deliberations over the Third Development Decade. The debt problem telescopes all the more general issues discussed in this chapter: an interface between the economic and political dependency in the South, and economic development for the poor nations. Nothing will move forward in the South unless the debt problem is viewed in both its economic and political contexts. Failure to do this will increase unrest and instability in the Third World.

The breakdown of the Bretton Woods international monetary system has revealed intensified difficulties with existing global economic institutions. Monetary instability, the storing of wealth in precious metals, the problem of petrodollar recycling, and debt in the developing countries are all symptoms of an international economic system operating without formal rules of the game. This system cannot obtain for too much longer. There will be an occasion for the convening of a new international conference that will establish certain new rules for the international economic system. Should this occasion arise, and this will be sooner than most think, then it becomes imperative to correct the deficiency of the Bretton Woods system by merging the economic and the political and by granting the South more participation than was the case at Bretton Woods. The United Nations should immediately prepare for such an eventuality by developing proposals and methods for a reconstructed monetary order.[2]

For the longer term, the nations of the world must come together and address the need for a new international monetary system. Such a system should be erected around several principles:

1. That the international monetary system promote economic growth in a noninflationary atmosphere.

2. That the system provide room for a plurality of economic systems in the industrial world and a plurality of development models in the Third World.

3. That power be shared more equitably than the present system in which some eight countries exercise over 50 percent of the voting power in the IMF. Some formula must be found that lies between the present weighted voting system, which favors the major industrial states, and the one nation, one vote principle advocated by the developing countries.

4. That the system promote economic self-reliance so that foreign debts do not become an overwhelming burden on the development strategies of poor countries.

5. That the international trading system be constructed around a new international trading unit that is to the largest possible extent independent of any nation's currency.

Developing countries' efforts to relieve their debt predicament over the longer term will require the realization of some elements of the New International Economic Order agenda. Commodity agreements and the Common Fund provide some hope for stabilizing export earnings in the Third World. Alterations in the voting power of public international agencies would enable Third World concerns to achieve a more responsive hearing in the important councils of the international financial system. More South-South cooperation, the term used to describe mutually advantageous economic arrangements that can be created among developing countries, can potentially provide a significant alternative to the present structure of dependency relations in the world economy. The OPEC nations bear a special responsibility to see that this happens, since they are the Third World countries with the resources to make South-South relations more of an economic reality. Countries in the Third World will have to fashion a development strategy that delinks them from the export-led dependency constructed during the 1960s. Responsibility will fall on the developing countries to experiment with techniques of delinkage. The public international institutions, such as the World Bank, IMF, and UNDP, should support such efforts with technical and financial assistance.

A bold step is required on the part of the members of the United Nations—both from the South and the North. But short of such an effort, the rhetoric used in the continuing debate over a New International Economic Order and the Third Development Decade will only become more vitriolic as the years pass without a resolution of the issues encompassed by the South's demands. Moving the debate to concrete action and merging economic and political issues will perhaps defuse this confrontation and provide the operational basis for a fair hearing on all sides. For the United Nations this means reassessing its role in international economic affairs; for the United States this requires bold new initiatives.

US FOREIGN POLICY INTERESTS, UN PRINCIPLES, AND THE NEED FOR A RECONSTRUCTED INTERNATIONAL ECONOMIC ORDER

What interest does the US have in taking steps toward a reconstructed international economic order, and how would such an order benefit the United States? This question is important because the United States has a large foreign policy interest in promoting economic development and political stability in the Third World. Indeed, these are the two pillars of American foreign policy toward the less developed nations of the world. There is a general consensus that economic stability is a prerequisite for political stability and that economic stability is enhanced through the process of orderly economic development.

In recent years, a form of economic justice has been added to this more general goal of economic development. "Basic human needs" and "growth with equity" are but two formulations of the proposition that economic development without attention to distributional questions is insufficient in terms of American foreign policy objectives.

To the extent that the New International Economic Order agenda put forward by the Group of 77 at the United Nations promotes economic development and economic justice it is consistent with American foreign policy objectives. This is the hub of the debate: Does the New International Economic Order agenda promote economic development with social justice and does it do so in the most efficient way?

There is no easy answer to this question, but it is the framework in which the debate should proceed. At least this would provide concrete, even observable, criteria upon which decisions could be based. Without such criteria, nations have fallen back on nationalistic policies based on self-interest, effectively stalemating the debate. If the deliberations about a New International Economic Order were couched in terms of economic development and social justice, the proposals would have a better chance of moving forward and a stronger mutuality of interest between the North and South could be forged. This could supplant the current posturing of various groupings in the deliberations.

In accepting the New International Economic Order dialogue in the context of American foreign policy interest, it should not be forgotten that the United States no longer is in a position to call the shots as it once was. Indeed, this is one of the premises of the call for a reconstructed world order and one reason it is so necessary. However, the United States can still play a crucial role in signalling a new approach toward the discussions, for unless the United States accepts the challenge of a meaningful dialogue, nothing will move forward.

Whenever these discussions occur, the question of voting rights rears its ugly head. This is the institutional form in which the issue of relative economic and political power is raised. As indicated earlier, the General Assembly of the United Nations is based on the principle of one nation, one vote; the economic institutions are based on the principle of one dollar, one vote. If a reconstructed international economic order is to occur through new institutional forms created through the United Nations or if it is to involve reforms of existing institutions, the structure of voting power must be changed. Neither the Third World demand for one nation, one vote, nor the industrial countries support of weighted voting based on economic contributions can prevail in a reconstructed world economic order. Attention should be given to the principle of bicamerality—of two legislative houses, one based on weighted voting, the other based on one nation, one vote.

Whether this should be done by reform of existing international economic institutions or the creation of new ones is a practical matter and should be considered in that frame of reference. The argument that we already have too many such organizations and the creation of new ones is inefficient does not hold up. The OECD and the International Energy Agency (IEA) are two relatively new international economic institutions on the world scene, both of which were created (or expanded in the case of the OECD) to handle specific problems that had fallen between the cracks of existing international economic institutions.

A distinguished foreign policy veteran once remarked to me: "The foreign policy of the United States is not made for foreigners!" Does a reconstructed world economic order benefit the United States? The answer to that question is: yes. The flashpoints on the world political scene have been in the Third World ever since the Korean War. Tensions in Europe have tended to fade as each succeeding decade has removed us further from World War II. Korea, Central America, Indochina, the Middle East, southern Africa—these are the places where global conflicts are most likely to occur. Economic instability and inequality contribute to the political instability that arises in those areas of the world. Stabilization in those regions of the world would be in the interest of United States foreign policy. A reconstructed world economic order would not guarantee such an outcome but it would provide the possibility for more economic and political stability, thus lowering tensions in the world system. Returning to first principles of both US foreign policy and the UN itself—the principles of economic justice, social progress, and world peace—clarifies the reasons for rolling up our collective sleeves and getting on with the serious business of moving toward a reconstructed world economic order.

Notes

1. Howard M. Wachtel, *The New Gnomes: Multinational Banks in the Third World* (Washington: Transnational Institute, 1977); and Howard M. Wachtel, "A Decade of International Debt," *Theory and Society* (1980), pp. 503–518.

2. I have written about such a reconstructed monetary order in the material identified in footnote 1 above.

UN STRUCTURAL REFORM: INSTITUTIONAL DEVELOPMENT IN INTERNATIONAL ECONOMIC AND SOCIAL AFFAIRS

RONALD I. MELTZER

Over the past several decades, the United Nations has undergone significant institutional growth and adaptation and in particular has come to exert a strong presence in international economic and social affairs. The shift in focus has been marked by significant institutional expansion in the myriad of organs, specialized agencies, regional and functional commissions, subsidiary bodies, and ad hoc structures that comprise the UN family, and spend over three billion dollars annually on economic and social programs. However, accumulated UN institutional and structural problems have called into question the continuing UN capacity to meet growing challenges in these areas. This chapter examines some of the shifts in UN priorities and their impact on UN structure and functioning.

The United Nations is a system that grew more from institutional inheritance and proliferation than from design. The UN of today is thus an amalgam of numerous diverse organizations, each with distinctive histories and their own constitution and governing authority, plus an accumulation of new structures designed to meet new programmatic needs. This basic pattern derives from vague Charter provisions regarding the organization of UN economic and social activities, an early emphasis on functional autonomy and decentral-

ization, and the addition of new institutions to conform to a broadened conception of United Nations responsibility. It is also the out-
growth of a system that often responds to new or persistent problems
simply by creating further machinery—even if these additional
structures have gone unaccompanied by any real policy initiatives.

United Nations institutional development has attempted to respond to a global environment remarkably different from that of 38
years ago. The growth and impact of new members in the world
body with significantly different priorities and needs than the original membership has had a profound impact on the UN's programs.
Dissatisfied with many existing United Nations organs, developing
countries preferred to create and utilize more sympathetic bodies,
such as the UN Conference on Trade and Development (UNC-
TAD), the UN Industrial Development Organization (UNIDO), and
other structures under the General Assembly. Thus, a side effect of
the tremendous increase in economic and social development activities has been the creation of various parallel units, resulting in
bureaucratic fragmentation and an exacerbation of already strained
relations among UN institutions.[1]

There have been many difficulties associated with institutional
development. In addition to problems of overlapping competence
and duplicative programming, there has been a lack of policy and
structural coherence emanating from the central United Nations organs, especially the General Assembly and the Economic and Social Council (ECOSOC). As new bodies were created, lines of authority to and between the Assembly and the Council became
increasingly complicated and disjointed, contributing to problems
of direction, identity, and control within the system, and reinforcing cleavages among the member states.

There has also been an absence of effective programmatic coordination and operational management within the United Nations
system. Even though there has been increasing recognition that most
international problems require system-wide action and integrated
planning, the United Nations has proved unable to achieve these
goals amidst entangled involvements by many different types of
agencies. Indeed, much of the United Nations effort to improve
coordination has led to added organizational burdens and uncertainties.

Finally, UN institutional diversity and growth have created critical problems in controlling and managing financial resources within the United Nations. The decentralized United Nations structure has meant that there is a wide variety of funding arrangements that support the different agencies and programs. Conflicting principles of financing as well as varied schedules and mandates for raising funds have impeded effective United Nations planning. Budgetary fragmentation has also fueled disputes over the amount and use of assessed contributions and the role of extra-budgetary financing.[2]

The problems of coherence, coordination, and efficiency associated with United Nations institutional development are closely attached to broader international political and economic currents. In recent times, the relationship between political and structural considerations within the United Nations system has become especially pronounced and complex. The political turbulence and cleavages within the United Nations, particularly involving North-South relations, had led to complaints in the West about voting and procedural abuses, "politicized" arenas, managerial breakdowns, and political one-sidedness and irresponsibility. Among developing countries, criticisms have focused on the United Nations' failure to achieve adequate representation, responsiveness, and authority on matters central to their needs. Differences among major groups of member states concerning the nature and structure of international decisionmaking have both fueled and impeded efforts to undertake UN institutional reform.[3]

These restructuring matters have far-reaching implications for the United Nations, dealing in effect with what Robert Gregg has called the "apportionment of political power" within the world body.[4] For this reason structural reform has been approached with great deliberation and controversy, especially since members' underlying political values and capabilities are so disparate. Indeed, fundamental questions about the nature and course of UN structural reform— its scope, its directions, its pace—remain unsettled, reflecting the divergent mix of institutional and substantive motives that have led to current restructuring efforts.

US PERSPECTIVES ON UN INSTITUTIONAL REFORM

American priorities for UN institutional reform have consistently emphasized achieving greater efficiency and rationalization within the UN system: the development of enhanced UN planning, programming, budgeting, and evaluation capabilities, improved central management and leadership in the UN Secretariat, and better policy analysis, research, and data-gathering assistance programs.[5] The US has also stressed the importance of consensus as a method for reaching decisions in UN global negotiations. Among other recommendations, the United States has sought to channel technical assistance through a strengthened UN Development Program (UNDP) funded on the basis of voluntary contributions and has voiced the need for better coordination by all nations of their policies within the different UN institutions.[6]

In general, this approach to UN institutional reform has been rather restrictive, reflecting an underlying ambivalence about the UN system. On the one hand, the United States strongly supports attempts to improve the functioning and management of UN activities in the economic and social sectors. But in a setting where US perspectives on international economic and social matters are now minority viewpoints, it has not been prepared to grant greater authority to UN organs and deliberations. Nor has the United States been ready to address broader "linkages" between UN institutional reform and a restructuring of the international economic system. As one observer has noted, the US has remained reluctant to deal with "structural reform" in international economic and social affairs from a framework that encompasses a full "blend of political, economic, and institutional objectives."[7] This position has limited the scope and course of prospective UN restructuring. However, the United States has not been alone in approaching UN structural reform with considerable caution and skepticism. In a global environment marked with uncertainty and division, it has been difficult for many governments to gain sufficient national resolve and perspective to assume the necessary risks of major UN reform.

STRUCTURAL REFORM ACTIVITIES

Almost from its beginning, the United Nations has entertained the notion of structural reform. For example, in 1949, the General Assembly noted that there was a need to rectify the proliferation of new programs, which weakened its control over United Nations activities and burdened its resources. At the same time, ECOSOC indicated difficulties in coordinating United Nations activities and in reconciling the autonomy of UN agencies with more general United Nations responsibilities. In 1969, the problems of coordination and management were given high level attention and comprehensive analysis by the UN. A report entitled *A Study of the Capacity of the United Nations Development System,* which came to be known as the Jackson Report, made numerous recommendations for restructuring UN machinery in the areas of technical cooperation activities and operations. Throughout the years, the United Nations system has also undergone incremental and informal adaptations in response to changing circumstances and pressures.[8]

However, more full-scale and effective movement toward United Nations structural reform was launched only in the wake of various proceedings concerning North-South relations and international development problems. In meetings leading to the 1975 Seventh Special Session of the General Assembly, United Nations restructuring in the economic and social sectors was identified as a major priority in order that the United Nations could become "a more effective instrument for the promotion of international economic and social cooperation and development." As then Secretary-General Waldheim noted, structural reform was to "proceed in the context of progress toward—and as an integral element in—the establishment of a new international economic order."[9] After the appointment in late 1974 of a group of experts on the structure of the United Nations, a pathbreaking report, *A New United Nations Structure for Global Economic Cooperation,* was issued. Following the Assembly's Special Session in 1975, an intergovernmental ad hoc committee on United Nations restructuring was established.[10] After two years of intensive negotiations, the committee produced a detailed set of "action proposals" on United Nations institutional reform that was adopted by the General Assembly in late 1977.[11]

The work of the Ad Hoc Committee on UN Restructuring represented a major effort to develop an integrated basis for updating and improving the structure and operation of the United Nations system in the economic and social fields. Its provisions called for: a strengthening and streamlining of the General Assembly and ECOSOC in order to develop more coherent UN deliberations and policies; improvements in system-wide planning, programming, budgeting, and evaluation of United Nations programs and activities; greater coordination of United Nations action at the intergovernmental and interagency levels; increased efficiency and integration of United Nations operational activities; and a significant reorganization of the UN Secretariat.

The overall thrust of these proposals reflected a shift toward a more coherent and consolidated United Nations system, after several decades of rapid organizational growth and uncoordinated institutional pluralism. Thus, the restructuring guidelines marked a significant development for the United Nations. Not only did they stand as the most comprehensive plans for UN institutional reform ever undertaken within the world body, but they also represented the first real occasion when developed and developing countries alike actively participated in redesigning those aspects of the UN system that are of fundamental importance to them.[12]

The Committee framed the agenda and scope of UN restructuring into eight problem areas. First, the roles and activities of the General Assembly were given considerable attention. Reflecting their influence and confidence in the General Assembly, developing countries gave a high priority to upgrading the GA's role, authority, and jurisdiction. However, Western countries predictably envisaged a much more restricted and recommendatory position for the General Assembly in the United Nations system. The Committee was able to bridge the differences in noting that the Assembly was the "supreme organ" in the economic and social fields, having responsibility for setting and harmonizing overall policy in these areas and for establishing guidelines for future international action.

The Economic and Social Council was a second major area of proposed reform. Despite its designated centrality within international economic and social affairs, ECOSOC has never realized its intended position and effectiveness within the United Nations. The Committee attempted to buttress ECOSOC functions and authority within the United Nations system by recommending actions that would make ECOSOC the central forum for discussing international economic and social issues and implementing UN programs and activities. However, no effective agreement could be reached on the size of Council membership—an issue central to any realization of ECOSOC reform.

A third major area of proposed restructuring entailed other forums of negotiation within the United Nations system. One critical consideration here was the extent of direction exercised by the Assembly and ECOSOC over negotiations occurring in other arenas. The Committee decided that other forums, including GATT, IAEA, and ad hoc world conferences, should give ''prompt and full effect'' to policy recommendations elaborated within the Assembly and Council. Furthermore, the role of UNCTAD as a major negotiating forum was reaffirmed.

A fourth area of proposed restructuring involved action at the regional level. United Nations activities have expanded considerably in these areas, and the five regional commissions (ECLA, ESCAP, ECA, ECE, ECWA) have taken on added responsibilities and importance over the years. The restructuring guidelines have noted these trends and have assigned to the commissions ''team leadership'' and coordination authority for their respective regions. There was also an emphasis on strengthening the links between the commissions and the rest of the system in order to integrate them more fully into global policymaking and implementation.

United Nations operational activities represented a fifth area addressed by the restructuring guidelines. These activities have burgeoned and became an increasingly contentious component of the United Nations system. The developing countries sought to ensure increased resources in this area, while Western governments desired greater consolidation and efficiency for programs and funds. Major reforms in this area call for the convening of a single annual pledging conference and for the establishment of more unified administrative, financial, budgeting, personnel, and planning procedures within the United Nations system. At the field level, it was proposed that United Nations activities become more integrated and coherent, relying upon UNDP country programming and a single United Nations official to coordinate system-wide activities within the recipient nation. Suggestions were also put forward concerning the creation of a unified governing body for UN operational activities.

Regarding planning, programming, budgeting, and evaluation, the United States declared that this sixth problem area represented ''the heart of the Ad Hoc Committee's mandate.'' The restructuring guidelines offered a number of specific reforms and principles to upgrade the United Nations' performance in this realm. The Committee emphasized that planning, programming, budgeting, and evaluation activities should be carried out on a system-wide and thematic basis, with the main responsibility given to the Committee for Program and Coordination (CPC). A major goal was the development of system-wide medium-term planning, and several reforms involving budget presentation cycles and work schedules among the system members were proposed toward this end. Another key focus for the CPC was improved internal evaluation procedures. Central responsibility for financial oversight was assigned to the Advisory Committee on Administrative and Budgetary Questions (ACABQ).

Interagency coordination has long been a subject of suggested reform, and the UN restructuring committee agreed upon a number of guidelines and steps toward achieving needed change in this seventh problem area. The goal was to achieve greater coherence of action among the many United Nations agencies and to increase coordination between the intergovernmental and intersecretariat levels.

In the final problem area, the UN restructuring guidelines proposed significant reforms in the organization of the United Nations Secretariat. The Committee's recommendations in effect dismantled the sprawling and controversial Department of Economic and Social Affairs and identified six major secretariat functions that were to be performed in three new units. In another key move, the restructuring guidelines proposed the creation of a new high-level post—Director General for Development and International Economic Cooperation—to coordinate system-wide action on development problems. The Director-General was also to ensure greater coherence and efficient management of United Nations activities in the economic and social fields.[13]

The action proposals of the Ad Hoc Committee represented a carefully constructed ''package'' intended to accommodate diverse priorities and interests. They were the product of intensive deliberations, relying heavily upon a chairman's consolidated text and voting by consensus. However, the report was only the initial step toward UN structural reform and lurking beneath this set of broad recommendations have been smoldering differences and continuing struggles over the path and emphases of UN institutional reform, especially between the Group of 77 and the Western governments. Despite Western efforts to decouple UN institutional reform and the disposition of substantive North-South negotiations, structural reform remains linked in the minds of many to substantive progress achieved elsewhere in the North-South dialogue. As the Ad Hoc Committee chairman advised, such reforms "could not replace, but must proceed pari passu with the elaboration of policies, priorities, and measures aimed at the realization of the new international economic order."[14]

Other important factors conditioning UN structural reform are the bureaucratic rivalries and vested interests which fuel an intense, ingrown, and growing competition among UN organs. As agendas became more intersectoral in nature, many potential conflicts have come to the surface, triggering not only protective efforts by existing United Nations bodies, but also intensifying organizational attachments and antagonisms held by different groups of member states. Also important is the extent to which national governments undertake symmetrical efforts to restructure their national participation in the UN system. In many instances, UN institutional sprawl and ineffectiveness have stemmed directly from incoherent and problematic representation by member states within the United Nations.

PROGRESS TOWARD UN STRUCTURAL REFORM

General Assembly Resolution 32/197 (1977) called for restructuring at all levels of United Nations activity—intergovernmental, interagency, and Secretariat. To facilitate this process, the General Assembly assigned each part of the reform package to the relevant United Nations bodies for action. Given the compromises and ambiguities found within the recommendations, however, it has proved difficult to keep this fragile package of reforms from unraveling or to gain decisive movement on implementation.

In large part, the reform plans contain two basic types of directives. One set of recommendations involves definitions of roles and responsibilities of UN organs and also provides guidelines to govern the substantive thrust of United Nations actions. A second type deals with more short-term, specific measures relating to the functioning, structural arrangements and methods of work for United Nations organs.[15] In general, more progress has been achieved on specific types of reform than on the broader, more policy-based directives. Among the different levels of United Nations activity, there has been more restructuring movement on UN Secretariat matters than in other realms.

In the structural reforms relating primarily to intergovernmental affairs—those sections principally dealing with the General Assembly, ECOSOC, and other forms of negotiation—relatively little real change has resulted from the restructuring exercise. This lack of progress attests to the importance of substantive North-South negotiations as a conditioning factor for institutional reform. It is at this intergovernmental level that the linkage is most direct and compelling.

There has been an attempt to gain more effective Assembly involvement in setting system-wide priorities and in directing negotiations on international economic and social policy. But the lack of progress at the Eleventh Special Session of the General Assembly and on global negotiations has kept action on structural reform in abeyance. Indeed, the impasse has exacerbated institutional problems at this level, raising further questions about the role of the UN system in international economic cooperation. At the base of these difficulties are complex ties between UN institutional and substantive developments. For some time, different groups of member-states, especially the Group of 77, have tended to pursue various forums and institutional paths in approaching international economic matters. While this has preserved negotiating flexibility, the practical results have been, in the words of one UN official, to "keep too many things afloat, avoid commitments, and impede any movement on restructuring."[16] This tendency has been reinforced by a frequent Western pattern of agreeing to the creation of new machinery as a substitute for substantive concessions.[17]

The difficulties of structural reform at the inter-governmental level have been clearly evident in ECOSOC matters. Member states have been largely unable to agree on the enactment of restructuring guidelines. The Group of 77 has remained unwilling to use the Council in considering important North-South issues. Moreover,

Council reform has been stymied by widespread government attempts to preserve various subsidiary organs of ECOSOC favored by different national bureaucratic constituencies.

The restructuring guidelines can be criticized for their failure to deal realistically with ECOSOC. In many respects, ECOSOC reform—the question of representation and of ECOSOC's relation to the General Assembly—remains at the heart of UN restructuring problems at the intergovernmental level. Past difficulties at ECOSOC have led repeatedly to the creation over the years of other UN subsidiary bodies intended to fill the Council's deliberative role. In the face of its admitted inability to respond to UN restructuring recommendations, significant reformulation of ECOSOC will be required to restore its effectiveness.[18] Various proposals, ranging from transforming the Council to an organ of the whole membership to making it a more modest program review and coordination body, have been put forward. Some of these actions would require formal Charter amendment, a prior constraint on UN reform efforts. But, as one UN official has suggested, "In the long term, no matter what happens the most effective way to deal with ECOSOC will likely require Charter revision, since its membership will either have to be expanded, or eventually it will need to be abolished."[19]

A major difficulty for UN negotiating forums has been a prevailing institutional rigidity within the UN system, predicated upon strong symbolic associations or political attachments to existing UN arenas. For example, the legacy of UNCTAD as a favored body to press for changes in international economic relations may well inhibit its ability to serve as a prospective negotiating forum—particularly since other negotiating arenas have not produced the types of results that would lead the Group of 77 to forego UNCTAD's value as an instrument of advocacy within the United Nations system. This severely limits the adaptability of various UN bodies to multiple use. Thus, when new deliberations are considered, there is pressure for creating additional entities to house them—not so much to build greater negotiating or administrative capacities as to avoid raising political objections tied to the use of existing settings. In addition, as a UN official has pointed out, "The United Nations really has not been programmed for negotiations—only presenting policy options. So when you get down to actual negotiation not only do you face problems about where to house them, but also about methods of ensuring their effective conduct.''[20]

At the interagency level, UN reforms are aimed chiefly at achieving greater coordination and integration among diverse United Nations bodies and operations. In the area of UN regional activities, some progress has followed from the restructuring recommendations. Steps have been taken to upgrade the regional commissions to ensure that more analytical and technical cooperation activities are carried out at the regional level, as well as to provide for greater involvement of regional bodies in global planning and programming.[21] In July 1978, the Secretary-General reported that the commissions had begun operating as executing agencies for a number of regional and subregional projects. UN headquarters units were also identifying research and analysis activities that could be transferred to the regional level. However, the Secretary-General noted that additional movement in this direction would ''require strengthening of the capacity of the regional commissions to take on added responsibilities.''[22]

The issue of decentralization has long been contentious within the UN system. It brings to the surface underlying UN bureaucratic conflicts, raising basic questions about the arrangement of organizational tasks within the system. It also highlights divergent objectives among member states regarding the appropriate level of control and focus of UN activities. Moreover, the issue of decentralization runs directly into long-standing UN controversies, such as competing definitions of regions and different locations for the regional offices of specialized agencies.

In the restructuring guidelines, there were clear connections between reforms intended for the regional commissions and those aimed at the UN Secretariat. In 1979, the Committee for Programme and Coordination, with the full support of the Secretary-General and the General Assembly, was asked to review ''the distribution of tasks and responsibilities between the regional commissions and other United Nations units, programmes, and organs concerned.''[23] Such a review may provide a significant first step toward meeting UN reform objectives in this area, for there is a growing appreciation of the potential role the regional commissions can play in the area of policy and program coordination.

In the area of United Nations operational activities, restructuring action has focused on two major provisions: the convening of a single pledging conference and the establishment of a United Nations resident coordinator at the country level. In 1978, the first annual pledging conference was successfully held, setting into motion standard procedures for future conferences. In addition, members also agreed to designate a single UN resident coordinator, normally the UNDP representative. However, there has been little progress on the recommended creation of a single governing board for the management and control of all United Nations operational activities or on integrating UN development programs and funds financed by extra-budgetary resources. Indeed, since the adoption of the restructuring resolution, there has been continued proliferation of special trust funds, which now together amount to almost as much as total UNDP resources.[24]

Beginning in 1980, the Security Council and the General Assembly undertook a comprehensive policy review of United Nations operational activities. This review has been framed in the context of the restructuring recommendations and could represent a significant step toward meeting UN reform objectives in this area. But, as one United Nations official cautioned, "This undertaking runs headlong into significant interagency differences, and it must still accommodate member states' continuing desires to specify where they want their contributions to go."[25]

Bureaucratic struggles can also be seen in other areas of United Nations reform aimed at the interagency level, particularly regarding issues of coordination. Relations between UN headquarters and the specialized agencies have long been difficult, and UN restructuring efforts have acted to highlight areas of sensitivity. For example, restructuring plans gave increased emphasis to combining coordination and programming functions. This has prompted concern that headquarters units will begin to interfere with programs of other agencies such as UNESCO, many of which have traditionally been rather self-contained within the United Nations system.[26] Thus, the objective of a more integrated and coordinated United Nations system must contend with the components that still see themselves in decentralized and polycentric terms. But progress has been made in bringing together different parts of the UN system and coordinating activities in common or related areas. But as one UN official cautioned, "Interagency coordination cannot be done by fiat (i.e., Resolution 32/197). It must be done through a slow process of exposure, added resources devoted to interagency work, and a positive bent by the secretariats involved."[27]

At the level of United Nations Secretariat matters, notable restructuring activity has taken place since 1977, but many uncertainties about eventual outcomes still exist. The establishment of the three new headquarters units has been completed, and actions have been taken to reorient Secretariat activities in line with the restructuring recommendations. One resultant problem, however, has been an increased institutional separation of research and analysis from technical assistance within the Secretariat. But the most significant element of intended reform deals with the new Director-General for Development and International Economic Cooperation. As might be expected, the establishment of a new, high-level post that seeks to provide improved overall management and policy guidance within the UN system has encountered many difficulties and areas of resistance.

During his tenure as Director-General, Kenneth K.S. Dadzie assumed an increasing workload of responsibilities. For example, he was entrusted with the coordination of all preparations for the 1980 Special Session of the General Assembly and given responsibility for guiding and coordinating all Secretariat contributions to the new International Development Strategy (IDS). Among his other key assignments were the direction of preparations for the 1980 United Nations Conference on New and Renewable Sources of Energy and the development of a report on United Nations operational activities for a policy review by ECOSOC and the General Assembly. In addition, he often was called upon to settle jurisdictional disputes within the economic and social fields.[28]

However, this broad range of activity belies an underlying weakness associated with the Director-General position. Although the restructuring guidelines contained the basis for developing significant Director-General authority, the capacities and influence of this new post were unveiled more as potentialities than as enumerated powers. Indeed, as a former UN official noted, the Director-General was given "little more than a pair of gloves."[29] Thus, he was required to draw upon certain implicit strengths, such as a high-level relationship with the Secretary-General, rather than actual authority vis-à-vis different UN activities. Partially to compensate for the initial institutional vacuum surrounding the post, Dadzie began amassing operational assignments and building upon the strength of his performance in these areas. But his success in these capacities was largely attributable to personal skills—not to the authority of his position within the UN system. The result was that the institutional standing of the Director-General has not been appreciably strengthened or clarified. This ambiguity reflects the competing institutional forces and unresolved relationships that make up the UN environment as well as the diverse demands and expectations of member states. For example, the Group of 77 has looked to the Director-General for substantive and policy initiatives, whereas the developed countries have preferred that he stress improved management and coordination within the UN system.

The evolution of the Director-General position can be seen as a microcosm of the entire restructuring exercise. Indeed, the Director-General's post is critical to the evolution of UN structural change. In his high-level capacity, the Director-General can ensure that UN institutional developments at various levels conform as much as possible to prescribed reform designs. To realize this potential, however, the Director-General may well need to function in a leadership role more aligned to and derivative of the Secretary-General's office. Acting as a prominent spokesman for global development issues, he could focus upon supervising the UN Secretariat to achieve a coherent framework for its wide-ranging activities and harmonize the work of the specialized agencies vis-à-vis central UN organizations. Even though much momentum has already been lost in the restructuring process, the current crisis environment provides a possible opportunity for such a leadership role. In the words of one UN official, "Everyone is looking for a constructive way out of the current impasse. Since the [Group of 77] doesn't have the resources and the developed countries [do not have] the commitment, it falls to the UN leadership to come up with ideas and bases for moving ahead. Although this has not been the Director-General's orientation in the past, he could still mount a more statesmanlike perspective and renew both his role and that of the United Nations."[30]

THE RELATIONSHIP OF RESTRUCTURING TO POLICY PRIORITIES

UN restructuring seeks to reorient present organizational arrangements and guide prospective institutional development in order to improve the performance of the United Nations system. Although this exercise is still unfolding, it is likely that eventual outcomes will be measurably different—and much more modest—than the initial designs. But certain trends and basic issues concerning the future of UN structural change can be discerned.

One key consideration is the emphasis within the restructuring guidelines on decentralization. The regional commissions have now been upgraded as executing agencies and as "development centers." As such, they are to become more important in policy formulation and coordination. Movement in this direction has also gone beyond a regional focus. There has been an effort to achieve greater functional decentralization as well, attempting to carry out more activities away from the center at the target areas. In large part, this institutional trend conforms to a growing emphasis on "collective self-reliance" as a policy orientation within the United Nations system.

However, UN restructuring has also stressed greater institutional coherence and responsiveness, that is to say, a countervailing trend toward centralization. This can be seen in attempts to harmonize Secretariat and agency work with central policymaking. It is also reflected in measures intended to achieve greater system-wide responsiveness to policy preferences, particularly regarding the creation of a new international economic system.

Underlying the issue of the extent of centralization *or* decentralization within the UN system is the desire by member states to ensure that UN activities do not extend beyond their express direction and consent. The fear that structural rearrangements may result in UN action deemed contrary to some states' national interests is at once caused and exacerbated by a lack of international consensus regarding the objectives of UN economic and social work. Indeed, there is some concern within the United Nations about tying future UN institutional developments too closely to current international economic deliberations. Reflecting a generally functionalist position, it is argued that the structure and character of UN economic and social work should be more insulated from the uncertain ebb and flow of North-South relations. Others see the situation as a trade-off of "risk vs. relevance" for the United Nations, a dilemma that the UN will continue to face as long as it seeks to have meaningful impact in a world of sovereign and diverse nations.[31] In any case, the desire to control evolving UN developments acts as a fundamental constraint on any type of structural change.

Another important issue is the capacity of the United Nations system to become more multidisciplinary in its approach to policy problems. For some time it has been argued that global development needs could not be adequately addressed in an institutional framework that remained structured along sectoral lines. The rearrangement of UN Secretariat units was intended to enhance a multidisciplinary approach to international economic and social affairs. But as one UN official noted, the multidisciplinary focus "has not advanced much beyond the slogan stage. No real methodology or design has been worked out yet to yield practical results."[32] Developing such a capability also runs directly into bureaucratic opposition at both the national and international levels. Bureaucracies within member states as well as throughout the UN system have not been structured to consider policies and programs in cross-sectoral terms and they have resisted steps in that direction. Moreover, efforts to build such a capacity raise fears that whole new sets of institutions would be created on top of existing sectoral arrangements.

Any attempts to strengthen multidisciplinary activities within the United Nations must also contend with their political implications for North-South relations. The Group of 77 has voiced support for a more cross-sectoral approach to UN programming and deliberations because this would enhance the prospects for collective bargaining and trade-offs across different issue areas, thus creating more leverage for developing countries. On the other hand, Western governments—especially the United States—have continued to stress a sector-by-sector approach in order to minimize the pressure to make concessions and to exercise more control over the bargaining process.

The issue of how and where global negotiations should be structured has significant implications for UN structural reform. Continuing differences about the institutional framework and procedures of such negotiations indicate once again how important and divisive structural preferences can be at the intergovernmental level. They also attest to the continuing significance of institutional venue questions in international economic and social affairs, as well as the problems of international economic decisionmaking. Indeed, issues about UN decisionmaking procedures have gained increased prominence, as the Group of 77 pushed for the United Nations to become "the forum within which all negotiations of a global nature relating to the establishment of the new international economic order should take place."[33]

The current debate and actions on North-South negotiations point up how closely UN institutional and substantive matters are linked. They also indicate how important different concepts of policy direction are for the shape of future institutional patterns within the United Nations system. As Robert Cox has noted, there are numerous viewpoints on what the substance of the new international economic order should be, and each of these implies different structural arrangements to implement policy priorities.[34]

From the beginning, UN restructuring was to proceed both as a result of and in support of broad policy objectives in international economic and social affairs. It was also to be accompanied by the necessary cooperation among members to ensure a strengthened UN capability to meet these objectives. However, at this point, there is no clear and specific understanding within the UN system about the direction in which any new international economic system will eventually evolve. In such a situation UN institutional reform can proceed only in fits and starts or could even become disconnected from its original designs and pursued for its own sake. If this were to occur, it would further exacerbate the types of problems that led member states to seek UN structural reform in the first place.

Future UN institutional developments will also be shaped by consideration of which roles the UN will emphasize in its future work on economic and social questions. Since the 1960s, the United Nations was mainly involved in identifying new problems, legitimizing norms and policy preferences, and providing arenas and instruments to pressure action in these directions. It generally has been successful in performing these roles, especially regarding global development issues. Recently, greater priority has been given to the conduct of negotiations and the management of numerous development assistance activities. However, to perform these roles effectively, a greater degree of international consensus is required than now exists.

Over time, different groups of states have wanted the United Nations to do different tasks. The ambivalences and even contradictions found in these notions account for the United Nations' sprawling structure and have important consequences for UN reform. As one UN official has remarked, "structural trends must follow from a clear concept of role, and there is no shared view that could shape institutional development at this time."[35]

Whatever new roles the United Nations may undertake in the 1980s, they are sure to affect UN structural developments. For example, key questions about meeting basic needs among the world's poor, facilitating structural adjustments within industrial nations, accommodating growing differentiation among developing countries, and resolving global resource problems will likely be high on the UN agenda in the next decade or so. Their eventual disposition will probably provide many opportunities and constraints regarding UN structural change. Indeed, some observers believe that the evolving international system will require the formation of completely new institutional components.[36] Thus, UN institutional reform needs to be closely attuned to the roles UN organizations can and must play. The goals of reform in this respect should be the creation of an ongoing institutional capacity to carry out valued services and functions effectively, as well as the avoidance of involvements that cannot be pursued productively within existing economic and political constraints.

NEXT STEPS FOR UN STRUCTURAL REFORM

Thus far, most UN members—including the United States—have shown little indication that they are prepared to undertake the challenges of full-scale UN structural reform. As one former US official commented, "Despite the UN restructuring designs, this may not be an era for grand reform. Indeed, such efforts could easily backfire."[37] In this context, a more incremental approach to UN structural reform may be necessary, one that would involve identifying specific areas of UN activity where modest restructuring action could produce tangible improvements acceptable to all major groups of member states. Clearly, these actions would need to go beyond simple organizational mechanics and would have to be responsive to prevailing North-South considerations. Proceeding in this manner could act to insulate areas of feasible reform from issues that remain unresolved.

To some extent, a limited approach to UN restructuring would present a departure from the original premises of UN institutional reform in that it would disaggregate what was intended to be an integrated approach to structural change. But if it is thought that effective restructuring action is only possible when full agreement is reached on all related matters—including contentious issues within the North-South dialogue—then the whole question of reform will be deferred indefinitely, in effect foreclosing any prospect of effective change.

In taking an incremental approach to UN institutional reform, priority should be given to remedying the most glaring institutional problems and building the groundwork for subsequent progress in other areas. For example, steps can be taken to ensure that no new or ad hoc structures are created whenever suitable existing arrangements and bodies are available. These strictures could apply to UN operational activities as well as to negotiating forums. Additional efforts can also be made to strengthen planning and evaluation capabilities within UN institutions, particularly for developing greater system-wide coordination and responsiveness. Furthermore, the reformulation of ECOSOC can be given priority attention, since the Council has been a major source of difficulty within UN institutional development. Transforming it into a more effective body would remove obstacles to other restructuring activities. The aim of such a step-by-step approach should be to produce results wherever the necessary political will can be mobilized, to resolve institutional difficulties existing in selected areas, and to foster reform movement in other, more intransigent domains.

The impediments to structural reform on any scale are significant. They include indecision and disagreement at the intergovernmental level concerning the identity and future authority of the UN system in economic and social affairs. At the interagency and Secreteriat levels, structural reform confronts an institutional environment marked by autonomous and uncoordinated entities operating without clear lines of authority or accepted procedures for interrelating. Finally, the eventual coherence of the UN system remains subject to the character of government participation. All these difficulties have weighed heavily upon the process of implementing UN reform. Indeed, in the words of one UN official, ''The UN restructuring exercise has turned into a major disappointment. A real initiative to revive the UN has been lost, as the process has become increasingly routinized, spurned or left suspended.''[38]

US POLICIES ON STRUCTURAL REFORM:
A LOOK AHEAD

For the United States, incremental action on institutional matters is clearly preferable to more comprehensive plans for UN reform. But even within this more limited agenda, the United States will need to reexamine its positions regarding UN economic and social affairs. At the policy level, the US has continued to stress a case-by-case, functional approach to issues and deliberations. At the operational level, the United States has emphasized increased rationalization and efficiency almost to the exclusion of other issues. Given the politics of the UN restructuring exercise and its relationship to North-South issues, the American positions have proved problematic. They have often applied concepts inappropriate to the setting or maintained too narrow a focus. Moreover, this perspective has generated precious little capacity for innovation or initiative, thereby reinforcing an increasing sense of defensiveness that pervades much of US involvement in the UN system.

Within the current political and economic climate, it may be difficult, if not impossible, to muster any support for new and positive steps in these areas. As a former US official remarked, ''the environment has grown particularly harsh for UN structural reform, largely because a key inducement to gaining restructuring activity—the promise of additional resources and commitment to economic development within the UN context—has been effectively precluded.''[39]

Clearly, UN structural reform does not offer a panacea for the problems of American participation within the UN system. UN institutional matters cannot be separated from many of the factors that have caused growing US disaffection with the United Nations. Furthermore, UN structural change by itself cannot produce progress and effectiveness for UN actions in the economic and social fields. Such outcomes—as well as any meaningful UN reform—remain ultimately tied to the evolving will, commitment, and cooperation of all member states. However, despite its limits, the pursuit of UN structural reform has been important. It has provided an essential basis for forging needed improvements in the UN's economic and social work. Restructuring activity can also lead to more systematic examination and planning regarding American participation within the UN system. Even in an era of minimal reform possibilities, attempts to identify specific US interests and facilitate their implementation within a changing UN system would constitute a significant—and long overdue—advance for the management of US foreign relations.

In the end, it is the way in which nations approach and use the UN system that will determine the course of structural change and the character of UN institutional capabilities in dealing with pressing global problems. Although the US role in shaping these developments has clearly changed since the UN's origins, the continuing demand and need for international organizations require a concerted American effort to ensure a strong UN institutional capacity for managing international economic and social affairs.

Notes

1. Martin Hill, *The United Nations System* (Cambridge: Cambridge University Press, 1978), pp. 24–42 and UN document OPI/624, November 1978, pp. 1–3.

2. Ibid.

3. David A. Kay, ''The United Nations and United States Foreign Pol-

icy,'' in David A. Kay, ed., *The Changing United Nations: Options for the United States, Proceedings, the American Academy of Political Science,* Vol. 32, No. 4, 1977, p. 14. See also the Atlantic Council Working Group on the United Nations, *The Future of the UN: A Strategy for Like-Minded Nations* (Boulder: Westview Press, 1977) for further writing on the perceived UN "crisis." Discussion of past US government views on UN problems can be found in Andrew Young, "United Nations: Serving American Foreign Policy Interests," *Department of State Bulletin,* Vol. 79, number 2007 (June 1979), pp. 47–48. For discussion of the current US representative's views, see Bernard D. Nossiter, "Questioning the Value of the U.N.," *New York Times Magazine,* April 11, 1982.

4. Robert W. Gregg, "The Apportioning of Political Power," in Kay, ed., op. cit., p. 69.

5. For a report on US positions on UN structural reform, as well as on broader UN reform matters, see "Reform and Restructuring of the UN System," *Selected Documents,* No. 8, The US Department of State, Washington, DC, June 1978, and *Reform of the United Nations: An Analysis of the President's Proposals and Their Comparison With Other Countries,* Report for the Committee on Foreign Relations, US Senate, Washington DC, October 1979. My article "Restructuring the United Nations System: Institutional Reform Efforts in the Context of North-South Relations," *International Organization,* Vol. 32 (Autumn 1978), pp. 1000–1004, provides a discussion of US positions in the Ad Hoc Committee on Restructuring the Economic and Social Sectors of the United Nations System, 1975 to 1977.

6. US Department of State, "Reform and Restructuring of the UN System," op. cit., pp. 8–11.

7. Roger D. Hansen, "North-South Policy: What is the Problem?" *Foreign Affairs,* Vol. 58 (Summer 1980), p. 1107. See "Reform and Restructuring of the UN System," op. cit., p. 5, for US recognition that a "purely engineering" approach to UN reform is inadequate.

8. Hill, op. cit., pp. 4–5 and 18–19, provides further references to these studies. In 1965, there was also more formal UN reform, as the Charter was revised to expand Security Council membership from 11 to 15 states. Similarly, membership in ECOSOC was increased to 54.

9. UN documents A/32/197, p. 1 and A/1005, 1975, p. 8.

10. For more background, see Meltzer, op. cit., pp. 994–999.

11. UN document A/32/197 and its annex.

12. Meltzer, op. cit., p. 1017, for reference to the importance attributed to this decisionmaking development by the Group of 77. See also UN document A/33/202, p. 1.

13. Much of the preceeding discussion has been drawn from UN document CPI/624, November 1978.

14. UN document A/31/34 Add. 2, p. 23.

15. UN document A/33/410/Rev. 1, p. 30, discusses this distinction.

16. Personal interview, United Nations official.

17. Mahbub ul Haq, "A View from the South: The Second Phase of the North-South Dialogue," in Martin M. McLaughlin and the Staff of the Overseas Development Council, *The United States and the World Development Agenda 1979* (New York: Praeger Publishers, 1979), p. 115

18. ECOSOC decision No. 1979/57.

19. Personal interview, United Nations official. See UN document A/C2/35/L2, for reference to Charter revision to expand ECOSOC membership as a basis for instituting needed changes and effectiveness.

20. Hill, op. cit., pp. 165 ff; also, personal interview, United Nations official.

21. UN document E/1979/81, pp. 7–8.

22. UN document E/1575/118.

23. ECOSOC decision 1979/64 and GA Resolution 34/213.

24. Personal interview, United Nations official. See also UN document E/1979/81, p. 13.

25. Personal interview, United Nations official.

26. Ibid. See UNESCO document 110/EX/19 (22 August 1980) for discussion of disturbing trends in this area.

27. Personal interview, United Nations official.

28. UN document E/1979/81, p. 22; also UN documents A/33/202, pp. 3–4, and E/1979/81, p. 21.

29. Personal communication, former United Nations official.

30. Personal interview, United Nations official. It should be noted that Jean Ripert became the new Director-General in 1982.

31. Personal interview, United Nations official.

32. Ibid.

33. UN document A/32/PV. 109, p. 13.

34. Robert W. Cox, "Ideologies and the New International Economic Order: Reflections on Some Recent Literature," *International Organization,* Vol. 33 (Spring 1979), pp. 273 ff. See also the arguments put forward by Cox in this volume.

35. Personal interview, United Nations official.

36. Mahbub ul Haq has asserted that growing global interdependence and distributional needs will result in the "inevitable" creation of international institutions for a worldwide taxation system, an international central bank, and a global planning system. See Mahbub ul Haq, "A View from

the South: The Second Phase of the North-South Dialogue,'' in McLaughlin, op. cit., p. 115. Many observers think that another institutional need in the future is the creation of an international Secretariat for the Group of 77 so that members can be adequately prepared for emerging deliberations and actions.

37. Personal communication, former US official.

38. Personal interview, United Nations official.

39. Personal communication, former US official.

3. THE UN SYSTEM AND HUMAN RIGHTS

THE DEVELOPMENT OF UNITED NATIONS ACTIVITIES IN THE FIELD OF HUMAN RIGHTS AND THE ROLE OF NON-GOVERNMENTAL ORGANIZATIONS

NIGEL S. RODLEY[1]

During the past three decades the intensity of United Nations activity in getting states to agree to international standards on human rights, then in taking action against violations of the standards, has increased. In general, the UN has been more active and effective in "promoting" human rights (its norm-creation function) than in "protecting" these rights (i.e., in implementing the norms).[2] Non-governmental organizations (NGOs) have been active from the beginnings of the UN both in the attempt to develop an internationally agreed code of behavior constraining governments in the treatment of their citizens and in urging the UN itself to help enforce respect for the code.[3]

In this chapter, major developments in the elaboration of international human rights standards will be reviewed, followed by reference to attempts to create various international mechanisms and to make them work. Consideration will also be given to assessing the continuing enthusiasm of NGOs for both promotion and protection of human rights at the UN level.

UN ACTIVITIES FOR THE PROMOTION OF
HUMAN RIGHTS

Having lobbied actively at San Francisco for the maximum incor-
poration of human rights among the concerns of the United Nations,[4] it is not surprising that NGOs were active in the UN's work
to develop an International Bill of Human Rights. Proclaimed on
December 10, 1948, the Universal Declaration of Human Rights
remains, and may be expected to remain, the moral touchstone for
all claims at the international level that justice has not been done at
the national level. Its broad scope, ranging from its guarantees of a
fair trial to those of a right to adequate housing, health care, and
education, enables its provisions to be invoked explicitly or by implication to virtually any unfair overreaching or negligence of governments toward the governed.

At the time of the Declaration's adoption it held itself to be "a
standard of achievement for peoples and all nations." Accordingly,
governments did not consider themselves to be undertaking legally
binding obligations when voting for it.[5] It is not by accident that
the Universal Declaration contains no instrument for its enforcement and that the Commission that drafted it had already decided
in 1946 that it had no power to take action on complaints of human
rights violations, a position subsequently ratified by ECOSOC.[6] This
was the beginning of the emergence of the practice whereby states
were to prove themselves more willing to enunciate desirable standards as long as this did not involve direct legal obligation or multilateral implementation of the standards than they were when their
commitment involved legal obligations to implement defined norms.

It was not until December 16, 1966 that the General Assembly
adopted the other components of the International Bill of Human
Rights: the International Covenant on Economic, Social and Cultural Rights; the International Covenant on Civil and Political Rights;
and the Optional Protocol to the latter Covenant. (The former Covenant only came into force on January 3, 1976, and the latter one
and the Optional Protocol came into force on March 23, 1976.) By
the end of 1981, 71 countries had ratified or acceded to the International Covenant on Economic, Social and Cultural Rights, 69
countries had ratified or acceded to the International Covenant on

Civil and Political Rights, and 27 countries had become parties to the Optional Protocol.

The caution evinced by the low incidence of ratification of these instruments is paralleled by the careful, confined definitions in their provisions. Thus, the articles guaranteeing the so-called fundamental freedoms (movement, conscience, expression, assembly, and association) are hedged about with provisos permitting restrictions on their exercise on such grounds as national security, territorial integrity, public policy, public morality, and protection of the rights and reputation of others (Articles 12, 18, 19, 21, and 22). The scope of these concepts remains to be defined at the international level. (The restrictive approach of the regional-level organs of the European Convention on Human Rights is not encouraging.)

Given the practice of some countries to justify the suppression of any activity against the officially approved policy on the basis of these exceptions, it would certainly appear that many parties to the Covenant may not feel that its obligations are unduly onerous. The same observation may be made about the provisions of the International Covenant on Economic, Social and Cultural Rights, most of whose obligations are framed in terms of recognition of a need to work to achieve progressively the full realization of the rights recognized in the Covenant. The essentially programmatic nature of the rights makes such an approach essential. But so does the fact that there is no international consensus on what national economic and social systems are best suited to the attainment of objectives that, inter alia, guarantee the right to work, to social security, to an adequate standard of living, to the highest attainable standards of physical and mental health, and to education.

The system of implementation of the Covenants[7] may also be characterized as prudent, given the restricted degree of international scrutiny to which parties submit themselves. Under the International Covenant on Civil and Political Rights, the only automatic monitoring is provided for by Article 40, which obliges states parties to submit periodic reports to the Human Rights Committee, an 18-member group of experts elected by the states parties to the Covenant. In 1981–82 the Committee was still in the process of examining the first reports of states parties; it is thus far difficult to see how the Committee will use its power to induce states to comply with their obligations.[8] Individual Committee members characteristically pose questions on generally self-serving reports to government representatives. The responses frequently increase in vagueness in direct proportion to the specificity of the question, and the Committee has not shown itself disposed to insist on adequate factual answers to its members' questions. Indeed, despite sending several "reminders," as of the end of 1981 it had not even been able to elicit the first report of one state party—Uruguay. Nevertheless, at this early stage, the potential of the Committee's review of states' reports cannot be dismissed. The mere fact that representatives of states are called to appear before and respond (however inadequately) to questions from members of an intergovernmentally established body on matters of the most extreme sensitivity for most governments is a development of some magnitude in a field that international law used to consign to the realm of domestic jurisdiction.

A further, so far untested, power is granted to the Human Rights Committee under Article 41 of the Covenant, which provides for states to make declarations whereby the Committee can receive complaints of violations by them of the rights contained in the Covenant from other states that have made a similar declaration. Since the tenth declaration required to bring the Article 41 procedure into force was only deposited with the UN Secretary-General on December 28, 1978, and, given the relative homogeneity of the 14 states that have now made such declarations, it will probably be some time before the Committee's powers to reconcile interstate disputes will be exercised.

The most radical aspect of the Covenant system of protection is that contained in the Optional Protocol to the International Covenant on Civil and Political Rights. Under this protocol individuals residing in states that have ratified it can lodge complaints ("communications" addressed to the UN Secretary-General) alleging violations by ratifying governments of the rights guaranteed them under the Covenant. As of its 1981 report to the General Assembly, the Human Rights Committee had had 102 complaints from 13 countries placed before it. The Committee reported to the General Assembly that it found violations by Uruguay in respect of 14 "communications."[9] In one case, it concluded coyly that it could not find that there had *not* been a violation by Uruguay.[10] Only the first finding of a violation was before the General Assembly at its 34th session (1979). The next five findings were before it at its 35th session (1980) and another eight at its 36th session in 1981. Uruguay ignored these findings and the Assembly did not address itself to the matter at either session. This is a serious challenge to the authority of the only UN body formally and explicitly mandated to deal with individual complaints of human rights violations. Even though the Committee, not being a judicial body, has no power to give binding decisions, it will be regrettable if the flouting of its findings entails no formal political costs within the UN. Whatever the outcome, the very fact of these findings will reinforce the work of NGOs on behalf of specific individuals and groups, in terms of the legitimacy and accuracy of their own denunciations.

The system for monitoring implementation of the International Covenant on Economic, Social and Cultural Rights[11] is even weaker than that of the International Covenant on Civil and Political Rights, for the monitoring body is the Economic and Social Council of the United Nations (ECOSOC), an intergovernmental body, and not a group of individual experts invested with international status and called upon to act impartially. Despite the nonperemptory nature of most of the obligations contained in the Covenant, ECOSOC's powers are confined to the examination of reports submitted by states parties under Article 16 of the Covenant. It took ECOSOC until 1979 to establish a procedure for dealing with the reports (a sessional working group composed of 15 ECOSOC representatives of governments that are also parties to the Covenant studies the reports). The working group started considering reports of states for the first time at ECOSOC's Spring 1980 session.[12]

In view of the none-too-demanding nature of many of the substantive obligations of both Covenants, the inherent weakness of the basic system of monitoring compliance through consideration of reports submitted by states parties, and the limited number of states accepting stronger (and still not fully effective) measures of implementation under the International Covenant on Civil and Political Rights, it may be wondered why NGOs are committed to working for the widest possible ratification of the Covenants and the Optional Protocol. The following factors are relevant. First, some substantive obligations (for example, the right not to be subjected to torture) are reasonably unambiguous and may not even be suspended even in time of emergency. Although states may nevertheless fail to comply with them, as illustrated by the findings of the Human Rights Committee on the situation in Uruguay, the mere existence of these legally binding standards may serve both to inhibit flagrant state disregard for their provisions and strengthen the legitimacy of the work of NGOs as they campaign to hold governments to their international promises. Second, the weakness of the basic monitoring mechanism and even of the voluntary improvement on it contained in the Optional Protocol must be seen as part of a process. Campaigning for respect for human rights is essentially a technique of step-by-step application of the pressure of international public opinion. The more steps that can be brought into play, however modestly, the greater are the chances of some kind of success.

In addition to the general human rights documents contained in the International Bill of Human Rights, the UN has promoted the adoption of a large number of instruments, both legally binding treaties and resolutions of debatable and varying legal force on specific areas of human rights. These have dealt with such areas as women's rights, children's rights, workers' rights, rights of the disabled and of the mentally retarded, educational rights, and religious rights. Some, such as those relating to the rights of aliens and migrant workers, are still in the process of being drafted. The first of these was the Convention on the Prevention and Punishment of the Crime of Genocide adopted on December 9, 1948. It basically singled out the major crime against humanity as defined at Nuremberg and made it susceptible of national jurisdiction in the territory where the crime was committed and of international jurisdiction before any competent future international tribunal.

It took a significant change in the composition of the UN before serious attention was given to a less sensational but related area of human rights violation, namely, racial discrimination. It was not until 1965 that the Convention on the Elimination of All Forms of Racial Discrimination was adopted. This followed the adoption on November 20, 1963 of the United Nations Declaration on the Elimination of All Forms of Racial Discrimination (General Assembly

Resolution 1904 [XVIII]). The Convention,[13] which defines and prohibits discrimination on the ground of racial origin, established an 18-member Committee on the Elimination of Racial Discrimination (CERD) empowered to examine periodic reports submitted by states parties. It can also receive interstate complaints under Article 11, although none has been made since the Convention entered into force on January 4, 1969. Under Article 14, it may also receive complaints of violations from individuals in countries whose governments have deposited a separate declaration with the UN Secretary-General. As of the end of 1981 this procedure was not yet in force, the Secretary-General now having received only eight of the required ten declarations.

Because of the anti-colonial political context in which the Convention was adopted, the reluctance of states to make interstate complaints, and their unwillingness to permit individual complaints, the focus of CERD's activities has been on states or territories whose governments are not bound by the Convention. This trend was continued by the General Assembly's adoption on November 30, 1973 (Resolution 3068 [XXVIII]) of the Convention on the Suppression and Punishment of the Crime of Apartheid which declares apartheid to be a crime against humanity, defines the offense in vague terms, criminalizes individual participation in it, and makes persons accused of the offense subject to trial in any state party or extraditable to another state party. A working group of the UN Commission on Human Rights composed of three government members of the Commission and parties to the Convention examines reports submitted by state parties. Needless to say, the country that gave the word apartheid to the world is not a party to the Convention. Yet the countries that have ratified the Convention have not reported the institution of any proceedings against any South African officials who may have visited their territories with or without diplomatic immunity.

General NGO involvement in the adoption and promotion of these instruments has not been marked despite the fact that a number of NGOs are committed to combatting racial discrimination. This may be explained by the fact that this particular cause already has a preponderant governmental constituency, which has made the NGO contribution less necessary. However, NGO promotion of declarations permitting individual complaints under Article 14 of the Convention on the Elimination of All Forms of Racial Discrimination could become more effective in the years ahead.

One area where there has been abundant UN activity in the standard-setting sphere is that of torture and areas related to it. This is also an area where NGOs have been particularly active inside and outside the UN and where UN bodies other than the Commission on Human Rights have played leading roles.[14]

The UN first took up the question toward the end of 1973, the year during which Amnesty International launched its Campaign for the Abolition of Torture and published a world survey of torture that attracted significant public attention.[15] On November 2, 1973, the General Assembly adopted Resolution 3059 (XXVIII), in which it rejected any form of torture and other cruel, inhuman or degrading treatment or punishment and decided to examine the question at a future session. Within a year the issue was back before the General Assembly which, by Resolution 3218 (XXIX) of 6 November 1974, requested the Fifth UN Congress on the Prevention of Crime and the Treatment of Offenders to draft rules on the question and to develop an international code of police ethics relevant to the question, and invited the World Health Organization (WHO), in cooperation with UNESCO, to draft similar principles for medical personnel. The Fifth Congress prepared a draft in 1975 of what was to become, with minor amendment, the General Assembly Declaration on the Protection of All Persons from Being Subjected to Torture or Other Cruel, Inhuman or Degrading Treatment or Punishment (Declaration Against Torture—Resolution 3452[XXX] of December 9, 1975). The Declaration did not go as far as some NGOs had wanted—namely, declaring torture to be a crime under international law—but it did condemn it as a denial of the purposes of the UN Charter and confirm its criminal nature, its unacceptability under any circumstances, and the importance of a number of legal safeguards in preventing its occurrence. NGOs were active at the 1975 Congress, by way of written submissions, oral interventions, and participation in the working group that amended the original draft declaration submitted by The Netherlands and Sweden.[16] For the NGOs, provisions such as those calling for the impartial investigation of evidence of torture, even where there has been no complaint, and for the inadmissibility in court of evidence obtained under torture would be of assistance in their efforts to make governments more responsive to NGO initiatives.

The Congress had recognized the need for a police code but had not been able to agree on one; [17] WHO had not acted on the Assembly's request concerning principles of medical ethics. Accordingly, on the same day as it adopted the Declaration Against Torture, the General Assembly (Resolution 3453 [XXX]), asked the 15-member Expert Committee on Crime Prevention and Control to draft a code of conduct for law enforcement officials, renewed its request to WHO concerning principles of medical ethics, and asked the Commission on Human Rights to prepare a body of principles on the human rights of persons under any form of detention or imprisonment. NGOs were very active in discussions of the drafts submitted to the Committee. Indeed, Amnesty International commented on a draft submitted by The Netherlands to the Fifth Congress that was before the Committee and was itself based on a draft prepared by Amnesty International. [18] The text of the final UN Code of Conduct for Law Enforcement Officials (General Assembly Resolution 34/169, December 17, 1979), while not as far-reaching as NGOs had suggested, did reflect a number of their proposals.

Faced with the new request of the General Assembly, the Executive Board of WHO went to an NGO, the Council for International Organizations of Medical Sciences (CIOMS), to ask it to prepare appropriate principles of medical ethics. The CIOMS, in turn, approached other NGOs, including NGOs in consultative status with WHO, such as the World Medical Association which had already adopted its own Declaration of Tokyo against Torture, and other NGOs not enjoying such status but expert in the field of working against torture. A draft prepared by CIOMS was forwarded by the WHO Executive Board to the UN General Assembly in January 1979 and is presently before the Assembly. Its Principle 4 goes to the heart of the matter: ". . . it is a contravention of medical ethics for physicians to apply their knowledge and skills in order to assist in methods of interrogation or to certify prisoners or detainees as fit for any form of punishment that may adversely affect physical or mental health."

The Assembly's request to the Commission on Human Rights to

draft a body of principles on the human rights of persons under any form of detention or imprisonment was potentially the most far-reaching. The Assembly's resolution had explicitly asked the Commission to take account of the Draft Principles on Arbitrary Arrest and Detention that the Commission had been working on in the early 1960s [19] but on which it had then been unable to reach agreement. The momentum of the torture issue was reviving concern for an area that was perceived to be closely related to torture, for experience had shown that torture occurs most frequently when detained persons are at the unsupervised mercy of those holding them and denied access to the outside world.

NGO observers were able to participate actively in the deliberations of the working group and the plenary discussion in the Sub-Commission on Prevention of Discrimination and Protection of Minorities. It is the clear view of a number of NGOs that the Body of Principles placed before the General Assembly would, if adopted, represent a major compilation of important internationally accepted limitations on those in authority to seize and hold those they govern without accountability. [20]

The General Assembly also undertook further initiatives in 1977. One of these was the adoption of a resolution of some legal ingenuity whereby states were encouraged to deposit with the Secretary-General unilateral declarations of their commitment to be bound by the Declaration Against Torture (Resolution 32/62 on December 8, 1977). As a contribution devised and promoted by Third World countries, this was seen as a welcome manifestation of concern in an area in which initiatives had been largely left to a number of Western countries.

Another initiative was the GA's request to the Commission on Human Rights to draft a convention based on the Declaration Against Torture. The draft submitted by the government of Sweden in 1978 is being worked on by the Commission. [21] It has many points in common with a draft prepared by the International Association of Penal Law (IAPL) and submitted at the same time. [22] The IAPL draft was framed by a specially convened group of experts, including legal experts from human rights NGOs and from governments, including that of Sweden. [23] Both drafts include the principle of universality of jurisdiction and the obligation to try or extradite suspected torturers. Meanwhile, the International Commission of Jurists has succeeded in persuading Costa Rica to introduce a draft optional protocol according to which governments would permit access to all places of detention by an international enquiry body.[24] It is too early to predict the outcome of this process.

UN ACTIVITIES FOR THE PROTECTION OF HUMAN RIGHTS

NGOs have been particularly enthusiastic in promoting and using available UN machinery as a way of dealing with allegations of human rights violations. Reference has already been made to the implementation mechanisms in the various human rights treaties. These do not, however, offer a direct role for NGOs except as victims themselves of violations of the treaty provisions. However, a number of mechanisms have been developed within the UN that have encouraged significant NGO efforts to supply relevant information.

While maintaining its long-standing policy of refusing to deal with the substance of individual human rights complaints, the Commission on Human Rights sought and received authorization from ECOSOC in 1967 to "examine information relevant to gross violations of human rights and fundamental freedoms" and to "make a thorough study of situations which reveal a consistent pattern of violations of human rights" (ECOSOC Resolution 1235 [XLII]). Within months NGOs had submitted information, not only on the expected southern African countries, but also on such countries as Greece (recently subjected to the regime of the colonels) and Haiti.[25] The Sub-Commission on Prevention of Discrimination and Protection of Minorities which first dealt with these complaints then duly referred them to the Commission.

This responsiveness to NGO information was perhaps too rapid. As a result of such vigorous NGO activity, the Sub-Commission and the Commission sought ways to restricting open NGO access to public UN procedures. This led to the adoption by ECOSOC of a new resolution in 1970 dealing with "communications," alleging the existence of "particular situations which appear to reveal a consistent pattern of gross and reliably attested violations of human rights requiring consideration by the Commission'' (ECOSOC Resolution 1503 [XLVIII]). This ''1503 procedure'' authorized the Commission to investigate or make thorough studies of situations falling within the scope of the resolution referred to it by the Sub-Commission, which in turn could only act on the basis of recommendations from a working group of five of its members. Until such time as the Commission decides to make recommendations to ECOSOC, all proceedings are to be confidential.[26]

It was not until 1979 that the Commission first brought one of the situations before it into the public domain, although one year earlier it had taken the step of making public the names of the countries it had been dealing with in confidential sessions. In this instance, the Commission sought and received authorization from ECOSOC to remove the restrictions on the file of Equatorial Guinea and to appoint a special rapporteur to make a thorough study of the situation in that country.[27] This move was made after it became clear over a period of six years that there would be little cooperation from the Macias Nguema regime, then in power. What is of special interest in this case is that the record of UN consideration of the case (contained in a report by a special rapporteur presented to the Commission on Human Rights on February 12, 1980) is the first of its kind to enter the public domain.[28] However it must also be noted that the authorization for the study was received on the eve of that regime's overthrow in a coup and that the study was then conducted with the agreement of the new government.

The dilatory nature of the procedures described in this case history hardly inspires confidence in its effectiveness. On the other hand, NGOs see some value in it as an additional means of pressure. Governments usually attend Commission meetings to defend themselves when being considered under the 1503 procedure and, indeed, some lobby extremely vigorously to avoid any Commission action. In other words, the cost to the governments of human rights violations is increased. It also may not be naive to hope that as the Commission accustoms itself to the idea of actually using the procedure, its inhibitions will diminish.

As can be seen from the final stage of the Equatorial Guinea case, it remains open to the Commission to take up cases in public session, for example, under ECOSOC Resolution 1235 (XLII). What this requires is a delegation willing to raise and document a case followed by a majority of votes for the proposal. Until recently, this had only happened, other than in connection with an international armed conflict, with regard to the countries of southern Africa and Chile. More recently the ranks have been increased to include Bolivia, Democratic Kampuchea, El Salvador, Guatemala, and (pre-Sandinista) Nicaragua. Indeed, in 1980, the case of Soviet Academician Andrei Sakharov's internal exile was discussed and, while no specific action was taken, the Commission formally decided to deal with it as a priority item at its 1981 session.[29] Although NGO written communications are dealt with confidentially, NGOs can supply information to individual delegations. They may also make oral interventions before the Commission and Sub-Commission where they are permitted to make explicit references to concrete country situations. In addition, the past three years have indicated a certain flexibility in the practice of the Secretary-General in permitting the circulation of short, written NGO statements that contain references to specific human rights situations. Both of these possibilities, while not capable of directly initiating Commission action, might affect the climate in which delegations discuss a particular country.

The Sub-Commission has had only limited success in trying to establish a special mechanism to deal with torture. Although it decided in 1974, as part of its annual review of the question of the human rights of persons subjected to any form of detention or imprisonment (Resolution 7 [XXVII]),[30] to request information on this matter from NGOs, the synopsis that was made available to the Committee did not mention the names of the countries whose barbarities were being described.[31] This may indicate why fewer and fewer NGOs are devoting resources to preparing material for this item. The Sub-Commission on a number of occasions sought authorization from its superior bodies to establish a working group to prepare its annual review.[32] Perhaps such a group would have been able to work in public and deal with the original versions of NGO submissions that remain theoretically available to the Commission. Unfortunately, each time the request went unheeded. Accordingly, in 1981, the Sub-Commission decided to establish a sessional working group on the topic.[33] The working group dwelt for some time on how it should operate, and general comments were made on various aspects of detention and the need for legal safeguards.[34] It was to be hoped that the precedent would be repeated, so that NGOs, which had this time been unprepared for the initiative, would be in a better position to contribute information and ideas.

The Sub-Commission has had more success on a narrower aspect of this area of its concerns. At its 1979 session it proposed that it should be authorized to establish a working group of its members to deal with the problems of what the General Assembly has called "enforced or involuntary disappearances." It would have been empowered to take emergency action on such cases. The recommendation went to the Commission on Human Rights, which, at its thirty-sixth session in 1980 decided to create a working group of its own members for a period of a year to examine the question. The group's powers were not spelled out, although it was expected to act in an "effective and expeditious manner." The working group met three times after authorization by ECOSOC and, from its report, seems to have interpreted its powers not only to examine the thousands of cases of disappearances already on file, but to take speedy measures to bring pressure for official recognition of new unrecognized captures, the facts of which were made available to the group by NGOs and others. It is to be hoped that its annual mandate will continue to be extended by the Commission and ECO-SOC.[35]

TRENDS: RHETORIC AND REALITY

Attempts by the United Nations to define its human rights role in programmatic terms have tended to cause gloom in human rights circles in the West. This is because a majority of UN members prefer to put the accent on economic and social development rather than on how much civil and political freedom they grant their citizenry. In 1968 the UN proclaimed:

Since human rights and fundamental freedoms are indivisible, the full realization of civil and political rights without the enjoyment of economic, social and cultural rights is impossible. The achievement of lasting progress in the implementation of human rights is dependent upon sound and effective national and international policies of economic and social development.[36]

At the time this statement was made, it could have been interpreted as providing balance to an earlier paragraph of the same Proclamation:

> The primary aim of the United Nations in the sphere of human rights is the achievement by each individual of the maximum freedom and dignity. For the realization of this objective, the laws of every country should grant each individual, irrespective of race, language or political belief, freedom of expression, of information, of conscience and of religion, as well as the right to participate in the political, economic, cultural and social life of his country.

By 1977, however, the General Assembly was reaffirming the first of the paragraphs just quoted, but not the second. In resolution 32/130 of December 16, 1977, for example, the Assembly put the accent on massive violations of collective rights and spoke of according priority to the realization of the new international economic order, since this was "an essential element for the effective promotion of human rights and fundamental freedoms."[37] Fifteen countries, mainly Western, abstained in the vote.

The main effect of this Resolution has only been to add an agenda item or two to the work of the Commission on Human Rights, while that body increased the amount of time it was already spending on the general question of violations of human rights and on the human rights of persons subjected to any form of detention or imprisonment, i.e., the two items of most interest to the human rights NGOs. Some of the major standard-setting advances and precedent-setting developments taken in these areas since 1977 have already been described above. So has the timid way in which ECO-SOC has embarked on its task, under the International Covenant on Economic, Social and Cultural Rights, of monitoring the far-from-stringent obligations of parties to that Covenant. Once the reality of governments' economic and social performance is open to scrutiny, this area of human rights concerns seems to assume a different priority for them. There is little reason to conclude that examination of civil and political rights has been sacrificed to economic, social, and cultural rights.

From the point of view of a human rights NGO, then, the history of UN activity in the field of human rights should be seen as one of achievement, particularly in the field of promotion of human rights standards, where progress has been more rapid. It is sometimes tempting to write off the standards as a manifestation of intergovernmental hypocrisy. But even if the standards represent no more than the tribute vice pays to virtue, they have constituted the bedrock on which NGOs have been able to base their work. They have permitted NGOs to say to governments that they are not seeking to impose their own morality on governments, rather, that they are merely insisting that governments abide by their own agreed values. This is no mean argument. Even in the field of human rights protection, the slow-moving creation and utilization of mechanisms have been an extra avenue of pressure on governments that violate the standards.

It is not unreasonable to expect that NGOs will continue their policy of looking to the United Nations for further developments in the fields of promotion and protection. For example, while Amnesty International has decided that it is no longer a priority to seek further international standards in the field of torture and the rights of prisoners, other than as regards those still in the process of elaboration, it is making a serious effort to induce the UN to adopt a stronger line in favor of the abolition of the death penalty.[38] Other NGOs are still working to have the Commission on Human Rights draft a convention on children's rights and to have it give full recognition to the right of conscientious objection to military service. Many NGOs will continue to seek to advance the institutional mechanisms available to protect human rights, for example by advocating the creation of a UN High Commissioner for Human Rights, or by advocating that the mandate of the new Commission on Human Rights group on disappearances be extended to cover all cases where the life or safety of a captured person is menaced. Similarly, they will certainly continue to submit information to the existing mechanisms in the expectation that these will still represent a source of pressure on a growing number of the governments whose practices are denounced.

Notes

1. The views expressed herein are those of the author alone. This chapter seeks to be accurate as of December 31, 1981.

2. In practice, the distinction oversimplifies what actually happens. The development of norms has sometimes been inextricably linked with the development of mechanisms of implementation. This is illustrated by the elaboration and adoption of the International Bill of Human Rights. There are other areas of activity that do not fall neatly into these categories. The *promotion* of human rights education and awareness, including dissemination of information about national and international standards and mechanisms, may well be considered a vital aspect of the *protection* of human rights.

3. Since NGOs are frequently established to work against particular practices of injustice, according to their respective mandates, their interest in the norm-creating side seems to suggest that they see this as, itself, an aspect of the protective function in which they are already engaged. The UN's work on standards for arrest and detention will be seen to illustrate this. See David Weissbrodt, "The Role of International Nongovernmental Organizations in the Implementation of Human Rights," in *Texas International Law Journal,* Vol. 12, No. 2/3 (1977), p. 293; Peter Archer, "Action By Unofficial Organizations on Human Rights," in David E.T. Luard (ed.), *The International Protection of Human Rights* (New York: Praeger, 1967), p. 160; Nigel Rodley, "Monitoring Human Rights Violations in the 1980's," in Jorge I. Dominguez, Nigel S. Rodley, Bryce Wood and Richard Falk, *Enhancing Global Human Rights* (New York: McGraw-Hill, 1979), p. 117; Antonio Cassese, "How Could Nongovernmental Organizations Use the UN Bodies More Effectively?" in *Universal Human Rights,* No. 4 (1979), p. 73.

4. See Archer, op. cit., p. 168.

5. See John Humphrey, "The UN Charter and the Universal Declaration of Human Rights," in Luard (ed.), op. cit., p. 39; "The Universal Declaration of Human Rights: Its History, Impact and Juridical Character," in B.G. Ramcharan, *Human Rights; Thirty Years After the Universal Declaration of Human Rights* (The Hague: Martinus Nijhoff, 1978), p. 21.

6. Indeed, the next stage of the development of the International Bill of

Human Rights was to be the elaboration of a treaty that would spell out the norms with greater precision and would contain a monitoring or enforcement mechanism. ECOSOC Resolution 75 (V), (August 5, 1947). See Jacob Möller, "Petitioning the United Nations," in *Universal Human Rights*, No. 4 (1979), p. 57.

7. See Bertie Ramcharan, "Implementing the International Covenants on Human Rights," in Ramcharan (ed.), op. cit., p. 159.

8. The Report of the Human Rights Committee to the 1981 General Assembly depicts the Committee in so far inconclusive discussions as to what form its "general comments" might take. However, there seemed to be no consensus in favor of country-specific comments. See UN Document A/36/40 (1981), pp. 81–84.

9. Ibid., p. 91.

10. UN Document A/35/40 (1980), p. 110.

11. See Ramcharan (ed.), op. cit., pp. 160–74; and also "Implementation of the International Covenant on Economic, Social and Cultural Rights," in *Netherlands International Law Review*, Vol. 23, No. 2 (1976), p. 151.

12. UN Document E/1980/60 (1980).

13. See Thomas Buergenthal, "Implementing the UN Racial Convention," in *Texas International Law Journal*, Vol. 12, No. 2/3 (1977), p. 187.

14. See Virginia Leary, "A New Role for Non-Governmental Organizations in Human Rights: A Case Study of Non-Governmental Participation in the Development of International Norms on Torture," in Antonio Cassese (ed.), *UN Law/Fundamental Rights—Two Topics in International Law* (Rockville, MD: Sijthoff & Nordhoff, 1979), p. 197.

15. *Report on Torture* (London: Amnesty International, 1975), Revised Edition.

16. See UN Document A/CONF. 56/10 (1975), Paragraph 291.

17. Ibid., paragraphs 254–258.

18. UN Document E/AC. 57/NGO 2 (1976).

19. "Study of the Right of Everyone to be Free From Arbitrary Arrest," UN Document E/CN. 4/826/REV.1 (1964).

20. See Niall MacDermot, "Report of the UN Sub-Commission on Discrimination and Minorities," in *Review of the International Commission of Jurists*, Vol. 21 (1978), p. 21.

21. UN Document E/CN. 4/1285 (1978). This draft has been considered by a working group whose 1980 report contains details of agreement so far. See UN Document E/CN. 4/1475 (1981), pp. 51–69.

22. UN Document E/CN. 4/NGO/213 (1978).

23. "La Prévention et la Suppression de la Torture" (The Prevention and Suppression of Torture), in *Revue International de Droit Penal,* Vol. 48, No. 3/4 (December 1977).

24. UN Document E/CN. 4/1409 (1980).

25. See John Carey, *UN Protection of Civil and Political Rights* (Syracuse, N.Y.: Syracuse Unversity Press, 1970), p. 86.

26. See Möller, note 6, above, passim; Nigel S. Rodley, "Monitoring Human Rights by the UN System and Non-Governmental Organizations," in *Human Rights and American Foreign Policy,* Donald P. Kommers and Gilbert D. Loescher (eds.), (Notre Dame, Ind.: University of Notre Dame Press, 1979), p. 157.

27. UN Document E/CN. 4/1371 (1980).

28. It was not, however, the first thorough study to have been approved by the Commission. As a number of governments, including that which took power in Kampala in 1979 have made public, that unannounced honor went to the Uganda of Idi Amin in 1978, several years after the International Commission of Jurists and, subsequently, Amnesty International, had submitted voluminous dossiers on the atrocities in that country. Even then Uganda was able to stall so long that the thorough study was not undertaken within the 15 months or so between the time it was authorized and the rather more radical remedy administered by the Tanzanian army.

29. See the *Commission on Human Rights: Report on the 36th Session,* UN Document E/CN. 4/1408 (1980), Chapter X. At its next session, the Commission decided "to take no decision" on a number of draft resolutions including one on the Sakharov case. UN Document E/CN. 4/1475 (1981), p. 102.

30. Kathryn Burke, "New United Nations Procedure to Protect Prisoners and Other Detainees, *California Law Review,* Vol. 64 (1976), p. 201.

31. Resolution 4 (XXVII), (September 10, 1975), UN Document E/CN. 44/Sub. 2/364 (1975), Chapter XXI.

32. For the last attempt, see Sub-Commission Resolution 17(XXXIII), (September 11, 1980), UN Document E/CN. 4/Sub. 2/495 (1980), Chapter XVII.

33. UN Document E/CN. 4/Sub. 2/495 (1981), p. 31.

34. Ibid., pp. 34–36.

35. UN Document E/CN. 4/1435 (1981).

36. "Proclamation of Teheran," in *Human Rights; A Compilation of International Instruments,* UN Document ST/HR/1/REV. 1 (1978), p. 18.

37. See Theo Van Boven, "United Nations Policies and Strategies: Global Perspectives?" in Ramcharan (ed.), op. cit., pp. 88–91.

38. See, for example, *The Death Penalty: Submitted by Amnesty International to the Sixth United Nations Congress on the Prevention of Crime and the Treatment of Offenders,* UNC Document A/CONF. 87/NGO/AI/1 (1980); Amnesty International Publication AI Index: ACT 05/17/80 (1980).

III

PUBLIC ATTITUDES AND PUBLIC PARTICIPATION IN THE UN

US PUBLIC OPINION AND THE UN

PAUL D. MARTIN

The tremendous importance of the role that the United States has played, and continues to play, in the United Nations is well-known. The US was a leader among the founders of the Organization, supplied much of its early funding, and helped to endow it with its moral and political legitimacy. These facts are thoroughly explained and analyzed in other chapters of this book.[1]

A significant influence on US policy towards the UN is, of course, public opinion. As with most government policies, foreign policy is an area of intense interest to many citizens. Some have emigrated from another country to the US, others have families in a foreign country. Americans have familial, business, and financial ties with virtually every nation on earth. Support or opposition to government policies by citizens interested in other countries has often been instrumental in shaping US foreign policy.

In the last few decades, the emergence of the US as the leader of the free world has served to heighten interest in foreign policy. Every citizen in the US has come to be aware of pressing international issues such as the East-West strategic conflict, the Arab-Israeli wars, and the attempts to limit nuclear proliferation. Fear has grown that local clashes may escalate into nuclear confrontation. The US is now perceived by its citizens to be more vulnerable than ever before to events elsewhere in the world.

In addition, the oil embargo by the Arab members of OPEC, and the subsequent attempts by the Third World countries to use their critical raw materials and commodities as a lever to gain political concessions, have accentuated this feeling of vulnerability and have brought home to Americans the interdependent nature of today's world. Farmers in Iowa now worry about grain surpluses and deficits in the USSR, China, and a host of other countries. Planners for aerospace industries nervously watch events in southern Africa, the source for many of the rare metals needed in the manufacture of their products. These factors have all served to make the American public aware, as never before, of the intricacies of US foreign policy.

American foreign policy deals with the United Nations, among other things. To say that the UN plays the central role in US foreign policy would be as untrue as to say that it plays no part at all. The US Ambassador to the UN does have cabinet rank, and the US does use the Security Council and General Assembly, when it can, as a forum for mobilizing world opinion in support of its position. The US government continues to spend a considerable amount of talent, time, and money on the United Nations.

Both because of its role as a focus for US policy, and because of its perceived legitimacy as a forum for world opinion, the UN is, quite naturally an institution of some interest to the American public. Public interest is undoubtedly heightened both by the proximity of the UN and by the crisis nature of many of the UN actions and discussions that are reported to the press. Since the late 1970s, and particularly since the Reagan Administration came to power, many more government officials and private groups and citizens have begun to express dissatisfaction with the UN.[2]

For over 35 years pollsters have been canvassing US citizens to try and determine their attitudes toward the UN. Polls, often the same polls, are cited as evidence both by those arguing for US withdrawal from the UN and by those arguing that the Organization should be strengthened. For example, news reports about the results of a 1980 Roper poll were variously headlined "UN Rates Poorly," "UN's Rating Drops in the US," "Americans Reject Isolationism," and "Poll: Americans Support UN."

How could such contradictory remarks be based on one set of data? What *do* Americans think of the UN and why? Is support for the UN increasing or decreasing? The answers to these questions are of critical importance, not only to US policymakers, but also to the UN itself, and to the future relationship of the US with the rest of the world.

THE 1980 ROPER POLL

In August 1980, the Roper Organization conducted interviews of 2001 Americans as part of a survey commissioned by the United Nations Association of the USA (UNA-USA).[3] Among the questions were standard polling questions that have been asked by a wide variety of pollsters over the last 30 years to assess public sentiment towards the UN, thus facilitating comparison of responses with those of other polls in the past (see next section). The survey sought both to determine public attitudes toward the UN, and to gain insights into the reasoning behind these attitudes. The results of this poll led to the odd assortment of newspaper headlines cited above.

The poll produced some striking results: although 53 percent of those surveyed believe the UN is doing a "poor job," fully two-thirds of the respondents favor maintaining or increasing US participation in the UN. Burns W. Roper, chairman of the Roper Organization, wrote in an article entitled "UN at 35: A Pollster Peers at a Paradox" that "these findings capsulize the American public's feelings about the UN. The majority who say it is doing a poor job are, for the most part, not condemning it. Rather, they are expressing their disappointment that it is not more effective than it is in dealing with tough world problems."[4]

In order better to understand public attitudes toward the UN and how they are measured, it is worth spending some time analyzing the Roper poll commissioned by the UNA. Respondents were asked six questions by the interviewer about their attitudes toward the UN. Two of these questions asked directly about their opinions of the UN and of US participation in it. The other four questions sought to establish the deeper beliefs underlying the first two answers.

When asked "In general, do you feel the UN is doing a good job or a poor job in trying to solve the problems it has to face?" a majority of respondents were critical:

Good job   30 percent
Poor job   53 percent
Don't know   18 percent

Yet, to the question "What is your opinion—should the US increase or should it decrease its participation in the UN?" the following results were obtained:

Increase   40 percent
Decrease   21 percent
No change   26 percent
Don't know   14 percent

The answers to these two questions present the apparent paradox referred to by Burns Roper above: a substantial majority (66 percent) want US participation in the UN to either increase or remain at the present level, while at the same time over 50 percent are dissatisfied with the organization. Critics of the UN, and those favoring a US withdrawal from the organization, tend to cite only the majority of responses giving the UN a "poor job" rating. UN supporters and those wishing to strengthen US participation in the UN sometimes downplay the high degree of criticism of the organization expressed by much of the public, and focus on the apparent commitment to the UN as expressed in the desire to increase US participation in it.

For these reasons the answers to the four in-depth questions that were included in the Roper poll are particularly enlightening. In general, they seem to offer some measure of support to the contention that the public would like to see a stronger, more effective UN.

The survey asked whether the US should try to get along on its own economically and politically, or whether it should work with other countries to solve the economic and political problems it faces. The three possible answers, and the percentage of responses in favor of each, were as follows:

Rely on our own economic and political strength,
even if this creates economic problems for us and
disagreements with our allies   17 percent
Work closely with our friends and allies to protect
our common interests throughout the world, even if
this means increasing our economic and military
commitments   42 percent

> Work with both our friends and enemies to further
> develop a system of international rules and organi-
> zations for solving problems together, even if we
> would sometimes have to go along with decisions
> we disagree with   32 percent

The answers to this question, with a total of 74 percent opting for
some form of multilateral cooperation, demonstrate a solid rejection
of isolationist policies by a margin of more than four to one. While
this suggests a strong preference for international cooperation in
general, it is important to note that only one in three Americans
specifically favors working through universal international organizations. Even so, that one-third of the public is willing to give first
priority to a foreign policy that presupposes compromise (i.e., "we
would have to go along with decisions we disagree with") is very
significant.

A fourth question sought to identify what types of issues respondents thought the US could handle better through the UN than
it could acting on its own. A list of issues was presented to the
respondent, who was asked whether he or she favored US use of
the UN on each issue. The following percentages on the six issues
were recorded:

Getting our hostages out of Iran	45 percent
Getting Soviet troops out of Afghanistan	39 percent
Settling our differences with the OPEC countries over the availability and prices of oil	36 percent
Handling the economic differences between richer and poor countries	35 percent
Resolving the racial and political problems of southern Africa	31 percent
None of them (volunteered)	14 percent
Don't know	11 percent

While the percentages favoring use of the UN on these issues were
large in many cases, on no issue did a majority believe that action
through the UN could be more effective than unilateral or bilateral
action by the US. It is interesting, however, that the percentages
favoring US action through the UN on such issues as the US hostages in Iran and the Soviet invasion of Afghanistan were substantially higher than one would have expected given the high percent-

age of "poor job" ratings the respondents gave the UN overall.

That 14 percent responded that none of the issues could be handled better through the UN than by the US alone can probably be strongly correlated with the 17 percent of the Americans which answered that the US should rely on its own strengths rather than seek international cooperation in solving the problems it faces (see the preceding poll question). These two results together suggest that there is a small but solid isolationist group who will oppose any form of international cooperation on virtually any issue.

The fifth question was in two parts and asked respondents to identify which of several possibilities listed were strong arguments for increasing and which were strong reasons for decreasing US participation in the UN. The following list of arguments in favor of *increased* US participation received the indicated results:

Smaller countries need a place to make their voices heard	42 percent
Some problems can only be solved by developing agreement among all nations, and the UN is in the best position to do this	40 percent
Without the UN the danger of war is greater	39 percent
UN agencies like the World Health Organization and the Food and Agricultural Organization have been very successful in doing such important things as eliminating smallpox and improving the production and distribution of food	38 percent
The UN is uniquely suited to develop rules of international behavior which help all countries get along better	28 percent
UN peacekeeping forces make a real contribution to peace	24 percent
Economic assistance through the UN is the most effective way to help poor countries develop	23 percent
None of them (volunteered)	7 percent
Don't know	10 percent

Again it is worth noting that none of these were rated by a majority of respondents as strong arguments for increased US participation in the UN. It is also interesting that the role of the UN as a forum and as a solver of universal problems was cited more often than its role in preventing war and peacekeeping, originally its primary mission.

The second part of this fifth question offered a list of arguments for *decreased* US participation in the UN. Among the reasons most often cited for decreased participation in the United Nations were the following (with the percentages indicated next to them):

Differences among member countries make it impossible for the UN to act quickly or decisively	42 percent
The UN has very little real power to enforce its decisions	41 percent
The money we give to the UN is wasted on bureaucrats and too little reaches those who need it	38 percent
The US is outvoted and criticized unfairly, especially by undemocratic countries	28 percent
Many of the things the US does in the UN could be done more effectively by working directly with individual countries or groups of countries	24 percent
The less developed countries have too much influence in the organization	15 percent
The UN is anti-Israel	8 percent
None of them (volunteered)	6 percent
Don't know	13 percent

Many of the reasons relate to the perception of the UN as a slow-moving, ineffective, and inefficient organization. Arguments reflecting the belief that United States interests could be pursued more effectively outside the UN were selected by smaller percentages. Given the criticisms regularly levelled against the UN in the press and elsewhere, it is remarkable to find Third World domination and anti-Israel bias ranking so low on the list.

The sixth and final question asked respondents whether or not they believed that the US should ratify various international treaties and covenants regarding human rights, genocide, racial discrimination, civil and political rights, and economic and social rights that have been prepared by the UN. Although some of these treaties date back as far as 1948, the US has consistently refused to ratify them for a variety of reasons. The results of the poll question were:

Favor ratification of the human rights treaties and covenants	48 percent

Oppose ratification   25 percent
Don't know   28 percent

The response to this question is of importance both in relation to the treaties themselves and with respect to the public's general attitudes toward such international undertakings. The results, while heavily in favor of ratification, are somewhat ambiguous due to the very large number of "don't know" responses.

In general, the survey demonstrated some interesting differences among various segments of the population. Younger respondents, between the ages of 18 and 29, were much more likely to be supportive of the UN than those in the older groups on all issues except peacekeeping. The existence of this new "UN generation," born during the lifetime of the Organization and favorably predisposed towards its work, is a hopeful sign for those supporting the UN.

Responses also indicate that women tend to be less critical of the UN than do men, and that blacks are generally more favorable than whites. Persons with higher education tend to be both more critical of the UN's shortcomings and to be more likely to support a strengthening of the UN.

There is no marked difference between conservatives, moderates, and liberals or between Democrats, Republicans, and independents in their assessments of the UN's performance and problems, although liberals and Democrats were somewhat more likely to see the value of talking problems out at the UN than were the other groups. Somewhat surprisingly, of the three party affiliations, Republicans register the greatest level of support for increased participation in the development of rules of international behavior in the UN, and show a high commitment to the work of the UN's specialized agencies.

The traditionally internationalist Northeast can no longer be clearly identified as such in this poll—indeed, the responses of people in the Midwest to many of the poll questions are as "internationalist" as those from the Northeast, while the West is now the region most likely to support the UN. The Northeast and the West are about equal in their level of criticism of the organization.

Despite wide variations, criticism of the UN can be found in all major demographic groups. However, in key groups such as those with incomes over $25,000, executives and professionals, and those identified as politically and socially active, positive assessments were generally much more common and in many cases actually constituted solid majorities of the responses.

Those groups with relatively large "don't know" responses—women, low income people, blacks, those who had not graduated from high school, and people living in rural areas—also gave the UN a relatively low percentage of negative ratings. Those groups that gave the UN relatively high percentages of positive ratings also appeared to be much more homogenous than the groups comprising the negative and "don't know" categories.

A considerable amount of attention has been paid to the results of the 1980 Roper Poll in the belief that this most recent poll is particularly relevant for those interested in public attitudes toward the UN. The data is both relatively current and detailed, and allows for a thorough analysis of what people actually do think about the UN. Writing about the poll, Elliot Richardson, a former cabinet officer who is now chairman of the UNA-USA, concludes that "these results suggest that Americans are looking with clear eyes at today's world, recognizing that the time is past when, unaided, American power and wealth could by themselves protect and advance American interests everywhere. They understand that the serious problems now facing the world can be solved only on a broad multilateral basis."[5]

While there is room for disagreement about what issues should be dealt with in what international forum and how much should be done on the regional level, as opposed to being done through universal international organizations, this poll certainly does seem to bear out those who wish to see the UN strengthened. However, a poll is nothing more than a snapshot of one instant in time. To fully interpret it, one must analyze it against the background of past polls in order to try and identify the direction of the various dynamics that a poll captures in stop-motion. In short, is support for the United Nations increasing or diminishing?

TRENDS IN PUBLIC OPINION

The 1980 Roper poll is only the latest in a long series of polls that have sought to measure public opinion of the UN.[6] As early as 1942, three years before the UN was founded, pollsters were exploring the nature and degree of public support for a postwar "union of nations."[7] When the UN was launched at the San Francisco Conference in 1945, an overwhelming majority of the American public supported it. A 1945 Gallup poll showed a 20 to 1 margin favoring Senate ratification of the UN Charter.[8]

Despite its auspicious beginnings, the UN soon ran into problems. As discussed in other chapters of this book, the wartime unity of the Allied powers broke down soon after the war, and the emergence of the Cold War virtually immobilized the UN Security Council.[9] As the Soviets extended their control throughout Eastern Europe, the international environment became one of increasing hostility between two ideologically and militarily competitive blocs.

The United States had, by the mid-1950s, extended its military, economic, and political leadership over much of the world, and this was clearly reflected in the UN. Votes in the UN were most often overwhelmingly in support of US initiatives and positions. In terms of US foreign policy, there is no doubt that this was the period during which the UN was most clearly meshed with the objectives of US foreign policy.

The emergence of a nonaligned bloc had already begun by the mid-1950s. By 1964, many of these developing countries had gained their independence and, as a group, had come to constitute a majority of the UN General Assembly. Increasingly, issues of economic and social justice became the central topic of discussion at the UN, and the US found itself more and more often in the minority of states voting against radical reform of the international system—a system that had served US interests very well for more than two decades. Actions taken by the UN General Assembly against traditional US friends and allies such as Taiwan, Israel, and South Africa underscored that the UN was no longer a US-dominated institution.

Against this background, it is hardly surprising that US attitudes toward the UN began to shift soon after the UN was established. The 20 to 1 margin of support of 1945 eroded gradually until, in 1977, it was only a margin of about 5 to 1. Table I summarizes the results of several polls taken between 1951 and 1977, which asked "Are you in favor of US membership in the UN, or are you opposed to it?"

Table I[10]

Pollster	Date	Oppose Membership	Favor Membership	Undecided
Roper	1977	13%	70%	17%
Roper	1976	15	77	8
Harris*	Nov. 1975	18	56	26
Roper	Aug. 1975	11	68	21
Gallup	Feb. 1975	11	75	14
NORC	1973	15	79	6
Gallup	Jul. 1967	10	85	5
Gallup	Nov. 1963	8	79	13
Gallup	Jan. 1962	9	86	5
NORC	1956	6	88	6
Gallup	Nov. 1951	13	75	12

*A Gallup poll in November 1975 gave different results (16% opposed, 74% in favor, and 10% undecided). The differences may be accounted for either by a slightly different wording of the question or by its being asked in a different order, either earlier or later in the interview.

Support for US membership in the UN slipped considerably between 1945 and 1951, probably due to the East-West stalemate in the Security Council, but by 1956 public support for continued membership reached an all-time high of 88 percent. The period of high support continued until the early 1970s; indeed, it was not until 1975 that support decreased to the levels of the early 1950s. The period of greatest support for the UN roughly coincided with the period of US domination of the organization. The level of support reached its lowest level point to date in 1975—at about the time the General Assembly adopted its resolution equating Zionism with racism. Yet it is also apparent that support for the UN had begun to decline before this issue arose.

Relatively large shifts in the percentage of those favoring membership have not been matched by similar fluctuations in the numbers favoring withdrawal. Even when the favorable rating dropped from 75 percent to 56 percent in 1975, the percentage favoring withdrawal rose from 11 percent to 18 percent. This finding is consistent with the 1980 Roper poll and suggests that there is a relatively small core of true isolationists among the general public.

Generally paralleling the responses concerning membership in the

Table II

Pollster	Date	Good Job	Poor Job	Don't Know
Roper	Aug. 1980	30%	53%	18%
Roper	1977	32	39	29
Gallup	Dec. 1975	33	51	16
Gallup	Jan. 1975	41	38	21
Harris	Jul. 1974	46	47	7
Harris	Sep. 1972	35	56	9
Harris	Oct. 1970	35	56	9
Gallup	Spr. 1970	44	40	16
Gallup	1967	49	35	16
Gallup	1956	51	37	12

UN, polls have indicated substantial shifts in American beliefs about the effectiveness of the UN. Table II shows the responses given between 1956 and 1980 when citizens were asked whether they would rate the UN as doing a "good job" or a "poor job."

There has unquestionably been a significant shift in public opinion on this issue, with a majority of Americans now believing that the UN is doing a poor job. Yet, here too, there are ups and downs, and these findings must be balanced against those of the 1980 Roper poll, which indicate a strong desire on the part of the public to strengthen the UN. What these findings show is that the public has no illusions about the UN's problems.

Other polls confirm the hypothesis that public support for the UN has decreased substantially from its high point in the early and mid-1960s. Table III shows the answers given when respondents were asked whether or not the US should cooperate fully with the UN.

Superimposed on Figure 1 are arrows indicating several events of the 1960s and 1970s that are often said to have had an impact on public opinion of the UN. It is clear that there was, in fact, a considerable drop in support in 1970 at the time when Taiwan was expelled from the General Assembly and was replaced by the People's Republic of China. Likewise, the adoption of the General Assembly resolution equating Zionism with racism appears to have had a strong negative (if short-term) effect on public opinion.

By contrast, events such as the two Middle East wars of 1967

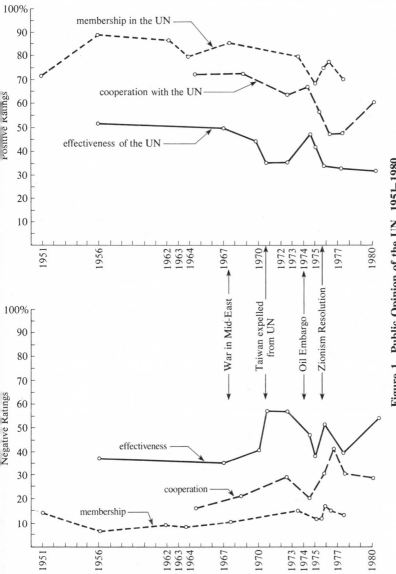

Figure 1. Public Opinion of the UN, 1951–1980

Table III

Pollster	Date	Cooperate Fully	Not Cooperate Fully	Don't Know
Civic Service	1980	59%	28%	13%
Roper	1977	47	30	23
Potomac Associates	1976	46	41	13
Potomac Associates	1975	56	30	14
Potomac Associates	1974	66	20	14
Potomac Associates	1972	63	23	9
Potomac Associates	1968	72	21	7
Potomac Associates	1964	72	16	12

and 1973, and the Arab oil embargo of 1973–74 appear to have had relatively little effect on US attitudes toward the UN, despite the UN being associated in some ways with each, at least in the public mind.

INTERNATIONALISM AND ISOLATIONISM

In an article titled "Internationalism Comes of Age . . . Again," Lloyd Free and William Watts analyze some of the poll results discussed above, together with some polls on more general aspects of public opinion on international issues. They write, "All the results point consistently to the mid-seventies as a watershed period in the recent history of American attitudes. The principal answer may be found in the fundamentally sober assessment Americans made at that time about the world around them and especially the effects of the tragedy in Vietnam." [11]

By combining the percentages of responses to a variety of questions, they established categories of respondents that they labelled as "Total Internationalist," "Mixed," and "Total Isolationist." Their results appear in Figure 2 below. [12]

Comparing Figure 2 with Figure 1 suggests that there may be an underlying upward trend in general internationalist sentiment that, by 1980, had only begun to have an impact on attitudes toward the UN. If this is in fact the case, then polls taken in the next few

Percent

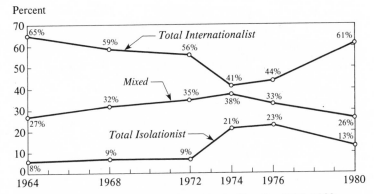

Figure 2. Internationalist/Isolationist Trends, 1964–1980

years may well show an increase in support for the UN in line with the increase in internationalism.

It seems unlikely, however, that any general increase in support for the UN will necessarily show up as a marked improvement in assessments of the UN's performance. At present, even groups most supportive of the UN's work and goals are extremely critical of the UN's present performance.

As part of its project on "The UN System at 35," the UNA-USA held discussions within its hundreds of local chapters across the US on the future of the UN and the US role in the United Nations. The UNA is an organization dedicated to increasing knowledge and support of the UN, and its members are among the most positive of groups regarding the UN. Idealism, however, is not coupled with unbridled optimism concerning either the present capabilities of the UN to mediate political strife between nations, or the UN's ability, without stronger support from its members for doing so, to establish priorities for dealing with emerging international problems. In a report summarizing the attitudes of UNA chapters across the country toward the UN, local members of the UNA are described as seeing the UN as caught between the demands thrust upon it by the Third World and pressures from many developed countries to resist radical reforms; its limited political authority is seen as inadequate to deal with regional instabilities or the momentum of the arms race.[13]

There is a sense that, with the increase in the economic and social problems of the world, "the need for the UN is greater, not less than it was in 1945," but that the shared vision which guided "what the UN should be or should be doing" in those years is irretrievably gone. The proper US response to these changes, according to many local UNA groups, "is not to give everything away out of guilt for having too much;" rather our "special role" is "to provide the resources, the technology and organizational know-how and the ability to take the initiative." By developing a "new consensus" within the UN sensitive to US priorities as well as to the national concerns of other countries, the process of change—political or economic—can be managed in a way that is not necessarily or inherently threatening to US national interests.[14]

As noted above, simultaneous support for and criticism of the UN is common to a variety of "elites"—the executives and professionals, the highly educated, the highly paid, and those people who are active politically and socially. Support from such groups has often been the cornerstone upon which American government policies, both foreign and domestic, have been built in the past. Those arguing for US withdrawal from the UN should be aware that they have little sympathy from those extremely important groupings. On the other hand, those concerned about how well international organizations are doing their job and interested in improving their level of performance will find much in common with elite opinion about the UN.

CONCLUSION

US public attitudes toward the UN seem at first glance to be paradoxical and even contradictory. There has certainly been a drastic decrease in support for the UN, particularly since the early 1970s, but there has also been a slight upward trend since 1976. The substantial increase in internationalist sentiment during the same period suggests that opinion of the UN may also be on the upswing. But it is also clear that the UN will have to get its house in order if there is to be any change in the American public's perception of how the United Nations does its job. The level of dissatisfaction is real and only a better run organization, one that is less politicized and less willing to take sides, can begin to deal with these criticisms.

The easy response to pressures for too much change too soon is to ''get tough'' or to disengage selectively from the UN's specialized agencies. This is often viewed in this country as a way to bring international organizations into line with US priorities. But the fact is that the United States can no longer control the UN, let alone world events, and that other countries will continue to use the UN as a forum for presenting and pressing their demands for change in the international system.

If the United States chooses to disengage or withdraw from the UN, disagreeable subjects will not disappear. This country will merely deny itself an opportunity to present its point of view on issues of concern to the world community, thus blocking lines of communication and eliminating the possibility of a constructive US role in international efforts to resolve tensions. The responses of the American public in poll after poll show an instinctive understanding that this country cannot afford to pursue such a defensive, ostrich-like policy.

The American approach to change, and to the future role of international organizations, will undoubtedly continue to emphasize incremental adaptations and reform as well as stricter control of UN activities and funding. As a result, the US will continue to find itself often in the minority, voting against radical economic reforms supported by the Third World or against resolutions that unfairly criticize our friends and allies. US public opinion will certainly be influenced, as it has been in the past, by this seeming isolation from other countries, and this will continue to be a source of dissatisfaction with the UN. On the other hand, if the United States is prepared to actively engage itself in the UN—and if the United Nations is prepared to meet it halfway—there is no question that the American public is willing, even eager, to support these efforts.

Notes

1. See especially the chapters by Leon Gordenker, Richard Bissell, and Donald Puchala in this volume.

2. An example of this criticism is the report issued by the Heritage Foundation under the title *The United States and the United Nations: A Balance Sheet,* Report No. 162, The Heritage Foundation, January 21, 1982.

3. The information in this section is taken from a report by the Roper Organization to the United Nations Association of the USA of the results to several questions asked by Roper interviewers as part of *Roper Reports* Survey, #80–8, August 1980. This information is summarized in a UNA-USA report, "Analysis of Data in the Roper Poll on US Public Attitudes Towards Foreign Affairs," October 1980.

4. Burns W. Roper, "UN at 35: A Pollster Peers at a Paradox," *The Christian Science Monitor,* October 24, 1980.

5. Elliot L. Richardson, "With a 'But,' Americans Still Back the UN," *New York Times,* October 17, 1980.

6. Information on other early polls on the UN can be found in William A. Scott and Stephen B. Withey, *The United States and the United Nations,* prepared for the Carnegie Endowment for International Peace under the auspices of the Survey Research Center, University of Michigan (New York: Manhattan Publishing Co., 1958), and in Alfred O. Hero, Jr., "The American Public and the UN, 1954–1966," *Journal of Conflict Resolution,* Vol. X, No. 4.

7. Scott and Withey, op. cit.

8. George Gallup, "The Gallup Poll," press release, March 16, 1975.

9. See especially the chapters by Leon Gordenker and Richard Bissell in this volume.

10. The data in Tables I–III are taken from polls released by the Roper Organization, the Harris Survey, the Gallup Poll, the National Opinion Research Corporation (NORC), Potomac Associates, and Civic Service Incorporated. The date of the polls are given in the tables.

11. Lloyd Free and William Watts, "Internationalism Comes of Age . . . Again," *Public Opinion,* April–May 1980.

12. Table reprinted from ibid., p. 49 with kind permission of the publishers.

13. Toby Trister Gati, *The UN System at 35: Chapter by Chapter,* UNA-USA, August 1981.

14. Ibid., pp. 7, 8, 13–14. Quotes are from the reports submitted by various UNA chapters throughout the country.

METHODS OF MULTILATERAL MANAGEMENT: THE INTERRELATIONSHIP OF INTERNATIONAL ORGANIZATIONS AND NGOs

ANGUS ARCHER [1]

Observers of the United Nations and other multilateral bodies are well acquainted with at least two distinct breeds of people who make these organizations function. The international civil servants are the economists and administrators, the writers and interpreters, the planners and bureaucrats who distill the information, prepare the reports, and administer the programs of one of the most complex systems of organizations in the world. The second group consists of the international diplomats, the ambassadors, delegates, and secretaries who serve as the official emissaries of their governments.

This chapter is about a third breed of people who inhabit the UN and other international organizations. They are the representatives of non-governmental organizations (NGOs), an awkwardly negative title coined by the United Nations to describe a vast range of international and national citizens organizations, trade unions, voluntary associations, research institutes, public policy centers, private government agencies, business and trade associations, foundations, and charitable endeavors. Many of these people are volunteers, retired, or representing their organizations in their spare time. A growing number are professionals with solid careers in their field of expertise. Some have been diplomats or civil servants; others will be in the future. Many are genuine idealists working long and hard for little recompense to promote goals or concepts in which they fervently believe and which, in most cases, are identical to the ideals of the United Nations itself. They all belong in the UN buildings and at the regular meetings no less than the civil servants or the diplomats, even though their role may be less obvious, and even less understood, and their outward appearance as a breed less uniform, less official, and less formal.[2]

Many of the international organizations these people represent have national affiliates in 80, 90, or 100 of the UN member states. A few of them have millions of members; most have thousands. Their relationship with the UN is embedded in the Charter itself and has been a constant feature of almost all aspects of the UN's work since the beginning.

Some observers tend to downplay the role of NGOs as a nuisance factor, as a fifth wheel on a four-wheel machine, as a collection of "little old ladies in tennis shoes." While there are aspects and incidences of the non-governmental–intergovernmental organization (NGO–IGO) relationship that have justified some of these attitudes, the relationship between the two is, on balance, clearly a mutually beneficial one. Many of the traditional ties with the NGOs from the early days of the UN are stronger and more important today than ever. Furthermore, there are several *new* forms of relationship between the UN and NGOs that have developed over the past ten years which will make the role of the NGO's even more important in the UN and in other intergovernmental institutions in the decade of the 80s.

Robert Cox, in a paper appearing in this volume, cites three new forms or levels of multilateral negotiation and management which, in his opinion, deserve attention:

1. Formal international institutions and their secretariats, both of which are used as instruments for aggregating positions by different groups of countries (UNCTAD by third world countries, OECD by rich developed capitalist countries, etc.);
2. Formalized coordinating bodies that serve as mechanisms

for arriving at common positions among different groups of countries (the nonaligned countries, the Group of 77, the Geneva group of principal contributors to the UN and other international budgets); and

3. Less formal networks created to do some of the initial thinking, planning and mobilizing of support (the Third World Forum, the Trilateral Commission, the Club of Rome, etc.).

Cox goes on to say that while levels 2 and 3 are the least studied, they "may be the most critical parts of the current political process of international organization."[3]

This chapter looks at level 3, using some examples of NGO networks, and illustrates both the inherent strength and the tremendous untapped potential for a much greater NGO role in the UN organizations. Dealing chronologically with the early forms of UN–NGO relationships (from 1945 on), the new forms of NGO involvement with the UN particularly manifested by NGO participation in the thematic UN Conferences (from 1970 on), and some new approaches of the UN towards NGOs (from 1975 on), the chapter then concludes with some recommendations for strengthening these relationships in the future.

TRADITIONAL FORMS OF NGO–UN RELATIONSHIP (1945 ON)

THE ECOSOC CONSULTATIVE STATUS RELATIONSHIP[4]

The origins of "consultative status" are to be found in the Charter of the United Nations adopted in San Francisco in 1945. If the San Francisco Conference was a "novum" in international relations, then Article 71 was a "novum" in intergovernmental–non-governmental relations. This Article specifically provided that:

The Economic and Social Council make suitable arrangements for consultation with non-governmental organizations which are concerned with matters within its competence. Such arrangements may be made with international organizations and, where appropriate with national organizations after consultations with the Member States of the United Nations concerned.

It is almost certain that the inclusion of this Article in the Charter was due to the advocacy of the United States delegation and that this advocacy was due, in turn, to strong NGO pressure. The very large US delegation had attached to it as "consultants" no less than 42 American non-governmental organizations. The consultants as a group met twice weekly with the US delegation to present and press their views. The Conference itself adopted Article 71 without opposition but without any marked enthusiasm.

An analysis of American NGOs attached as consultants reveals that no less than 29 were concerned with broad social problems and the attendant issues of human rights and peace. This emphasis may well explain why consultative status was granted exclusively to and by the Economic and Social Council (ECOSOC) and not, for example, to the Trusteeship Council, the Security Council, or the General Assembly itself.[5]

This consultative status relationship is clearly the most important of all the traditional (or formal) ways in which NGOs relate to the UN. Close to 700 organizations, most of them international, a few national, are so listed. About 150 of them are members of the Conference of NGOs in Consultative Status (CONGO) which has committees and sub-committees in New York and Geneva that wield considerable NGO power and influence.

It is fair to say that the effectiveness of this formal relationship, and certainly the enthusiasm with which it has been embraced by either side, has fluctuated over the years. In the 1940s and early 1950s the relationship was strong. The most active and effective international non-governmental organizations were those concerned with social and humanitarian concerns. ECOSOC, too, was primarily concerned with these issues. Of its seven functional commissions at least five were of vital importance (and still are) to NGOs, namely the Commissions on Human Rights, the Status of Women, Population, Social Development, and Narcotic Drugs.[6]

In the late 1950s and the 1960s several developments occurred that tended to weaken this basic relationship. In the first place, because international economic issues at the UN tended to be diffused throughout the UN system, the specialized agencies wooed NGOs to their respective folds. Secondly, many of the "status" NGOs seemed to be more concerned with the mechanics and prestige of their status than their role in the issues. Some international NGOs began to lose contact with or respect for their national affiliates or to lose effectiveness as organizations altogether. Thirdly, the level of governmental (diplomatic) representation on the "NGO committee" of ECOSOC dropped to very junior grades and the committee itself decided to meet much less frequently, thereby slowing up the process of accreditation and the granting of status. The amount of prior notification of ECOSOC agenda points and the opportunities for NGO inputs either before or during ECOSOC sessions were curtailed. In general, by the end of the 1960s the consultative status relationship was at a low ebb.

Events in the 1970s precipitated new forms of UN–NGO relationships. The result was a resurgent interest in the formal "consultative status" relationship coupled with renewed questioning of some of its early assumptions and narrow constrictions. Concurrent with the moves toward restructuring of the UN and the changes in the role and relationship of ECOSOC[7] has been the beginning of a sweeping review of the non-governmental organizations in consultative status and some rethinking of the "status" relationship altogether. This review is still under way.

RELATIONS WITH THE UN'S DEPARTMENT OF PUBLIC INFORMATION

Less than a year after the creation of the UN, in February 1946, the Office (now Department) of Public Information (DPI) established an NGO section to provide a regular and systematic flow of information on UN activities to interested NGOs. A procedure for "listing" NGOs was established, which included those in consultative status and also many national NGOs with a particular interest in UN programs. The listing procedure was and still is much less formal than the procedure for the granting of consultative status (approval is granted by an in-house Secretariat committee rather than by an intergovernmental committee).

The advantage of the DPI–NGO relationship is its outreach (actual and potential) to a large number of NGOs, the regular weekly briefings provided for NGO representatives in New York, and special facilities such as NGO lounges and documentation supply in New York and Geneva. Some of the 60 UN Information Centres scattered around the world try to duplicate these services in their own countries and renewed efforts are now being made to expand this outreach still further.

The major drawback in this relationship is its inevitable one-way flow. Being part of the Department of Public Information, the NGO section is a part of the outflow of information on the UN to the various disseminators such as press, radio, television, NGOs, and the interested public. Because there is little opportunity for input from the NGOs *to* the UN, the relationship has tended to perpetuate the notion that the UN provides information and "expertise," and that NGOs are passive recipients. While this function is practical and necessary, it should be noted that it is only part of the overall process of NGO involvement in global management. With the advent of new forms of NGO–UN relationships at the various world conferences and the General Assembly Special Sessions, the NGO section of DPI has been able to involve NGOs in many aspects of these events. As a result, this DPI–NGO relationship has taken on new forms.

SPECIALIZED AGENCIES—SPECIAL RELATIONSHIPS

Many of the specialized or related agencies of the UN system, particularly the larger ones such as FAO, UNESCO, WHO, UNHCR, and UNEP have developed quite elaborate relations with NGOs interested in their particular fields of competence. Since the specialized agencies have their own governing councils and conferences, they have established procedures for inviting particular NGOs as observers to these meetings. UNEP, the UN Environmental Program, has established an Environmental Liaison Board in Nairobi. Some of the other specialized agencies have conducted particular campaigns that have relied heavily on NGO involvement and support such as FAO's Freedom from Hunger Campaign/Action for Development and UNESCO's World Literacy Campaign. UNDP took an early initiative to foster field-level cooperation between operational NGOs and multilateral development projects. Other agencies of the UN system, including the World Bank, encourage their field staff to work more closely with NGOs on development projects, particularly since NGOs in many developing countries are the best carriers of social services, including credit schemes, to rural populations.

Of all the campaigns of the specialized agencies, FAO's Freedom from Hunger Campaign during the 1960s was the most dramatic and effective in terms both of mobilizing public support in the rich countries for solutions to the problems of world hunger, but also for developing and encouraging indigenous field-level NGOs in the rural areas of the poor countries.

NEW FORMS OF UN–NGO RELATIONSHIPS DEVELOP IN THE 1970s

No other form of United Nations activity over the past ten years has generated so much interest and participation on the part of NGOs as their involvement in the special United Nations conferences related to international development. Partly because the conferences themselves were designed to attract public attention and to disseminate information as widely as possible, and partly because NGOs were ready to take a global approach to development problems, the special conferences of the United Nations have become rallying ground for many different NGOs. The conferences have illustrated the full, and in many instances a new, potential of NGOs in international cooperation for development.

Many of the NGOs, particularly those with origins in the Western industrialized countries and having a "missionary" base, can claim involvement in the process of international development dating back to the nineteenth century. Their concern was motivated by humanitarian ideals and their activities largely confined to transferring resources, ideas, or technical skills from the developed to the developing countries. Generally speaking, NGOs shunned any broader "political" role, either nationally or internationally. This began to change with the coming of the first United Nations Decade for Development in the 1960s as more and more NGOs broadened their basic humanitarian concern to include the root causes of hunger, poverty, and underdevelopment and the more political but highly relevant issues of international trade, commodity arrangements, transfer of technology, world food policy, and international economic and social justice.

The UN series of special conferences have, in varying degrees, focused United Nations activity and public attention on specific aspects of development. They have brought together in one place and at one time the various and often scattered United Nations interests in one particular issue and they have dealt with the issue from all perspectives—the humanitarian and the conceptual, as well as the economic and the social. Some of these special conferences, such as the first and the second World Food Congress organized by FAO (1963 and 1970) were designed in large part for NGOs. But more often these international gatherings have been intergovernmental conferences, with an NGO component or "parallel activity."[8] It seems clear that many lessons learned from the involvement of NGOs in these UN-related conferences of the last ten years could be applied to the whole relationship of NGOs to the United Nations system.

The first NGOs to indicate interest and preliminary involvement in these conferences have been the international NGOs in consultative status, either with ECOSOC or a specialized agency or both.[9] Among these, the largest group has been that of NGOs based in the Western industrialized countries. Many of these NGOs feel a real identity with the needs and aspirations of the Third World and, in fact, have made efforts to include third world representatives of their organizations at these special conferences. NGOs such as the World Council of Churches, the International Chamber of Commerce, or the International Confederation of Free Trade Unions have fielded quite large and diverse delegations to attend the special United Nations conferences.

International NGOs based in Socialist countries have also played an important role in planning NGO activities (particularly the parallel activities) and have been represented at the special conferences both by persons from their developed member countries and from the Third World NGO affiliates. Most active throughout the series of special conferences have been organizations such as the World Peace Council, the World Federation of Democratic Youth, the World Federation of Trade Unions, and the World Federation of Democratic Women.

A most interesting and new phenomenon, particularly among NGOs from the Western industrialized countries, is the increase in numbers of participants from national NGOs. Because of the ad hoc and often less rigid attitude of the conference Secretariats with regard to invitations to NGOs, many national-level NGOs received special invitations to attend, participate in, or observe the conferences. Where there were parallel activities, national-level NGOs were often encouraged to participate either in addition to or in conjunction with the international NGOs with which they were affiliated. In fact, most of the parallel activities were open to all, with or without organizational affiliation. For many national NGOs without such affiliation, the invitation to attend a special conference was their first direct contact with the United Nations system.

Indigenous NGOs from the Third World have also been represented, but to a lesser extent, in the special conferences. The main limiting factor is always travel funds. Where special efforts have been made to pay travel costs of Third World NGOs to the parallel activities, such as the Population Tribune at Bucharest or the International Women's Year (IWY) Tribune at Mexico City, new and active NGO representatives from developing countries have made a significant impression on the meeting and have been able to forge new links with NGO representatives from the industrialized countries.

Rather than providing a chronological account of NGO involvement in each conference, the next section of this chapter will group conferences on similar themes together in order to illustrate the kind of new relationships which have developed.

FOOD AND HUNGER ISSUES

It is significant that two of the early examples of NGO involvement in United Nations special conferences dealt with the issues of food and hunger and were sponsored by FAO. The food issue from early on was one that appealed to a wide spectrum of NGOs.

The first World Food Congress in Washington, DC in 1963 brought together some 2,000 concerned individuals. Most of them represented NGOs, but the Congress also included government officials and international civil servants. It was not an official intergovernmental conference, but many of its conclusions and recommendations, particularly the proposed Indicative World Plan for Agriculture, were heeded by governments and by FAO. The Congress marked the mid-point of the first five-year phase of FAO's

Freedom from Hunger Campaign (FFHC) and did much to sustain NGO interest and involvement in that campaign during the decade of the 1960s through the mechanism of 80 national FFHC committees.

This was the first really large international NGO gathering to look at the goals and targets of the United Nations Decade for Development. Because it focused on the agricultural aspects, it attracted the largest segment of NGO interest in development at that time, for most development-oriented NGOs in the industrialized countries either had field programs in rural development or were vitally concerned with the rural sector in developing countries. Indeed, most NGOs in the Third World were actively engaged in rural development projects.

Seven years later, FAO sponsored the second World Food Congress at The Hague. This time there were 3,500 participants. Once again they acted as individuals but came from both NGOs and national governments. What was interesting about the 1970 meeting was the evolution in thinking of the NGO participants. There was much more talk about the root causes of hunger, about hunger as a symptom of world poverty, and about the quest for international economic and social justice. Three hundred participants were youth representatives (under 30 years of age) housed in a special camp called "New Earth Village" on the outskirts of The Hague. Their impact on the Congress in support of the aspirations of the Third World was significant. Much of the rationale for the work of the United Nations in development education—both in school and out of school—was laid out in recommendations and conclusions from the New Earth Village at the second World Food Congress.

The two World Food Congresses were successful primarily as training grounds for NGOs. They provided one of the first opportunities for NGO representatives from East and West, North and South with a common interest in development issues to meet and exchange experiences. They provided an inspirational boost and a broader perspective for the individual NGO representatives working on particular projects in their own countries. The second World Food Congress, particularly the youth component, encouraged national-level NGO representatives to interact with officials from their own governments and to feel that they might wield some influence over national policy.

More by accident than design, the NGO activities around the United Nations-sponsored World Food Conference in Rome in November 1974 became integrated to an unprecedented extent with the Conference itself. Lack of time and money made it impossible to organize any large-scale parallel activities. In addition, space was available for NGO facilities in the main conference building, the Palazzo dei Congressi in Rome. These two factors combined to throw over 400 NGO representatives of 150 organizations into the corridors, lobbies and public meeting rooms of the Conference itself. (Even though daily briefings and some "parallel" type panel discussions were held in the NGO meeting room of the conference site and a small program was organized in a conference hall within walking distance of the Palazzo, these activities were considered out of the mainstream and were rather poorly attended by the NGOs.)

Partly because of their early training at the second World Food Congress in The Hague in 1970, and partly because of intense national level information/education/action on the issue of world hunger, several groups of national level NGOs from countries such as Canada, the United Kingdom, Sweden, The Netherlands, and Australia were prepared at the World Food Conference to conduct systematic monitoring of their own delegation's performance. The Canadian experience is best known. A group of 13 Canadian NGO representatives, chosen at a national food conference in Ottawa a month before, descended on Rome with a systematic plan to monitor and influence the Canadian delegation. Dialogue had started in Canada with the official delegation and this continued almost daily in Rome. On some important issues, such as the amount of Canada's contribution to emergency food supplies, the NGOs were visibly successful in urging the Canadian authorities to alter their original position in favor of the needs of the developing countries. An effective communications system (telephone and telex) was established between the NGO representatives in Rome and a network of NGO information points throughout Canada. Pressure from NGOs and influential citizens in Canada was directed at the cabinet-level leaders of the Canadian delegation in Rome, and questions about the Canadian role in Rome were asked by opposition members in the Canadian Parliament in Ottawa.

In general, the World Food Conference in Rome was the first example of widespread involvement of NGOs in the inner workings, including committees, of a world conference. To quote one NGO representative in Rome:

> While NGOs in consultative status with the Economic and Social Council have certain well-defined prerogatives, such as making written or oral statements, other lobbying activities depend more on luck, circumstances or just plain enterprise. Seldom have NGOs had such privileges as some made for themselves at Rome. The International Organization of Consumers Unions, for example, was one of several NGOs that spoke to one of the three Conference committees. Others, such as Church World Service and the World Conference on Religion and Peace, were made members of drafting committees. The traditional women's and population lobbies were also active at Rome and can take credit for tangible, if modest successes.[10]

TRADE AND DEVELOPMENT ISSUES

There had been some NGO monitoring of the UNCTAD III session in Santiago in 1972. The Dutch, British, and Canadian NGO groups sent observer teams that reported back to their countries. After the World Food Conference a group of the more activist NGOs (in the political lobbying sense) from the Group B countries (Western Europe, North America, Japan, Australia, and New Zealand) got together to plan a joint strategy for UNCTAD IV. This grouping of national-level NGOs, known as the International Coalition for Development Action (ICDA), met in Geneva several times before UNCTAD IV and compared notes on developments in the trade and commodity fields and on the positions of their respective governments. As a result, NGO involvement at UNCTAD IV and UNCTAD V expanded, and improved upon, the new relationships established at the World Food Conference.

At Nairobi in 1976 and three years later in Manila (UNCTAD V) there were about 200 NGO observers from developing and developed countries, of which 100 were members of ICDA. The ICDA group worked together from a common base in Nairobi and in Manila, shared briefings together, and divided up the responsibilities of monitoring, reporting, and lobbying. While mainly from the Group B countries, they were supportive of, and in close touch with, the position of the Group of 77 (developing countries).

National-level NGO action on food, trade, and development issues had spearheaded this new form of NGO interest in the activities of the UN on those issues. At the present time, the important relationship for the national-level NGOs is to the issues, not to the structure of the UN. In fact, the UN-sponsored world conferences on these issues have been used (as, in part, they were intended to be used) as a hook or a catalyst for more intensive action at the national level and for better networking (through organizations like ICDA) at the international level.

A similar interaction was undertaken by ICDA-related NGOs at the 1980 Eleventh Special Session of the General Assembly on International Economic Issues and, to a lesser extent, at the 1982 Special Session on Disarmament. By 1980 NGOs had learned better techniques of interacting or "lobbying" with delegations and, perhaps even more important, relating to the media. Often during the Eleventh Special Session of the General Assembly the media focus was on parallel activities taking place in the Church Center across the street from the UN rather than on the central (often repetitive) debate in the General Assembly hall. During the recently concluded UN Special Session on Disarmament, non-governmental groups received the lion's share of media coverage, particularly those groups actively engaged in public demonstrations and marches.

ENVIRONMENT, LAW OF THE SEA, AND HABITAT ISSUES

The very first example of a major NGO parallel activity was at the Stockholm Conference on the Environment. Because it was the first, some traditional rules of the United Nations meetings were set aside and some significant precedents were established for future conferences. Most important was that the Conference Secretary-General, Maurice Strong, was eager to have as wide a representation as possible from the NGO community. He believed that there were many NGOs vitally involved in the environmental issues which were not in formal consultative status with the United Nations. His invitation list included many "new" international and national NGOs not seen at previous United Nations meetings. The short lead time for organizing NGO activities led to considerable confusion about the role of the NGOs right up to the opening of the Conference, but, in retrospect, it is clear that broad-based NGO participation sparked continuing commitment by NGOs to environmental issues.

One interesting NGO event was organized before the Stockholm Conference itself. An International Youth Conference on the Environment, held a few months before in Hamilton, Canada, adopted a statement that was read in the plenary of the United Nations Environment Conference. During the Conference itself, the NGO Forum was the largest parallel activity, an event that was officially sanctioned by both the United Nations and the Swedish government. The Forum was attended by about 400 NGO representatives who listened to panel sessions on the main themes of the Conference. Very little attempt was made by the Forum organizers to influence the Conference; it was seen as an ancillary event for the intellectual satisfaction of the NGO members and many of the Conference delegates. In addition, it was held at a site several miles from the Conference.

Other less formal and definitely "unofficial" parallel activities included the Hog Farm Commune (a gathering of activist youth and student NGOs in a camp at the Stockholm airport); the Pow-Wow, a grouping of international environmental NGOs; and Dai-Dong, a type of counter-conference organized by the International Movement for Reconciliation.

What was intriguing about the Stockholm experience was that all these disparate NGO activities (which it was feared at one point might disrupt the Conference) were, in the end, of considerable positive support to the objectives of the Conference and its follow-up activities. By providing high-quality briefings early each morning to all the NGO groups and by allowing the NGOs collectively to present a statement directly to the Conference, the Conference Secretariat ensured that the NGO presence was felt in a forceful and positive manner at a major United Nations event.

The NGO daily newspaper, *Echo,* was produced by Friends of the Earth, the Sierra Club and *Ecologist* magazine. It broke ground as a new type of conference information vehicle and gained credibility with delegations and the Secretariat. This NGO newspaper tradition has continued during subsequent conferences.

When the United Nations Environment Program was created as a new UN agency after the Stockholm Conference, the relationship of environmental NGOs was built in to the structure as a most important feature. A broad-based and effective Environmental Liaison Board of NGOs oversees this new, practical UN–NGO relationship.

The third Law of the Sea Conference, which started meeting in Caracas in 1974, continued in Geneva in 1975, and in New York from 1976 to 1982, attracted the special interest of NGOs involved in legal and environmental questions. At the New York sessions the number of NGO representatives who followed the Conference was approximately 30. A group of interested NGOs based in Washington, DC took the lead in coordinating Law of the Sea information for NGOs and publishing a periodic newspaper called *Neptune*. The specialized NGOs interested in these negotiations both from the legal and the environmental standpoint have been credited by delegates with much of the success in perpetuating the idea of a World Heritage Fund for some of the profits from deep-sea mining.[11]

The large scale parallel NGO activity around the United Nations Conference on Human Settlements was the Habitat Forum at Jericho Beach, Vancouver, Canada, held in June 1976. Over 6,000 NGO representatives were reported to have taken part, although that figure was probably inflated by a large number of local Vancouver citizens who were encouraged to become involved in the Forum events.

The representatives at the Forum far outnumbered those at the UN Conference and the event was more spectacular for newsmen, for local citizens, for NGO representatives, and for many of the conference delegates. The largest group of the participants came from North America, many of whom were primarily—or even solely—concerned with North American problems.

The Chairman of the NGO Committee for Habitat, Mr. J. C. van Putten, assessed the input of NGOs to the Conference in the following manner:

As the input of the Forum into the Conference had to take place in an informal way, it is difficult to measure exactly what its influence has been. There is no doubt, however, that the wording of the HABITAT documents on such subjects as land policy, participation of the population in decision-making by all levels of government, the supply of clean water, the involvement of NGOs in the implementation of the Conference decisions, and the interrelationship between human settlement issues and the problems of economic and social development, was changed because of non-governmental action.[12]

WOMEN'S ISSUES

In what must be considered the largest parallel event ever held, 6,000 persons from more than 90 countries gathered in June 1975 in Mexico City for the IWY Tribune, running parallel to the United Nations World Conference for International Women's Year. The Tribune included probably the most widely representative group of women (and some men) leaders ever assembled.

The Tribune was designed for maximum communication between individuals of the greatest possible diversity. Renowned scholars, administrators, politicians, and activists mingled with villagers and rural workers. The program consisted of 25 half-day sessions planned in advance, 192 extra meetings held at the request of participants, daily morning briefings on the work of the Conference, films, exhibits, and a daily newspaper called *Xilonen*. The Tribune was held at the Convention Hall of the National Medical Centre, a site five miles from the United Nations Conference.

The planning group, as in the Population Tribune, was a committee of the Conference of NGOs in Consultative Status (CONGO) with ECOSOC. The evolving form of the parallel meetings at previous United Nations Conferences in Stockholm and Bucharest and the experience of NGO representatives in organizing these events gave the IWY Tribune planners a head start.

This was the third parallel conference for NGOs in as many years and attests to the snowballing popularity of these occasions. The tremendous attendance was a source of excitement for the Tribune, but it also contributed to serious management problems as the conference proceeded. Much of the follow-up activity was channeled through CONGO, which created a special sub-committee to coordinate subsequent NGO involvement in an even more effective form in the mid-Decade World Conference on the UN Decade for Women (Copenhagen, July 1980).

These four issue topics are used only as illustrations of the new kinds of UN–NGO relationship forged by participation in world conferences throughout the 1970s. There are other, more technical, subject areas such as water, science and technology, industrialization, technical cooperation among developing countries (TCDC), crime prevention, social services for youth, disabled and the aging, and outer space, where the same dynamics are taking place. In sum, no major United Nations conference dealing with any aspect of economic or social development during the last ten years has been held without either a large-scale or at least a significant involvement of NGOs. Nor is it likely that one could be held in the future without such involvement.

That NGOs are around a conference has an impact in and of itself. In some cases, where attendance at the parallel activities far outnumbers the attendance at the conference, the effect of NGOs is to make an event a "happening." In all cases, whether the numbers of NGOs in the vicinity is large or small, their presence adds flavor, a sense of excitement, and, in some cases, a sense of reality to what might otherwise be a dull intergovernmental meeting.

But what is the effect of the NGOs on the final outcome of the conferences? Do NGOs add significantly to the conference objectives? Are the new relationships that are forged useful over the long term?

If we assume that one of the major reasons for the UN having a conference in the first place is to focus world attention on the issue being discussed, then NGOs should be seen as a vital and necessary parallel component. If the main purpose is to achieve some progress through negotiations, then an NGO role that is more closely integrated with the conference can also be valuable.

In general, the effect of the NGO contribution on the conference proceedings depends to a large extent on the timing, level, and form of the initiative. Whenever a UN conference Secretariat recognized the need for a significant NGO involvement, NGOs have had a profound effect on the preparations for the conference, particularly in the formulation of position papers and documentation. During the conferences, it is doubtful whether, on balance, the NGO statements made at some of the plenary sessions or the joint declarations emerging from parallel activities had much impact on the proceedings. The exception might be well-prepared, high-caliber statements by eminent persons such as those presented at the World Food Conference and at the Habitat Conference. Usually, a more useful approach for NGO groups has been to get their points of view incorporated in resolutions sponsored by a government delegation, as was done by the Population Crisis Committee at the World Food Conference.

Often overlooked in the consideration of the role of NGOs in the United Nations affairs is the effect of United Nations conferences on the regular ongoing work of NGOs. Many international meetings, such as the World Food Congresses, became important training grounds for NGO leaders. A world conference is of immeasurable value for NGO representatives in terms of meeting one another, sharing information and techniques, and planning coordinated action. Frequently the agenda of a world conference is used by NGOs as a guideline for their national program planning and provides a thematic focus for their activities. Pre- and post-conference actions are often much more important, and sometimes more productive in terms of changing public attitudes, than the actions of the conference itself.

Perhaps most important is the follow-up role of NGOs. Along with the major actors in a conference (government representatives and the Secretariat), NGOs are interested in and capable of undertaking a systematic follow-up of the conference resolutions and recommendations. In this role they are more consistent than the media, the other major actor during a conference. Now, with the formation of international coalitions of NGOs such as ICDA to follow up on meetings such as UNCTAD IV and V, this traditional role of NGOs has been made more exciting and relevant.

SOME NEW UN APPROACHES TO NGOS (1975 ON)

As noted earlier in this chapter, rethinking is presently going on in the UN with regard to the formal consultative relationship with

NGOs. Like the business of restructuring the UN itself, this is a long, slow process. Suffice it is to say that the effect of NGOs on the various world conferences of the 70s and the increased visibility of NGOs in UN General Assembly events such as the two Special Sessions on Disarmament and the Eleventh Special Session on International Economic Issues have injected a new dynamism into the way the UN system relates to NGOs.

During the last several years some other developments at the UN have had a bearing on this changing relationship. The most important has been the adoption at the Sixth and Seventh Special Sessions of the New International Economic Order (NIEO). The NIEO has not only given a framework and focus to the North-South dialogue, but has catalyzed the UN system into looking more holistically at development issues. Whether the particular perspective was women, trade, habitat, industrialization, or technology, each of the world conferences of the 70s have reiterated the basic premises of the NIEO.

The advent of the NIEO has had at least two effects on the relationship of the UN to NGOs. First, NGOs are becoming more adept at relating the various sectoral issues of development (and even the related issues of human rights, decolonization, and disarmament) to broader economic concerns. There is now more interest in the affairs of the General Assembly and in major global negotiations and strategies such as were discussed at the Eleventh Special Session. Even in particular sectors, for example the Conference on Women, the NGO involvement in the 1980 Copenhagen conference followed the lead of the UN Secretariat and took a broader, more NIEO-oriented view than was evident with the NGO involvement in Mexico City in 1975. Secondly, NGOs are tending to take a more activist, issue-oriented, even political approach to international development questions. The humanitarian-based aid and charity approach so characteristic of some NGOs in the 60s is giving way to a more pragmatic issue-oriented approach more compatible with the premises of the NIEO.

Partly as a result of the introduction of the NIEO and partly for reasons of common sense and plain good management, the information departments of the various UN agencies (which have the major responsibility for implementing relations with NGOs) joined together in 1974 into a common planning function called the Joint United Nations Information Committee (JUNIC). One of JUNIC's most successful projects has been the creation and joint (inter-agency) sponsorship of two Non-Governmental Liaison Services, one in Geneva servicing NGOs in Europe, and one in New York servicing NGOs in North America. The focus of the work of these services has been on activist NGOs who are interested in the issues of the NIEO.

The notion of "development education," i.e., increasing the awareness of people (particularly people in the developed Northern countries) of the issues of world development, is one that has sprouted in the last several years. With it has arisen the need for a closer relationship with relevant parts of the UN system. One of the most useful projects of the Non-Governmental Liaison Service in Geneva has been the publication of a small volume, *UN Development Education Directory for NGOs in Industrialized Countries*.

An innovative project of the Non-Governmental Liaison Service in New York is the assistance to a series of large-scale conferences (with appropriate preparatory activities and follow-up action) on the issues of the NIEO in various regions of North America—specifically around Los Angeles, Seattle, Minneapolis, Atlanta, and Denver. At these events the global issues of the UN agenda have been directly related to the local or regional economy in order to make them more relevant and understandable. These events have clearly emphasized the increasing role of NGOs in interacting with governments at the national and even sub-national levels.

CONCLUSION

The process of change in the UN–NGO relationship is an evolving one. What is clear is that the role of NGOs in intergovernmental bodies such as the UN is increasing and should become more significant in the future. The potential is there. The third breed, that diverse group of NGO representatives, will be seen much more in the corridors of the UN and the conferences and workshops of international agencies.

Some concluding thoughts and recommendations on how this potential can be realized might be useful:

NGOS NEED TO REDEFINE THEIR ROLE IN THE 1980S

The decade of the 80s is going to be infinitely more difficult for multilateral management than the 70s. Under these conditions, the role of the NGOs is threefold:

1. *To monitor developments and to contribute to the process of discussion by means of research, studies, and consultations.* NGOs often bring a human or social perspective to what is otherwise a strictly economic approach, often defined narrowly in terms of national interest. Many NGOs are traditionally concerned with the effect of economic decisions on people as well as governments, with the poor and underprivileged, with the role of women, with the humanization of institutions. These concerns should continue to be raised by the NGO community.

2. *To clarify issues and represent public interest constituencies for decisionmakers both at the national and international levels.* On many of the problems of global management—trade, finance, science and technology, industrialization, food, cooperation between developing countries—NGOs can mobilize the mass support required before changes in the international system are made. On some issues, such as aid levels, the role of the multinational corporations, and human values, NGOs have developed a special expertise coupled with the desire and ability to exert influence. Sometimes this is done by suggesting new approaches or solutions. More often it is done simply by showing policymakers that a proportion of interested people support alternate approaches.

3. *To inform and educate their own constituencies and the public at large.* Almost by implication, this enormous task is left to the NGOs because of their connection to local communities, their expertise, and their independent role.

THERE IS NEED FOR GREATER FLEXIBILITY ON THE PART OF THE UN IN ITS DEALINGS WITH NGOS

This process has already begun in conjunction with the world conferences held during the 1970s. But as the UN restructures itself in the 80s, streamlining some of its circuitous lines of command and communications, there is an excellent opportunity to modernize its relationship with NGOs as well. NGOs relate to the UN and other intergovernmental organizations on the basis of genuine ability and their willingness to follow issues and contribute to problem-solving. Official status by grade or degrée should be less important than ideas and inputs and more of a two-way flow of information and news of activities should be encouraged. The UN should seek out NGO involvement in policy formulation and implementation (and not only for the dissemination of information), rather than waiting for NGOs to come to the UN. A more flexible approach to NGOs needs to be promoted not only by the civil servants who implement UN programs, but also by the diplomats who legislate the form and extent of UN–NGO relations. This is particularly so for diplomats from countries where NGOs are active contributors at the national level.

MORE NEEDS TO BE DONE ON FIELD-LEVEL (PROJECT) COLLABORATION

UNDP has taken some initiatives in this regard and has alerted resident representatives in developing countries to press for more NGO involvement in project implementation. More of a coordinated effort, similar to the coordination of efforts around development education cited earlier, needs to be done at the field level, perhaps even on a country-by-country basis.

THERE IS NEED FOR MORE RESPECT FOR THE CREATIVE DYNAMIC RESULTING FROM BETTER UN–NGO RELATIONS

Too often the civil servants and the diplomats at the UN look upon NGO representatives with condescension. Likewise, NGO representatives look at the intergovernmental process as cumbersome and unproductive. Stereotyped impressions abound. What is needed as the UN system gears itself for the decade ahead is a better mutual respect and deeper appreciation of reciprocal strengths and weaknesses. NGOs should be seen as a valuable component of the process of multilateral management, not as an appendage to it.

Notes

1. The views expressed in this paper are those of the author alone.
2. Many of these people have offices within a few blocks of the UN

buildings in New York, one of the most often used buildings being the Church Center for the UN, a 12-story building directly across from the UN's General Assembly Building. This building houses a diverse group of organizations such as the World Council of Churches, the International Peace Academy, the Institute for World Order, Interlink (IPS) Press Service, and PACT (Private Agencies Cooperating Together, Inc.).

3. See Robert Cox, "Problems of Global Management," in this volume.

4. Much of this section is drawn from a paper by the late Elfan Rees, "A Critique of the Consultative Process between ECOSOC and NGOs," UNITAR, 1978 (paper No. 2. in a series on "Non-Governmental Organizations in International Cooperation for Development").

5. Two subsequent resolutions of ECOSOC, 288 B (X) and 1296 (XLIV) have further defined the relationship of NGOs to the Council and divided them into three levels (degrees) of Category I, Category II, and Roster.

6. The other two Commissions or Standing Committees of ECOSOC are the Commission on Statistics and the Committee on Program and Coordination.

7. For more details on the role of ECOSOC in the UN, see Ronald Meltzer's chapter in this volume.

8. Parallel activities are usually in the form of non-governmental conferences which take place at or near the formal, intergovernmental conference. They generally focus on those aspects of the formal agenda that are most relevant to NGOs and they often interact with the intergovernmental conference both at a formal and an informal level.

9. A detailed study providing a profile of the various relations between NGOs, the UN system, and the ad hoc conference has been prepared by UNITAR.

10. Jack A. Homer, "A Persistent Species at Rome: NGOs," in *America*, March 1, 1975.

11. Perhaps the failure of the US government to sign the Law of the Sea Treaty—in part because of the implications of the NGO-inspired World Heritage Fund—is indicative of the problem when a small group of competent NGOs work so hard at the international (UN) level that they do not have enough energy or resources to work (lobby) at the national level.

12. J.C. van Putten, Chairman of the NGO Committee for Habitat, Forum Report (The Hague: Habitat Forum, September 1976).

IV

US POWER AND INFLUENCE IN THE UN OF THE 80s

THE UNITED NATIONS IN TODAY'S WORLD

CHARLES WILLIAM MAYNES

The U. N. has ten years to become effective or disappear.
—SECRETARY-GENERAL U THANT, 1969[1]

More than ten years have passed since U Thant made his prediction. The UN has neither become more effective nor has it disappeared. Nevertheless, U Thant's statement is striking in the face of
the dangers confronting the UN today. Consider the UN's current
plight.

In the Middle East and southern Africa, conflict is assuming an
increasingly unrestrained viciousness. This development is both
awkward for the United States and dangerous for the UN. The Middle East and southern Africa arouse strong but conflicting emotions
among the American people. Both issues tap deep emotions that in
certain unfavorable circumstances could persuade the United States
to leave the UN. Both also kindle angry frustration among the larger
UN membership because of the slow pace of progress toward a
solution that is both sensible and just.

In the field of international security policy, there are equally ominous trends. The Soviet Union continues on the greatest military
buildup in peacetime. The Reagan Administration, in response, has
refused to ratify the SALT II agreement, shows no interest in the
Comprehensive Test Ban Treaty, and proposes to increase defense

spending in the period 1981–84 by an amount greater than the entire US defense budget of 1978. This combative counterpoint between the two superpowers is not only damaging to their own relationship but is also likely to weaken further the restraint most of the rest of the world has shown in foregoing the opportunity to acquire nuclear weapons. Pressure in Pakistan and India to acquire nuclear weapons is mounting rapidly. Israel may already have them. Iraq and Libya probably are trying to acquire them. It seems safe to assume that substantial nuclear proliferation will shortly take place and that this proliferation will increase significantly the danger of a relatively early use of nuclear weapons. Any use of nuclear arms, no matter how limited, will deal an irreparable blow to the UN as an institution relevant to the issues of peace and security.

Finally, in the area of economic policy, another watershed seems to be approaching. The wealthier industrialized countries are turning inward. Major Western countries have sharply curtailed their aid programs in real terms. Protectionism is on the rise. The Tokyo Round, which was supposed to address the trade problems of the developing countries, failed to do so, and opposition to penetration of industrial markets by Third World countries is mounting. In addition, the energy crisis is placing extraordinary adjustment demands on the developing countries. Some are spending virtually all their export earnings on energy imports. As a result, traditional aid donors look upon their development efforts as increasingly marginal and therefore harder to sustain politically in Western parliaments. An international economic crisis disturbingly similar to that of the 1930s—a reduction in international cooperation precisely when the common danger is the greatest—seems to be emerging.

So the dangers the UN faces seem unusually ominous. If U Thant were alive, he might argue that his prediction had been all too tragically accurate. Yet, all this said and the dangers notwithstanding, there is a paradox anyone studying US attitudes toward the UN must face: In the face of its failures, most Americans continue to regard the UN as a compelling ideal. Why is this so?

The answer relates as much to the way Americans see themselves as to the way they see the world. Historically, Americans have always viewed their country as the nation of the fresh start. Americans feel they alone have avoided the excesses and flaws of the old continent. Yet Americans, like most individuals, live by example and extrapolation. So it is natural that they would conclude that if a fresh start worked so well domestically, there is at least a reasonable possibility that a fresh start might work internationally.

Perhaps most Americans, looking at the current state of the United Nations, may be reluctant to declare that the institution in its currently configured state represents the "last, best hope of mankind." Nevertheless, most Americans probably continue to believe that the United Nations stands in supportable contrast to the traditional approaches to international problems, which have pushed whole regions of the globe into war innumerable times. The spring of Wilsonian optimism, in other words, remains an important feature of American political life even in the face of UN setbacks.

So it should be no surprise that a recent Roper poll commissioned by the UNA found that Americans by a roughly two to one margin believe both that the United States should increase its participation in the United Nations and that the United Nations is doing a poor job.[2] That cruel juxtaposition unfortunately reflects rather accurately both the enduring faith of the American people in international organizations and the precarious state of the organization itself.

Asserting that the UN is in a precarious state is not to suggest that the United Nations does not give the United States good, even irreplaceable, value in innumerable areas. For example, the international community would have been much less effective in helping Thailand to cope with the flood of refugees from Cambodia had institutions like the UNHCR and UNICEF not existed. The UN peacekeeping role in Cyprus and the Middle East has at times been irreplaceable. The technical work of many UN agencies—ICAO in air safety, IMCO in marine safety, WHO in disease control, WMO in weather prediction, and the IMF in monetary policy—is priceless and should never be forgotten. Nevertheless, the American people sense that on the central issues of peace and security and the promotion of economic cooperation and welfare, the UN is now stumbling.

As it has stumbled, US dissatisfaction with the UN has begun to reflect more prominently a hitherto submerged US ambivalence toward the world organization. This might be formulated in the following way: The United States values the UN primarily when it is used to manage more efficiently, or even more humanely, the international system as it already exists. It views the UN with growing skepticism verging on hostility when it is used to promote change in the system itself.

Conforming to this ambivalence, the US can be in the forefront of pushing the UN agencies to undertake traditional development efforts; it can pioneer various forms of international cooperation along functional lines within the UN system; and it can be the most vocal of all UN members in championing the organization's role in the field of peacekeeping. In these respects, the US can remain among the most enthusiastic and constructive of UN members. But the US has also been the most negative of all the Western countries to Third World demands for fundamental economic reform. It has strongly resisted the trend to turn the specialized agencies from institutions primarily concerned with research, expert dialogue, and standard-setting into development institutions that channel resources from the rich to the poor, and it has successfully resisted all efforts to give the UN a significant role in the field of disarmament, which could affect the real balance of power between the weak and the strong.

This sense of ambivalence is not unique to the United States. The primary objective of most UN members has always been, not the welfare of the globe as a whole, but the protection and enhancement of national security and living standards as traditionally conceived and narrowly viewed. US leaders usually conclude that this goal can best be pursued through better management of the status quo. The leaders of most members of the UN with its Third World majority usually conclude that this goal can only be obtained through a degree of change in the system that the US has traditionally resisted.

For both groups of leaders, however, the sense of commitment to world peace, the international community, or mankind's future seems to be in a process of progressive decline. Those who wrap their demands for change in the ideals of the Charter or the sanctity of UN majorities increasingly seem to dismiss the Charter or world opinion the minute that UN actions begin to conflict with more short-run considerations of national interest.

India, Indonesia, and Morocco regularly applaud UN resolutions calling on South Africa to withdraw from Namibia or on Israel to withdraw from the West Bank. They have denounced just as persistently UN resolutions condemning their own respective actions in Bangladesh, East Timor, and the Spanish Sahara. Turkey joins enthusiastically in UN calls for fundamental economic reform along North-South lines. It rejects the UN as a "tyrannical majority" when members repeatedly and overwhelmingly call on Turkey to respect the rights of the citizens of Cyprus. Israel applauds the UN decision in 1949 to recognize Israel's right to exist as a sovereign state by admitting it as a UN member. It cannot accept a similar decision for the Palestinian people even within the narrow confines of the West Bank. For most UN members the organization has increasingly become a tool, not an ideal. It has turned into an instrument that a government employs when it is useful and that it casts aside when it is not.

This membership-wide attitude toward the UN has given rise to a particularly troublesome problem: the so-called double standard. It is an obvious and painful fact that the UN follows a double standard. The UN has been as eager to condemn South African abuse of human rights as it was hesitant to take even the modest steps it finally took to criticize Idi Amin's abuses in Uganda. It has been more concerned with Israel's treatment of the Palestinians than Iran's treatment of the Bahais.

Of course, member states also follow double standards. Indeed, the Reagan Administration initially attempted a public defense of the double standard. It argued that it was appropriate to look on human rights violations by authoritarian states more tolerantly than the same human rights violations committed by totalitarian states on the asserted, but unprovable, grounds (particularly after China, Poland, and Yugoslavia) that the former have the potential to evolve into more democratic regimes whereas the latter never change.

Other states, however, do not feel under the compulsion to defend the double standard, perhaps because a nation state that attempted to avoid a double standard altogether in its foreign policy would almost certainly fail. It is hard enough to avoid a double standard in domestic affairs where the central government theoretically has the power to apply a common standard to similar problems throughout the land. But in international life that kind of power from the center does not exist. So a demand for a complete end to the double standard (or for total consistency) can quickly become a call for either policy passivity or policy crusades.

But if that is true of a nation state, is it also true of an international organization? There are some similarities. Like a nation state, the UN would be reduced to impotence if it could not act in a particular crisis unless it was prepared to act similarly in *all* comparable crises. Moreover, as a general rule, the UN can only act when its member states authorize it to act. So if member nations are following a double standard in their diplomacy, this practice will be reflected in their UN policy and a double standard will develop in the various policies the UN is ordered to pursue.

Nonetheless, the existence of the double standard is much more damaging to the effectiveness of the UN's mission than it is to the efficacy of a member state's foreign policy. The effectiveness of the UN depends on a perception of impartiality, whereas a nation state's depends on a perception of reliability. It is this perception of UN impartiality that has been steadily eroded in recent years.

There are many reasons for this erosion. Among them has been the eagerness of all member states, including the United States (indeed in the Cold War period particularly the United States) to exploit temporary majorities for diplomatic advantage. But the principal cause, which few want to acknowledge, is the institution's response to the problem of apartheid.

Apartheid, as an issue of UN concern, has been with the world organization from the beginning. The spiritual father of India, Mahatma Gandhi, spent many years of his life in South Africa; it was India, appropriately, that first raised the issue.

At first, apartheid was considered a special kind of question. The very name, apartheid, symbolized something out of the ordinary, something apart, something separate. The UN's approach to the subject conformed to the definition. Separate tools were developed for a separate problem. Thus, it was only in the case of apartheid that it was deemed appropriate for the UN to take a "biased" position. The Secretariat report of the Soviet invasion of Hungary in 1956, though in the end critical of the Soviet action, contained a chapter that presented the crisis as the Soviets saw it. No such evenhandedness was permitted in the treatment of apartheid, which, as racism, could not be viewed objectively.

The General Assembly authorized propaganda programs designed to press the case against apartheid. The Secretary-General took pains to establish that he and his colleagues in the Secretariat were working to eradicate apartheid. As a final step, to establish definitively that South Africa was beyond the pale because of the abhorrent racial policies it followed, the General Assembly decided in 1975 to block South Africa from exercising its rights of membership. As a result, South African representatives were denied the right to speak in various UN forums.

All of this took place over the opposition of the Western states, but that opposition was passive. The reason was two-fold. Western states were at least formally opposed because many of the steps taken against South Africa violated UN rules of procedure or even the Charters of the UN and its agencies. They were also passive because South Africa's substantive case was so difficult to defend in any guise and they were all unwilling to take any concrete action against South Africa. Acquiescence in a questionable or even illegal vote in the UN was easier than taking the more courageous action of expressing opposition to the policy of apartheid through action in bilateral channels.

There is a sense, in other words, in which the Western states agreed that the UN system should be permanently mobilized, and thus distorted, against apartheid. If it was pointed out that other member states also violated the ideals of the Charter, the not unreasonable reply was that these states made excuses, hid the facts, or cited extenuating circumstances. Only South Africa proclaimed that blacks in that country would *never* be given full political rights. Only South Africa decided in this way to establish that it was beyond redemption. In these circumstances, over many years, UN members that opposed illegal actions against South Africa voiced their concern about illegal procedures but then concluded that a country like South Africa did not merit more than this immediate, but ineffectual, form of support.

The way the organization addressed the issue of South Africa, if understandable, would be controversial in itself. What in recent years brought the UN to the brink of disaster was the use of similar techniques in other subject areas, particularly the Middle East and the New International Economic Order. In both these areas, there was a concerted effort, by the Arabs in the first instance and by the developing countries in the second, to compel the Secretariat to take sides in the same way that it had taken sides on the issue of apartheid. Despite occasional breakthroughs, this effort has on the whole not succeeded, but preventing overall victory has been a "perils of Pauline" exercise for more than a decade.

This is the true background to the Zionism-racism issue that raised such a storm in this country. This resolution is less an effort by itself to delegitimize Israel than an effort to justify, within the UN context, the resort to the same kind of total political warfare against Israel that has been employed against South Africa. If Israel is judged a racist state, then it is permissible for the membership to order the Secretariat to choose sides as it has in the case of apartheid.

The developing country approach to the North-South dialogue also can be viewed in this light. If the industrialized countries can be induced to acknowledge that they *owe* the developing countries a larger amount of aid in payment (reparations) for the curse of colonialism, then the membership can *order* the UN system to mobilize against the industrialized countries. Precisely for this reason, the industrialized countries have vigorously (and rightly) rejected any suggestion of guilt or obligation rooted in colonialism as opposed to concern or mutual interest based on participation in a single world economy.

What can be done? Not only is the genie now out of the bottle, but so long as Western members both oppose apartheid and are unwilling to translate their opposition into action in bilateral channels, there is little alternative to acquiescence in UN warfare against South Africa. At the same time, it is unrealistic to expect Arabs not to try to use strategies that have worked so successfully for the Africans. Nor will the Group of 77 readily abandon a strategy for putting the West permanently on the defensive.

One resolution of the dilemma, which should be rejected, is to surrender to the pressure. Even if one believed—and it is certainly intellectually respectable to concede this point in some cases—that the Western countries did many developing countries a unique historical injustice by colonizing them, it would be a mistake to accept a Western obligation in the form of a UN resolution now to compensate them. That would destroy the future utility of the UN as an instrument for promoting the common economic interest of North and South. Western publics would not support an institution that appeared so biased in favor of one party. A similar point can be made regarding the Middle East. Israel's current attitude toward the UN—which, in fact, has done much in a longer perspective to assist Israel—is an example of the damage that can take place. The Israelis have acquired an hysterical, yet understandable, view of the UN because of the bias they perceive not just in UN decisions but in Secretariat actions. They may misinterpret Secretariat intentions, but with the apartheid model in mind, thay have reason to fear the worst.

Another answer is to address the core of the substantive problem that lies behind UN treatment of a particular issue. The United States, for example, was pained by the way that Panama was able to use the UN to bring pressure against the Americans on the issue of the Panama Canal. The minute a treaty was signed, however, the issue disappeared from the UN agenda. Would a homeland for Palestinians or full political rights for the blacks of South Africa have the same effect on UN treatment of the Middle East and southern Africa? It is not inconceivable. By contrast, a major breakthrough in North-South relations would have a less permanent, even if impressive, impact. The issues involved in the North-South dialogue are by definition of a recurring nature. Realistically, however, none of these problems can be solved as easily as the US solved the issue of the Panama Canal, which itself took years of negotiations.

A three-prong strategy, therefore, seems in order to prevent the destructive spread of the apartheid model. First, it is important to continue to make progress in resolving the core, substantive issues involved in issues like the Middle East or southern Africa. This should be done not to avoid UN embarrassment, but because this is the right and wise thing to do. Nevertheless, there is a UN dividend worth taking into account when policy is developed.

Second, in order to preserve the UN as an important instrument of international cooperation and negotiation, the United States should, for example, be prepared to suspend its membership in bodies where the membership succeeds in directing the institutional machinery to favor one cause over the other. This is not just an issue involving Israel. In UNCTAD, the developing countries have tried to use funds from the general budget to schedule meetings open only to the developing countries. The United States must hold firm to the position that the UN is most useful to its members when the Secretariat and general program are perceived to be serving the general interest of the membership and not just one portion of it.

This does not mean that the United States should always support Israel on Middle East questions or the right wing of the US business community in North-South debates. If Israel undertakes actions of which we disapprove, we should not hesitate—as sometimes we have—to vote the US position. But we must make clear to UN members that there is a sharp difference between a vote that records the political position of member states on a substantive issue and an effort to restructure permanently the Secretariat of the UN so that it will, in effect, choose sides. It is the latter measure that is doing permanent damage to the UN. Combatting this trend is an issue the US should have discussed in a very concrete way with the new Secretary-General prior to his selection in December 1981.

There is a third step to take. The US must do more to reestablish a firebreak between apartheid and other UN issues. South Africa itself has chosen to be a pariah country and should be treated as one unless it gives a clear commitment to move rapidly toward fundamental reform. It is controversial to say this, but it must be said: Both the Soviet Union and South Africa have treated their Third World minorities with great cruelty, but even the totalitarian Soviet Union has done more for its Central Asian population in terms of education, health, and housing than South Africa has done for its blacks. Indeed, Seweryn Bialer, Soviet expert at Columbia University, looking at the Soviet record, concludes in the Summer 1981 issue of *Foreign Affairs* that "the Uzbek peasant [now] lives far better than his Russian counterpart,"[3] a claim no expert looking at the status of South Africa's blacks versus its whites could ever make about that country.

The policy advocated would not require the US to move immediately to impose economic sanctions on South Africa through the UN Security Council. But it would require the US to make clear that its sentiments clearly lie on the side of justice and that it sympathizes with the political struggle of blacks in that country. Under this policy the executive branch would actively discourage US investment in South Africa. It would state clearly that it favors full political participation of blacks in South Africa. It would withdraw all military attachés from South Africa. It would undertake programs to provide educational opportunities in the United States for blacks that escape from South Africa. And at some early point, if no change took place, it would even be prepared to support suspension of South Africa from the world community through action in the Security Council. The dogma of universality should not apply in all cases. While many states do not live up to the ideals of the Charter, there is a difference when a state both defies those ideals in its organic laws and states that it will ignore them on a permanent basis.

At the same time, the United States should make it clear to the whites of South Africa that this country is prepared to help them through a difficult period of transition if they choose the path of racial conciliation. The idea would not be to close off communication and cooperation with South Africa, but only to make it clear that the United States can never be politically close to the regime in its current form even if it is prepared to provide assistance for a courageous program of transformation.

The policy outlined, however, is one of mere survival. It is designed to get the UN through a difficult period. Can the aim be higher? Can the UN not only survive but become more effective?

Many scholars of global issues have pointed out the increasing irrelevance and inappropriateness of the old statecraft based on the "realist" paradigm of international relations. Under this paradigm, change takes place primarily in the wake of system breakdown. It takes a world war to persuade statesmen to create a United Nations. It takes a collapse in the world money system to persuade people to consider monetary reform. It takes an ecological disaster to persuade people to give some attention to planetary issues.

Who can lead us beyond this crippling form of realism? For most of the postwar period, the US sporadically attempted to do that.

The US was so dominant and so rich that it believed that, although a status quo power, it could manage at least modest change. It was, therefore, willing to play more of a leadership role than now.

One of the major challenges for those who wish to see a vibrant UN system is to find an alternative policy locomotive to the United States. For budgetary reasons and because it is passing through a period of intense nationalism from which it is unlikely to emerge soon, the US will not return quickly to its former role. Moreover, the US may simply be unable to lead the international community in the UN framework as it once did. Europe and Japan have regained their influence on the world scene, and new states with great power have emerged in the developing world. India is now the tenth industrial power in the world. Saudi Arabia is more important monetarily than Britain. Brazil's motor car industry is as large as Britain's.

Could Europe be the new policy locomotive? In this regard, the Brandt Commission report on North-South relations was encouraging less for what it said than what it symbolized.[4] A prominent German, representing a country with great influence within the Common Market, was taking the lead on an issue of global importance.

There are many reasons why Western Europe might be in a better position to play a leadership role than the United States. The key to policy leadership in the UN is a country's relationship with the developing countries, which constitute a majority of UN members. For a variety of reasons the Europeans now enjoy better relations with those countries than the United States.

In part because of the colonial tradition, the West Europeans have an emotional bond to the developing countries that does not exist in the United States. This bond makes possible a more permissive public attitude toward such sensitive issues as North-South relations. European politicians win elections by promising higher levels of foreign aid; US politicians lose them by promising the same thing.

The West Europeans are also highly dependent on the developing countries for economic markets. In the case of France, 25 percent of its industrial exports go to the developing countries. With dependence comes concern and with concern policy involvement. No West European foreign minister would ever state, as Alexander Haig did in his confirmation hearings, that there is no such thing as a "third world."[5] The area is too important for European statesmen to ignore the strong emotional ties that bind the areas of the world that their countries had formerly ruled.

Finally, economically now of age but politically still at the margin, particularly on non-European issues, many West European states are looking for a diplomatic vocation. The Scandinavians have sought such a role in the United Nations itself. The Europeans in general might seek it in the broader area of North-South relations. Certainly there are signs of ferment. Not only has the French government made North-South relations a top priority, but the West German government has at times shown signs of independent action in such areas as Western policy toward Namibia.

At the same time Europe with all its strengths is not a superpower and it may take the shoulder of a superpower to make the UN function more effectively. At some point on every key issue, it is necessary to deal with the Soviet Union, and only the US is powerful enough to do this. But here also Western Europe may have an advantage. While not a superpower, it does have an important voice in influencing the policies of one superpower, whose underlying instincts remain profoundly Wilsonian for reasons already cited. It is therefore possible that positive leadership from Western Europe could in time elicit more positive responses from the United States.

But for a more positive posture to appear, both Western Europe and the United States would have to insist on a higher standard of political leadership than either has seen in most of the postwar period. On both sides of the Atlantic, leaders would need to follow a form of realism that looks to the future, that goes well beyond present day Realpolitik.

Under present circumstances one can only be very pessimistic that such leadership would arise on either side of the Atlantic. Governments everywhere are turning inward and shirking international obligations. After two years of a new Administration in Washington, U Thant's prediction seems more relevant than ever.

Notes

1. U Thant, cited in Lester B. Pearson, "The UN At 25," *Saturday Review,* Vol. LIII, No. 26, June 27, 1970, p. 16.

2. See Paul D. Martin's article in this volume for a detailed analysis of public attitudes toward the UN. See also *Analysis of Data in the Roper Poll on US Public Attitudes Towards Foreign Affairs,* A Background Paper Prepared by UNA-USA, New York, October 1980.

3. Seweryn Bialer, "The Harsh Decade: Soviet Policies in the 1980s," *Foreign Affairs,* Summer 1981, p. 1001.

4. Willy Brandt, *North-South: A Program For Survival.* Report of the Independent Commission on International Development Issues (Cambridge, Mass.: The MIT Press, 1980).

5. US Senate, Committee on Foreign Relations, *First Session on the Nomination of Alexander M. Haig, Jr. to be Secretary of State.* 97th Congress, 1st Session (Washington D.C.: US Government Printing Office, January 1981), p. 15.

US NATIONAL INTERESTS AND
THE UNITED NATIONS

DONALD J. PUCHALA

For more than 35 years it has been the policy of the United States to support the United Nations by participating in multilateral policymaking, by favoring and furthering institutional growth, and by helping to finance general UN activities and special programs. The US government's positive posture toward the United Nations has met with public approval as evidenced in opinion polls, widespread mass media endorsement and political party platforms. United States presidents of both parties have reaffirmed our commitments to international organizations. "The ideals of the United Nations," then Secretary of State Alexander Haig, Jr. told the 36th UN General Assembly, are "also American ideals. The Charter embodies American principles. It will always be a major objective of our statecraft to make the United Nations an instrument of peace."[1]

Continuing support for the United Nations and deepening involvement in its processes, policies, and programs remain in the American national interest. Yet criticisms of the United Nations and questions about United States participation are being voiced today by some analysts of American foreign policy.[2] Their main argument is that the United States is currently subject to considerable rhetorical abuse in the United Nations General Assembly and in other large multilateral forums where majorities of countries are pressing for world political and economic changes that appear to be inimical to US interests. In addition, these critics contend that the

343

United Nations seems to operate on a double standard by condemning actions of the West while condoning similar behavior by the East. While the United States is ridiculed and slighted at the UN, the critics say, our government continues to pay a substantial share of the organization's bills. Do we get our money's worth from the UN? What has the world organization done for the US lately?

In addition to legitimate questions and concerns, some of the current criticism of the American involvement in the United Nations is ideologically slanted and is motivated in part by domestic politics in the United States. It must be interpreted, therefore, in light of its source. Furthermore, some bemoaning the failures of the United Nations follows from regrets about the end of American global dominance and the passing of Western cultural universalism. Such positions are symptoms of a broader dissatisfaction with trends in world affairs. However, venting frustrations by attacking the UN hardly seems appropriate, since the organization cannot alter the fact that the world is mostly non-American, non-Western, and non-Caucasian.

With regard to the more reasoned criticisms of the UN, it should be emphasized that there are two fundamental flaws in American critics' assessments. First, they tend either to misrepresent or to misperceive the nature of the international organization, attributing to it capabilities that it does not have. This enables critics to decry the UN for being unable to perform according to the impossibly high standards they themselves have established. Second, critics confuse rhetoric at the UN with performance by the world body. Clearly, much of the harsh language spoken in UN deliberative organs nowadays tends to be anti-American or anti-Western, and much of it is unfair and untrue. But, as is the case in most parliamentary bodies, the weakest members shout the loudest, the most radical seek the most attention, and the most paranoid are the most critical. In these regards, UN forums are almost archetypical. Rhetoric is important, but so is performance. Looking at the record, when actual UN decisions and programs of action are examined, what emerges in fact is a marked congruence between UN policies and US preferences.

Having said this, there are still plausible and very real questions to be asked about the United States and the United Nations. There are also many legitimate concerns about the UN expressed even by its supporters. The questions deserve a reasoned response and the problems call for corrective action by the United Nations itself. Both of these points will be addressed in this chapter.

THE UN TODAY: REFLECTIONS OF A DANGEROUS AND FRAGMENTED WORLD

Those who have called the United Nations "a dangerous place" are correct only in that the United Nations is a microcosm of the cleavages, contentions, insecurities, and volatilities of a very dangerous world.[3] Rivalry between superpowers, the nuclear specter and frustrating efforts at disarmament, racial, ethnic, and class antagonisms, and festering, explosive political issues are some of the stuff of United Nations affairs. Governments go to the UN to deal with matters that divide them, although they do not often reach lasting agreements because incompatibilities beneath issues are real. There is no remedial magic in the Security Council or in the General Assembly. Conflicts between the United States and the Soviet Union are no more soluble within the UN than without, and Cold War issues in general remain practically immune from UN influence. But governments do sometimes find accommodation through multilateral diplomacy in the UN, and when they do—as for example in Zimbabwe, earlier in Suez (1956), in the area of nuclear testing and non-proliferation, in the Latin American nuclear-weapons free zone, and until recently in the creation of the United Nations Interim Force in Lebanon—the world becomes incrementally *less* dangerous.

Governments also go to the United Nations to deal with matters that unite them. Many of the most pressing problems of our planet are transnational in origin and impact, and most defy unilateral solutions. Preserving peace among nations, facilitating international commerce, protecting the global environment, ordering the use of the seas, airways, and airwaves, alleviating hunger, and accommodating global movements of information, resources, and people are beyond any single country's capacities. These are tasks for collective action, and governments have assigned many of them to the United Nations.[4] Global policies toward global problems are not easily or quickly formulated at the UN because members' consensus is essential for enforcement, and this consensus is elusive in a fragmented, politically charged world. But when consensus is reached—as, for example, in GATT's trading rules, the IMF's lending rules, UNCTAD's commodities program, the Food Aid Convention and IFAD's rural development program, the allocation of airwaves, and important aspects of the Law of the Sea—the world becomes less anarchic, more predictable, and thus safer.

The United Nations is not a world government, and there is no evident desire by its members to have it evolve toward greater supranationality. Most Americans hardly want yet another level of political authority reaching down into their lives. But along with recognizing that the UN is not an independent power beyond the nation state, it must also be accepted that the international organization has limited capabilities. It has no power beyond that which its members grant it, and no legitimacy beyond that which its members accord it. Furthermore, as an association of sovereign states, every one equal under international law, majority rule, consensus, or unanimity must be the principles of UN decisionmaking. Where majority rule prevails, no member can hope to be part of a winning coalition on every decision, and the organization is therefore bound to make policies that some members will not agree with. When policy is formulated by consensus, as it is most frequently at the United Nations, compromises produce "common denominator" agreements acceptable to all members but often less than ideal for most. Where unanimity is the rule, decisions will often not be taken at all and impasse will prevail. In addition, because UN members are sovereign states, enforcing the organization's decisions is ultimately a national matter for each of them. The UN cannot compel any member to act or to react in any specified manner. Nor can the United Nations move militarily, politically, financially, or otherwise onto the territory or into the domestic affairs of any member state unless the organization is specifically invited to do so. In light of this, the answer to the question, "Why didn't the UN do something?" is often simply that the member states had not given it either the authority or the power.

US PREFERENCES AND UN POLICY: LOOKING AT THE RECORD

In the United Nations, talk is too often substituted for action, mainly because action demands consensus, while talk requires only word-smiths, mass media agents, and attentive home-country audiences. Currently, some of the talk is critical of the US, but this was not always so. During the 1950s much of the rhetoric was anti-Communist as Western Europe, Latin America, and much of the rest of the UN membership echoed Washington's themes.[5] There is also some reason to expect that the volume of the anti-American rhetoric will also diminish in the years ahead, partly because time puts the Western colonial period further and further into history and because current events focus attention on the expansionist tendencies of other types of regimes, particularly the Communist ones. Furthermore, economic development in coming years will create more and more states with interests and economic and political systems akin to ours, so that gaps in perception and interests between the West and the South could narrow appreciably. Even today, the so-called newly industrializing countries (NICs) are increasingly uncomfortable with the more radical themes, demands, and accusations of the Group of 77 (G-77), and the anti-American utterances of the NICs are accordingly subdued. During the next two decades many more newly industrializing countries will emerge, and present ones will look, behave, and increasingly talk more and more like the developed Western countries.

The United States could not afford to tolerate the charges made against it at the UN and resolve merely to ride out the present rhetorical storm if there were a direct connection between what extremist orators say at the General Assembly and what the United Nations actually does in terms of policy and program. But this connection is at best tenuous; in some cases, there is no connection. UN programs (as opposed to UN rhetoric) reflect the consensus that produced them, and consensus usually requires wooing the United States. Little of substance can happen in the UN system without American cooperation—and little happens without American resources—so that it is not very surprising that negotiators often defer to United States preferences. Examples abound:

• Security Council resolutions are frequently modified to court the approval of the United States, as, for instance, with Iraq's compromises on the 1981 resolution that protested the Israeli air attack on an Iraqi nuclear reactor.[6]

• A similar episode in 1981 concerned a Security Council resolution of condolence for three Nigerian soldiers who were killed in UN service in Lebanon. The US government preferred that the resolution not single out Israel for condemnation and strong contrary stands by other members of the Security Council eventually gave way to the American position.[7] When the approval of the United States cannot be gotten, an American veto is sufficient to kill any possibility of Security Council action.

• On questions of economic development, US influence is linked to US resources, and American preferences often prevail. For example, the Third World stance on the question of world economic restructuring was modified dramatically between the Sixth and Seventh Special Sessions of the General Assembly after it became apparent that the United States was neither going to support schemes of redistribution nor be swayed by confrontational tactics.[8]

• Similarly, the agreement on an International Development Strategy (IDS) for the United Nations Third Development Decade was a bargained compromise that took account of American preferences for free trade and open markets, American insistence that agriculture be a central target of development, and the American position that the first responsibility for development rests with the developing countries themselves.[9]

• The final form of the Integrated Program for Commodities agreed to at the United Nations Conference on Trade and Development (UNCTAD) was largely a Group of 77 deferral to the American position.

• Earlier, the conciliation or cooling-off mechanism that modifies UNCTAD decisionmaking by moving it away from straightforward majority voting was another case of American preferences taking precedence over G-77 desires.[10]

• The system of "graduation" that links eligibility for assistance to levels of economic development, agreed upon at the June 1980 meeting of the Governing Council of the United Nations Development Program (UNDP), was yet another G-77 concession to an American position.[11]

• The structure and functioning of the International Fund for Agricultural Development (IFAD) are of American design.

• American positions have consistently prevailed in the area of population activities within the United Nations and in the disposition of the United Nations Fund for Population Activities (UNFPA).

• When it became apparent that the United States would not accept international restrictions on the freedom of the press, or anything in the nature of a codified New International Information Order (NIIO), Third World countries in UNESCO readily accepted an American plan for an International Program for the Development of Communication. The intent of this program is to help developing countries improve their capabilities in mass communications.[12]

• The voluntary rather than binding nature of the United Nations Code for Restrictive Business Practices is yet another deference to American preferences, and work on the Code of Conduct for Transnational Corporations also appears to be evolving in directions that American firms and the United States government can accept.

• Important, but ultimately insufficient, concessions were offered to the United States in 1982 on controversial aspects of the draft treaty on the Law of the Sea.

• The United Nations Interim Force in Lebanon (UNIFIL) was accepted largely in the form that the United States proposed.

More generally speaking, throughout the UN's 38-year history the Organization's principles and most of its actions have been consistent with United States interests.[13] Americans, for example, certainly have no trouble with the UN's principle of self-determination. Woodrow Wilson was its early American champion, and the rapid and peaceful dissolution of our fledgling colonial empire was its embodiment in policy. The illegitimacy of armed intervention is another UN principle that Americans can readily accept, although our own record as regards gunboat diplomacy is somewhat blemished. The promotion of peaceful change is a cornerstone of American diplomacy; it is also a first principle of the United Nations. Protecting and promoting human rights are central to US political theory, just as they are central among United Nations objectives.

Conflict resolution through negotiation, mediation, conciliation, and adjudication are main elements of the American political process, and also main features of UN decisionmaking. That human affairs should be ordered by codes of law rather than by contests of power is another tenet of both US and UN political thinking.

Principles are fine, but what about practice? To be sure, there is considerable slippage between principles of the United Nations and the domestic and international practices of some of its members. But the day-to-day actions of the organization and the behavior of some of its members should not be confused. In fact, the United Nations itself has expressed disapproval of some of its members' actions. During the 1950s France and Britain were censured for their invasion of Egypt; Israel was likewise censured; so too was the Soviet Union for its invasion of Hungary.[14] The 1960s saw the beginning of the UN's public disapproval of apartheid in South Africa, Ian Smith's usurpation in Rhodesia, and Chilean denial of human rights. In the 1970s, United Nations members decried the atrocities of Idi Amin's Uganda and the genocide perpetrated by the government of Kampuchea (Cambodia). More recently the General Assembly voted sharp disapproval of the Khomeini regime's imprisonment of United States diplomats; it condemned the Soviet Union's invasion of Afghanistan by an extraordinary majority of 104 to 18; and it censured Israel for its de facto annexation of the Golan Heights.[15]

These negative actions are important because they forcefully assert the limits of the international community's tolerance. But sanctions against deviant members are only a very small part of UN activities. Through the years, actions to strengthen the international community in the areas of peacekeeping and peaceful change, economic development, and the preservation of the earth's resources have been the UN's main concerns. Here again, in most of these areas there has been rather close correlation between UN policies and American preferences.

IN DEFENSE OF PEACEFUL CHANGE

In the realm of peacekeeping, the United Nations has on several occasions physically inserted international military contingents to monitor and enforce ceasefires between warring countries and factions. Some of the better-known peacekeeping missions include the United Nations Truce Supervisory Organization (UNTSO), established in 1948 to monitor the ceasefire between Israel and neighboring Arab states, the United Nations Emergency Force (UNEF I and UNEF II), stationed to enforce Egyptian and Israeli ceasefires in 1956 and 1973; the United Nations Operation in the Congo (ONUC) executed to quell civil anarchy and to prevent fragmentation immediately following the former Belgian Congo's passage to independence; the United Nations Force in Cyprus (UNFICYP) dispatched in 1964 to separate parties locked in Greek-Turkish communal conflict; and most recently the United Nations Interim Force in Lebanon, sent to separate contestants in the Lebanese civil war and to deter terrorist activities along the Israeli-Lebanese border. UNIFIL is the international organization's second peacekeeping mission to Lebanon.

The primary purpose of these UN missions have been to deter renewed fighting, to gain time for diplomacy, and to discourage external, and especially superpower, intervention that could lead to escalation into larger wars. The United States has supported each of the peacekeeping ventures, and their results have largely supported the American interest. The different ventures in the Middle East, particularly UNEF II, bought some of the time that American statesmen required to promote Egyptian-Israeli reconciliation. The Congo operation contained anarchy in Central Africa and thwarted Soviet interference in the political turmoil there. The mission to Cyprus has discouraged two NATO allies from attacking each other, and the diplomatic time purchased by the monitored ceasefire may now be yielding first conciliatory results.

In each of these cases escalation was controlled, and more frequently than not, keeping the superpowers out meant excluding the Soviet Union. The Soviet refusal to pay United Nations assessments for peacekeeping operations caused considerable financial stress for the Organization, but it also denied the Soviet Union legitimacy as a mediator and an opportunity to share credit for peacekeeping that has been successfully executed. American support for UN peacekeeping, on the other hand, has enabled the United States to participate in the diplomacy of conciliation that both preceded and followed peacekeeping episodes. This has been especially important for American policy in the Middle East. The United States initially challenged the Soviet Union on the question of payment for peacekeeping operations, but when the so-called Article 19 crisis threatened to destroy the United Nations, the issue was left unresolved and Washington announced that it too would henceforth support only those UN peacekeeping missions that were in the American interest. To date, however, the United States government has continued to support all UN peacekeeping activities. The US Ambassador to the UN, Jeane Kirkpatrick, recently indicated that the Reagan Administration "would like to see the role of the UN in promoting and preserving and maintaining peace expanded."[16]

Threats to the peace nowadays come as often from terrorists, guerrillas, mercenaries, and other transnational troublemakers as from hostilities between governments. The United Nations is devoting considerable effort to finding ways to control such lawlessness. But building international consensus has been difficult because groups abhorred as terrorists by some are acclaimed as freedom fighters by others. There is widespread agreement, however, that innocent people should be protected from indiscriminate violence, and toward this end the United Nations has drafted conventions concerning airline hijacking, the protection of diplomats, and the taking of hostages. Basically, these commit signatories to either prosecute or extradite captured terrorists. A UN committee is presently drafting a convention against the recruitment, use, financing, and training of mercenaries. Naturally, these codes are only as effective as governments permit, but many countries are adhering to them because prescriptions against terrorism are in almost everyone's interest. Since Americans abroad seem particularly vulnerable to terrorism and disproportionally chosen as targets by terrorists, our people benefit by whatever deterrents the UN can contrive. For example, incidents of air piracy involving Americans have dropped off markedly since the adoption of the Hijacking Convention in 1977.

Decolonization has been the primary expression in United Nations policy of the principle of peaceful change. In historical perspective the end of the great European overseas empires represents a universal political change of monumental proportion and import. In a period of somewhat less than 30 years the entire structure of the international state system changed, distributions of power and wealth among states changed, the agenda of diplomacy changed, and global affairs became truly global for the first time. Despite its enormity, the change from a world of a few empires to a world of many states was unexpectedly peaceful, quite unlike decolonization during the eighteenth century, where Britain and Spain were ejected from the Americas at considerable cost in human lives. There were some wars of independence in the 1950s and 1960s; a few, such as those in Algeria, Indochina, and Angola, were long and bloody. But most countries in Africa, South Asia, the Pacific, and the Caribbean moved to self-government without much bloodshed.

The story of the UN's role in twentieth-century decolonization has been told many times.[17] To monitor the Declaration on the Granting of Independence to Colonial Countries and Peoples, the United Nations General Assembly appointed a Special Committee on Decolonization in 1962. For nearly two decades this group, which came to be known as the Committee of 24, oversaw the decolonization process and pushed it forward by prodding metropolitan powers toward planned, orderly withdrawals. Britain and France did not entirely appreciate the Committee's zeal, and the United States, too, soon lost its enthusiasm for it. But in many ways the UN was but a handmaiden to history, since colonialism had already lost legitimacy and since the power to maintain empires was drained from Western Europe during World War II. What the Committee of 24 did was to put the handwriting on the wall in bold script, while counseling expedition and order in the midst of what might otherwise have been delay and chaos.

Except for our brief flirtation with imperial grandeur at the end of the nineteenth century, anti-imperialism has been a main tenet of American foreign policy. Our own country broke away from the British empire; self-determination was part of Wilsonian idealism; American refusal to endorse the reconstitution of empires after World War II was a source of inter-allied dissension in wartime diplomacy.[18] In light of our tradition, decolonization was something that Americans could understand and welcome. Peaceful decolonization was even more welcome, since this spared the United States countless agonizing decisions about policies toward European countries that were NATO allies on the one hand and contestants in colonial struggles on the other. The United States had difficulties with the Committee of 24, abstaining from voting on most occasions because the issues raised continually compelled choices between Western allies and advocates of colonial independence, and because of the way in which the issues were raised. But had these been choices about battles that our allies were losing rather than about resolutions on which they were being outvoted, the US dilemma would have been infinitely greater. The battles were many fewer because the United Nations guided decolonization in a peaceful way. We sometimes tend to forget this.

There is no denying that some of the new countries that emerged from decolonization are now among the harshest critics of the United States. Collectively they compose the Group of 77, now about 125 strong, vocally volatile, politically and economically impatient, outwardly single-minded, and narrowly self-interested.[19] They are also highly dependent upon the West financially, commercially, and technologically, and almost powerless in their efforts to effect changes on the issues that interest them most—world economic restructuring, independence for Namibia (Southwest Africa), the abolition of apartheid in South Africa, and statehood for the Palestinians.

On economic questions the fundamental division between the United States and the Group of 77 stems from relative wealth: the industrialized countries of the so-called North are rich and the developing nations of the South are poor, in many cases very poor. Southern ideologies centered on doctrines of equality and restructuring schemes involving international leveling reflect the poorer countries' economic conditions and aspirations.[20] Both of these will probably temper as economies develop. At this juncture the United States may either contribute to the pace and scope of Southern development or remain passive and watch it happen anyway, albeit more slowly and haphazardly. Contributing to third world development by accommodating some of the interests of the Group of 77 may not yield immediate political gains for the United States, since allies are no longer to be bought and the appeal of nonalignment grows as dangers in the East-West relationship mount. But contributing to development will establish economic partnerships and international market-oriented relationships "out there," where two-thirds of the people in the world live, work, and consume, and where marketing and investing opportunities are vast. Our West European and Japanese friends seem to understand this much better than we do. So does the Soviet Union, although in a more devious way. Those who promote Marxist revolutions make their views most convincing where people are miserable and frustrated, and the more strained the relationship between the United States and the Group of 77, the slower the probable course of development and the higher the likelihood of revolutions in the Third World.

The major political questions in United States relations with the Group of 77—Namibia, apartheid, the fate of the Palestinians—are complex and dangerous since each conflict could escalate into a large-scale war. Namibia is an issue of self-determination, a decolonization matter with international legal implications. Apartheid is fundamentally a matter of human rights being denied to a people by a racist doctrine that is enforced by an obstinate regime. The Palestine question involves issues of self-determination, conflicting territorial claims and security interests, and disagreements about the legitimacy and representativeness of the Palestine Liberation Organization (PLO). It also involves broader matters having to do with ways and means to a comprehensive Middle East settlement. On each of these issues of great concern to the Group of 77, the United States has an opportunity to exercise considerable influence because our government remains able to deal directly with almost all contending parties. If there are keys to peaceful settlement, Washington certainly holds several of them. However, our effectiveness resides in our willingness to accept and to play the mediator's role, or, where that is not possible, in our willingness and ability to protect opportunities for institutions like the United Nations to do so.[21]

IN SUPPORT OF ECONOMIC DEVELOPMENT

By any measure of volume or intensity, the bulk of the United Nation's current work is in the realm of economic development. Here, United Nations policies and programs emerge not only from the banging of American and G-77 heads but also from negotiating processes that involve the rest of the Western countries, sometimes some of the Eastern countries and increasingly China, and often officials of the United Nations Secretariat and the specialized agencies. Contrary to what North-South rhetoric might suggest, there has been substantial agreement between North and South at the United Nations on development issues and considerable activity at the operational level. Since the United States has been a party to most of the development agreements and indeed is the author of some of them, it is more appropriate to explain *why* they are in the American interest rather than to ask whether they are.

United Nations planning for global development is a decade-by-decade effort. In 1980 the UN entered its Third Development Decade and negotiated and published a most ambitious plan to guide its agencies and member governments toward 1990.[22] Bearing in mind that the plan lists aspirations only, that it obligates no one, and that its goals are loftier than its accomplishments will be, Americans might nonetheless ask whether they would welcome the future that UN planners project. The UN's International Development Strategy (IDS) assigns "primary responsibility" for development of developing countries to "those countries themselves," although it also encourages increased North-to-South financial flows and transfers of technology. It projects a world of increased economic interdependence, "an open and expanding trade system," and "the realization of the dynamic pattern of comparative advantage." It also calls for enhanced cooperation among developing countries under the rubric "collective self-reliance" and a more efficient allocation of industrial production globally. Responsibility for world economic growth and well-being is assigned to developed and developing countries jointly for "in an interdependent world economy, it is the responsibility of all Governments to contribute to the goals and objectives of the Strategy." Linkages between agricultural and industrial development are affirmed, and developing country investment in agriculture, "agrarian reforms," "national food policies," and the "eradication of hunger" are called for. Linkages between development and improved social conditions are also acknowledged, and population, health, and education policies, as well as special efforts on behalf of women, children, and youth are prescribed. "The ultimate aim of development," according to the plan, "is the constant improvement of the well-being of the entire population." According to the IDS a number of institutional reforms are in order, especially in international monetary affairs, where developing countries are seeking more influence over decisionmaking.

If the IDS for the Third Development Decade represents the UN's interpretation of the New International Economic Order (NIEO), a catch phrase that has raised much alarm in the West, it may surprise many Americans to find so little in the development strategy that is particularly objectionable. Passions surrounding the acronym NIEO have distracted many in the United States from actually studying the substance of the UN development plan. Clearly, some of the UN's aspirations are controversial. How much more aid would flow, whose technology would flow to whom on what terms, how much of whose industrial production would be relocated and how fast, and what kinds of institutional reforms would be feasible in light of American interest remain to be determined. But these are much more matters for negotiation than confrontation, and indeed the West holds most of the bargaining chips because the industrial countries need only say no to third world demands when such denials are reasoned to be in the Western interest.

Furthermore, the controversial issues are not the central features of the development strategy, which is basically aimed at improved well-being for poor countries and poor people and calls for greater international cooperation to accomplish this. The IDS does not call for the redistribution of the world's wealth, nor would the West ever permit this. It does, however, look to a narrowing of the income gap between industrialized and developing countries in the context of a general increase in world prosperity through the development of new resources, productive capacities, and markets. What the United Nations aspires toward in its development planning is notably different from what G-77 extremists advocate, but it will also turn out to be different from what some extremists in the West believe that they can accept.

Whether or not the development strategy succeeds will depend upon UN members' separate and collective policies and actions during the next decade. Meanwhile, a great many development programs are currently under way under UN auspices. For example, as a result of the World Food Conference in 1974 an International Fund for Agricultural Development was established, partly financed by the United States, but mostly by Arab countries. IFAD has been paying particular attention to small farmers in poor countries. Rural development efforts of the World Bank under Robert McNamara's presidency were also focused on small farmers. Projects financed by the United Nations Development Program are primarily intended to develop economic infrastructure—roads, dams, port facilities, public utility systems, training schools, etc.—that are essential to economic modernity but unattractive to private investors. Efforts have been mounted by the United Nations Industrial Development Organization (UNIDO) to encourage third world investors to keep their funds in their own countries and to encourage inflows of foreign funds. UNIDO is also promoting the development of indigenous industrial technologies. UNCTAD is seeking stabilized markets for internationally traded agricultural and mineral commodities, which are mainstays among third world exports and are also crucial exchange earners. The International Labor Organization (ILO) is pressing for development that is oriented directly toward meeting basic human needs, such as food, shelter, sanitation and health facilities, and education. With the exception of activities like famine relief and aid to children via the United Nations Children's Fund (UNICEF), little of what the UN is doing in development can be interpreted as the doling out of international welfare. Economic development is a multifaced process, with each phase and element related to every other one. UN programs are directed toward welding these interrelationships.

The United Nations is promoting development in the Third World, and development is taking place. By many indicators, growth in the South has been outpacing growth in the North, although, of course, huge income gaps remain.[23] Whether what the UN is doing is in the US interest depends upon whether economic development in the Third World is in the US interest. Outside of all the obvious economic reasons why better-off people make better neighbors, customers, borrowers, and general all-round partners, there are political reasons for encouraging development. The correlation between economic desperation and political turmoil is very high, and turmoil in third world countries tends either to promote local demagogues with "quick fixes" (and usually anti-Western ideologies) or to invite outside meddling. Neither of these situations should be particularly welcome to the United States. In addition, there are domestic political costs to pay in the United States as a result of turmoil in third world countries, as Americans tend to be quite divided about how our government should respond to such situations.

PRESERVING THE EARTH'S RESOURCES

Increasingly during the last decade the United Nations has been led by its members into issues concerning the disposition of the global commons. The commons are those domains possessed by no nations but used by many or all. These include the high seas, regional seas, the seabed, international river basins, the atmosphere, the ionosphere, and outer space. A generation ago, the exploitation of many of these common domains was technologically unfeasible and their despoilation was unimaginable. But today we can mine the oceans and the moon, direct electronic signals and laser beams through the ionosphere, and travel in outer space. We can also pollute the oceans, change the rains to acid, destroy the earth's ozone layer, squander reserves of fresh water, contaminate the atmosphere with radioactivity, and station nuclear weapons on the floor of the sea and on platforms orbiting in outer space. Moreover, because some countries are more technologically able to accomplish these feats than others, there is currently danger that the exploitable commons will disappear as the pioneers scramble to extend their national jurisdictions. There is also some danger that present-day polluters will pass a highly contaminated earth on to future generations.

The thrust of United Nations efforts on issues of global commons has been to attempt to regulate these domains under international law. Some law-making in the form of treaties, conventions, and codes has been directed toward forestalling the closure of the commons by guaranteeing access to all countries regardless of present power positions or technological prowess.[24] This, for example, was a major element of the United Nations-directed effort to draft a new treaty codifying the Law of the Sea and institutionalizing the principle that the oceans are the "common heritage of mankind." Forestalling closure is also a key element in negotiations concerning the allocation of radio and television frequencies, as taken up at the World Administrative Radio Conference in 1979.[25] A similar question has to do with the parceling out of satellite space in the earth's geostationary orbit. In 1980, United Nations members concluded an Agreement Concerning the Activities of States on the Moon and Other Celestial Bodies, which stipulates that neither the moon's surface nor its subsurface shall become the national property of any state. (Outer space as well as the seabeds were demilitarized by UN-sponsored treaties in 1967 and 1971.) As esoteric as some of these matters may appear to be, they are but hints of the world affairs of the future that are being fashioned now by advancing technology. Current efforts to establish legal regimes are actually attempts to provide for the resolution of conflicts of the future by adjudication rather than by force.

Law-making about environmental matters promoted by the UN is designed to elicit commitments from states either to refrain from polluting or to cooperate in cleanup efforts. By UN agreement, for example, oceangoing oil tankers are regulated by international law and owners are held responsible for the pollution their ships may unleash. A major United Nations treaty, the Treaty Banning Nuclear Tests in the Atmosphere, in Outer Space and Under Water, is aimed primarily at slowing the nuclear arms race. But it also stems contamination by radioactivity in the atmosphere and the oceans. Ocean contamination is also the target of the United Nations Environmental Program's emphasis on regional seas, where activities are under way to combat pollution in the Mediterranean Sea, the Caribbean Sea, the Red Sea, the Persian Gulf, the Gulf of Guinea, and other areas of the Pacific.[26] All the programs involve commitments to common action by littoral states and all are funded by international trusts established to finance UN environmental activities. In 1977, the United Nations adopted a Plan of Action to Combat Desertification at the perimeters of the Sahara, as well as a global plan to preserve the earth's fresh water resources.[27]

US interests in the global commons are consistent with the intent and direction of United Nations efforts. Americans use the global commons much more than most other peoples. The United States would probably benefit from a short-run scramble to close off the commons and parcel it into national jurisdictions. Since our technology permits us to exploit now what others can hope to exploit only in the future, we would for a time command the lion's share of the parceled-out commons. But there should be no doubt that such a policy will invite challenge and conflict in the future—much as colonizers' territorial conquests in the past invited later decolonization. A commons that is regulated by law, protected from contamination, and exploited under a regime that allocates shares among users (including the United States and other industrialized countries) and that provides an equitable division of benefits between present and future generations, promises greater international tranquility. Far from contradicting American beliefs in free-market behavior (since abusive exploitation is regulated even in our own country), United Nations programs concerning the global commons affirm the fundamental American belief that law and not force must be the basis of public order.

AMERICA'S FUTURE AT THE UN: CRITIC, SUPPORTER, LEADER

The United Nations system of international organization that emerged after 1945 was in considerable measure the product of American idealism, imagination, and political creativity. Others read our cues, accepted our visions, followed our lead, and took steps away from traditional international anarchy not only because they believed that the United States was powerful but also because they believed that the United States was right. A great mistake of those who specialize in rewriting the history of the postwar era is to attribute America's leadership, or "hegemony" as some call it, solely to this nation's power. Certainly, the United States was powerful and its might was widely respected, particularly by the Soviet Union and its allies. But, among non-Communist countries, the moral leadership of the United States was equally compelling. Washington's initiatives were accepted and acclaimed because they were viewed as legitimate, with legitimacy flowing from projected values that people almost everywhere could accept: freedom, human dignity, the rule of law, anti-imperialism, non-aggression, and peaceful change. US endorsement gave a critical measure of legitimacy to the United Nations, and in this sense the UN very much still needs US approval.

The organization also needs the United States as an anchor. We remain among the very few countries in the world that both share the values upon which the United Nations was founded and are capable of acting in the interest of world order. Without us, the UN becomes a parade of small countries largely unable to act upon their aspirations, plus some Communist states that continue to reject the principles of the organization. When Eastern countries use the UN at all, they attempt to use it solely as an instrument of their revolutionary foreign policies, and they almost always fail. We may applaud this failure, but if that is all we can expect from international organizations, the world would indeed be a more dangerous place. The United Nations requires American power and authority behind its programs for world order and peaceful change.

The UN also needs a constructive critic, sympathetic to its goals but realistic about its shortcomings. The United States must take on the critic's role, as indeed it has already, both to protect our national interests and to keep the international organization true to its original purposes. In many ways the United Nations is less than most of its supporters would like it to be, and emphasizing its accomplishments, as has been done in this chapter, must not distract us from looking at the organization's problems. As Vice President George Bush told the United Nations Association in 1981, there is an urgent need for an "immediate and meaningful reduction in political rhetoric throughout the UN system," since it is impossible to politicize every issue and still hope to create humanitarian and developmental programs that benefit the international community.[28] The primary victim of the harsh rhetoric exchanged in UN forums is the organization itself, for it loses credibility and efficiency when its deliberations turn into global shouting matches.

The UN, moreover, must be prevented from straying from its own ideals or from being used by overzealous members for ends that are not prescribed in the Charter. Recent attempts by some in UNESCO, for example, to push international authorities toward attempting to limit freedoms of the press distort UN principles concerning the free flow of information. Similarly, the double standards evident especially in the General Assembly, and the persistent attempts to make scapegoats of a few governments, do little either to advance the causes of the accusers or to enhance the stature of the United Nations. Such behavior contributes only to polarization; it is wholly out of place within an institution chartered to promote international conciliation.

That UN activities are costly, that budgets need to be more tightly controlled in times of economic austerity, and that such controls have been less than effective in international organizations in recent years are all true statements. Former Secretary-General Kurt Waldheim's call for "no growth" budgeting for the next biennium and his insistence that program administrators make their priorities explicit are steps in the right direction. So too are expanded Secretariat efforts at evaluation and assessment and more deliberate attempts to terminate ineffective or redundant activities. But much more such monitoring and control are necessary in the administration of the UN, and some of this could be prompted by donor countries, such as the United States, watching and questioning the ways in which their international contributions are used.

If the United Nations needs the United States to do all these things, it is also true that in these last decades of the twentieth century, the United States also needs the UN, for the organization has become a legitimizer in its own right.[29] Most members currently respect the United Nations, accept commitments contained in its policies and programs, adhere to UN-inspired conventions and codes, and accord authority to resolutions that follow from consensus. The US must therefore watch very closely what happens at the UN. For the United States, as for other countries, power plus legitimacy remain the keys to leadership. As underlined throughout this chapter, American values and foreign policy interests are largely consistent with the principles and policy directions of the UN. A more positive United States official attitude, then, together with greater willingness to work within the organization, more flexibility and imagination in parliamentary diplomacy, and indeed more diplomacy and less unilateral posturing, could help to recreate a situation where US foreign policy works in tandem with the UN to build legitimacy for both. It is time to again identify the United States with the goals and aspirations of most of the peoples of the world. The United Nations is one place where this can be done.

Notes

1. Alexander M. Haig, Jr., "A New Era of Growth," US Department of State, *Current Policy,* No. 314 (September 21, 1981), p. 1.

2. Juliana Geran Pilon, "The United States and the United Nations: A Balance Sheet," *Backgrounder* (Washington, D.C.: The Heritage Foundation, January 1982).

3. Cf. Abraham Yeselson and Anthony Gaglione, *A Dangerous Place: The United Nations as a Weapon in World Politics* (New York: Grossman Publishers, 1974); Daniel Patrick Moynihan, *A Dangerous Place* (New York: Berkley Books, 1980).

4. United Nations Secretariat, Department of Economic and Social Affairs, Office of Financial Affairs, *Proposed Medium-Term Plan for the Period 1984–1989* (future A/36/6) 1982.

5. Thomas Hovet, Jr., *Bloc Politics in the United Nations* (Cambridge, Mass.: Harvard University Press, 1960), passim.; Hayward R. Alker, Jr. and Bruce M. Russett, *World Politics in the General Assembly* (New Haven: Yale University Press, 1965), pp. 50–54, 70–80, et passim.

6. Resolution 487 (1981); See also *Issues Before the 36th General Assembly of the United Nations* (New York: United Nations Association of the United States, 1981), pp. 18–19; *New York Times,* June 20, 1981.

7. Dorothy Rabinowitz, "Reagan's 'Heroine' at the U.N.," *New York Magazine,* July 20, 1981, p. 38.

8. Branislav Gosovic and John Gerard Ruggie, "On the Creation of a New International Economic Order: Issue Linkage and the Seventh Special Session of the UN General Assembly," *International Organization,* Vol. 30, No. 2 (Spring 1976), pp. 320–321 ff.

9. United Nations, Department of Public Information, *International Development Strategy for the Third United Nations Development Decade* (New York: United Nations, 1981).

10. Richard N. Gardner, "The United Nations Conference on Trade and Development," *International Organization,* Vol. 22, No. 1 (Winter 1968), pp. 114–120.

11. Cf. Statement of Elliot Abrams, Assistant Secretary of State for International Organization Affairs, before the Subcommittee on Foreign Operations, House Committee on Appropriations, May 12, 1981.

12. *Issues Before the 36th General Assembly of the United Nations,* op.cit., p. 126.

13. Flora Lewis, "The Value of the U.N.," *New York Times,* May 23, 1982.

14. United Nations, Department of Public Information, *Yearbook of the United Nations, 1956* (New York: United Nations, 1957), pp. 25–62, 67–89.

15. See S/RES/46 (1979); A/RES/ES–6/2, A/RES/35/37; *New York Times,* December 18, 1981.

16. "US Positions to Change Under Reagan, Reflect More Realism," *Diplomatic World Bulletin,* April 6, 1981, p. 2.

17. David A. Kay, *The New Nations in the United Nations, 1960–1967* (New York: Columbia University Press, 1970); David A. Kay, "The United Nations and Decolonization," in *The United Nations: Past, Present and Future,* James Barros, ed. (New York: The Free Press, 1972), pp. 143–170; Rupert Emerson, *From Empire to Nation* (Boston: The Beacon Press, 1967), passim.

18. Robert Beitzell, *The Uneasy Alliance: America, Britain and Russia, 1941–1943* (New York: Alfred A. Knopf, 1972), pp. 142–143.

19. Robert L. Rothstein, *The Weak in the World of the Strong: The Developing Countries in the International System* (New York: Columbia University Press, 1977), pp. 3–72 et passim.

20. Roger Hansen, "The Political Economy of North-South Relations," *International Organization,* Vol. 29, No. 4 (Autumn 1975), pp. 925–929 ff.

21. Oran Young, *The Intermediaries: Third Parties in International Crises* (Princeton: Princeton University Press, 1967), passim.

22. *International Development Strategy for the Third United Nations Development Decade,* op. cit., passim.

23. Martin M. McLaughlin, ed., *The United States and World Development Agenda 1979* (New York: Praeger Publishers, for the Overseas Development Council, 1979), pp. 149–182.

24. Seyom Brown, et. al., *Regimes for the Ocean, Outer Space and Weather* (Washington, DC: The Brookings Institution, 1977).

25. *Issues Before the 34th General Assembly of the United Nations* (New York: United Nations Association of the United States, 1979), p. 115.

26. Conference of Plenipotentiaries of the Coastal States of the Mediterranean Region for the Protection of the Mediterranean Sea against Pollution from Land-Based Sources, 1980, *Final Act* (United Nations, 1980); *Issues Before the 35th General Assembly,* op.cit., pp. 103–104; *Issues Before the 36th General Assembly,* op.cit., p. 107.

27. *Report of the United Nations Conference on Desertification, Nairobi, Kenya, 29 August–9 September, 1977,* A/CONF.74/36; *Report of the United Nations Water Conference, Mar del Plata, Argentina, 14–25 March, 1977,* U.N.P. Sales No. E.77.11.A.12; see also *Yearbook of the United Nations 1977,* pp. 509–514, 553–563.

28. Remarks of Vice President George Bush before the United Nations Association, 1981 Spring Dinner, New York Hilton, New York City, May 26, 1981.

29. Inis L. Claude, *The Changing United Nations* (New York: Random House, 1967), pp. 73–104.

BIOGRAPHICAL INFORMATION

Angus Archer is presently Coordinator of the Non-Governmental Liaison Service of the United Nations. The Service is funded by several agencies of the UN system and is mandated to promote "development education" among NGOs in the industrialized countries. He is a Canadian citizen. Before coming to the UN in 1974 he was Executive Director of the Canadian Council for International Cooperation, a coordinating body of all NGOs in Canada concerned with world development. He also served as a program officer with the Freedom from Hunger Campaign of FAO (Rome) and the Overseas Institute of Canada (Ottawa). He is a graduate of Carleton University in Ottawa.

Richard E. Bissell is presently Director of Program Development at the United States Information Agency (USIA). He was formerly Professorial Lecturer at the Johns Hopkins School of Advanced International Studies (SAIS) in Washington, DC. He was also Managing Editor of *Orbis,* Coordinator of Economic Security Studies at the Foreign Policy Research Institute, Philadelphia, and taught at the University of Pennsylvania. Among his many publications is *Apartheid and International Organizations.*

Robert W. Cox is Professor of Political Science and of Social and Political Thought at York University, Toronto, Canada, and was formerly (1972–77) Professor of International Organization at Columbia University, New York. Prior to taking up academic work full time, he was an Assistant Director-General of the ILO and Director of the ILO's International Institute for Labor Studies in Geneva. He is co-author with Harold K. Jacobson of *The Anatomy* *of Influence: Decision Making in International Organization* (Yale University Press, 1972) and has published a number of articles on international political economy and world order issues.

Jock A. Finlayson is a Research Associate, Institute of International Relations, University of British Columbia, Canada. He has contributed articles to *International Organization, International Journal, International Perspectives,* and *Orbis.* He is presently writing a book on the politics of international commodity regulation with Mark W. Zacher.

Toby Trister Gati is Deputy Vice President for Research and Policy Studies at the United Nations Association (UNA-USA). She has written extensively on international affairs, with special emphasis on Soviet-American relations and multilateral foreign policy issues. (Among her most recent articles is "The Soviet Union and the North–South Dialogue," *Orbis* (Summer 1980).

Leon Gordenker is Professor of Politics and Faculty Associate at the Center of International Studies, Princeton University. He is the author of many books and articles on international organization, including *International Aid and National Decisions, The UN in International Politics,* and *The UN Secretary General and the Maintenance of Peace;* he is also an editor of *World Politics.* He was one of the first American members of the UN Secretariat in 1945. He earned his A.B. at the University of Michigan and his Ph.D. at Columbia University.

Stephen D. Krasner is Professor of Political Science at Stanford University, California. He has also taught at UCLA and Harvard. His main area of interest is the political determinants of international economic behavior. He is currently completing a manuscript on the political economy of relations between developing and industrialized states. He earned his Ph.D. from Harvard University in 1972.

Paul D. Martin has a Master's in International Affairs from Columbia University's School of International and Public Affairs with a specialization in economic and political development and African studies. He has worked at the UN as an intern and as a consultant. He is currently Assistant to the President of the AFS for International/Intercultural Programs.

Charles William Maynes is the Editor of *Foreign Policy* magazine. He served as Assistant Secretary of State for International Organization Affairs from 1977–80.

Robert F. Meagher is Professor of International Law at the Fletcher School of Law and Diplomacy, Tufts University, specializing in law and development. In addition, he is a private consultant to various governments, international organizations, and private business groups. During 1975–76 he was Visiting Fellow at the Overseas Development Council and in 1981 he was a Visiting Professor of Law at both Melbourne and Monash Universities Law Schools in Australia. Educated at the City College of New York, Yale Law School, and the Bombay School of Economics (Fulbright Scholar), he has lived in Asia, the Middle East, Africa, and Europe. He is author of *An International Redistribution of Wealth and Power*, co-author of *International Financial Aid,* and has published a number of monographs, articles, and book reviews.

Ronald I. Meltzer is Assistant Professor of Political Science at the State University of New York at Buffalo. His areas of specialization include international organization, North-South relations, and US foreign economic policymaking. He is co-author with Stephen D. Cohen of *U.S. International Economic Policy in Action: Diversity of Decision Making* (Praeger, 1982) and a number of journal articles and book chapters in these fields. He has also co-directed an international conference on human rights and development in Africa, which was sponsored by the National Endowment for the Humanities and other funding sources. He has edited a volume on this topic, with Claude E. Welch, Jr., entitled *Human Rights and Development in Africa: Domestic, Regional, and International Dilemmas* (State University of New York Press, forthcoming 1983).

Debra L. Miller is Assistant Professor of Political Science at Barnard College, Columbia University, where she teaches courses in international relations. She also teaches at the Graduate School of International and Public Affairs at Columbia. She has written articles about North-South technology transfer, as well as other political and economic subjects. In the past she has served as a consultant on international organization and political economy to the Department of State and the Department of the Army.

Donald J. Puchala is Professor of Government and International Studies at the University of South Carolina and Director of the University's Institute of International Studies. He is the author of *International Politics Today,* co-author of *Global Food Interdependence,* and editor of *Issues before the United Nations General Assembly.* Professor Puchala has served as a consultant to the United Nations and to US agencies dealing with international organizational affairs.

Nigel S. Rodley is the Legal Adviser at the International Secretariat of Amnesty International. He also lectures at the University of London (London School of Economics and Political Science). A former Associate Economics Affairs Officer at United Nations headquarters in New York, he has held teaching or research positions at New York University (Center for International Studies), the New School for Social Research (Graduate Faculty, Department of Political Science) and Dalhousie University, Faculty of Law, Halifax, Nova Scotia. He has written widely in the field on international law and organization. The views expressed in this article are his own and may not necessarily be attributed to Amnesty International.

Ivor Richard was the United Kingdom Permanent Representative to the UN between 1974 and 1979. Prior to that he was a Delegate to the Council of Europe. He is now Member of the Commission of the European Communities responsible for Employment and Social Affairs, Tripartite Conference, Education and Vocational Training. He has contributed a number of articles to various political journals and is co-author of *Europe or the Open Sea,* published in 1972.

Howard M. Wachtel is Professor of Economics and Chairman of the Department of Economics at the American University. He has been Director of the International Economic Order Project of the Transnational Institute, where he wrote *The New Gnomes: Multinational Banks in the Third World*. He has written over 30 articles which have appeared in major academic journals and magazines throughout the world. He is the author of *Workers' Management and Workers' Wages in Yugoslavia* and is currently finishing *Labor and the Economy*, a book to be published by Academic Press. Dr. Wachtel is a frequent lecturer for the US Agency for International Development and has participated in meetings of the Aspen Institute for Humanistic Studies, the International Association for Research in Income and Wealth, and other professional organizations.

Sidney Weintraub has been Dean Rusk Professor of Public Policy at the Lyndon B. Johnson School of Public Affairs, the University of Texas at Austin, for the past six years. He had been a career foreign service officer for 27 years and served, in his last ten years, as Director of the Economic Mission in Chile, Deputy Assistant Secretary of State for International Finance and Development, and Assistant Administrator of the Agency for International Development (AID). He was a Senior Fellow of the Brookings Institution in Washington, DC. He is the author of numerous articles and books on international issues.

Mark W. Zacher is Professor of Political Science and Director of the Institute of International Relations, University of British Columbia, Canada. He is author of *Dag Hammarskjöld's United Nations* (1970) and *International Conflicts and Collective Security, 1946–1977: The United Nations, Organization of American States, Organization of African Unity, and Arab League* (1979), co-author of *Pollution, Politics and International Law: Tankers at Sea* (1979), and the co-editor of *Conflict and Stability in Southeast Asia* (1974) and *Canadian Foreign Policy and the Law of the Sea* (1979). He is presently writing a book on the politics of international commodity regulation with Jock A. Finlayson.

INDEX

Abrams, Elliot, 4, 5

Acheson, Dean, 84

Afghanistan, Soviet invasion of (1979), 6, 51, 55, 124; war with Pakistan (1960-61), 166

Africa, 15, 16, 19, 171-172, 220

African Development Bank (AFDB), 220

Aggression, 49-50

Aid (*See* Development assistance)

Algeria, 19, 54, 110; war with Morocco (1963), 165

Amin, Idi, 333

Amnesty International, 270-271, 278; Campaign for the Abolition of Torture, 270

Antarctic Treaty (1959), 178

Apartheid, 269, 333-336; UN Convention on, 269

Argentina, 20; dispute with United Kingdom over Falkland Islands (1982), 31, 136

Arms control, 30, 33, 132-135, 156-157 (*See also* Disarmament)

Atoms for Peace Program, 150

Bangladesh, 40, 43

Bank for International Settlements (BIS), 187

Baruch Plan (1946), 150

Belgium, intervention in the Congo (1960), 117, 168

Berlin Blockade (1948), 30

Bialer, Seweryn, 338

Biological Weapons Treaty (1972), 137

Bizerte crisis (1961), 167, 168

Blix, Hans, 151-152

Brandt Commission Report, 157, 207

Brazil, 340

Bretton Woods, negotiations and institutions, 66, 69, 71, 227-237

Buckley, James, 106

Burma, 18

Bush, George, 108, 362

Cambodia (*See* Kampuchea)

Camp David Agreements, 55

Canada, 119, 313-314

Carter, Jimmy, 151

Chad, 88

China, People's Republic of (PRC), 11, 71, 106, 108, 296

China, Republic of (ROC), 102, 105, 106, 123, 296

Churchill, Winston, 48, 49

Cleveland, Harlan, 53

Club of Rome, 78, 305

Cold War, 13, 14, 16, 52, 68, 131, 134, 162-163, 294, 345

Collective security, UN system of, 50, 162-183 (*See also* Peace and security issues)

Committee of 24 (*See* Decolonization)

Committee of the Whole (COW), 187, 190, 192

Commodity issues, 23, 188, 195, 231; International Commodity Agreements (ICAs), 188, 217, 231; Integrated Program for Commodities (IPC), 217, 348; Common Fund, 188, 192, 195-196, 217-219, 221

Common Fund (*See* Commodity issues)

Comprehensive Test Ban Treaty (CTB), 329